BUILDING A
LEARNING
NATION

With my compliments

Chris Pratt

BUILDING A
LEARNING
NATION

A new approach for the 21st century

CHRIS PRATT

with ALLISON CHIN OBE

BROWN
DOG
BOOKS

Published under licence by Brown Dog Books and
The Self-Publishing Partnership, 7 Green Park Station, Bath BA1 1JB

www.selfpublishingpartnership.co.uk

ISBN printed book: 978-1-78545-387-8

ISBN e-book: 978-1-78545-388-5

Cover design by Kevin Rylands
Internal design by Andrew Easton

This book is printed on FSC certified paper

Printed by CPI Group (UK) Ltd, Croydon CR0 4YY

Contents

PREFACE: A PERSONAL NOTE

The book has its roots in our personal and professional backgrounds. Between Allison and I we have enjoyed around eighty years of working with young and adult learners, much of the time in senior leadership roles. We also have the invaluable perspective of parents. But, the explanation of why we have written this book starts with our own learning journeys.

Neither of us came through what might be seen as the traditional route. We were born into working class northern families. Our parents were manual workers on low wages. Had they had the opportunities afforded to our generation, I am sure their lives would have been qualitatively different; more prosperous, and most likely they would have lived a lot longer than they did. Despite our parents' poor circumstances they provided us with the love, values and encouragement that enabled us to make our way in life.

My schooling was in pre-comprehensive days. I failed my 11+ and went to a secondary modern school. Because of supportive, but not pushy, parents I can honestly say that I survived this 'failure' unscathed. In my latter days at secondary school comprehensive education came in and helped me get some O level equivalents. I left school without A levels but the few O levels I secured plus my passion for sport were sufficient to get me into a teacher training PE course. I qualified as a teacher, worked in further education (later on as a college principal); and as a senior education and children's services officer, serving as the director of education and children's services in two local authorities, and the deputy in another. In my early 40s I acquired a master's degree at my own expense through part-time study. I retired in June 2013 and published my first book, *Re-inventing Leadership*, in 2016.

Due to her Chinese heritage, Allison, like her siblings, was repeatedly subjected to racist bullying and her educational experience was severely restricted by the stereotypical attitudes that society then had towards working class girls. Allison left school with only three O level equivalents and worked in shops, a factory and as a farm labourer. She went to 'night school' at the local further education college, and was successful in getting an A level and a couple more O levels that enabled her to train as a primary school teacher. Allison taught in a number of schools and worked as a local authority advisor. For twenty-four years Allison was the Headteacher of an inner-city primary school, rated outstanding by Ofsted on three separate occasions. As a National Leader of Education she worked with other schools, including as an Executive Headteacher. In 2011 Allison was awarded an OBE for services to education. She retired in 2017.

Allison and I have been married for twenty-seven years with three grown-up daughters, of whom we are very proud. We were both fortunate to have supportive parents and to grow up at a time when many youngsters from poor working class families were able to move into skilled and professional jobs. It is deeply concerning that the social mobility of the latter decades of the 20th century seems today to have all but dried up. This slow-down in social mobility is inextricably linked to the UK's high levels of educational underachievement. The prime cause of this 'long tail of underperformance' is that poor quality home lives mean that too many children start and go through school at a massive disadvantage. Unfortunately our national education system, with its narrow academic focus, obsession with testing rather than promoting a love for learning, and dividing people into 'successes' or 'failures' from the earliest age, compounds this disadvantage.

We felt inspired, therefore, to tackle these concerns in a serious and substantial way, which meant comprehensively and objectively evaluating our current state of learning, and articulating and advocating for a better alternative. The result is this book, which we hope will help in opening up a debate about learning and its importance for the future of our country.

Chris Pratt
January 2019

INTRODUCTION

It is the learners who inherit the future. The learned find themselves equipped
for a world that no longer exists.
Eric Hoffer[1]

At a time when we have a fascination with mythical super heroes who have
super powers, we can easily forget that in the real world, human beings
have the greatest power on earth – their immense capacity to learn. It is this
power, developed over hundreds of thousands of years, that has been the most
important force for human endeavour and progress. So much so that learning
has become the lifeblood of our modern society; as it has shaped our past, so
it will inexorably define our future. Given the centrality of learning in our
society, how well we learn has by far the greatest influence on people's quality
of life, be it in families, organisations or nations. This book explores how good
we are at learning in the UK, and specifically in England. We ask and do our
best to answer two fundamental questions. How well prepared are we to meet
the knowledge and skill requirements of the present day and, more importantly,
those of the future? And, what changes can be made to ensure that learning has
the most positive impact on everybody's lives?

We deliberately use the language of 'learning' rather than 'education'.
While you can define the two terms as being the same or very similar, many
perceive 'learning' as the broader function of acquiring skills and knowledge,
as well as shaping behaviours and personalities, through a variety of formal
and informal means. 'Education' is seen as the relatively narrower and more
formal process, usually involving a 'teacher' to structure how people learn. In
practice, therefore, 'education' is one vehicle for learning, albeit a critically
important one. This is not just semantics. One of our main arguments is that
in national policy making there has been a failure to properly recognise the
massive influence that factors outside of school and post-school education

have on learning, particularly the powerful impact of family life on children's learning as they grow up. From birth, children have an insatiable appetite for learning, something that should be nurtured and built upon. Often learning goes wrong when adults, mainly unconsciously, stifle or fail to nurture this natural desire to learn.

The book looks in some detail at our 'national system of learning', by which we mean the whole range of learning opportunities and experiences that are available to people. These include both the formal education settings in England (such as early years placements, schools, colleges, youth services, adult education centres and universities, as well as distance or e-learning), and the more informal ways in which we learn from our day-to-day experiences.

Part 1 explores how fit for purpose our national learning system is, using three key measures – the contribution learning makes to people's *mental health* and well-being, whether we have sufficient of the right *skills*, and how the knowledge and skills of the UK population *compares internationally*. We then examine the main factors affecting the efficacy of learning – the influence of *family life*, the effectiveness of *schools* and the impact of social and economic *inequalities*.

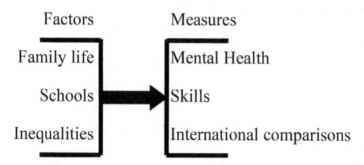

Part 2 sets out an alternative approach to learning and, amongst other things, calls for a systems approach involving promoting lifelong learning, long-term work with families, changing the conditions within which schools have to operate, and vigorously tackling the country's skills deficit and educational underachievement. Our findings are heavily evidence- based – some of which is referenced in the main text, and much of it in the extensive notes at the end of the book.

The time is right to undertake a fundamental review of learning in our country. Society is deeply divided – socially, educationally and economically.

There has been a cross-party consensus to the national direction of education for the last thirty years. A significant proportion of young people continue, year-on-year, to be disaffected from education, and leave school without marketable qualifications and skills. There are major skills shortages, which act as a drag on our economy and prevent many from accessing quality employment. UK education performance lags behind those of most other developed countries. Morale amongst teachers is generally low, with increasing numbers of teachers and school leaders leaving the profession. The current government's response (and that of previous governments) does not fill us with confidence that these concerns are properly recognised and understood. They are defensive, complacent and often deliberately ignore the available evidence. Government policy is narrowly focused on 'academic knowledge', rather than the broader nature of learning and skills. It is driven by ideology and structure, for example wanting to make all schools academies and a return to the grammar school system. Implementation is through a 'command and control' style including constant testing, setting targets, regular inspections and forcing schools to become academies.

Such a review could be facilitated through a 'great learning debate' similar to 'the great education debate' that the then Prime Minister, James Callaghan, initiated over forty years ago[2]. This would enable the widest possible public engagement, in pursuit of finding the most powerful ways of tackling underachievement and educational disadvantage, and providing the country with the skills it needs to meet the social and economic challenges of the future.

1
WHAT IS LEARNING AND WHY IS IT SO IMPORTANT?

Learning how to learn is life's most important skill
Tony Buzan

A brief canter through the history of our planet gives an appreciation of how the human's enormous capacity for learning has set it far apart from all other animals. It was not always the case. Humans first evolved around two and a half million years ago. For nearly two million years humans were no different than other animals. 'Prehistoric humans' explains Yuval Noah Harari 'were insignificant animals with no more impact on their environment than gorillas, fireflies or jellyfish'[1].

Advent of modern human learning

How did it all change? It started around 800,000 years ago, at a time when there was still more than one species of human. Somewhere, most likely in East Africa, our forebears made two discoveries that probably are the most important in humankind's relatively short existence on earth – the ignition and control of fire, and its use for cooking. Less energy was required to eat cooked food, and over hundreds of thousands of years this helped in the development of larger and larger brains. Thus humans evolved in a dramatically and fundamentally different way than other animals. About 70,000 years ago this led to what is often called the cognitive revolution[2] – large brains providing humans with the capacity for sophisticated thinking and problem solving and the capability for accelerated learning. From that time we started to radically distinguish ourselves from other animals. It was the advent of modern learning, which became of growing importance to human life.

Since then humans have demonstrated the incredible things they are capable of, many for the good, others sadly that have severely harmed our planet and the life on it. We have inhabited all continents of the earth; developed sophisticated forms of oral and written language; domesticated plants and animals; and through science developed a growing understanding of the physical and natural world, as well as the wider universe of which our planet is only a small part. This learning has been used to lengthen human life; ease pain; vastly reduce poverty, hunger, plague and wars; construct great buildings, towns and cities; develop instant worldwide communication; travel in space; and walk on the moon. On the other hand we have used our learning to cause the wide-scale extinction of other animal and plant species and human races; to pollute and endanger the earth; and to invent and use weapons of mass destruction. This demonstrates clearly that learning is not value free – it depends on what you learn and how you apply what you have learnt.

What is learning?

There are different definitions of learning and associated terms such as knowledge, understanding, skills, education and training. In order to be as clear as possible about our use of these and other terms in this book, we provide our own definitions.

Learning can be defined as the acquisition of knowledge, understanding, skills and behaviour including emotional development, through experience, study, or being taught. It allows us 'to make sense of the world' and 'effective learning leads to change, development and the desire to learn more'[3]. To be meaningful, learning has to be contextualised, that is relevant to the modern day and the foreseeable future. The process of learning can be represented diagrammatically, as below:

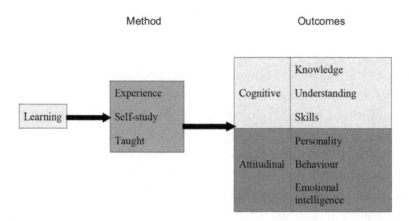

Knowledge is about being aware of, acquiring and becoming familiar with facts and information, again through experience or more structured means. For example a child may become aware at an early age that some objects float in water and some sink.

Understanding is about comprehending the knowledge you have acquired, for example the child at a later stage understands the reasons why some objects float in water and others don't.

Skills are abilities, competencies and techniques that enable people to apply their knowledge and understanding practically – that is to actually do things, for example the child will be able to build an object that will float in water. Skills are wide-ranging including *cognitive* skills (involving the application of ideas, for example putting an objective argument together); *technical* skills (involving manual dexterity, for example plumbing); and *interpersonal* skills (involving working with people, for example team working).

Learning, therefore, can be explained as an interplay of knowledge, understanding and skills.

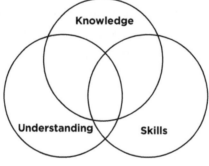

Virtually all actions we take have been learnt previously. We learn the basics of life – eating, attracting attention and communicating with others, crawling then walking and, as we grow and mature, a vast range of functions and skills. Learning is a continuous process from birth, what is commonly referred to as from 'cradle to grave' or 'lifelong' learning. Most learning occurs randomly from our day-to-day life experiences, particularly in our early and most formative years, in contrast to the more formal learning processes of school, college, university and training.

Education is the process of facilitating learning. The most common understanding of education is that which is directed, guided or structured by an 'educator', such as a teacher.

Training is usually associated with organised activities that provide people with particular proficiencies, skills or fitness. It is commonly used in an employment context, in training someone to do a particular job to a certain standard (for example, brick-laying or being able to code). Another use is in sport i.e. training sessions to improve performance both of individual athletes as well as teams.

Why is learning so important?

Through evolution, learning has made human beings the highly organised, intelligent and technologically-driven race that we are today. The quality of learning and how we apply its lessons, more than anything else, influences the nature of individuals, families and organisations, and of the local communities and broader societies we live in. Learning is critically important then, because it enables society as a whole to progress, and individuals to lead a fulfilling life – emotionally, socially, economically and culturally. More specifically learning provides the knowledge and the skills that are needed for the economy and public services, and individuals with the marketable skills needed to secure and sustain employment.

The enormous advances and changes to the way that we currently live that have been made possible by learning, will almost certainly continue, and undoubtedly accelerate in the future. As Harari so aptly puts it, 'There are three kinds of resources: raw materials, energy and knowledge. Raw materials and energy are exhaustible – the more you use, the less you have. Knowledge, in contrast, is a growing resource – the more you use, the more you have.'[4] It is imperative for people to flourish in what will be an increasingly knowledge and skills-rich society. The larger the number of those who are not able to keep pace with this learning challenge, the greater will be the scale of social and economic exclusion, and the consequent human and societal costs. Lack of relevant skills excludes people from more qualitative work. Parenting skills, often learnt from our own parents, greatly influence the type of future that the next generation will have. People's broad awareness of the world and current affairs helps them as citizens to participate in democratic society.

Going forward, as technology and science advances, knowledge and skills will be increasingly more important. How well we learn and are enabled to learn will be crucial to the kind of society we build in the future, and how well individuals fare within it.

Part 1

HOW WELL ARE WE DOING?

How fit for purpose is our national learning system? How has it impacted on people's mental health and skills, and how does education in the UK compare to that in other countries? How influential are family life, schools and the level of inequality on the quality of people's learning?

2
MENTAL HEALTH

Exam stress major cause of growing children's mental ill-health, impacting negatively on learning

We are addicted to exams … but measuring success by exam results is fuelling stress, anxiety and failure among pupils, teachers, and schools. We are sleepwalking into a deepening crisis when it comes to the mental health of kids and we need to drastically change the way we assess kids. It's a fundamental thing about what constitutes a successful life.
Lord Gus O'Donnell, former Cabinet Secretary[1]

Mental health is defined as 'A state of well-being in which every individual realizes his or her own potential, can cope with the normal stresses in life, can work productively and fruitfully, and is able to make a contribution to her or his community'[2]. Given that more than anything else, a person's mental state defines the quality of life s/he has, it is an apt starting point for examining how well our system of learning is working. You can be highly qualified with an affluent life-style, but these advantages will mean little if your day-to-day life is riven by anxiety and depression. It is fitting to ask, then, how far our learning system is contributing to people's mental health, both positively and negatively.

In this chapter we evidence that:

• Poor mental health impedes learning.
• Incessant testing and pressure to succeed in examinations contributes significantly to child mental ill-health.
• Substantial and increasing numbers of people, including children, suffer from

poor mental health.

• Child mental health services are under-resourced and over-stretched, and the response of successive governments to the escalating child mental ill-health problem has been totally inadequate over many years.

Poor mental health impacts negatively on learning

Mental ill-health has a significant impact on education attainment[3], particularly where there are failures to identify and treat poor mental health in children[4]. In girls the main symptoms of mental ill-health are 'anxiety and depression' and 'excessive worrying and difficulty controlling this' and in boys 'loss of confidence or self-esteem'[5]. Children with emotional worries are more likely to have problems at school with punctuality, attendance and being excluded[6]. Pupils with poor mental health find it difficult to 'concentrate in class [and] participate fully in lessons or make friends'[7].

Exam pressure fuels child mental ill-health

Failing at school is one of the main worries that children have[8]. Examination pressure (along with social media interactions) is cited as a major cause of the increasing numbers of children and young people experiencing anxiety, eating disorders, self-harm and suicidal thoughts[9]. The House of Commons Education Select Committee came to the conclusion that 'SATs [in primary school] as they currently operate, are affecting the well-being of both pupils and teachers'[10]. One consequence of the pressure of SATs on primary schools is the significant amount of homework being set for these young children including four and five-year-olds. One in eight primary school children, for example, spends at least five hours a week on homework[11]. Significant numbers of children express anxiety about and unhappiness with school[12]. For example, 8 in 10 twelve to sixteen-year-olds 'experience emotional distress' after starting secondary school, being most anxious about exam worries and work overload[13].

Schools are witnessing 'unprecedented levels of school-related anxiety... particularly around test or exam time' caused by 'increased pressure from tests/ exams; [children's] greater awareness at younger ages of their own "failure"; and the increased rigour and academic demands of the curriculum'. Symptoms include panic attacks, loss of eyelashes, sobbing, sleeplessness, fear of academic failure, lower self-esteem and depression[14]. As a result counselling sessions for children for examination stress have rapidly increased[15].

Mental ill-health – major and growing

Two-thirds of adults in the UK have experienced mental ill-health at some point in their lives, higher than in most other countries[16]. Most mental health conditions in adults started when they were children[17]. Those with mental health problems are more likely than the rest of the population to be unemployed, not do well educationally, be homeless and be involved in crime[18].

Like adults, all children and young people from time to time experience negative feelings such as being upset and unhappy. This is part of the 'ups and downs' of life. What is concerning is when children are unable to effectively manage these negative feelings, and they become severe and are sustained. UK children are less satisfied with their lives than those in most other countries[19]. Serious mental health conditions are prevalent in children of primary[20] and secondary school[21] age, university students[22] and young adults[23]. One in three teenagers suffer from mental health problems such as depression, anxiety, negative feelings, inability to focus and restless sleep[24]. 720,000 children and young people in England (one in 10) have a diagnosed mental health disorder[25]. Nearly half of all young women, and just over a quarter of young men, have self-harmed[26].

Far more children have mental problems today than they did thirty years ago[27], and there have been substantial increases in the past ten years[28]. Eating disorders, body image anxieties, hyperactivity, problems with sleeping, bed-wetting, substance addiction, worries about friendships, family difficulties, depression, general anxiety, cyberbullying, self-harm and suicidal thoughts have all increased significantly[29]. The number of children and young people in England being treated for mental health problems is the highest ever[30]. Sadly, the number of children visiting accident and emergency for mental health treatment has more than doubled since 2010[31].

Government response ineffective

Increasing demand and shortage of funding and specialist staff mean that services are not responding adequately to the growing mental health problems being suffered by children and young people[32]. Inadequate resources force higher service thresholds[33], resulting in more than a third of children and young people (nearly 125,000) referred for specialist treatment, including those with life-threatening mental illnesses, being turned away by child and adolescent mental health services (CAMHS)[34]. Even those with the most serious mental health problems are waiting up to 18 months to be treated by CAMHS[35]. Severe shortages of hospital beds in some areas of the country mean that large numbers of children with complex mental health problems are being provided with treatment far away from their family homes. Sending these children so far from their family and friends 'can be frightening for them, reduces their chances of recovery and increases their risk of self-harm'[36]. 'The poor access to specialist services', says the NHS regulator, the Care Quality Commission, is 'damaging the health of young people with anxiety, depression and other conditions'[37] and is a major cause of the doubling of the number of those with psychiatric conditions who report to hospital Accident and Emergency units[38]. In addition CAMHS, the main specialist service for treating those children and young people with the most serious mental health problems, seems to be in a poor state, with 'high staff turnover, poor morale and poor working conditions'[39].

As can be seen, many children are not getting appropriate support early enough[40]. This, combined with cuts in school pastoral staff[41] and the virtual dismantling of local early intervention and prevention services[42], inevitably means the numbers of children with mental health problems will continue to increase. This is a concern highlighted in a report by the House of Commons Education and Health Committees that points out that 'stress and anxiety are rising among schoolchildren and yet services to head off mental health problems are being stripped back'. The report concludes that 'with half of all mental illness starting before the age of 15, it is a false economy to cut services for children and young people that could help to improve wellbeing, build resilience and provide early intervention'[43].

What has the government's response been to this ongoing deterioration of children's mental health? There has been plenty of rhetoric, but little practical action to improve matters[44]. For example, there has been a lot of talk about mental health having parity of importance with physical health within the NHS. Less than one per cent of the total NHS budget, however, is spent on children's mental health, and this is only six per cent of the total mental health budget[45]. In 2015 the government committed an 'additional' £1.4 billion over five years for children's mental health[46], but it seems that much of this hasn't found its way into front-line services[47].

Prime Minister Theresa May has said that she will 'put Britain's schools on the front line of the fight against child mental illness' including plans to train staff, review services and link schools to mental health workers to aid speedy intervention[48]. At the end of 2017 the government issued a consultation paper[49] and announced an additional £300 million for child mental health. Proposals include a pilot maximum four-week waiting time for children accessing mental health services[50]; specialist mental health teams working directly with schools[51]; a lead person in each school and college co-ordinating the referral of students to services; mental health awareness training for schools and colleges; and having mental health and well-being as part of the school curriculum[52]. On the surface the government's proposals seem positive. But, given the scale of need, £300 million is unlikely to be sufficient to fund the proposals, never mind address current shortcomings including the shortages of specialist personnel such as child psychiatrists[53]. Disturbingly, a review by the National Audit Office in late 2018 warned that 'the government ha[d] not set out and costed what it must do to achieve' its plans[54]. And a thorough review of the consultation paper by the House of Commons Education and Health Committees concluded that the government's plan 'lacks any ambition and fails to consider how to prevent child and adolescent mental ill health in the first place... put[s] more pressure on the teaching workforce without sufficient resources, and ... the funding... is not guaranteed'[55].

Furthermore there is a limit to what schools can reasonably be expected to do. Schools are ideal places for identifying children with poor mental health and referring them to specialist services; something they do now. The notion, however, that schools will be able to 'secure treatment promptly'[56] (as the government foresees) shows unbelievable naïveté about the reality of the current state of specialist child mental health services[57]. With no extra funding and cuts to school budgets, it is also totally unrealistic to think that every school could employ an 'on-site mental health professional'. There are serious concerns about how equipped teachers are to identify and respond appropriately to children's mental health problems; for example more than half of primary school teachers 'do not feel adequately trained in supporting pupils with mental health problems'[58]. It is also clear that the government hasn't bothered to talk to young people about what they want. Teenagers say teachers don't have the skills to help them, the vast majority of young people preferring to access professional mental health services external to, and not within, the school[59].

Conclusion: children's mental health – a serious cause for concern

It's self-evident that good mental health has a positive effect on the quality of people's lives, socially, educationally and employment-wise, and that mental health is a key factor influencing how well children and adults learn and achieve educationally. Increasing numbers of children, however, are suffering from mental ill-health and a major cause of this is the pressure on schools and their pupils to secure high grades in national examinations and tests.

Children's mental health services are under-resourced and, therefore, not able to meet the current demands being placed on them, and this contributes to young people's mental health conditions deteriorating. There can be little confidence that the government understands why this is happening, including the adverse effects of their own education policies; nor have they an appreciation of the huge scale of the problem; nor do they know what is required, over time, to make the substantial improvements that are needed. In virtually every year since 1998, there has been a national initiative aimed at improving children's mental health. None of these has made any lasting impact, and in all those years children's mental health, and the services meant to support them, have deteriorated. While the good intentions and rhetoric have been plentiful, effective action to improve matters has not.

3
SKILLS

Skill shortages holding back economy and people's life chances

I travelled across the country talking to all types of businesses and asked them what the single biggest threat to their future success would be. I got the same answer every time – skills.
Sir Keir Starmer MP[1]

Skills enable people to make their way in life. They are key to the quality of our relationships with family and friends, being good parents, and how we earn a living. Economic prosperity and the standard of public services are increasingly dependent on the skilled personnel available to employers. A critical test of the fitness of the learning system, then, is how well it provides the country and its individual citizens with the skills that are needed, which this chapter now assesses.

Skills take many forms. In chapter 1 we suggested these fell into three broad types - interpersonal, cognitive and technical skills. In studying the evidence, which we cite below, it is clear that the country has major skills shortages, negatively affecting economic growth and productivity, and causing there to be a significant number of low-skilled, poorly paid and insecure jobs.

Growing skill shortages across key sectors of the economy

There is a great deal of coverage in the media about the recruitment difficulties in particular areas of work such as the building trade and health service. These problems, affecting a wide range of occupations in both the private and public sectors, are at the heart of what has become a national skills crisis. The growing skills shortage the country faces, however, is a much more diverse and multi-dimensional phenomenon. At the root of the problem is the substantial number of people with poor numeracy and literacy skills, and what are termed as 'work-readiness' or 'employability' skills. These 'basic' skills, together with the other key issues that impact on the nation's skill shortages - vocational and technical education; apprenticeships; the number of science, technology, engineering and mathematics (STEM) graduates; and digital skills, will be explored later in this chapter. There is one area, however, generic higher level skills, where the UK is a world leader.

UK leading in generic higher level skills

Since the 1960s there has been a quadrupling of university students[2], with over a quarter of adults in the UK now having a degree[3]; a greater proportion of graduates than most other developed countries[4]. This abundance of workers with degrees and generic high-level skills has helped to grow the UK economy and cause productivity to be better than it otherwise would have been[5].

Millions with low numeracy and literacy skills

Conversely just under a half of sixteen-year-olds are leaving school without good GCSEs in English and/or mathematics, and a fifth don't achieve even the most basic levels in mathematics and reading[6]. These are the main reasons why one in seven young people are not in education, employment and training (NEET)[7]. England has nine million people of working age, one in four, who have low literacy or numeracy skills[8], and alarmingly for our long-term prospects, it is the only country in the developed world where the youngest adults are less literate and numerate than the generation approaching retirement[9].

Deficiencies in employability skills

Most employers say that there are too many young people they cannot employ because they lack the necessary disposition to be productive employees[10]. This is to do with poor basic cognitive skills (particularly numeracy and literacy), a lack of mature-enough interpersonal, social and communication skills, and what employers see as poor attitudinal and behavioural skills (such as commitment, punctuality and flexibility). Young people NEET in the UK face the biggest barriers to entering work in the industrialised world because of their lack of employability skills[11].

Of equal concern is the fact that employers report that there are deficiencies in the employability skills and work-readiness of a sizeable proportion of graduates who (at least at the start of their careers) experience difficulties in finding jobs requiring graduate-level skills[12]. Around one in two employers believe that the graduates they consider for jobs don't have the skills to start work, lacking 'people skills and a fundamental understanding of the world of work' and 'the ability to work with people and get things done when things go wrong'[13]. One cause of poor employability skills cited is the decline in school students taking up part-time jobs[14].

Dire shortage of vocational and technical skills

While the UK has a high number of young people with general education qualifications, such as GCSEs and A levels, just over one in three have 'upper-intermediate and lower-intermediate vocational qualifications', which has not changed in recent years[15], and compares very poorly with other countries[16]. This disadvantages the country, as research shows that an economy only benefits from skills stemming from general education at the 'upper end of the skills spectrum [i.e. degree level and above]'[17]. The UK also has one of the lowest proportions of people with technical subjects as their highest qualification, out of all developed countries[18]. It is 'losing ground' in respect of 'qualifications with a more technical and vocational focus' compared to other European countries[19], which is no wonder given the funding cuts to further education, the sector that provides most of the technician and vocational programmes[20].

In March 2017 the government announced plans to simplify what they correctly see as an 'over-complex system' of technical and professional education for sixteen to nineteen-year-olds[21]. Under the proposed new arrangements, called T-levels, up to twenty specific professional and technical routes lasting two years will be created, to be phased in from 2020[22]. (The government has also proposed introducing higher technical qualifications from 2022 as a progression from T-levels)[23]. These plans, however, may not go far enough. The UK's dire shortage of technical and scientific skills at graduate and pre-degree level is a long-term problem that will not be solved solely by changing the structure of 16-19 vocational qualifications, in isolation from the rest of the curriculum. There is a cultural bias against technical and vocational education that is embedded in the school curriculum and examinations system. This bias has been heightened by the government's use of what is called the English Baccalaureate (EBacc), a secondary school performance measure of 'core subjects' that excludes technical and vocational studies. The introduction of T-levels is likely to reinforce the bias as the Education Secretary, Damien Hinds, has made it clear that these new qualifications 'are predominantly a college-based system'[24]; that is, they are not for school sixth forms, which will continue with a largely A level offering for the 'most able' youngsters. Unless this bias is tackled the UK will continue to have substantial skills gaps in vital economic areas.

Insufficient good quality apprenticeships

Apprenticeships are paid jobs that combine training in the workplace with continuing education. They operate at three main levels – Intermediate (Level 2, roughly equivalent to GCSEs); Advanced (Level 3, roughly equivalent to A-levels); and Higher (Level 4 and above, pre-degree, degree level and post-degree). In many countries apprenticeships are a major vehicle for providing skilled jobs for individuals, particularly young people, and contributing to the skills their economies need. In Germany around sixty per cent of young people are on vocational training programmes, and the Chinese are doing something similar[25]. In the UK the number of apprentices shrank dramatically in the latter part of the twentieth century[26], but more recently government and business have started to re-vitalise them.

Apprenticeship numbers were increasing up to 2017 when they took a dramatic downturn as a result of the introduction of the government's 'apprenticeship levy'. The levy made it statutory from April 2017 for large companies[27] to pay 0.5% of their salary bill towards the funding of apprenticeships[28]. Under the previous system the government fully funded all sixteen to eighteen-year-old apprentices; nineteen to twenty-four-year-olds were fifty per cent funded; and older apprentices forty per cent funded, irrespective of the size of the company[29]. Since the levy was introduced there has been a substantial drop in apprenticeship starts in every successive quarter, compared to 12 months earlier[30]. For the period September 2017 to May 2018, for example, apprenticeship starts had declined by thirty-four per cent compared with the same period the previous year[31]. It might be instructive to ask what the public reaction might have been had there been a similar cut in the numbers of student places at university[32]? Probably a major outcry with demonstrations, petitions and debates in parliament. Another indication of the considerable bias in this country against vocational and technical education. It is highly unlikely therefore that the government's target of having three million apprenticeships by 2020 will be reached[33].

Worryingly, there is evidence that many organisations are 'exploiting' the new funding mechanism by training up existing employees rather than taking on new young people as apprentices. It is estimated that 'two-thirds of apprenticeships are... 'converting' existing employees and certifying existing skills, rather than focusing on expanding expertise'[34].

Probably a bigger concern is that apprenticeships are heavily skewed to those over twenty-five, more than young people[35], to the service sector rather than technical and scientific occupations[36], and to the lower (level 2) and not the higher end (level 3 and above) of the skills spectrum[37]. Interestingly, level 3 programmes are the mainstay of apprenticeships in other European countries[38]. In the UK, however, less than a quarter of young people starting an apprenticeship at level 2 progress to level 3[39], and large numbers of apprenticeships for young people are in jobs such as hairdressing or retail, where there is low pay and poor career prospects[40]. Far more women start apprenticeships than men[41], although male apprentices on average are paid more[42]. There is a small but growing number of higher level apprenticeships[43], whose graduates are twenty-five per cent more employable than those from traditional university courses[44]. The vast majority of higher level apprentices are aged over twenty-five[45].

Most small businesses say that their biggest challenge in recruiting apprentices is the quality of applicants they have to select from[46]. Many apprenticeship schemes are of poor quality, with over half of training providers judged by Ofsted as requiring improvement or inadequate[47], and more than a quarter of apprentices not completing their programmes[48]. The National Audit Office found that that there were no success measures to evaluate the quality or impact of the apprenticeship programme, and recommended that the government's approach should be more about the type of apprentices that are required rather than the overall number[49].

Following a review, the House of Commons Education and Business Select Committees[50] issued a scathing indictment of the national apprenticeship programme including the government's stewardship of it. The committees reported that 'There continues to be a worrying lack of focus [of apprenticeships] on the sectors of the economy where training or upskilling are, and will be, most needed. The government has not set out how its increase in apprenticeship numbers will help fill the country's skills gaps. The current balance of provision is skewed towards sectors with low wage returns and few skills shortages. As a result, the contribution that apprenticeships can make towards solving skills shortages and improving productivity is undermined'.

Not enough STEMs (Science, technology, engineering and mathematics)

STEM skills are of critical importance to a growing range of businesses including manufacturing, construction, research and development, and information technology and computing, as well as contributing to scientific and technological processes across all sectors of the economy. The proportion of UK graduates with degrees from 'courses of a practical or occupation-specific nature' is lower than many of our competitor countries[51]. There is a shortfall of about 40,000 STEM graduates each year[52], restricting economic growth[53]. It is also predicted that the problem will get worse in the next few years with 500,000 STEM workers retiring, and an additional 142,000 STEM jobs being created[54]. It is estimated that there will be 1.3 million more STEM jobs needed by 2030[55].

Growing skill shortages across key sectors of the economy

For the reasons outlined above, the UK suffers from major skill shortages in such areas as engineering[56], construction, information technology[57], the NHS[58], haulage[59], boat building[60], foreign languages[61] and the creative industries[62]. It is estimated that by 2022 the British economy will be short of three million skilled workers[63]. As a result, organisations are facing increasing problems in recruiting staff[64], which may be exacerbated when the UK leaves the EU in 2019. And more and more high-level skills, and fewer low-level skills are required in the UK; since 2001 there have been two million additional high-skilled jobs and 500,000 fewer low-skilled jobs[65].

In future as technology advances, especially automation, 'demand for skills will rocket' say the manufacturers' umbrella group, EEF[66]. According to Sir James Dyson, the UK needs an additional one million engineers with skills in software, hardware and electronics by 2020[67], which 'are badly needed if UK companies are to remain competitive'. Next to accessing finance, a shortage of surveyors, bricklayers and other construction workers is the biggest single factor holding back building work. This is at a time when there is a great need for more houses[68]. The rapid speed of technological and scientific change also contributes to the growing skills gap, as will the record numbers of skilled workers who will be retiring in the next five years from jobs where there are already major shortages[69].

The Fourth Industrial Revolution and digital skills

While the UK struggles with basic skills and has insufficient numbers of skilled personnel to fill well-established occupations such as engineering, construction and medicine, the world is deep into a 'Fourth Industrial Revolution', which is radically transforming the sets of skills that individuals, businesses and countries need. This latest industrial revolution is driven by digital power generating emerging technologies such as artificial intelligence, robotics, drones, autonomous vehicles and 3-D printing, creating innovative solutions in such areas as medicine, manufacturing, transport, entertainment, retail, marketing and communication. Billions of people across the globe, nearly a third of the world's population[70], are connected through computers and mobile devices, with access to what is virtually unlimited data storage capacity and knowledge. We are at a stage where 'digital skills are now necessary life skills'[71].

The government estimates that the digital sector in the UK is worth over £100 billion, and research suggests it might be double this[72]. While there is a growing demand for those with high-level specialist digital skills such as coding, in the near future 'almost all jobs will require some level of digital skills'[73]. The growth in the digital economy will require increasing numbers of digitally skilled workers if the UK is to capitalise on the available business opportunities[74]. About 138,000 new entrants a year are required to fill specialist digital roles[75], with a predicted 500,000 needed in the next few years[76]. However, there are already major shortages of such skills. More than half of the country's technology companies have vacancies which they are finding difficult to fill[77], and in excess of three-quarters of UK employers report a shortage of digital skills[78]. It is therefore very worrying that nearly one in five adults don't have basic digital skills, more so for those aged 45 plus, and in the north of England[79].

Skills crisis has multiple negative effects on country's way of life

The skill shortages have multiple adverse effects on the life of the country, including on economic growth and productivity, the general quality of employment, and the real value of wages. Investors tend to grow businesses around what skills are available. As a result there has been a substantial increase in the UK in the last ten years of low-skilled, low-paid jobs that have 'fuelled a slowdown in Britain's overall economic efficiency', weakening economic growth, eroding public finances and reducing the real value of the pay of many workers[80]. Businesses report that there is a widening skills gap (exacerbated by continuing falls in unemployment) which is one of the biggest 'barriers to growth' that they face[81].

Skill shortages = low productivity

Increasing productivity is essential for securing the long-term economic wellbeing of the country and its citizens, particularly in lifting the real value of wages, which have generally declined since the 2008 financial crisis. UK productivity has 'stagnated for a decade'[82], slowing down to a greater extent than in other major economies[83]. The productivity gap with other countries is increasing[84], graphically illustrated when the Chancellor of the Exchequer, Philip Hammond, reported that 'It takes a German worker four days to produce what we make in five'; which means that too many British workers work longer hours for lower pay than their counterparts[85]. While the UK ranks seventh in the world in terms of infrastructure, in education we are sixty-fifth out of 181 countries[86]. Education and skills are therefore seen as the country's 'Achilles' heel' when it comes to productivity[87].

Skill shortages = growing number of low-skilled, low-paid, insecure jobs

There is a clear link between skill shortages and the fact that the UK has a larger proportion of low-skilled, low-paid jobs, and fewer high-skilled jobs, than virtually any other northern and western European country[88]. Poor skills are the single biggest factor contributing to poverty, with a fifth of the entire workforce paid at or below the Living Wage[89] - over five million people[90]. There has also been a growth in jobs that are less secure, including self-employment and 'non-standard' employment contracts[91] such as 'zero-hours contracts'[92].

Conclusion - skill shortages due to cultural bias and disaffection

How does the UK measure up in terms of skills? It's a mixed picture, but overall there are serious shortfalls. The UK does well, compared to other developed countries, in supplying generic high-level skills. This is complemented by the increasing number of degree apprentices, seen by employers as highly employable.

We have, however, insufficient STEM graduates, and a major shortage of people with advanced technical and vocational qualifications. Apprenticeships are heavily skewed to those over twenty-five, the service industries and low-level qualifications, far more than young people, technical and scientific occupations, and the high end of the skills spectrum. Many apprenticeship schemes are of poor quality and nearly a third of apprentices drop out before completing the programme. Too many school leavers and graduates do not have adequate 'employability' skills. Although there has been a significant reduction in recent years, there is still a substantial number of young people not in education, employment and training (NEET). All of this results in substantial and growing skill shortages in several vital business sectors and public services.

These shortcomings have major consequences for the UK. Economic growth would be higher if the skill shortages were not as acute. Skill shortages contribute crucially to our low productivity and to the increasing number of low-paid and insecure jobs and, therefore, to the substantial economic and social inequalities there are in the country. The causes of these skill shortages are multi-faceted, including a strong bias in our education system against technical and vocational education. Only a comprehensive strategy, addressing all the main reasons for the skill shortages, will be capable of providing the country with the skilled personnel it requires for the future. In chapter 12 we outline what the main ingredients of such a strategy might look like.

4

INTERNATIONAL COMPARISONS

UK education lagging behind other countries

If we don't act with speed to close the gap in [education] performance, our country risks becoming an underachieving offshore island which in the next decade or two will watch much of the rest of the world go racing by[1]

Sir Richard Lambert

In seeking to understand the strength of our learning system it is important to know how the UK's education performance compares with that of other countries. Having an appreciation of where we stand internationally is even more vital when you consider that the UK is a highly developed country with the fifth largest economy in the world, competing for business in a globalised world. Comparisons with other developed countries show that:

- The UK performs far less well than a large number of other developed countries.
- The UK's international performance has been broadly stagnant for nearly ten years.
- High performing countries have three main characteristics:
    - Learning is highly valued in families
    - Teachers are held in high regard by society
    - The gap between the highest and lowest achievers is relatively small.

These findings stem from analysis of a number of studies comparing the respective performances of developed countries, including the Programme for International Student Assessment (PISA) of fifteen and sixteen-year-olds in mathematics, science and reading; Progress in International Reading Literacy Study (PIRLS) of ten-year-olds; GCSE world class standards; and basic literacy and numeracy skills of 16 to 19-year-olds and graduates. The key outcomes of these studies as they affect the UK and England are outlined below.

The learning tower of PISA – no improvement in UK since 2006

Every three years the Organisation for Economic Co-operation and Development (OECD) carries out a worldwide study of education in its member and partner countries, PISA, which is the most commonly used tool for comparing education standards in the developed countries of the world. Fifteen-year-olds in each country sit identical tests in mathematics, science and reading. Results for the last two PISA studies are show below:

Year	Participating countries	UK Ranking		
		Mathematics	Science	Reading
2012	65	26	20	23
2015	72	27	15	22

As you can see, PISA in 2015[2] shows only marginal changes for the UK from 2012. Science has traditionally been one of the UK's strongest subjects in international comparisons, and we moved to fifteenth in the PISA rankings, despite having a reduced average test score (other countries' results also declined)[3]. There was a very small improvement in reading[4], but in mathematics both the average score and the ranking fell[5]. European countries such as Poland and Germany are now significantly better than England and the UK[6]. Nations like South Korea, China and Singapore have made substantial advances in all subjects, increasing the gap with England and the UK[7]. There was a large gap between the highest and lowest achievers; one of the widest internationally[8]. It is interesting to note that one of the highest performing regions in England, London, is ranked 21st in science, 24th in reading and 26th in mathematics, out of thirty-seven cities, six months behind leading world cities[9]. Overall the OECD has concluded that:

PISA 2015 shows there had in effect been no material improvement in the past three years, nor indeed much change since 2006 in the UK's results[10].

Primary school pupils achieve highly in international tests

When they are of primary school age, English children seem to fare better in international tests than they do when they reach the end of their compulsory schooling. In literacy tests taken in fifty countries[11] in 2016, England's ten year-olds were placed joint eighth, compared to tenth in 2011 and 15th in 2006. These literacy tests, however, evidence a greater gap in England between the highest and lowest achievers than in most other countries[12]. In mathematics tests taken in forty-five countries in 2015[13], English ten-year-olds were joint ninth, with Ireland ahead of England in the rankings[14]. What is striking is that when analysed, the results of these tests show that 'England has one of the biggest gaps in the developed world between high and low achievers in maths'[15]. We know that this achievement gap widens as children go through their school life, and this may be the main explanation as to why England's ten year-olds achieve far better in international tests than they do at aged fifteen and sixteen.

Just over third of English students meeting world class standard in GCSEs

The new GCSE grade scale, which started to be introduced for examinations in 2017, is 'pegged to international standards'. On the scale of one to nine, where nine is the highest, grade five is deemed as the 'world class standard', calculated as being that 'achieved by the average student in countries at the top of world education'. Analysis of the 2016 GCSE results, marked under the A*-G scale, shows that only thirty-five per cent of students would have achieved this 'world class standard'. The results of the analysis 'illustrate how far British teenagers have fallen behind their peers in countries such as China, South Korea, Germany and Poland'[16].

Literacy and numeracy of UK 16-19-year-olds and graduates amongst worst in developed world

English sixteen to nineteen-year-olds, based on an international assessment of their ability to read and answer questions on a text, and numerical ability, are ranked as the worst-performing of twenty-three OECD member countries for literacy, and the second worst for numeracy[17]. Alarmingly, these tests show that the number of low-skilled sixteen to nineteen year-olds in England is three times more than the best performing countries such as Finland, South Korea and Holland[18].

Although the UK is a leading country in supplying generic higher level skills, as reported in chapter 3, it has a significant proportion of graduates with low levels of numeracy and literacy skills[19]. As a result the OECD has poignantly concluded that 'England has a large university system relative to a poorly skilled pool of potential entrants'[20].

Conclusion – underperforming UK must do better

Given the highly competitive globalised world we live in today, and the criticality of learning and skills for social and economic wellbeing, it is important that the UK understands how well its citizens are educated compared to other countries. The faster economic growth of countries such as India and Brazil means they are likely to surpass us within the next decade. There is also an imperative for the UK to have sufficient of the right workplace skills to be able to better compete in global markets when it leaves the European Union in 2019.

Our conclusions have been informed by the analysis of PISA and other international research. These have been supplemented by a more in-depth comparison of the UK with two other countries – Finland and Canada, which we have undertaken, drawing from accounts of those who have had first-hand experience of what, according to PISA, are the best performing countries in Europe and America[21].

Comparing countries is not straightforward and we should be careful not to draw simplistic conclusions. Nevertheless, the outcomes of the five sets of triennial PISA studies into education in the world's most developed countries show the UK as a consistent mid-table performer, and make very clear that the

UK can and must do better than it has been doing for at least the last seventeen years. It is concerning that the education performance of the UK, and England in particular, has virtually stood still since 2009 and, in the critical subject of mathematics, appears to be going backwards. Although science is the UK's strongest subject in PISA tests, not enough young people are studying science or science-based subjects beyond age16[22], which (as described in the previous chapter) is a major cause of there being insufficient graduates to fill growing numbers of STEM jobs. The international comparisons also show that the UK has a bigger gap between its highest and lowest achieving young people than most other countries. This results in the UK having one of the highest proportion of sixteen to nineteen-year-olds with poor literacy, numeracy and other skills.

The countries that consistently do better than the UK all have different systems and policy approaches to learning and education. It would not be sensible to take one of the high performing countries and simply transfer what they are doing to the UK. There are, however, some key characteristics of many of the high performing countries that we need to take serious heed of if we are to significantly improve educational achievement in the UK and match the best in the world. There are three main circumstances that seem to be common to most of those countries that do well educationally:

• Learning and education is highly valued by families, and children are actively encouraged to work hard and do well at school. There are too many families in the UK where this is not the case, and the poor quality of children's upbringing puts them at a disadvantage in their learning and their progress in education.
• Teachers are held in the highest regard and respected as the important professionals they are[23]. The increasing difficulties that schools in the UK have in recruiting and retaining teachers, which is covered in more detail in chapter 8, indicate that teachers generally are dissatisfied with the undue pressure on them, constant organisational changes and heavy workload, and that they feel undervalued by parents, government and the wider public.
• There are good results for children from poorer and immigrant backgrounds, and less inequality of educational outcomes. The gap between the highest and lowest attaining pupils is a great deal narrower in these high performing countries than it is in the UK.

We need also to consider why countries do far better than the UK without some of the features of an education system that have been so cherished by successive UK governments. For example neither Finland nor Canada have public tests, or examinations for pupils until the age of eighteen, or systematic external inspections of schools.

In the UK we are overly-obsessed with structure – what schools are called, who governs them, whether they are selective or not; as well as constantly changing the curriculum, national tests and examinations. This appears not to be the case in high performing countries, where the main focus is on developing the best conditions for children to learn and teachers to teach. Elsewhere what macro-structures are in place seems to matter a lot less than what is happening in school classrooms. In the UK, education policy and structures are highly centralised; in Canada very much de-centralised; and in Finland a mixture of both. Pupils in countries where schools are deemed (by the PISA analysis) to have relatively less autonomy seem to do as well as those from countries whose schools are seen as having more autonomy. It is interesting that both in Finland and Canada local authorities have a significant role, far more than in the UK, where since 1990 the function of local councils in regard to education has continuously been diminished by central government. What really counts is whether the professionals on the front line, both school leaders and classroom practitioners, feel they have enough discretion to use their professional skills in the way that they believe best suits children's learning and welfare.

Renowned Finnish educator, Professor Pasi Sahlberg, succinctly describes the essence of what the international education research tells us in saying that:

> *What Pisa surveys, in general, have revealed is that education policies that are based on the principle of equal opportunities and equality in education and that have brought teachers to the core of educational change have positively impacted the quality of education systems*[24].

5
FAMILIES

Family life the most significant influence on learning

Families are the bedrock of our society. The family provides both a safety net and a springboard from which to make a place in the world.
National Institute of Adult Continuing Education[1]

The quality of their family upbringing is the single biggest influence that shapes children's lives and their adulthood, including how well they learn and achieve educationally. This is an important matter in the context of this book, because we believe that in their approaches to learning and education this crucial factor has been largely ignored by successive governments. Former school head and university vice-chancellor, Sir Anthony Seldon, puts it more candidly in saying that:

> *Families are largely forgotten ... Governments are afraid to talk about this area. We champion the liberty of adults to have children, how they want, but not the liberty and the right of the child to have stable and secure parenting. The pleasure and rights of parents are lauded over responsibility for children. Children need not only security but firm expectations of their behaviour. Parenting is a lifelong responsibility, and the better the parenting – ie love and security with firm guidelines – the less likely the child will be to develop mental problems. We need a massive drive towards responsible parenting[2].*

For many children positive changes to their home life would have very beneficial effects on their learning, their engagement with and outcomes from school, and consequently their ability to make good the opportunities they are presented with later on in life - further and higher education, skilled employment, and positive mental and physical health. This chapter looks at the links between children's home life and their general development, and more specifically their learning and education outcomes. It also assesses the success of recent government initiatives to improve family life.

Children's future shaped mainly by their home life

The experiences of childhood, particularly the early years, lay the core foundations for the rest of people's lives. Children's development is shaped by a whole range of experiences, behaviours and events that happen in their family life. How well are they cared for? Do they feel loved? How safe, secure and stable do they feel? Are they taught to behave well, to respect and care for others? Is the relationship with adults a positive and responsive one? Do adults respond positively to children's inquisitiveness and questions about what they are observing, experiencing and feeling? Do adults engage with them in exploring the world around them? Are there positive adult and older sibling role models, both male and female? Is there stability in the family unit? Are there generally good relationships between the adults, and between adults and children, in the family? If the answers are generally positive then children will develop the basic social, emotional and communication skills for healthy development and build the necessary resilience to overcome the challenges they will face in the future. On the other hand, children who experience negative parenting and a poor-quality home life usually become vulnerable and are at high risk of poor outcomes, including in regard to their physical and mental health, education and employment.

Family upbringing most important determinant of education success

There is a great body of research that supports how critical parenting and home environment is to quality of life outcomes for children and adults. The role of parents plays a large part in performance at school, as the more they engage, the better their children do[3]. One study[4] concludes that 'before even starting school, differences are found in children's cognitive and behavioural development'[5]. These differences, however, are more to do with what parents do with their children with regard to education activities and parenting style than with family income levels[6]. For example, when parents eat the main meal of the day with their children and discuss matters like homework, this increases their children's sense of belonging[7]. Research findings draw a distinction between parenting skills and poverty; both have 'important but independent effects on children's outcomes'[8]. Wilkinson and Pickett's research suggests that 'good schools make a difference', but 'the biggest influence on educational attainment, how well a child performs in school and later in higher education, is family background. Children... do better if they come from homes where they have a place to study, where books and newspapers are available, and where education is valued.'[9] The International Reading Literacy Study backs this up, finding that 'children whose parents had engaged them in literacy activities – reading books or playing word games – from an early age are better equipped with basic reading skills when they begin primary schools and go on to have higher reading achievements'[10].

The qualitative involvement of parents, particularly mothers, on their children's cognitive development can be discerned from as early as three months onwards[11]. Children whose mothers believe that 'their fate lies in their own hands' do better in GCSEs, even when family background, mother's education and the child's sense of control are taken into account. This is because such mothers have a 'more hands-on approach to parenting' as they 'strongly believe that their actions will make a difference in their child's life'[12]. Fathers' involvement 'is associated with a range of positive outcomes for children including educational and emotional attainment, and... mental health'[13]. Babies' learning is accelerated if their fathers engage with them in their first few months, and 'confident fathers, who embraced becoming a parent, were less likely to have children who displayed behavioural issues before the teenage years'[14].

Another factor demonstrating the importance of the quality of home life to children's learning is the increasing amount of homework that school pupils are set by their teachers. Many parents ensure that their children complete this homework and will help them do it. Other parents won't, and this adds to what is a growing gap in educational progress between children depending on their home circumstances. 'Every time I sit down with my children to do the bit of curriculum that school hours can't cover' says children's novelist, Michael Rosen, 'I am widening [the attainment gap]'[15]. On average parents in the UK spend less time helping their children with homework than in most other developed countries[16].

Many children and young people in the UK are experiencing vulnerabilities within their families. Shockingly, nearly a third live in poverty and 188,000 are homeless or living in temporary accommodation[17]. 670,000 live in high risk family situations (such as high levels of substance addiction and domestic violence); 500,000 are supported by public services; and 200,000 have experienced trauma or abuse[18]. It is not surprising then that large numbers of children are ill-prepared to start school and benefit from what education offers[19]. For example, almost a third of four-year-olds have such poor speech, language and communication skills that they are not ready to start school[20]. Research by Ofsted found that many children start school knowing only a third of the words they should, and quickly fall behind in their learning[21]. This worrying situation prompted one primary school headteacher to quip that 'some children know how to swipe a phone but haven't a clue about conversation'[22]. Another vivid illustration of this lack of school-readiness is the reports from teachers that an increasing number of three to seven-year-olds are wetting or soiling themselves at school, the main reason being the rise in parents failing to toilet-train their children before they start school[23].

Children's traumatic home experiences are, very sadly, growing, with huge increases in the numbers of children being referred to social care[24], on child protection plans[25] and going into care[26]. Levels of education attainment of those children referred to social care lag behind their peers, even when they are no longer assessed as being 'in-need', showing the 'lasting negative impact' of poor family life experiences[27].

The abuse and neglect being suffered by children and young people is likely to get worse as local services are diminished because of population growth, increasing demand for support, and central government cuts to council budgets. Since 2010 there have been severe budget cuts in the funding for early intervention, to help children and families prior to reaching 'crisis point', and other services involved in protecting children such as children's centres, youth centres, teenage pregnancy advice and family support[28]. These budget reductions have resulted in real spending on children's services falling dramatically, particularly in the areas of greatest need[29], despite increasing demand pushing up spending on children's social care by almost ten per cent in the last four years[30]. It is estimated that by 2020 there will be a shortfall in these budgets of £2 billion[31].

What is especially concerning is that we have now reached a situation where half of all the spending on children's services goes on the 73,000 children who are in care, and another thirty per cent on those with child protection plans, leaving only a fifth for more preventative work[32]. As a result, thresholds to trigger social service intervention where children are being neglected or abused have risen substantially[33]. One and a half million children living in families with 'very high needs'[34] are not getting 'any form of substantial help'[35]. And research shows that if children are not supported at an early stage their problems worsen[36]. At the same time it is deeply concerning that services for children appear to have been de-prioritised by the current government with the downgrading of the role of the children's minister[37].

Both Labour and Conservative ministers have failed to understand the fundamental importance of family life on children's education outcomes. When family background is mentioned, ministers have often retorted that this is an excuse used by teachers for having low aspirations for children from low-income groups. However, as anyone working with children from different backgrounds understands, and as research proves, parenting and family life has a major impact on children's life chances, including educational achievement. While we should guard against professionals using family background to depress their ambitions for children, a critical ingredient for raising educational outcomes for those who currently under-achieve, is sustained activity aimed at improving the quality of home life for these children.

Government family initiatives not effective

Over the years there have been a number of major government initiatives to support families.

Sure Start was launched by the Labour government in 1998 to give help and advice to families on health, parenting, financial management, training and employment. The programme was originally conceived to meet locally assessed needs, with core elements including children centres, play and healthcare, and outreach services for families. Some centres also provide early learning and full day care for children of pre-school age. Under Labour, Sure Start became a universal service and children centres were put on a statutory footing. In 2010 the coalition government introduced a core purpose, focusing on the neediest families and on early intervention[38]. As a consequence of removing ring-fenced funding and considerable grant reductions, since 2010 the number of children centres has been reduced by around a third, causing a major diminution in service levels to children and families[39].

Government-commissioned evaluations of the effectiveness of Sure Start[40] show some positive impacts on parenting and the home learning environment; and on some health indicators including immunisation rates. More telling, however, is that the centres appeared to make no difference to behaviour, and 'school-readiness' defined as 'early language, numeracy and social skills needed to succeed in schools'. An Audit Commission review found the health improvements had been 'limited'. While between 1998 and 2011 £10.9 billion, including £7.2 million in Sure Start, had been spent on initiatives to improve the health of children under the age of five, some health indicators, for example obesity and dental health, had actually worsened, and there had been no real reduction of the gap in health inequalities. In addition, the evaluations could not evidence that Sure Start had made a discernible difference to children's general and cognitive development. Nor did Sure Start positively change the employment situation within families[41].

Think Family, introduced in 2007, was about 'secur[ing] better outcomes for children, by co-ordinating the support they receive from children's, adults' and family services'[42]. It generally promoted joined up multi-agency work with families across the country. The independent evaluation of Think Family's pathfinder programmes showed that there had been 'significant improvement in outcomes for nearly half of [all] families supported' and 'savings to local partners'[43], and that there was 'a compelling case for LAs [local authorities] and their partners to develop and implement intensive family intervention with families with multiple and complex needs'[44].

The coalition government, however, ceased the Think Family policy and in 2012 launched the Troubled Families Programme (TFP) aimed at 'turning around' the lives of 120,000 'troubled families' by 2015[45]. Under the programme, councils were paid to work in a multi-agency way with families that had multiple problems, including worklessness and truancy. The aims were to reduce antisocial behaviour, get truanting children back into school and get parents into jobs. By 2015 £448 million had been spent on the programme, with a further £200 million earmarked for 2015-20. Local authorities are paid up to £4,000 on a payment-by-results basis when they 'turn around' a family[46]. In March 2015 the government proclaimed that TFP had been a great success, turning around the lives of 105,000 people and saving £1.2 billion[47]. A subsequent independent evaluation[48], however, totally contradicted the government's claims[49], concluding that there was 'no evidence that the programme was having any significant or systematic impact on employment prospects, performance at school, crime and antisocial behaviour or dependency on benefits'[50]. The claim of virtual total success of TFP was based on information from local councils, who were financially incentivised to make positive returns[51].

The House of Commons Public Accounts Committee criticised the government for its 'misleading' report overstating the benefits of the TFP, which did not achieve long-term change in families' lives[52]. One of the independent evaluators of TFP, Jonathan Portes, was scathing, saying that 'the Troubled Families Programme [is] a perfect case study of how the manipulation and misrepresentation of statistics by politicians and civil servants – from the Prime Minister downwards – led directly to bad policy and, frankly, to the wasting of hundreds of millions of pounds of taxpayers' money'[53].

Conclusion: Home life critical for children's future, but government family programmes have had little impact

The evidence undoubtedly shows that the quality of their parenting and home life is the most significant factor determining how well children develop and learn. How far children derive the benefits of what schools offer depends greatly on their experiences during their earliest and most formative years in the family home. Increasing numbers seem ill-prepared to start school, and many do not receive the parental support they need during their time at school.

It is surprising and disturbing, then, that successive governments have not seen family life as the major focus for improving children's life chances and in particular their education outcomes. Instead, governments have preferred to place the main responsibility on schools for turning round the fortunes of children who from the earliest ages have had their lives blighted by poor parenting. And the problems faced by children at home are likely to get worse. There are signs, including increases in reports of neglect and abuse, that more and more children are experiencing home lives that are chaotic and dysfunctional. Recent government interventions, because they have been short-term and driven by a requirement for quick results, have had negligible or no impact on the lives of children and families. The high levels of educational underachievement in the UK will not be effectively tackled without a long-term strategy for influencing the quality of family life for those children who are at risk of poor social, health and education outcomes. How this might be done is covered in chapter 10.

6
SCHOOLS

30 year political consensus leaves 'long tail of underperformance'

Since 1988, all governments with the best of intentions, but in ignorance and deafness, have trammelled schools with excessive testing, obsessive inspection and a restrictive curriculum which has taken from schools their professional autonomy, damaged the status of teachers in the public eye, and in consequence endangered the all-round education of the nation's young.
Professor Michael Bassey[1]

The quality of family life is the most important determinant of how well children do educationally. We now consider the second most crucial factor – schools. This chapter examines government policy on schools over the last thirty years, and how effective this has been. We have found that:

- Over the last thirty years there has been a political consensus on national education policy.
- During this time the numbers of people with good academic qualifications and those going to university have risen.
- The control that successive governments have exerted on schools, however, has contributed significantly to growing mental ill-health in children, large numbers of young people underachieving, critical skill shortages, poor education outcomes compared to other developed countries, and a disenchanted and understrength teaching workforce.

Since the 1988 Education Reform Act, governments of all political parties have broadly had the same policy approach to English education and increasingly directed what happens in schools through the national curriculum, nationally designed tests and examinations, external inspections, and the push for schools to become academies. Over this time the continuing demise of the education role of local authorities has been matched by increasing central government control over state schools.

The 1988 Act provided the mechanisms for most of the changes that took place in the following three decades. In the 1990s the Conservatives brought in self-governance and management of schools, the national curriculum, grant maintained schools, Ofsted to systematically inspect schools, publishing of test and examination results, and powers to intervene in schools perceived as 'failing'. From 1997 the Conservative's reforms were continued and extended by the Labour government. 'What is remarkable' says Professor Alan Smithers 'is how little [the Labour government] differed at root from the policies of the previous Conservative administrations. Many of the education reforms which the Conservatives had introduced from 1988 onwards... now became the backbone of the Blair programme. The national curriculum, tests and league tables, financial delegation to schools, and a beefed-up inspection service were all enthusiastically adopted by New Labour'[2].

From 2010 the Conservative/Liberal Democrat coalition government built on Labour's work. The chief architect and driver of the coalition's schools' policy, Education Secretary Michael Gove, expressed his admiration for both Tony Blair[3] and his key education adviser, Andrew Adonis[4], and their education policies, particularly the academies programme. This consensus has continued with the Conservative governments elected in 2015 and 2017.

There are a number of positive features of this thirty-year political consensus. The principle of the national curriculum is a very sound one, which if used appropriately can provide a consistent learning entitlement to all school pupils throughout the country. But, as explained later, how the national curriculum has been applied, particularly in conjunction with high stakes testing, has led to a narrow, 'overcrowded' curriculum. Self-governance and management has proven to be a sensible way of running schools, with those closest to the service making the key decisions. School 'autonomy', however, has been undermined by the growing influence of central government in how schools are run.

Another dimension of the political consensus, at least up until 2015, is the priority given to funding schools. The 1997-2010 Labour government doubled school funding in real terms[5], and the coalition government (2010-15) protected school budgets at a time when most other public services were being savagely cut. Since the Conservatives were elected in 2015, cash allocated to schools has not kept pace with inflation and increased pupil numbers, leading to real terms budget reductions for individual schools[6]. An additional £1.3 billion has been added to the schools budget for 2018 and 2019[7]. Despite the cuts, spending on UK schools is above the OECD average[8]. The government has also decided to introduce a national funding formula[9] which, whatever its merits, is the latest in a long-line of measures to impose central government control over schools.

Being tough with schools

The policy consensus over the last thirty years can best be described as governments being 'tough with schools'. It is an approach based on the belief that exerting pressure on schools forces teachers and pupils to perform better, thus raising educational standards. There has been 'tough' rhetoric from the various education secretaries. David Blunkett (in 1997) 'named and shamed' eighteen 'failing' schools and threatened their closure, saying 'difficult situations demand tough solutions'[10]. Nicky Morgan (in 2015) said there would be 'tough targets for coasting schools' and headteachers of 'coasting schools' would be sacked[11]. Ofsted regularly join in the tough talk, 'naming and shaming' whole areas of the country including the worst-performing region, worst for early years and worst for disadvantaged children[12]. In 2016 Sir Michael Wilshaw, Ofsted's then chief, publicly castigated Birmingham as 'a rotten borough' with 'awful schools' that were 'beyond redemption'[13], and opined that 'lower standards in schools in the Midlands and north of England contributed to a sense of resentment behind the Brexit vote'[14]. The rhetoric has been backed up with a package of measures depicted below.

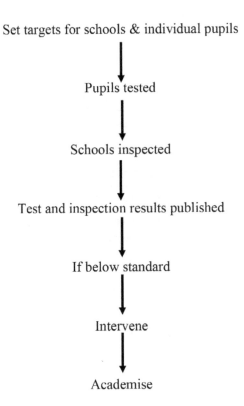

Set targets for schools & individual pupils

↓

Pupils tested

↓

Schools inspected

↓

Test and inspection results published

↓

If below standard

↓

Intervene

↓

Academise

Together these measures represent the heavy hand of government scrutiny and control over schools. Each of these measures is now explained, including their impact on schools. To provide a complete picture, two other main pieces of government education policy over the last thirty years – the belief in market forces, and constant change – are also unpicked.

Testing for school accountability, not children's learning

From the earliest age up to young adulthood, children and young people in England are formally tested virtually every year, and are amongst the most tested in the world[15].

Age (years)	Test
0-5	Early years learning goals
4-5	Baseline check in basic literacy, reasoning and cognition
6	Phonics reading and spelling screening check
7	Phonics check again, if required standard not met
7	Key Stage 1 SATs in mathematics, reading and writing (ending in 2023)
9	Times table tests (from 2019/20)
8,9 & 10	'Optional' SATs (which many schools use)
11	Key Stage 2 SATs in spelling, punctuation and grammar, reading, and written and mental mathematics
13	Optional Key Stage 3 SATs tests in English and mathematics
14	Optional Key Stage 3 SATs tests in science
15	Mock GCSEs
16	GCSE and equivalents
17	GCE AS levels
18	GCE A levels and equivalents
18+	Degrees and other higher education courses – annual examinations

The government sets minimally acceptable levels of attainment for all schools; for eleven- year-olds in reading, writing and mathematics; and for sixteen year-olds for GCSEs[16]. Schools are also classed as underperforming if a sufficient proportion of pupils do not achieve expected progress between Key Stages one and two (primary) and Key Stages two and four (secondary). How these progress measures are calculated is quite complex and is explained in glorious detail in government instructions to schools[17]. Schools falling below these 'floor targets' are 'named and shamed' in 'performance tables', and are then subject to intervention. This puts schools under such pressure that some go to extremes to meet the targets. One example is that in 2017 fifty-four secondary schools entered pupils for GCSE mathematics with two examination boards, a practice that is banned[18].

There is no link between how much a country tests its children and its level of educational achievement[19]. As evidenced in chapter 2, however, the increase in testing in English schools has led to rising mental health problems amongst children[20]. Most tests and examinations serve to judge and hold schools to account, rather than giving helpful feedback to children and teachers.

In 2018 the government introduced a baseline test of pupils in Reception classes, which 'has only one overriding purpose… to hold schools in England to account for the progress that pupils have made at the end of key stage 2'[21]. According to an evaluation by the British Educational Research Association this assessment, costing in excess of £10 million, is 'flawed, unjustified, and wholly unfit for purpose' and will be 'detrimental to children, parents, teachers, and the wider education system in England'. The test will not even serve its sole purpose, as 'any value-added calculations that will be used to hold school to account will be highly unreliable', and certainly 'will offer no formative help in establishing [children's] needs and/or in developing teaching strategies capable of meeting them'. The evaluation rightly concludes 'that the assessment of very young children is hard to justify when it is not being used to support a child's learning'[22].

Another example are Key Stage 2 SATs[23], held at the end of children's primary schooling and, therefore, offering little or no diagnostic information to teachers or children to aid improved learning. Schools minister, Nick Gibb, confirms that 'Sats [are] about holding schools to account'. He astonishingly goes on to say that 'the results [of SATs] will have no impact on a child's future education'[24]! Furthermore, because secondary schools believe that SATs are too narrow and 'over-coached', they buy in other testing arrangements, such as Cognitive Abilities Tests (CATs), to provide baseline information, inform individual learning plans, and organise pupils into sets for certain subjects. Nevertheless, Key Stage 2 SATs results act as the main accountability measure for primary schools, and provide the baseline for the progress measure for secondary schools. Despite SATs having 'no impact on a child's future education' the Conservatives in the run-up to the 2015 general election promised that children who had 'poor' Key Stage 2 SATs results would have to re-sit them, possibly twice, in their first year of secondary school[25]. Thankfully, in late 2018 the government made a low key announcement that it would 'not proceed' with the re-sits[26].

One unintended and perverse effect of this immense pressure on schools to succeed in external tests is the fourfold increase in teachers caught cheating to obtain better examination results[27]. Another perverse consequence is what the chief inspector of schools, Amanda Spielman, reports as an increasing number of schools who are exerting pressure on parents to take their children with special needs and behavioural difficulties and home educate them, in 'an effort to boost exam performance'[28]. As the rationale for external testing and examinations is school accountability, they inevitably determine the priorities of what is taught and how it is taught. There are two major consequences of this 'teaching to the test' – a narrowing of the curriculum, and significant numbers of young people becoming disengaged from education.

Despite contrary evidence ministers continue to operate in the mistaken belief that having a raft of statutory national tests improves children's learning. The latest, stemming from its inclusion in the Conservative party's 2015 manifesto, is the decision to test year 4 pupils' (eight and nine-year-olds) knowledge of times tables from 2019/20. The justification for this, according to the schools minister, is that the 'multiplication tables check will help teachers identify those pupils who require extra support'. He goes on to make the extraordinary claim that this online test (that will take only five minutes) 'will ensure that all pupils leave primary school knowing their times tables by heart and able to start secondary school with a secure grasp of fundamental arithmetic as a foundation for mathematics'[29]. The stark reality is that this national test will not tell teachers anything more than they already know about their year 4 pupils. We don't know of any primary school that doesn't teach the times tables and regularly assess the progress that each of its pupils is making. The government's mandatory multiplication test then is a sheer waste of time and money: resources that could be better allocated to more pressing needs in our schools.

Inspecting for accountability, not to improve schools

The systematic inspection of schools is central to the overall approach to education that different governments have pursued for over twenty-five years. Ofsted[30], established in 1992, is responsible for school inspections, and also inspects and regulates a vast range of other provision and services[31]. It has a huge remit that some consider too wide. The organisation is headed by Her Majesty's Chief Inspector. Following an inspection, four grades – outstanding, good, requires improvement and inadequate – are used by Ofsted to make judgements about a school, both overall and for the different aspects of the inspection i.e. leadership and management, governance, behaviour and safety, quality of teaching, achievement, and the sixth form[32]. There is invariably 'intervention' in schools deemed 'inadequate', usually in the form of the dismissal of the headteacher and/or governing body (being replaced by an Interim Executive Board) and forced 'academisation' under the control of an existing academy trust.

Successive governments have had an unshakeable conviction in the power of inspections, believing they provide objective accounts about school performance, show how schools can do better, and enable parents to make an informed choice about which schools to send their children to. Those with faith in the marketisation of education see this as a powerful way of raising standards. However, there is a counter view. The evidence casts real doubt about how well inspections hold schools to account, helps them improve or drives standards up through market forces.

There is a tendency for judgements made by Ofsted to be seen as the absolute truth and beyond challenge. As researcher and journalist, Robert Colvile, pithily says 'The Ofsted verdict has the weight of Scripture. Schools that fail are thrown to the wolves. Those that pass put up giant, boastful banners'[33]. But, Ofsted's judgements can be flawed. Schools with lower numbers of children from poorer families and higher prior attainment are more likely to be judged as outstanding when inspected. Conversely, schools with higher proportions of poorer children are more likely to be rated inadequate. Schools with the fewest pupils on free school meals were the most likely to improve their inspection grades from good to outstanding[34]. In 2014 Ofsted discontinued its outsourcing of inspections to private companies[35], and in 2015 didn't re-engage forty per cent of additional inspectors, because they were 'not good enough to judge schools'[36]. These dismissals of inspectors call into question the consistency of Ofsted findings overall.

Inspection reports make dramatic judgements about schools – from 'outstanding' to 'inadequate', and highlight schools' strengths and what they believe is wrong. They don't, however, put forward the practicalities about how schools can actually improve what is wrong. The system has become heavily weighted towards inspections rather than improvement work. According to headteacher, education adviser and author, Will Ryan, this means that school leaders have been 'looking backwards at what they should have achieved or looking over their shoulder to protect their backs, rather than looking forwards and steering the school towards an outstanding future'[37].

Current ministers regularly quote that ninety per cent of schools (or 1.9 million pupils) are now good or outstanding, as a way of demonstrating the success of government education policies. It is the case that – 'the proportion of schools judged good or outstanding *at their most recent inspection*[38]' has risen from sixty-five per cent in 2010 to ninety per cent in 2017. But, how have school inspection grades improved so much when over the same period test and examination results, and how well we compare with other developed nations, have flat-lined? Undoubtedly, due to the skills and hard work of school leaders and their staff, many schools have improved, and this is reflected in better inspection outcomes. The statistic, however, is misleading as not every school is inspected each year. The ninety per cent figure includes schools that have not been inspected for a number of years, some as long as 12 years ago, having been judged to be good or outstanding at the time. Outstanding schools are not routinely inspected; only about ten per cent are inspected each year, and many have not been inspected since 2006, and then under a different Ofsted framework[39]. In fact, of the schools actually being inspected there are far fewer than ninety per cent returning good or outstanding judgements; only fifty-four per cent, for example, in 2017/18[40]. Worryingly, secondary schools are faring far less well than primaries and the gap between the two phases is growing[41]. Research shows that more than a quarter of the rise in pupils attending good or outstanding schools is due to the overall increase in school rolls[42], and not an expansion of the number of schools achieving high inspection grades.

What difference do all these inspections make? The research, both for England and internationally, gives mixed findings. A review of relevant research concluded that Ofsted inspections have a powerful influence on schools' actions, but whether this influence is overall positive or negative depends on the type of school inspected and the quality of inspections'[43]. One study showed that there were 'slight' improvements in GCSE results where 'achievement was already much higher or lower than the average (e.g. selective schools)' but in all other schools (the majority), no improvement[44]. Other studies found 'no relation between inspections and student achievement, or even a decline in student achievement results after inspection visits'[45]. From their review of research, Ehren et al concluded that there was 'no clear picture of the impact of school inspections on student achievement' [46]. There were other important findings from the research. Teachers teach to the test and to the inspection criteria, which narrows the curriculum[47]. Schools in disadvantaged areas are less likely to improve from one inspection to the other[48]. Inspections take insufficient account of the context within which individual schools operate (particularly disadvantage)[49], and 'highlight what needs to be done' but not 'how to do it' [50]. Conversely, the countries with the best educational performances in Europe and America – Finland and Canada – do not have national external inspections of their schools.

Another concern is that the framework within which inspections are carried out changes every few years. This is not only frustrating for schools, but causes major re-training for inspectors, school leaders and teachers, diverting vital staff time and resources away from children's learning. Yet more, very substantial, changes to the inspection framework are planned to be introduced from September 2019[51], with schools having only a few months to adjust to the new framework once it is finalised.

And, finally there seems to be a perverse relationship between the inspection system and the interests of more vulnerable and underachieving pupils. Research shows that 'school leaders regularly felt incentivized to prioritize the interests of the school over the interests of particular groups of, usually more vulnerable, children' [52] and that there is 'no significant evidence' that effective schools (as judged by Ofsted) are 'reducing the gap in attainment between children from affluent and poor backgrounds'[53].

No evidence that the education market drives up standards

Conservative, Labour and coalition governments have all believed in the power of the market to raise school and pupil performance. The market theory goes something like this. Test and examination results and inspection reports are published. These help parents to make informed choices about the schools their children go to. Parents choose the best schools, which acts as an incentive for the poorer schools to work harder and make their establishments better.

School-by-school SATs and GCSE results are published by the government as 'performance tables'[54]. National and local media then create league tables of schools and local authorities[55]. If you are an anxious parent looking for a Reception place for your four-year-old, it will not be of much comfort to you knowing that you don't live anywhere near to the Sun's top ten English primary schools. Even worse if you live somewhere in the East Midlands, a huge area of over 6,000 square miles, named by the Sun as being at the bottom of England's nine regions. Nor will the national league tables of the 'top' 1,000 or 100 schools (in the Telegraph and Times) be of much practical help to the vast majority of parents.

Reports of inspections are posted on Ofsted and school websites. Schools with 'outstanding' and 'good' outcomes use these to market the school. Those judged as 'inadequate' or 'requires improvement' are generally treated to negative media publicity, with headlines such as 'school plunged into special measures after failing inspection'[56]. Particularly at a time of teacher shortages, it becomes even more difficult for schools with poor inspection reports to attract teachers and managers, which limits their capacity to make necessary improvements.

Research on the impact of league tables shows their negative effects, such as a narrowing of the curriculum, focusing on particular groups of pupils or teaching to the test[57]. There is no evidence either that the introduction of market forces into education has driven up standards. The idea that parents have a real choice about which school they send their children to is largely mythical. Parents can express a preference, but at a time when pupil numbers are rising, and there is a shortage of school places in many areas of the country, choice is extremely limited[58].

Wide-sweeping powers for government to intervene in schools

Target setting, tests, examinations and inspections give the government the reasons and justification to intervene in schools considered to be 'of concern'. Both the local authority and education secretary have wide-sweeping statutory powers to intervene in the running of state schools – the secretary of state for all schools and local authorities only for schools they maintain (and not academies). These powers include issuing warning notices, requiring schools to have external support, appointing additional governors, suspending delegated staffing and finance budgets (to be managed by the local authority), and replacing governing bodies with interim executive boards. There is also a 'catch-all' definition allowing intervention in 'other maintained schools about which the local authority and/or Secretary of State have serious concerns'[59]. In addition the education secretary is able to require schools to be part of named academy trusts, and close 'underperforming' schools.

Legislation in 2016[60] created Regional Schools Commissioners (RCS), responsible for exercising the Secretary of State's intervention powers. The RCS has virtually unbridled power, for example in determining intervention in a school, and which multi-academy trust should take it over. Statutory guidance makes this explicit: 'Ultimately, in maintained schools, if there is any disagreement between an RSC and the maintained school governing body, or the local authority, about what should be taken into consideration and what conclusions should be drawn, the RSC's powers to intervene take precedence, and the RSC will make the final judgement' [61].

Independent State Schools

Since 2010 governments have seen academies as the only way of 'turning around' those schools that are seen to be 'failing'. The origins of academies stem from the 1988 Act, which allowed schools to opt out of the local authority to become grant maintained schools or city technology colleges. In 1997 the Labour government converted grant maintained schools into foundation schools and brought them back into the local authority orbit, and then established academies. Labour, with some success, used academy conversions to provide new leadership for struggling schools. In 2010 the coalition government introduced free schools (which can be set up by various groups and in governance terms are academies). As at May 2018 there were 7,317 academies and free schools[62] – forty per cent of all schools in England. £745 million has been spent on converting schools into academies since 2010/11, an average of £106,000 per school[63].

Since 2010 academies have become an ideological crusade for the government and in 2016 they were only prevented from legislating for all schools to be academies, by opposition from a significant number of their own back-bench MPs[64]. The current government's preferred, and now single, intervention vehicle then is forcing 'schools causing concern' to be run by multi-academy trusts and, in the absence of a legislative mandate, cajoling all schools to become academies. Even when schools have been judged by Ofsted to have made significant improvement they are still being forced into multi-academy trusts, threatening their continuing progress[65]. When closely examined the case for academies as *the main or sole driver* for school improvement is a weak one.

A case is often made for academies that state schools should be more like private schools. Such an argument is based on a belief, held by many, including politicians of all parties, that private schools are better than state schools. This was the justification initially made by Labour in 2005 in describing academies as 'state funded independent schools'[66]. But this is a flawed proposition. On the surface private schools do better than state schools, as measured by examination results, university entrance and employment destinations. But you can't, with any sense of objectivity or fairness, compare largely selective schools with high-level parental support in the private sector, with state schools that cater for all needs and parental aspirations. Furthermore, private schools are far better funded than state schools with much smaller class sizes. In fact when socio-economic differences are taken into account, state schools do as well or better than private schools[67]. Research shows that the 'impressive results at independent schools [are] partly due to the greater affluence and expectations of the parents who sent their children there' and that, contrary to popular myth 'the management was better and more efficient at state schools' than at private schools[68].

There are many cases where academies and academy trusts have made and are making a positive difference to school performance and pupil outcomes. A range of evidence, however, casts serious doubt as to whether academies and academy trusts constitute an effective and sustainable national improvement model. A recent and very thorough piece of research by the Education Policy Institute concluded that overall there was 'little difference in the performance of schools in academy chains and local authorities'[69]. For example, in the 2017 Key Stage 1 SATs and the 2018 Key Stage 2 SATs, average results for academies and local authority schools were very similar[70]. And it seems that academies do not add any greater value to pupils' attainment than do local authority schools[71]. Attainment in two-thirds of academy chains is below the average for disadvantaged children[72].

Overall local authority schools fare no worse and sometimes do better in Ofsted inspections than academies[73]. For example, seventy-five per cent of schools judged inadequate by Ofsted in 2013 that continued to be local authority maintained were rated good or outstanding when re-inspected, compared to fifty-nine per cent of those that became academies[74]. Between 2010 and 2016, 160 academies were placed in special measures[75].

The former Prime Minister David Cameron justified his call for all schools to become academies by saying he wanted 'teachers, not bureaucrats, deciding how best to educate our children'[76]. And yet the argument that academies 'free from local authority control' enjoy greater autonomy is a bogus one. Since 1990 local authority schools have been self-governing and self-managing, including setting their own strategic direction and budgets, appointing and managing staff, and having direct control over buildings and other resources.

In reality 'control' comes from central government in the form of the national curriculum, examinations, statutory testing, inspections and forced 'academisation', rather than local government. Former teacher and Education Secretary, Baroness (Estelle) Morris, sums this up so well when she says that while the government 'claim to be devolutionists [and] rally around a banner of freeing schools ... teachers are working with a curriculum, assessment and pedagogy that are increasingly directed by ministers' own priorities and prejudices. Poignantly Baroness Morris points out that 'when the government talks about freedom, it only means freedom from its bete-noire, local authorities, not freedom from Whitehall. The irony is that much of the control government attributed to councils ceased to exist years ago; ministerial control is present and real.'[77] The Institute of Education research bears this out, finding that while the government promised "'high autonomy' and 'high accountability'" for schools and "to "trust" the profession, reduce bureaucracy and "roll back"' the state... any increase in operational autonomy for schools is more than balanced out by changes to the accountability framework, which have allowed the state to continue to steer the system from a distance and to increasingly intervene and coerce when and where it deems necessary"[78].

There are growing concerns about the academy system itself. Ofsted has been critical of a number of large multi-academy trusts[79]. Many academy trusts have had to give up some of their schools, and several trusts all of their schools, because of poor standards and poor financial management[80]. As a result 260 academies transferred from one academy trust to another in 2017-18 alone[81]. Rapid expansion by some academy trusts (encouraged by the government) has led to many of them being ineffective and their schools consequently suffering[82]. Various parliamentary reviews of the academy system[83] challenge whether it is working effectively. One such review says that 'academisation is not always successful nor is it the only proven alternative for a struggling school'[84]. Another that that there is a 'high degree of uncertainty about the effectiveness of Mats [multi-academy trusts], and there is not yet the evidence to prove that large-scale expansion would significantly improve the school landscape'[85]. The Public Accounts Committee found that the government 'in the rush to convert large numbers of schools to academies, did not pay enough attention to ensuring that its scrutiny of applicants was sufficiently rigorous' and was not 'learning the lessons from high–profile academy failures that have been costly for taxpayers and damaging to children's education'[86].

A very disturbing example of the government's continuing failure to 'learn lessons' is the incident of a primary academy, removed from the control of one academy trust and offered by the government to another (called 're-brokering'), which turned it down. The government then gave another academy trust two days to decide whether it wished to take over the primary academy! Aptly summing up this debacle, the Chair of the Public Accounts Committee said that, 'A 48-hour fire sale for our children's future doesn't seem like a good way of running things'[87].

At the same time, the government has no plan for how schools would be held accountable and supported as the number of academies grows. And there is real doubt whether there are enough sponsors of sufficient quality for the growing numbers of academies[88]. This is evidenced by the ongoing difficulties there are in finding new academy sponsors for academies that have been judged inadequate by Ofsted[89]. Two in three schools judged as 'inadequate' at inspection, for example, are taking more than nine months to open as academies[90]; some as long as eighteen months, and one school was 'left in limbo' for seven years![91] A review by the National Audit Office (NAO) found that there was 'a shortage of sponsors and multi-academy trusts with the capacity to support new academies'[92]. The NAO concluded that the government 'is likely to face a challenge in finding enough suitable sponsors in the coming years' and because of this questioned the feasibility of continuing to convert large numbers of schools to academies[93]. Ofsted expressed concern that 'a severe lack of capacity to sponsor [academies], has led to a mismatch in available support'[94].

There are an inordinate amount of governance concerns about academies, including in respect of financial management[95], fraud and misuse of public funds[96], exam-fixing[97], illegal admissions practices[98], pupil exclusions[99], and paying out excessive salaries (of between £143,000 and £500,000) and awarding massive pay increases to the trust chief executives and headteachers[100]. Also the National Audit Office has reported that 'civil servants do not carry out checks to ensure that all academy trustees and senior leaders are fit and proper people'[101].

It appears also that the government is struggling to deliver on its two main stated objectives for launching the free schools programme – facilitating parents to set up schools in their local areas, and bringing in an 'innovative ethos and curriculum' to the running of schools. According to a major review, 'only one in five free schools has had parents involved in their inception, and the proportion of parent-led schools has decreased over time'. In fact nowadays the vast majority of free schools are being established by multi-academy trusts, and only one-third of free schools have demonstrated a 'novel (innovative) approach'[102].

Furthermore, free schools are being set up in the way that doesn't represent good value in the use of public funding. Half of free school places are being established in 'areas where there is no demographic need', creating spare capacity at other schools, at a time when pupil numbers are rocketing[103], resulting in many schools being 'overcrowded' with two-fifths of secondary schools at or in excess of their capacity[104]. On average the government pays a fifth more on procuring accommodation for free schools than the market value[105], and almost £140m. has been spent on free schools, University Technical Colleges (UTC) and studio schools that have closed or did not open[106]. At the same time, the condition of existing schools is worsening, and it is estimated that nearly £14 billion will be needed to bring school buildings to a 'satisfactory to good condition'[107], whilst since 2010 capital spending on school buildings has fallen from £8.8 bn. to £5.2 bn.[108]

In addition to this, too few children from poor backgrounds attend free schools, which have a much smaller proportion of pupils from low-income families, including poor white British children, than the local areas in which they are located[109]. The academy programme takes responsibility for schools away from the local communities they serve, placing it in the hands of central government; counter to the stated intent of all political parties to devolve more powers to local areas.

Back to the future

In September 2016 Theresa May presented plans to create new grammar schools and expand existing ones. She claimed, despite overwhelming evidence to the contrary[110], that more grammar schools would help 'build a great meritocracy in Britain'[111]. Mrs. May's plans, included in the Conservative manifesto, died a death when she failed to gain an overall majority in the 2017 general election. In May 2018 the education secretary, Damien Hinds, announced that existing grammar schools would be able to expand (by an additional 16,000 places), reversing a ban on grammar school expansion by the last Labour government[112]. In fact the number of grammar school pupils in England has increased by 11,000 since 2010[113].

Does the school curriculum meet the nation's needs?

In this section we explain how pervasive the national curriculum is; the impact of testing on what is taught; and how far the curriculum is meeting the needs of individual children and young people, and the social and economic needs of the country.

National Curriculum omnipresent

The content of what children and young people study between the ages of five and sixteen in England and to a large degree how they are taught this, is determined by the national curriculum and the tests and examinations that stem from it. The national curriculum was introduced into schools in 1989, as part of the implementation of the 1988 Act. While the basic structure of the national curriculum has remained broadly the same, there have been major and constant changes to its detailed content. One of the more recent changes is that the national curriculum only applies to local authority schools and not to academies. This is supposedly one of the additional 'freedoms' that schools acquire when they become academies. But, what's the rationale of having a *national* curriculum for some state schools and not others?

The main aim of the national curriculum is to provide 'pupils with an introduction to the essential *knowledge* they need to be educated citizens'. Government guidance misleadingly says that 'the national curriculum is just one element in the education of every child. There is time and space in the school day and in each week, term and year to range beyond the national curriculum specifications'. In the real world, however, the heavy content of the national curriculum makes it in effect the totality of the school curriculum. This omnipresent national curriculum, combined with testing requirements that create high risks for schools, leaves very little flexibility for differentiation and innovation. The national curriculum is organised into five key stages:

Key Stage	Ages	School Year Group
Foundation	0-5	Nursery & Reception
1	5-7	1 & 2
2	7-11	3, 4, 5 & 6
3	11-14	7, 8 & 9
4	14-16	10 & 11

The Early Years Foundation Stage (EYFS) sets out welfare and developmental goals for children from birth to five years old[114]. For each of the Key Stages one to four there is a list of subjects that schools must teach. English, mathematics, science, computing, religious education and physical education are compulsory at all Key Stages; art and design, design and technology, geography, history and music for Key Stages one to three; a modern foreign language for Key Stages two and three; and citizenship, sex and relationship education for Key Stages three and four, no less than 12 subject areas. The education secretary agrees a programme of study for each statutory curriculum subject in each Key Stage, which determines the content and matters which must be taught. The most recent programmes of study were published in September 2014.

Following the 1988 Act, a panel of 'experts' designed programmes of study for each subject, resulting in an 'overcrowded' curriculum, which teachers found difficult to deliver. Since then there have been constant changes to the national curriculum causing schools and teachers to continually adjust what they teach and how they teach it. There have been four major revisions to the national curriculum in 1994, 1997/98, 2008 and 2011; causing schools and teachers to divert precious time from children's learning to understand the new requirements imposed upon them.

Ministers determine detail of curriculum

Over time the powers of the education secretary have grown and grown, including for the curriculum – not just its broad parameters, but the detailed content. As a result, what is taught in schools has been increasingly determined at the will of the education secretary and her/his ministers. There are many examples of where ministers have used their powers to take forward a particularly narrow ideological approach; two that particularly stand out are briefly summarised below.

Back in 1992 the then Education Secretary, Kenneth Clarke, in reviewing the history curriculum made a decision, seemingly unilaterally, that only events preceding 1972 could be taught. The process by which Mr. Clarke made the decision, however, was quite bizarre. The then Chief Executive of the National Curriculum Council, Duncan Graham, recalls that Mr. Clarke's decision that 'history should end before the present day[115]... was the result of a Dutch auction between Clarke and his officials. His opening bid was 1945'[116]. The curriculum council, established by law to provide independent advice to ministers, 'was not consulted' [117]!

Michael Gove changed the literacy curriculum from 2014 to include the requirement for four to eleven-year-olds to learn a range of niche syntax and grammar terms that many graduates of English have never heard of, such as graphene-phoneme correspondences, fronted adverbials and expanded noun phrases[118]! Many teachers, journalists, authors, academics and linguists are adamant that there is 'no evidence whatsoever' that this obsession with 'linguistic labelling... as an end in itself' benefits children's writing[119]; a view shared by the House of Commons Education Select Committee[120].

Given such severe criticisms, how did these changes come about in the first place? Michael Gove had set up a panel to advise him but, incredibly, none of its members 'had much experience of primary education' [121]. In unusual openness, all four of the panel have now expressed 'serious reservations' about the changes[122]. One panel member described the process as 'chaotic' and 'shambolic'[123] and said that the panel's proposals were not based on research evidence, and that they 'were guessing'[124]!

These examples expose the dangers of an education secretary, exercising all-embracing arbitrary powers, advised by only a few people, making decisions about what children have to learn and what teachers have to teach.

Testing narrows curriculum

Given the high stakes involved in testing, it is not surprising that schools concentrate on those aspects of the curriculum that are nationally tested and that 'teachers teach to the test'. Former senior chief inspector of schools, Professor Eric Bolton, suggests that 'Ministers' influence over testing… borders on the undesirable. If they say only three things will be tested in primary schools then you can be sure only three things will be taught in primary schools'[125]. There is firm evidence that 'high stakes testing' has led to a narrowing of the curriculum in many schools.

As described previously, knowledge of complex English language terms has been introduced into the primary literacy curriculum. Since 2016 as part of 'tougher' Key Stage two SATs, children's knowledge of this terminology has been tested. These new requirements, according to a review by the House of Commons Education Committee[126], are 'putting [children] off reading and writing' and 'diminished focus on composition and creativity'. The committee concluded that 'the close link between primary assessment (Sats) and school accountability creates a high stakes system which can negatively impact children's teaching and learning. It can lead to a narrowing of the curriculum and teaching to the test'. One English teacher describes how children arrive at her secondary school 'having not written a proper story for over a year. They knew what a fronted adverbial was [but when] I asked them to write a story… they couldn't do it.'[127]

Chief inspector, Amanda Spielman, confirms that the primary school curriculum is 'narrowing, especially in upper key stage 2, with lessons disproportionately focused on English and mathematics'. 'Sometimes', says Ms. Spielman, 'this manifested as intensive, even obsessive, test preparation for key stage 2 sats that in some cases started at Christmas in Year 6'[128], and in our experience even earlier. This obsession with meeting targets also squeezes the fun and interest out of learning for children in the latter part of their time in primary school.

The English Baccalaureate (EBacc) was brought in by the coalition government in 2010 as a measure of school performance. Pupils are deemed to be meeting the requirements of the EBacc if they achieve at least a GCSE C grade (now grade 4) in English, mathematics, science, a modern foreign language, geography and history. Because a whole range of subjects, including creative and vocational ones, are excluded, EBacc has narrowed the curriculum for students from aged fourteen, when GCSE subject choices have to be made[129]. Due to school budget reductions, teaching posts in subjects not included in the EBacc are the most at risk of not being filled when they become vacant[130]. In the vast majority of secondary schools the EBacc performance indicator is 'limiting opportunities for pupils with vocational or technical aptitude' and more than half of schools are offering far fewer vocational courses[131].

Between 2014 and 2017 entries for non-EBacc GCSEs fell by thirteen per cent, most notably design & technology, drama, home economics, media, performing arts and religious education[132]. Increased pressure to produce good examination results has led to significant reductions in the time pupils spend in physical education, and personal, social health and economic education, and 'children [are] being pulled out of PE lessons for tutoring'[133]. Anecdotal evidence suggests that young people are being 'pressured' into taking EBacc subjects that they 'dislike least', leading to increases in demotivated and badly behaved pupils[134]. There has been an avalanche of concerns expressed by leading industrial figures about the adverse impact of EBacc on the school curriculum and as a consequence on the skills businesses need[135], to which ministers have turned tin ears to.

Because schools feel so pressurised into getting good examination results, many start to teach the GCSE syllabus a soon as children start their secondary education in year 7, consequently providing a more restricted curriculum than they would normally have[136]. This includes 'drilling children for GCSEs' from as early as age eleven; sitting tests modelled on GCSEs, having them marked and the results fed back to them[137]. In addition, around a quarter of secondary schools are starting hundreds of thousands of pupils on GCSEs at the age of thirteen, extending the two-year courses to three years. To accommodate this, pupils have to drop subjects they would normally be studying at this stage[138]. Amanda Spielman says that the actions of schools to introduce GCSEs early to pupils is resulting in a 'whittling away [of] the broad curriculum… for younger pupils'[139]. She has admitted that 'school inspectors have put too much weight on tests and exam results when rating schools', which 'has added pressure for schools to deliver test scores above all else'[140]. Ms. Spielman goes further in saying that 'focusing too narrowly on test and exam results can often leave little time or energy for hard thinking about the curriculum, and in fact can sometimes end up making a casualty of it'[141].

What is studied after GCSEs has also been narrowed. The so called 'tougher' A levels (fully introduced in 2018 examinations) with no opportunity for re-sits and no marks from AS-levels contributing to the overall final A level grade, have led to students following a narrower range of subjects than previously. Three subjects rather than four are the norm now, and these tend to be all mathematics/science or all humanities based[142]. There has also been a significant reduction in the number taking A-levels in the arts, modern languages and social sciences[143], and design and technology[144].

Education ministers should start taking note of their chief inspector, Amanda Spielman, when she says that 'good examination results in and of themselves don't always mean that the pupil received rich and full knowledge from the curriculum. In the worst cases, teaching to the test, rather than teaching the full curriculum, leaves a pupil with a hollowed-out and flimsy understanding'[145].

Curriculum heavily weighted towards acquiring knowledge rather than skills

The national curriculum is largely knowledge-based, suited to learning facts and regurgitating them in tests and examinations in a way that can be fairly easily scored and graded. There is obviously a need for people to acquire underpinning knowledge. But people need to have an understanding of the knowledge they have, and the necessary skills to apply it productively in the day-to-day reality of their personal and professional lives. Because of this there are many, including those in the business world, who are calling for a more skills-based curriculum. 'Our education system is failing young people' because 'children are being trained for tests rather than how to succeed in work and life' believes entrepreneur & Dragons' Den panellist, Peter Jones. 'It is critical' he says 'to equip young people with the business acumen and soft skills (such as resilience, leadership and ambition) that they need to flourish in the real world'[146]

Curriculum biased against technical and vocational education

We evidenced earlier the strong bias there is in the school curriculum against vocational and technical education, reinforced by their exclusion from the EBacc. Following the Tomlinson review in 2004[147], which proposed replacing GCSEs, A-levels and vocational qualifications with a new single diploma, the then Labour government missed a golden opportunity to unify 16-19 curriculum and qualifications and end the false division between vocational and academic education. The government at the time decided not to implement Tomlinson's proposed changes out of fear of being accused of dumbing down the so called 'gold standard' of A-levels. Peter Finegold, Head of Education at the Institution of Mechanical Engineers, is absolutely right when he says that 'without change, the dominance of A-levels will continue to scupper initiatives to bring about improvements in technical education'[148].

Curriculum inflexibility leads to disaffection

Disengagement at school is the main reason quoted by young people as to why they are not in education, employment or training (NEET). These youngsters have been turned off learning by the education system, have low levels of attainment, lack confidence and see themselves as failures. The vast majority want to work, but are not motivated to go back into full-time education[149]. Large class sizes, meaning individuals don't get the personal attention they feel they need, and boredom due to the pace of teaching, were major causes of disengagement. Teaching style is a contribution to teenagers being disillusioned, with many quoting that there is too much reliance on repetitive worksheets, listening, reading and copying. Young people NEET report that the requirement to complete the lesson as planned often outweighs the needs of individual students (the consequence of a heavily prescribed examination-driven curriculum), resulting in some being 'left behind'. Many feel that a structured school classroom environment (listening and recording information) doesn't suit them, as they would prefer 'learning while doing'[150].

Change, change, change and more change

In the latter years of the twentieth century and the early years of the twenty-first, the key tenets of national education policy, irrespective of government, have remained constant. Another thing that has been a constant throughout this time, and proved very debilitating to schools, is change. This is not change in the overall national direction of education, which has remained remarkably consistent, but in the more detailed day-to-day ways in which schools are organised and run. Space constraints don't allow us to do justice to the sheer enormity of changes that successive governments have imposed on schools over many years. Here we try to give you a flavour of what has happened.

A major cause of these non-stop changes is the high turnover of education ministers, each wanting to make their political mark in what they realise will most likely be a short-stay in office. Since 1979 there have been eighteen secretaries of state for education, seven being in the job for less than two years. These ministers have steered through forty-one major Acts of Parliament devoted to education, resulting in headteachers and their staff having to continuously effect change in all aspects of school life[151], including the curriculum; examinations and testing; pupil discipline; staff appointments, remuneration, conditions and appraisal; school places and admissions; governing body functions and membership; inspections; special educational needs; relationships with parents; safeguarding; pupil attendance; and budgets. A consistent theme of legislation over this time has been to give greater and greater powers to the Secretary of State. The 2009 Act[152], for example, gave the Education Secretary 153 new powers, in contrast to the three powers[153] allocated to the minister of education in the 1944 Act[154]!

In addition to the Acts (primary legislation) we have secondary legislation - statutory instruments that are determined by ministers. A committee of the House of Lords examining the regulations when Ed Balls was secretary of state urged him 'to stop deluging schools with new regulations' [155]. In 2006-7 the education department and its agencies sent schools over 760 documents to consider. The head of one of the school leaders associations at the time said that a 'juggernaut of policies, laws and regulations hurtles at ever increasing speed towards [schools], seemingly out of control'[156]. Despite the concerns expressed then, this onslaught of paper going into schools has continued. Invariably when you talk to headteachers they place having to deal with the ongoing bureaucratic changes imposed by government as their number one frustration.

Workload and stress causing growing teacher and school leadership shortages

We have seen the impact that the 'being tough' approach has had on children's well-being. There has been a similar impact on the school workforce with mounting dissatisfaction amongst staff, causing increasing difficulties in retaining and recruiting teachers and school leaders, which in many schools has now reached crisis proportions.

Teachers leaving profession at record high

One in 10 teachers each year leave the profession, the highest rate on record[157]. An increasing proportion, one in 12, leave for 'reasons other than retirement'[158]. What is particularly concerning is the wastage of those in their early years of teaching. A quarter of newly qualified teachers are not in teaching within a year of qualifying[159]! In 2016 thirty per cent of those newly qualified had left after only five years[160]; by 2018 this had increased to forty per cent[161], and to fifty per cent in particular subjects such as physics and mathematics[162]. Half of teachers trained by Teach First, the biggest graduate recruiter, leave the profession after two years[163]. The vast majority of schools are experiencing major difficulties in recruiting and/or retaining teachers, and believe this will get worse[164]. Retaining teachers is particularly problematic in secondary schools. Following a thorough review, the House of Commons Public Accounts Committee concluded that 'secondary school teachers deserting the profession have triggered a crisis in education'[165].

The most cited reasons for teachers leaving are long hours, heavy workload, teacher bashing in the press, constant changes, pupil behaviour, inspections, and adverse impacts on their mental health[166]. More than three-quarters of teachers give high workload as the main reason they are considering leaving[167]. On average teachers in England are working over 54 hours a week[168], longer than in any other developed country, bar two[169]. Senior school leaders are working an average of around 60 hours a week[170]. The cause of the longer working hours is marking and administrative duties, not extra teaching time[171]. Research shows that the primary causes of increased workload are government changes to inspection, curriculum and assessment; and changes to the accountability system and school structures[172]. In 2017/18 a quarter of graduates left the Now Teach programme (which trains those from other professions as teachers) blaming the 'data-led, assessment-heavy culture' in schools[173]. And between 2017 and 2018, the numbers of teachers seeking 'crisis' support due to workload and depression increased by more than a third[174]. It is not surprising therefore that teachers in the vast majority of developed countries have much higher job satisfaction than teachers do in England[175].

A review by the National Audit Office concluded that government initiatives to retain teachers were 'relatively small scale' and not working[176]; and the House of Commons Education Committee criticised the government for focusing 'too much on attracting new teachers and too little on preventing experienced teachers quitting'[177].

Teacher vacancies up; year-on-year shortfall in trainee teacher numbers

Because since 2010 the retention and supply of teachers has not kept pace with the increase in pupil numbers, teacher vacancies are growing and the pupil-teacher ratio has increased[178]. In 2015, for the first time, the number of teachers leaving the profession was higher than the number entering[179]. As a result the total number of teachers employed in schools is falling[180]. At the start of the 2017/18 academic year recruitment agencies reported major increases in the number of teaching vacancies compared to two years previously[181]. These increases prompted the head of one of the largest agencies to comment that 'In my 20 years of working with schools on teacher recruitment, I have never seen so many unfilled vacancies'[182]. By 2018 there was a shortfall of

30,000 classroom teachers in England[183]. One in 10 of the vacant posts is left unfilled[184], an increasing number is filled by temporary personnel[185], and half are covered by staff who do not have the relevant 'experience and expertise'[186]. It is particularly difficult for secondary schools to recruit mathematics, physics and chemistry teachers[187].

The workforce problem is aggravated by major shortfalls in the numbers of trainee teachers recruited against the numbers that are needed in schools, in each of the five years since 2011-12[188]. In 2017 only eighty per cent of places on teacher training programmes were filled[189]. Applications for post-graduate secondary teacher training courses for 2018 fell by a third compared to the position twelve months previously, with subjects such as design and technology, history, French, mathematics and English faring particularly badly[190]. There was a reduction of nearly a half in applications to primary school teacher training courses for 2018[191]. Growing pupil numbers are exacerbating the teacher supply problem[192]. In just one year, between 2016/17 and 2017/18, the school population increased by 66,000[193]. By 2020 there will be 615,000 more pupils of compulsory school age than there were in 2015[194]. Pupil numbers are expected to continue to rise significantly at least up until 2025[195], by when it is estimated an extra 47,000 secondary teachers will be needed[196].

As a consequence of the severe shortage of teachers, schools are spending £835 million annually on supply agencies[197], offering major incentives to attract new recruits[198] and spending in the region of £200 million a year on recruitment[199]. The government is funding a campaign to recruit teachers from overseas[200] to plug teacher shortages in physics, mathematics and modern languages, which will cost £10 million – £16,000 per overseas teacher recruited[201]. Fewer newly qualified teachers are responding directly to advertisements placed by schools because recruitment agencies are 'snapping [them up] before they graduate', dramatically increasing the fees they charge to schools[202]. And, these efforts to retain and recruit teachers will not have been helped by the ten to twelve per cent real terms decrease there has been in teachers' pay in the last ten years in England[203] (a loss of around £5,000 per annum[204]).

More school leaders leaving; vacancies increasingly difficult to fill

The enormous pressure on headteachers causes insecurity. A typical comment from serving headteachers is 'Being a head is like being a football manager. One bad season and you're out'[205]. Headteachers believe that headship is becoming less and less attractive[206]. As a result, increasing numbers are leaving, resulting in headteacher retention rates falling in every year since 2012[207]. Retention rates are lower in schools with low levels of attainment[208]. The school leadership retention problem is unlikely to ease in the short term as significant numbers of headteachers and other school leaders say that they are planning to leave within the next few years[209].

The vacancies created by headteachers leaving their jobs are also becoming harder and harder to fill[210]. Nearly a third of headteacher posts advertised attract no applicants[211]. Four in ten school governing bodies have difficulties attracting suitable candidates for headteacher and other leadership posts[212]. Headships in schools deemed to be 'underperforming' are especially hard to fill[213]. The pool from which future heads are drawn seems to be getting smaller as senior teachers find headship far less attractive than they used to; the main reason being that 'the extra responsibility, exposure and stress of running a school is not worth the modest pay rise or uncertain job satisfaction'[214]. As a consequence of worsening retention and recruitment it is forecast that there will be a shortage of 19,000 school leaders (heads, deputies and assistants) by 2022[215].

Alienation of teaching profession

At a time when growing pupil numbers mean that far more staff are required in schools, teachers and their leaders are leaving in their droves and replacements for them are increasingly difficult to find. The reasons for this are clear – the excessive pressure placed on schools by successive governments is proving unbearable for too many teachers and leaders, and turning off those who might aspire to the classroom and to lead our schools. To make matters worse in 2011 the then Education Secretary, Michael Gove, relinquished central government's responsibility for teacher supply, the consequence of which is that the government 'has no clear idea how many teachers it needs as it has abandoned [teacher supply] planning'[216]. How can schools be expected to maintain, never mind improve, what they are doing, faced with such a dramatic turnover and shortfall in practitioners and managers? The government seems to be deaf to the cries from schools for a change in direction, and complacent about doing something positive about this retention and recruitment crisis. Chair of the Industrial Society, Will Hutton, sums it up graphically:

> *What should be one of the noblest professions of all has been turned into the country's poor relation, endlessly criticised, indifferently paid and in the front line of stewarding and caring for children as much as teaching them. To have a stable pool of teachers offering continuity, especially in subjects such as maths, is becoming a rarity. The new norm is a high turnover of teachers with pupils taught by a succession of supply teachers*[217].

Conclusion: successive governments' command and control approach is failing

For thirty years governments of different political persuasions, with the intent of raising educational standards, have increasingly controlled what schools do. The main instruments of exerting this control have been the national curriculum, testing, inspections and intervention (particularly through academisation), as well as a constant barrage of policy changes and regulations. This coercive unremitting approach has had major consequences. In 'real-life' measures i.e. comparisons with other developed countries and skills sufficiency, the UK has been found wanting.

The country consistently languishes as a mid-table performer in international tests with a growing gap between the UK and its major economic competitors in Europe, America and particularly Asia. The UK has critical skills shortages caused primarily by a curriculum biased against technical and vocational skills, and the significant number of youngsters disaffected from education and leaving school without marketable skills and qualifications. Mental health problems are growing amongst children and young people, a major contribution being the pressures of an incessant examination and testing regime. Political changes to the national curriculum have led to a narrowing of learning experiences for pupils, including in creative and vocational studies. Inordinate pressures on teachers have caused a massive retention and recruitment problem, which acts as a considerable constraint on schools' capacity to maintain, let alone improve the quality of teaching and learning. The policies of successive governments have alienated the teaching profession, which dramatically contrasts with conclusions reached from analysis of school improvement reforms internationally that 'the most effective policies are those that are designed around students and learning, build teachers' capacity, and engage all stakeholders'[218].

The consequences of the command and control, that successive governments have assiduously exercised over schools in the last thirty years, powerfully highlights the need for radical change. Such change should be concerned with fundamentally changing the conditions under which schools have to operate. In chapter 11 we put the case for a more supportive and collaborative approach to helping schools improve and holding them to account.

7
EQUALITY

Inequality thwarts learning for all

We may have all come on different ships, but we're in the same boat now
Martin Luther King Jr.

The highest performing countries educationally are also those that have the greatest equality of outcomes; that is the gap between the highest and lowest attaining students is narrower than that in less well performing countries. There is also a clear link between a country's overall equality and how well it does educationally. In more unequal countries, compared to more equal countries, there is a strong tendency for there to be greater ill-health and social problems[1]; more people suffering from mental illness[2]; higher infant mortality[3]; and lower levels of life expectancy, child well-being[4], and mathematics and literacy skills[5]. The UK is amongst the most unequal of developed countries in the world[6]. In this chapter we highlight the deep inequalities there are in families, the economy, education, employment and health, and culturally and ethnically. There is a major gap in the UK between those with the highest and lowest education outcomes, and this plays a significant part in creating the major economic, health and social divides we have.

Advantage and disadvantage starts in the family

As evidenced previously, the home environment is by far the most significant determinant of children's future life chances including the progress they make at school and their educational outcomes. Advantage and disadvantage starts in the family. Parents playing, reading and helping children with their homework is a major factor in how well they do educationally, and middle class parents generally spend more time on these activities than those who are less well-off[7]. These differences lead to five-year-olds from poorer families on average being nearly two years behind those from better-off homes in 'school-readiness' and abilities such as reading, concentration, self-management and co-operation[8]. Significant numbers of children then start school already at a massive disadvantage. The education achievement gap widens as children go through school, due primarily to the varying levels of support they get from their families[9]. Such support includes greater use by some families than others of private tutoring for their children[10].

For children suffering severe neglect or abuse within their family setting, the alternative is for them to be looked after in the public care system. This, sadly, doesn't necessarily guarantee positive outcomes for these youngsters. The education attainment of children in care is far lower[11], and they are more likely to be not in education or training[12], suffer mental ill-health[13], be excluded from schools[14], be involved in crime[15], end up in prison[16], and die in early adulthood[17], than other young people. One of the causes of generally poor outcomes for children in care is the regular disruption they face in their lives, including changing social workers, homes and schools. These upheavals adversely affect children's emotional health, behaviour and academic performance[18]. The outcomes of those who are adopted, the most stable of circumstances for children in care, are often not much better[19].

Economically, UK one of the most unequal countries

In the UK the top two-fifths of earners take four-fifths of the total income distributed[20], one of the highest levels of income inequality in the developed world[21]. The richest ten per cent have forty per cent of the wealth, with half of the population owning less than a tenth[22]. While the total wealth in the UK is increasing, for the poorest fifth of households it is actually reducing[23].

Low pay and poverty can be debilitating for families, particularly for children, often meaning frequent house moves, long journeys to school, and staying indoors because of safety concerns in the area where they live[24]. A fifth of people in the UK are low paid, one of the highest proportions of developed nations[25], and an increasing number of people (19 million, including six million children) live on less than what is considered to be the Minimum Income Standard[26]. Relative child poverty[27] is growing[28] and is expected to continue to do so in the next five years[29]. Being in temporary accommodation can have a destabilising effect on children including regularly changing schools, and on their 'ability to focus on school studies and form friendships'[30]. There is rarely a smooth transition between schools, and children forced to move home can be out of school for a number of months. Over 120,000 children live with their families in temporary accommodation, a dramatic increase since 2014[31].

Experience of cultural and sporting activities help raise the aspirations of children and young people and get them into jobs and university. Those from more affluent families, however, are more likely than those from poorer backgrounds to go on trips to galleries, theatre and the cinema, adding to the advantages they have in life[32]. Equality of access to cultural activities may in fact have worsened; for example, today young people from better-off families are more likely to go to the cinema than their poorer counterparts, while in the 1960s those from all backgrounds, including from low-income families, went to see films[33].

Education attainment gap between poorer and wealthier growing

There is already a substantial ability gap between children from poorer families and better-off peers when they start school, and this gap widens as they proceed through school[34]. While around six in ten of all pupils achieve good grades in English and mathematics GCSEs[35], only around one in three from poorer backgrounds do so[36]; a gap that has widened over the past five years[37]. Only one in ten pupils on free school meals achieve the EBacc measure (i.e. achieve good GCSEs in the government's 'core' subjects) compared to the national average of one in four[38]. In fact, pupils from poor families are more likely to be excluded from school than meet the EBacc standard[39]. What is especially disturbing is that nearly half of children from low-income families who had high attainment at the end of primary school, do not achieve good grades at GCSE[40]. In recent years[41] there has been little change in the gap in school attainment between disadvantaged pupils and their peers[42]. According to research by the Institute of Education[43], on current rates of progress it will take well over 100 years to close the attainment gap in GCSE English and mathematics!

Those from low-income families are far more likely to discontinue their education at sixteen than those from better-off families with the same GSCE results[44], with declining proportions of disadvantaged pupils entering sixth forms[45]. Only one in 10 young people from the poorest backgrounds goes to university[46], and those from more disadvantaged backgrounds drop out of university at a greater rate than students from better-off families[47].

Increasingly girls are doing better in education than boys. Girls get better GCSE results than boys and this gap is growing[48]. Since 2012 a greater and greater proportion of women have entered higher education, mainly because girls are getting far better A-level results than boys, and also due to the acute underachievement of white working-class boys[49]. These higher levels of educational achievement, however, are not reflected in pay, with men on average continuing to be remunerated better than women. For example, the pay of female apprentices is significantly less than that of their male counterparts[50], and across all subjects, male graduates are paid more than females only five years after graduating[51].

While the quality of children's family life is the key force influencing education outcomes, there are other issues that impact including school admissions, pupil behaviour and private education. Children from poorer families are significantly less likely to gain admission to schools with the best examination results and those that have been judged 'outstanding' at inspection[52], even if they live closer to the school[53]; and they are more likely to misbehave and be excluded from school[54]. Whilst constituting only about seven per cent of the school population, the private sector provides a quarter of students going to so called 'top universities'[55], and a disproportionate number of those employed in what are often referred to as the 'elite professions' such as doctors, barristers, senior military officers, senior civil servants, journalists and senior executives[56]. Also, if you have special needs, a disability or a temporary illness in a private school you are on average given more extra time to sit GCSEs and A levels than if you are in a state school[57].

Odds stacked against children from poor and working-class backgrounds gaining quality, well-paid employment

There is an increasing gap in the employment market between those from the poorest and better-off backgrounds. For example, only one in eight children from poor families is likely to become a high earner when they grow up[58]. Young people from more affluent families are more likely to take up apprenticeship places than those from low-income households[59]. What jobs people end up doing is heavily influenced by the adult role models they have around them in their families as they are growing up. Even with levels of employment at record levels, it is startling that today there are three million households (one in seven) that have no adults working, and six times more children living in families where no one has ever worked than there were in the 1990s[60]. Those brought up in workless households are far less likely to be in work than those raised in working families[61].

While disadvantage transfers within families from generation to generation, so does advantage. This is reflected in the type of careers that people follow and the remuneration they receive. The professions are still overwhelmingly dominated by those from affluent backgrounds[62]. Those with parents who have professional occupations are two and a half times more likely to be employed in the professions than those from less advantaged backgrounds[63]. One of the main reasons is that gaining employment in 'Britain's most competitive professions' is highly dependent on young people being able to undertake unpaid internships, as employers say that candidates without work experience 'have little or no chance of receiving a job offer'. Accessing these largely unadvertised internships greatly favours those who have parents who are working in the professions, have the connections with employers, and the financial means to support their children (with almost half of internships being unpaid)[64]. Even those from working-class backgrounds employed in the professions are on average paid less than those from better-off families[65].

Young people who have contacts with employers while at school (including visits from employers, job shadowing or work placements) are far more likely to be in education, employment and training when they leave school. Engagement with employers is particularly strong in private and grammar schools[66]. As Dr. Anthony Mann of the Education and Employers charity says, 'Those with greatest need to experience the world of work while in education received it least'[67].

Poor suffer more ill-health and die younger than better-off

The Marmot Review[68], published in 2010, highlighted the large and growing health inequalities in England. Compared to those in higher income groups, on average, people on low incomes live seven years less[69], suffer from disability for seventeen years longer during their lives[70], and are much more likely to have experienced mental ill-health[71]. This health inequality has a particular impact on children, with those from the lowest income families far more likely than those from higher income groups to attend Accident and Emergency[72], be obese[73] and have poor oral health[74]. The UK also has higher rates than in many other European countries of child deaths, obesity, general ill-health and smoking in pregnancy[75].

Poor white and black Caribbean pupils do worst educationally; black and minority ethnic people discriminated against in employment

Thirty years ago black and Asian pupils had very poor GCSE results and were behind their white counterparts. The situation today is remarkably different, although the position of black Caribbean pupils, unfortunately, hasn't changed a great deal. Those from Indian[76], black African and Chinese[77] heritage perform above the average at GCSE, while white and black Caribbean pupils (particularly boys)[78] are below the average[79]. White pupils from low-income households and those from Gypsy and Roma families perform the worst educationally[80] and, alongside those from black Caribbean backgrounds, have the lowest proportion of any group going to university[81]. Black students are least likely to achieve good degrees and most likely to drop out of university[82]. Black Caribbean youngsters (predominately boys) are more likely to be excluded from school[83], be arrested[84] and go to prison[85].

Family behaviour is an important factor explaining why the attainment of white British working-class pupils' attainment is so low. Research indicates that along with Roma, Gypsy and Traveller groups, white working-class families 'tend to be less engaged in their children's education than other ethnic groups'[86]. Immigrant parents are generally better at supporting their children doing their homework, accessing a computer at home, insisting that they have reasonable bedtimes and eating together as a family[87]. This is probably the main reason why there is a much narrower achievement gap between the poorest and better-off within ethnic minorities, than in white families[88].

Although those from minority ethnic groups are achieving much better than they did thirty years ago, many from these backgrounds continue to be discriminated against in employment. Despite similar and better qualifications, there is a smaller proportion of people from minority ethnic groups in employment than white people[89], and this is particularly acute in the professions and managerial jobs[90]. Minority ethnic people also generally earn less for doing the same type of job as white people do[91].

Major regional differences in jobs, income, health and education

Regional economic differences in the UK are growing. There is also a new 'geography of disadvantage', not just a north-south divide, but deprivation in coastal towns such as Blackpool, Great Yarmouth and Minehead, and older industrial towns such as Mansfield and Stoke[92]. There are already massive income and wealth disparities between the two most prosperous regions, London and the south-east, and the rest of the country. These disparities are likely to grow as it is forecast that in the next five years the proportion of national output from London and the south-east will continue to rise while that of all other regions will decline[93]. Incomes in the vast majority of the regions of the country are currently more than ten per cent lower than in the south-east[94]. While fifteen per cent or more of school children in Yorkshire and Humberside, the north-west, west Midlands and the north-east were claiming free school meals, less than ten per cent in the south-east were doing so.

There are dramatic health differences between the regions, with people in the north of England much more likely to die before the age of seventy-five than those living in the south[95]. Regional differences in examination results are growing, being highest in London and lowest in Yorkshire and the Humber[96]. There is a much stronger link between attainment and where people live, than family background and income, for young people today than there was thirty years ago. The most likely reason for this is that there are now higher levels of relative poverty in areas such as the north-east and the Midlands[97]. There are nearly twice as many children (per head of population) in care in the north-east of England than there are in the east of England[98].

The proportion of young people going to university varies significantly from one area of the country to another; nearly half of sixteen to eighteen-year-olds in London go to university compared to just over a third in the Midlands and north[99]. These regional educational disparities have been aggravated by a migration of better educated people from the north to the south over the last two centuries![100] It is startling also that in recent years there has been a shift of government spending from the north to the south. Since 2009-10, while public expenditure in the north of England reduced by £6.3b., it increased by £3.2b. in the south-east and south-west[101].

Conclusion: UK deeply divided society – economically, educationally and social

International research shows that the overall level of inequality in a country is a major factor influencing educational standards, and that the best performing countries have narrower gaps between the highest and lowest achievers. The UK is a deeply divided society, economically, educationally and socially.

Quality of family life is crucial in determining children's future prospects. Yet there are wide variations from family to family in what children experience, from highly supportive parenting that gives children great advantages, to abuse and neglect, which blights children's futures. In terms of income and wealth the UK is one of the most unequal of countries. Poor people generally suffer more ill-health than those who are better-off. Those whose parents are middle class and employed in the professions fare better in education and employment than those from working-class backgrounds.

The education attainment gap between poorer and wealthier pupils in the UK is wider than in most other developed countries. Children from low-income families access cultural experiences far less than those from wealthier homes. Of all the ethnic groups, white children from poor families and black Caribbean pupils have the lowest educational achievement levels. Although most black and minority ethnic groups do as well or better educationally than their white peers, they are discriminated against in employment. There are glaring differences between the different regions of the UK in regard to employment, income, education and family stability, with outcomes for the south-east of England far better than all other regions.

Government efforts to narrow the inequality gap and improve social mobility, although often implemented with the best of intent and having some positive impact, overall have 'failed to significantly reduce inequality between rich and poor'. There has been a great deal of regression since the 2008 financial crisis, with child poverty rising and wages stagnating in real terms, with the poorest most affected[102]. In fact the research shows that income inequality in the UK has widened since the 1990s, and that compared to other countries 'intergenerational mobility is relatively low, particularly in terms of earnings and education'[103].

How we tackle the deeply embedded inequalities, and social and economic divisions in the country, are well beyond the scope of this book and the knowledge and expertise of its authors. It is clear, however, that reducing education and skills inequalities would make a substantial contribution to creating a much fairer society overall. In pursuit of addressing these inequalities, we set out proposals in the following chapters for promoting lifelong learning for all, strengthening family life, supporting school improvement, enhancing the nation's skills and tackling educational underachievement.

Part 2

DEVELOPING AN ALTERNATIVE

There are major concerns about our current system of learning. Is there a better alternative? How can we promote lifelong learning for everyone, provide all children with stimulating family lives, give schools the support they need to continuously improve, meet the nation's skill requirements and tackle educational underachievement?

8
THE ARGUMENTS FOR CHANGE

A systems approach

The world as we have created it is a process of our thinking.
It cannot be changed without changing our thinking
Albert Einstein

2018 marked the thirtieth anniversary of the passing of the Education Reform Act 1988, the main progenitor of the schools system we have today. The Act had many positive features, particularly the devolution of strategic and operational decision-making powers to schools, and the principle of having a national curriculum. There has been some significant progress since 1988, for example in the rise in the proportion of GCSEs achieved at the top grades[1] and the substantial increase in the number of people going into higher education[2].

But there have also been some worrying trends. Successive governments have taken an ever-tightening grip on the day-to-day running of schools. This approach, administered with remarkable consistency by eight successive governments, involving three political parties since 1988, has significantly contributed to growing child mental ill-health, a large proportion of young people leaving school disaffected from education and having underachieved, major skills shortages, and consistently poor education performances compared to other developed countries. It has also failed to recognise and address the increasing problems experienced by children growing up in many households, which negatively impact on how well they engage with and achieve at school. The 'get tough' stance with schools is also causing a worsening teacher and school leader retention and recruitment problem, undermining the capacity of schools to maintain, never mind improve learning and educational outcomes.

At the same time governments, and particularly the ones since 2010, have been obsessed with the 'academic route' as the predominant means of defining education success. Leading business and educational figures have argued that the school curriculum lacks modernity and is out of touch with the needs of the economy[3], and it is abundantly clear that the learning system is not fit for purpose, either for the country as a whole or for many of its individual citizens. There has been massive technological and social change in the past thirty years. In front of us is an uncertain and ever-changing future driven by digitalisation, artificial intelligence and robotics, where lifelong learning, and rational thinking combined with creativity and interpersonal skills, are likely to be valued more highly than any other attributes.

Powerful case for change

All of this makes a sound case for a review of our learning system, and exploring whether there are better alternatives. The analysis points to seven major problems with the current state of learning, which help to shape what those alternatives might look like:

- Increasing numbers of children and young people suffering from mental ill-health, restricting their capacity to learn.
- A substantial section of the population without appropriate skills including basic numeracy and literacy; school leavers and graduates without the necessary employability skills; and significant and growing skill shortages in key business sectors adversely impacting on economic growth and productivity, and the quality, pay and security of employment.
- The UK being a consistent mid-table education performer amongst developed countries, having not improved since 2009, with a bigger gap between its highest and lowest achievers than most other developed countries.
- Increasing numbers of children experiencing chaotic and dysfunctional home lives, leading to poor life outcomes, including in education.
- A curriculum that is too narrow (particularly in secondary schools), which is knowledge and academic orientated, with insufficient focus on developing skills, and a marginalisation of vocational, technical and creative studies.

- A 'great minority' of school pupils underachieving – a 'long tail of underperformance'.
- A substantial and growing teacher and school leader retention and recruitment problem.

The evidence, as outlined so far in this book, clearly indicates that there are a number of key causes of these problems:

- Incessant high stakes testing.
- Substantial numbers of young people leaving school disaffected and without marketable skills and qualifications.
- Cultural bias in the curriculum favouring academic education, and discriminating against creative, vocational and technical education.
- Too many apprenticeships that are of poor quality, and that don't meet the country's skill requirements.
- The quality of home life (the most important single factor influencing how children learn) not being given sufficient attention by successive governments in their education policies.
- The government's 'command and control' style and 'be tough with schools' approach.
- The wide inequality gap in the UK.

In developing an alternative, it is crucially important to look at the system of learning as a whole rather than via its separate parts. A 'systems approach' has therefore been taken, and this is briefly explained below.

Systems approach

A set of beliefs held by successive governments has moulded the system of learning we have today. Firstly, 'command and control' – that the government and individual ministers know best, and impose their will on schools, teachers and pupils. Secondly, that schools and teachers will only perform well if they are constantly pressurised to do so, and that there are 'carrots and sticks' to incentivise them. This particular belief is founded on a 'negative view of... human nature'[4] – that for people to do a good job they need to be heavily directed, controlled, supervised and monitored. Thirdly, that competition between them will drive schools to improve. And, finally, a lack of understanding of the dynamics of the whole system within which learning sits, for example the influence of family life. This latter belief is based on a view that to best manage complex issues you have to break them down into manageable separate parts.

Systems thinking[5] is fundamentally different from the hierarchical and fragmented methods that successive governments have used to manage schools and other services, and effect change, in these important respects:

- *Policy* is formulated and implemented in a holistic way by gaining an understanding of, and utilising, the whole environment within which services and organisations operate. Through this approach it is possible to identify the factors that are most influential, both positively and negatively, and assess the impact particular actions taken in one part of the system have on others. People involved have an appreciation of the core purpose of the whole project and, therefore, are able to make sure that their contributions are tailored to this. The primary aim is to 'improve overall system performance, as judged by end-users [customers], not just ministers and civil servants'[6].

- The predominant *leadership* style used is concerned with actively engaging people and organisations and channelling their energy, skills and ideas behind the mission to be accomplished, rather than 'command and control'. Systems thinking recognises the reality that 'different individuals and organisations... have significantly different perspectives, based on different histories, cultures and goals', which 'have to be integrated and accommodated if effective action is to be taken by all the relevant agents'[7].

- Continuous *learning* - taking a range of actions, honestly and objectively evaluating the results, learning what measures are most effective, and making adjustments[8].

From the above, three basic tenets of a systems model have been identified to help shape our proposed alternative:

- Taking a *holistic view*. Underpinning this is a recognition that humans have an innate desire to learn, and we need, therefore, to promote independent lifelong learning and nurture learners. A holistic perspective enables us to understand and shape all the major environmental factors that influence the quality of learning including family life, people's day-to-day experiences, formal education and work. In particular we need a 'lifelong long learning for all' strategy that systemically tackles educational underachievement.

• *Building capacity*. We need to continuously strengthen the capabilities of the two environments that most influence children and young people's education outcomes – families and schools.

• *Collaborative working*, between all key stakeholders including children and young people, parents, schools, national and local government, academy trusts, employers, colleges, universities and voluntary organisations. Partnership working facilitates the sharing of expertise, ideas and resources, to develop a high quality and continuity of learning for everyone.

By identifying the major problems with the current system and their principal causes, and using a systems approach, we can now propose an alternative way to take the nation's learning forward, based around five main drivers:

• Promoting lifelong learning for all.
• Supporting families.
• Changing the conditions within which schools operate.
• Improving skills.
• Tackling underachievement.

These five areas provide the focus for the remainder of the book.

9
PROMOTING LIFELONG LEARNING FOR ALL

Learning is a lifelong process of keeping abreast of change. And the most pressing task is to teach people how to learn
Peter F. Drucker[1]

Can you conceive of a time when your learning began? Most of us can recall early memories from around two or three years of age. We can probably remember our first day at school and certainly when we started working. But can we recollect when we learned to talk, or first listened to music, or disliked a certain noise, or started to walk? Learning is continuous, from the moment we are born to the moment we die, commonly referred to as 'cradle to grave'. In fact 'womb to grave' might be a more accurate descriptor, as there is strong evidence that babies start learning before they are born from sounds they hear in the latter stages of pregnancy![2]

Lifelong learning challenges the common perception that learning is only about what happens in schools, colleges and universities, and that if you don't do well at school, learning stops at the age of sixteen or even before then. Unfortunately the pass/fail nature of our current education system reinforces this common perception, producing high levels of disaffection and underachievement. That is why, in setting out an ambitious alternative to the present learning system, we start with lifelong learning. We do so believing that there is a latent force behind lifelong learning which, if promoted vigorously and inclusively, can be a powerful driver for tackling educational underachievement, and breaking down the social and economic divisions in our society.

As important, there is an uncertain and rapidly changing future before us, where individuals, organisations and whole nations will have to adapt nimbly and continuously to ever-advancing science and technology. It is no longer the case that schools, further and higher education can equip people with the knowledge and skills they will need for the rest of their lives. People need to be able to constantly re-skill and learn how to adapt to a continuously changing world. The duty, then, of parents, teachers, employers and governments is to help people develop the personal and cognitive skills to become independent lifelong learners. This is a huge challenge. Many people are lifelong learners. They have a natural appetite for learning, which has not been diminished or extinguished, and they have an enthusiasm and energy to continue learning. But there are too many others who have been 'put off learning' by their past experiences (particularly in the home and at school) and do not go out of their way to broaden their horizons or learn new things.

We have coined the headline 'learning nation' to symbolise the ambition and leadership that the national government and other key policy makers need to have. At the forefront of such leadership needs to be developing a culture of lifelong learning embedded in the day-to-day life of the country – in individuals, families and organisations. This has to be backed up with practical actions, campaigns and initiatives, led by the government and delivered through our major national and local institutions. That is why we are calling for a major national programme promoting lifelong learning. In this chapter we explain what lifelong learning is and put forward some ideas about how we might make this imperative of modern life real for everyone.

Lifelong learning - everything that people learn across their entire lifespans

Put simply, lifelong learning is 'everything that people learn across their entire lifespans'[3]. Our more comprehensive definition is:

> *Continuous learning throughout people's lives to acquire knowledge and skills for personal and/or professional reasons, which benefits individuals' social and personal development, promotes active citizenship, and supports the economy and employability.*

You can distinguish between 'intentional' learning, where people set out in advance to acquire particular knowledge or skills, and 'incidental' learning, which occurs in an unplanned way from the day-to-day events and experiences in our lives. Although this is a largely un-researched area, it is probable that far more learning happens from 'incidental' than 'intentional' learning, including the most important skills and behaviours we need in order to make our way in life. A great deal of learning comes from 'informal' activities as opposed to those that take place in formal educational settings such as schools, colleges and universities[4]. Lifelong learning, then, is a mix of intentional, incidental, formal and informal learning, as the diagram[5] below illustrates.

	Intentional	Incidental
Formal	A course at school, college, university or an e-learning programme where the learning objectives and the structure of the learning process are determined by the teacher or organising body	Learning which arises from an organised course, but which is unplanned and not necessarily linked to the pre-determined learning objectives
Informal	Learning where there are objectives, but the activities learners are engaged in are informal, with little or no teacher direction. Good examples would be structured play in an early years setting, and a high quality youth service session.	Learning that happens as part of everyday life experiences, where behaviours, knowledge and skills are picked up unintentionally without pre-planned aims

Desire and self-belief imperative for continuous learning

There are two key conditions for people learning effectively – their desire to (motivation) and self-belief (confidence). Humans have a natural propensity to learn. Where parents and other adults in a family understand this and encourage young children's inquisitiveness, those children are likely to develop highly positive attitudes to further learning. On the other hand negative adult intervention, for example ignoring children's questions or telling them to be quiet, blunt their curiosity and ability to learn, particularly language and conceptual development. Today, technological tools such as iPads and tablets are often used as 'passive babysitters', limiting children's conversation with adults and other children, restricting their social, emotional and language development.

Only about a fifth of adults participate in formal learning, whether this is for basic skills, occupational purposes or leisure courses[6], and later on we make some suggestions about how more people could be encouraged to access learning. Any plan for promoting lifelong learning needs to be built on people's natural desire to learn. It will be necessary to do some 'rehabilitative' work for those who, because of their previous negative experiences, have been turned off learning and need to be re-engaged. Key to actively engaging people in learning and sustaining that involvement, is sparking and nurturing their motivation and confidence. People's participation is also dependent on how accessible learning opportunities are in terms of timing, location and environment, as well as the teaching and learning styles used.

Making a national lifelong learning programme real

The leadership role of the government should, therefore, be no less than the pursuit of activating the whole nation in lifelong learning. In pursuit of building a learning nation the crucial nature of the learning that takes place in the family, particularly for children growing up, needs to be fully recognised and understood. Those establishments that have a statutory responsibility for the education of children, young people and adults – nurseries, schools, youth services, colleges, universities and adult education centres – obviously play a massive part in the country's overall learning provision. Alongside these the great institutions of the country, including businesses, public and voluntary sector organisations, trade unions and cultural venues, already make, and potentially can make an even greater, contribution to people's learning. Let us now explore how we can develop a learning nation through what are the four major strands of lifelong learning - learning from life's experiences; learning families; structured learning; and learning organisations.

Learning from life's experiences is 'unavoidable'

Learning is most commonly associated with that which happens in schools and other education establishments i.e. learning that is intentional and structured. But most of what we learn comes from our day-to-day life experiences – the reality that learning is 'unavoidable' and that 'individuals [constantly] learn everywhere and all the time, in any kind of settings'[7]. Informal experiential learning takes place outside the formal learning system - in the home, at work and socially. There are numerous mediums through which we learn from life's experiences including from role models (for example parents, friends and work colleagues), the media, cultural activities, volunteering, and doing DIY jobs around the house and learning to do these better. Sometimes non-formal learning from experience has goals, particularly for acquiring technical skills such as riding a bicycle or cooking a meal. More often than not, the learning that stems from our life experiences has no pre-determined outcomes or structure. This latter form of learning most importantly includes learning to speak, which we do in our earliest years by mimicking the language of parents and others around us. Particularly through our relationships with other people, we develop the social and behavioural skills needed for everyday interactions that enable us to live socially and economically meaningful lives.

Informal experiential learning, by its very nature, goes largely unnoticed and is, therefore, little understood or appreciated. In seeking to make lifelong learning work for everyone, therefore, it is important to actively support the principle that 'all learning has value and most of it deserves to be made visible and recognised'[8]. Alongside side this it has to be recognised that learning can have negative as well as positive outcomes; for example children growing up in family situations where there is little structure or discipline tend to learn poor behaviour.

How, then, can we improve the quality of how people learn from their ongoing life experiences? An indispensable first step is to facilitate an understanding amongst people that they are learning all the time and can acquire knowledge and learn vital skills from their every-day experiences, and make positive choices. The second pre-requisite is the personal motivation and commitment that individuals need to have to learn positively and effectively from their life experiences. Without this it is simply not possible to take advantage of the learning opportunities that life presents. Alongside this goes resilience – the ability to keep going when you face setbacks or resist peer pressure to make poor choices. This enables people to learn from their mistakes and errors, which is how a great deal of learning occurs.

Many young people and adults lack the self-esteem and confidence to pursue further learning. Actively and skilfully encouraging people who have 'turned off' education to re-engage with learning has to be a key aspect of any strategy to make lifelong learning real for all. Once people are motivated and want to engage with learning, many of them will need support in developing the skills that will help them to learn effectively from their life experiences, as well as accessing more formal ways of learning. Some basic communication, numeracy and computer skills will certainly be required. There will also be a need for people to be able to reflect on and analyse experiences in order to maximise learning from them.

Re-engaging people with and enabling their continuing learning is a mammoth task and will involve identifying those individuals who need help and then providing them with the most appropriate support. This will necessitate the commitment of the major organisations within each local area, including further and adult education providers, universities, cultural venues, employers, and voluntary and community groups, and the ongoing deployment of their resources and expertise. A major role is envisaged for the local family support services, which we look at in some detail in the next chapter. Given that these services would have a remit of developing long-term, trusting relationships with families, we see them as having a prime role in linking individuals with the support they may need to improve their learning. It will be vital that the efforts of the different agencies are effectively co-ordinated to ensure maximum impact. Lifelong learning partnerships, which we propose will be statutorily established for each local area, would provide the means of co-ordinating the activities of these different organisations.

Finally, it is important to recognise that there is already a wealth of learning resources in most local communities provided by various venues and facilities, many of which do not charge for access, such as libraries, art galleries, museums, buildings and grounds of historical interest, and parks and woodlands. A lot of these facilities offer talks and presentations (often free). There are also sports and leisure facilities, run by local councils and increasingly by the private sector, which generally charge for use. The aim must be to widen the range of people who make use of what are generally wonderful and inspiring learning resources. Barriers to access are people's desire to visit (as they may believe that such cultural venues are 'not for them'), the prohibitive cost to those on low incomes to use some of the facilities, and the practicalities and cost of getting there, again for those on low incomes and/or who are reliant on public transport. Overcoming these barriers will be a major challenge for local services seeking to widen participation in lifelong learning.

Learning families

Children's first and most influential learning takes place in the family. In theory the government recognises this in articulating that 'the role of parents during a child's earliest years is the single biggest influence on their development' and that 'good quality home learning contributes more to children's intellectual and social development than parental occupation, education or income'[9]. In reality, however, governments, in designing and acting out their education policies, have largely ignored the criticality of family life to children's learning.

It is the unintended learning in the family environment – how children are treated and what they hear and see – that is most significant, particularly in the immediate years after birth, when they develop at the fastest rate of their whole lives. That is why in chapter 10 we advocate the development of a major national family strategy, at the heart of government policy, including local services to support families generally and in particular to form long-term relationships with those households where children are most at risk of not doing well at school and in employment. Central to this national strategy and the work of the local services will be facilitating positive learning within families. How we practically enable all families to be 'learning families' is developed further in chapter 10.

Structured learning

Currently structured learning offering lifelong learning opportunities for tens of millions of UK children, young people and adults are provided by:

	Age range
Early years and childcare services	0-5
Primary schools	3-11
Secondary schools	11-19
Youth service	13-19
Sixth form colleges	16-19
Further education colleges	16+
Adult education centres	18+
Universities/higher education establishments	18+
e-learning	all ages

Early years and childcare services

The early years of children's lives, between birth and five years, are the most formative, strongly influencing the quality of their later life – educationally, economically, socially, and in respect of their physical and mental health[10]. While their home life has the most significant impact[11], good quality education and care services for very young children can be very influential[12], particularly for children from disadvantaged backgrounds, by helping 'parents to develop effective home learning environments'[13]. Given the crucial relationship they have with parents, the wide range of early years and childcare services is reviewed in chapter 10 when we examine how best families can be supported.

Schools most critical part of formal learning system

Given their mandatory and universal nature the 28,000 schools in the UK, attended by 7.5 million children, are the most critical part of the formal learning system and, next to families, act as the biggest influence on how well people engage with learning throughout their lives.

Although many more young people are achieving at a high academic level and going to university, there are significant numbers who have become disaffected from education, underachieve and leave school without the qualifications and skills to acquire quality employment or continue into further and higher education. For many people, sadly, their lifelong learning stops when they leave school at sixteen years of age. The main causes of this 'long tail of underperformance' are children's family experiences, and a national schools system that fails to meet the needs of all pupils and the skill requirements of the country. That is why in chapter 11 we argue for a radical overhaul of the conditions under which schools are operating, to facilitate the development of a curriculum that inspires and meets the needs of all children and young people.

Private schools must take on wider responsibility to justify charitable status

The 2,500 private schools are part of the country's diverse range of formal education provision, catering for around 615,000 children, seven per cent of school pupils[14]. These establishments are funded largely by the fees they charge parents, augmented by gifts and charitable endowments. The average annual fee for a day pupil is more than £13,000 a year, compared to the average funding for state schools of £4,500 per pupil[15]. A third of private school pupils receive 'some form of support for paying their fees', but only about one per cent pay no fees[16]. Most private secondary schools select their pupils by ability.

In chapter 7 we briefly looked at the part played by fee-paying schools in the growing social and economic inequalities we have in the UK, highlighting the grossly disproportionate number of privately educated people at what are considered 'top' universities and employed in the so called 'elite' professions[17]. There appears to be no political appetite nor pragmatic case for abolishing private schools. It is argued that in a free society parents should be able to choose to have their children educated privately, and the additional cost to the state of educating the numbers currently in fee-paying schools would be around £3.6 billion. Private education also contributes substantially to the national economy[18].

However, these schools because of their charitable status have business rate relief[19] and the fees they charge are exempt from VAT[20]; a total tax payer subsidy of around £1.8 billion. This substantial tax relief obviously helps many private schools to provide generous resources for their pupils, including small class sizes. Parliament could legislate to require private schools to make more of a contribution than they do now to the greater 'public benefit'. Other options proposed would be to remove their charitable status and/or make VAT payable on tuition fees, or introduce a special tax on private schools[21], using the funding raised to help extend educational opportunities. The Charities Commission issued guidelines on what private schools would have to do to justify their charitable status, but a successful legal challenge in effect removed the Commission's ability to enforce this guidance[22].

The Conservatives promised to require private schools to justify their charitable status by sponsoring academies, having partnerships with state schools and providing bursaries to children from low-income families, but following the 2017 general election this was 'quietly dropped'[23], so fresh legislation would be required to ensure that private schools justify their charitable status in a meaningful way. In its 2017 general election manifesto the Labour Party proposed applying VAT to school tuition fees. Caution would have to be exercised about the amount that might be made available from such changes, as they would result in schools charging significantly higher fees, causing some parents to stop using private education and transferring their children to the state sector, with additional costs to public spending and lower than anticipated tax revenues[24].

A pragmatic approach would be tightening up on what private schools have to do to justify their charitable status. This would better facilitate the active and meaningful participation of private schools in working with state schools and other stakeholder organisations in developing lifelong learning for all. In return for charitable status and the financial rewards this brings, private schools would be required to use their facilities and staff to work directly in an extra-curricular way with children who need additional support and/or helping adults return to learning.

Strengthen supplementary education

There are around 3,000 supplementary schools in the UK providing education programmes for children and young people outside of and in addition to mainstream schools. A large number are run by minority ethnic groups to boost the education attainment of children in their local communities. Supplementary schools vary in the curriculum they offer, with many focusing on the core subjects of mathematics, English, science and information technology; and others on religious studies, heritage languages, sport and performing arts. They run throughout the week in the evenings, or at weekends, and are not permitted by law to teach children of compulsory school age for more than eighteen hours a week, in excess of which they have to register as private schools.

Although they vary in quality we are generally supportive of the concept of supplementary schools and have worked with them productively during our careers. Lord Adonis has called for schools and local authorities to strengthen their support for supplementary schools, including use of premises, training volunteers and grant funding[25]. Additionally, it would be helpful for government to provide a policy framework for supplementary schools, and contribute to the funding of the National Resource Centre for Supplementary Education[26].

Home education – need to ensure children are literate, numerate and safe

Another aspect of the compulsory school system is home education. Parents have the legal right to educate their children at home and not send them to school[27]. In these circumstances parents are required to provide their children with 'efficient full-time education, suitable to his [or her] age, ability and aptitude and to any special education needs he [or she] may have'[28]. There is no obligation to follow the national curriculum. Local authorities, if they have evidence that children of compulsory school age are not receiving a full-time education, can issue parents with school attendance orders. In reality this is extremely difficult to implement as local authorities have no powers to monitor home education. Unless the child was previously on the roll of a state school, parents are not even required to notify the local authority that they are home-educating. Against a total school population of 9.5 million, the nearly 58,000 being educated at home is relatively small, but the numbers have increased dramatically in the last few years[29].

Parents choose to home educate for a variety of reasons including religious, cultural, philosophical or ideological beliefs; dissatisfaction with what is happening in schools (either generally or in their local schools); children's refusal or reluctance to go to school; special educational needs; bullying; and behavioural difficulties. Many parents who home school do their very utmost to provide their children with the best education possible. There are, however, widespread abuses of this long-standing parental right. Both the current chief inspector and her immediate predecessor have reported that significant numbers of children who are officially home educated are in reality attending illegal (i.e. unregistered) private schools, often run along strict faith lines, which are unregulated and without any form of public accountability[30]. And, as we will explain in chapter 11, parents of some children who have behavioural difficulties are pressurised by some secondary schools to remove their children from school rolls and 'home educate' them [31].

There are two particular questions that arise from these abuses of home education – are children being educated at all, even in the basics, and are they safe? We make two proposals that will help to address these two concerns. Firstly, a legal obligation should be placed on parents to notify the local authority as soon as they have decided to home educate their children, and when this is to start. This will enable the local authority to establish and maintain a register of those being home educated in their area. Secondly, a duty should be placed on and powers given to local authorities to visit households where parents have elected for home education to ensure that children are receiving at least a basic level of education and that they are safe. In circumstances where it is clear that children are not being educated and/or where there are safeguarding concerns, local authorities would be able to issue school attendance orders compelling parents to send their children to school. The government is reviewing its home education guidance, but it is unclear how far, if at all, this will be strengthened[32].

Youth service – invaluable asset in re-engaging youngsters

The immense strength of youth services is that unlike schools they are voluntary and largely free of testing and examinations. In our experience youth services are generally staffed by highly competent workers (be they hired by local councils, charities or community groups; paid or volunteers) who have the skills necessary to positively engage with and win the trust of young people. This mix of voluntarism and young-people centredness, combined with the informal nature of the activities offered, makes the youth service an important vehicle for re-engaging disaffected youngsters with learning. Theoretically providing a youth service is a statutory duty on each local authority[33], but in reality there isn't a common or standard youth service provision across the country. (The Labour Party has proposed that there should be a statutory minimum level of youth services[34]). What is offered depends on the priorities and historical provision of each local area, and is usually a mix of what is provided by local authorities and the voluntary sector (such as uniformed organisations, charities, church and community groups). Most local youth services are for teenagers, the main aim being to develop their personal and social skills.

Services are provided in the evenings, and also at weekends and during school holidays. Some schools contract youth services to work with their pupils in the school day. Facilities used include discrete youth centres, community buildings, schools, mobile units and health centres. There is also detached or outreach work, involving youth workers engaging with young people 'where they choose to gather', including on the streets and in parks. A lot of provision continues to be organised through youth centres, where young people 'drop in' to take part in activities such as games, use of computers, organised programmes such as cooking or motor cycle maintenance, or just to talk and socialise. Depending on access to funding and specialist facilities and equipment, the youth service offer can be enriched by young people's participation in sports, outdoor education (including the Duke of Edinburgh's Award scheme), performing arts, residentials, and leadership and volunteering experiences. An important role for the youth worker is providing mentoring and advice to young people of both an informal and structured nature. More specialised youth services support young people with the major issues they face such as physical and mental health, sexual health and relationships, drugs, alcohol and bullying.

There has been an ongoing debate about how far the youth service should be universal (i.e. open to all young people) or targeted (i.e. focusing on those who are most vulnerable such as those from disadvantaged backgrounds, with special needs, or at risk of being NEET or offending). In more recent years youth services have taken responsibility for promoting the 'young person's voice' through facilitating discussion and debate on topical issues, and encouraging participation in youth councils and parliaments.

Funding is a major limiting factor that influences the range of activities offered and how many young people can be involved. The Albemarle Report[35], published in 1960, was the harbinger of what turned out to be the heyday of the youth service in the 1960s and 70s. Since then funding has been progressively reduced to an extent that youth services generally have a limited range of services engaging only a small proportion of local young people. There was some respite during the period of the 1997-2010 Labour government, with the youth service benefitting from some specific grants aimed at helping vulnerable young people. Since 2010 there has been an estimated £413 million cut from youth service spending, over 630 youth centres closed, 4,452 youth work jobs lost and 183,898 places for young people cut[36].

Current government policy is set out in *Positive for Youth*, published in 2011. Given the weak guidance provided by the government and the debilitating spending cuts, the national policy has proved to be meaningless. This is summed up succinctly in a review carried out by the National Youth Agency:

> *There is no longer a common form of youth service across England - everywhere services are different. Councils are rapidly re-shaping services according to local circumstances rather than a national vision. There is an absence of national youth policy. The youth work 'offer' is diminished and has little currency. The uncertainty around current funding means there is little investment in programmes that build long-term relationships and support for young people[37].*

Re-engaging young people with learning in its broadest sense should be at the heart of what in the future needs to be a re-vitalised national and local youth service. Towards this end we would urge the government, in partnership with young people and service providers, to set out a clear and positive national direction for youth services. Such a strategy should include the issuing of meaningful statutory guidance, backed up by sufficient additional funding to support local youth services in working with those young people who have become disaffected from education or who are at risk of doing so.

Further education – mass educators

The sheer size and diversity of its student body and vast range of courses offered makes the further education sector one of the largest and most important contributors to lifelong learning, third only to families and schools. Tuition is usually free for those under twenty-four studying for their first qualification equivalent to GCSE or A level and many on basic education programmes. In English further education there are:

- 2.7 million students in 189 general further education colleges including 75,000 apprenticeships.
- 1.9 million adult learners.
- 153,000 students on higher education courses.
- 79 sixth form colleges with 162,000 sixteen to eighteen-year-olds on A level or vocational programmes.
- 26 specialist colleges (including art and design, and agriculture). [38]

Further education is thus a mass educator, with a record of working successfully with people from all backgrounds and with the full range of abilities, including those who have not done all that well at school, and adults who are returning to learning to better their lives and career prospects. Colleges are also the biggest supplier of vocational programmes and apprenticeships. The contribution of further education to lifelong learning, however, has been badly dented in the last ten years with a thirty per cent cut in funding[39], and a huge fall in the number of adults taking college courses[40]. Because it is central to meeting the country's skill requirements we take a more in-depth look at further education in chapter 12.

Adult education challenges the bias that learning is a once in a lifetime chance

A major cultural bias in our system is that learning is a once in a lifetime chance – that if you don't do well in school you are stuck with this for the rest of your life. Unfortunately for the vast majority of people who leave school without good qualifications this tends to be the case. The concept of adult education challenges this bias, and enables individuals to return to learning, often in a more mature and motivated state, with the aim of maximising their potential in the way they didn't at a younger age.

Adult education enables people to adapt to changing circumstances in society (including in employment and skills) and in their personal and family circumstances. It also provides opportunities for those who simply want to pursue personal interests to fulfil their thirst for learning. The record of adult education, then, in re-engaging learners and helping them succeed in their chosen courses of study, and in the process transforming the lives of millions, makes it an absolutely vital part of the lifelong learning continuum. There are 238 providers (including those run by local authorities, and voluntary and community sector; and nine specialist designated institutions[41]) whose core aim is to provide adult education. Nearly nine in ten of these providers have been judged good or outstanding by Ofsted[42]. Courses are run in colleges and school buildings, community halls, libraries, children's and health centres.

The massive economic and social changes taking place in modern society make continuous learning for adults more important than ever. Being in employment, particularly well-paid work, will in the future be increasingly dependent on skill level[43]. Also the UK population is growing. There is an increasing proportion and number aged sixty-five and over, and the number of young people is declining[44]. We have an ageing society with people living longer, and being economically, physically and cognitively active into their seventies, eighties and beyond. These radical demographic shifts, together with changes in state and occupational pensions, will almost certainly mean more and more people working well past what used to be considered retirement age. It is highly likely that all of this will result in people having an increasing number of significant transitions in their lives that they will have to manage, including developing new skills.

These considerable skill and demographic changes therefore pose a major challenge for the country, its people, businesses and public services. The evidence, however, suggests that we start from quite a low and worrying baseline, with nine million adults (a quarter of those aged between sixteen and sixty-five) having low literacy or/and numeracy skills[45]. Over nine million are without basic digital skills[46] and one in five lack basic financial capabilities[47]. Also, half of businesses report that some of their employees have such poor basic literacy, numeracy and IT skills that it affects the efficiency of their businesses[48].

The level of skills in the UK has historically lagged behind that of many other developed countries[49]. And the country's skills are unlikely to improve, and are more likely to deteriorate, as the number of adults on level three and four courses has declined dramatically[50]. Equally concerning is the record of successive governments, particularly since 2010, in how they have treated adult learning. It would appear that the government and national politicians generally regard adult education as a low priority. Between 2010 and 2017 education was discussed in the House of Commons on 339 occasions, but there was only one debate and one question to ministers on adult education[51], and the adult education budget was cut by forty per cent[52]. There was a four-year cash funding settlement for adult education (from 2016-17 to 2019-20) of £1.5 billion a year[53]. No account, however, has been taken of inflationary costs and so in reality there will be further reductions to adult education provision up until 2020[54].

Adult education has enormous potential for tackling some of the serious shortcomings in our system of learning that we highlighted in the first part of this book, including the UK's 'long tail of underperformance' and damaging skills shortages. But to do so will require a fundamental change in the government's attitude towards this colossus of lifelong learning.

Firstly, the government must give far greater priority to adult learning. The incontrovertible rationale for this is that improving economic growth and productivity, and creating more skilled and better paid jobs, is conditional on upskilling the adult workforce. Giving priority means that the government should be much more active in promoting the benefits of adult learning, encouraging participation, and giving tangible support to education providers, businesses, and voluntary and community groups to engage adults in learning. The more practical manifestation, following a nationwide consultation, would be to develop a national strategy that sets out a clear core purpose and priorities for adult learning. Employers and learners in particular need to be meaningfully involved on an ongoing basis in influencing adult education provision to ensure it meets business and individual needs[55]. To deliver the national strategy there will be a need for local plans, with lifelong learning partnerships co-ordinating the designing and implementation of these.

Secondly, the government has to move to stabilise and then start to increase funding. A first step would be to halt the continuing real terms reductions by providing additional cash to inflation-proof the adult education budget for the current funding settlement up to 2020. Alongside this there should be a more medium-term plan, say over five or ten years, to invest more in adult learning with a focus on improving adult basic skills and meeting skill shortages.

Thirdly, the government needs to be instrumental in building an infrastructure that stimulates and enables adults to access learning opportunities, and then provide them with the long-term support needed to sustain and progress their studies. Adults wishing to re-enter learning want 'highly visible and accessible information and career guidance', but the majority are not aware of the services provided by the National Careers Service[56]. That is why in chapter 12 the case is made for major improvements to advice and guidance services for adults. There is then a need for specific targeted programmes aimed at 'getting people hooked on learning', such as 'bite-sized' short courses[57] and, given the crucial importance of reading, initiatives to encourage adults to read, or to read more often[58]. Finance is often a barrier for adults wanting to re-start or continue their education. There are advanced learning loans, but given the poor take-up[59] and the dramatic fall in adult student numbers[60], the government should look how these can be made more attractive. Other ideas for financially supporting adult learners have been proposed, such as an 'education savings account'[61], a 'lifelong learning fund'[62] and a 'flexible loans system'[63], all of which need to be explored as alternatives or additions to current financial support arrangements.

Finally, to stand any chance of tackling the huge adult skills deficit the country has, it will be necessary to put some major national programmes and pathways in place. In this regard the Learning and Work Institute have made three substantial proposals[64] that are worthy of serious consideration:

- A 'Citizen Skills Entitlement' programme aimed at providing all adults with the 'core capabilities needed for life and work in 21st century Britain'– literacy, numeracy, digital, health and financial capability – by 2030[65].
- Personal Learning Accounts' setting out the learning opportunities and entitlements for each adult, and the public funds and loans they are able to access[66].
- A 'Career Advancement Service' aimed at helping the UK's five million low-paid workers to progress and increase their earnings, and employers to boost productivity[67].

Much more to do on widening participation in higher education

Catering for over 2.2 million students, of which 1.84 million are from the UK[68], universities make an enormous contribution to the nation's overall learning provision. The numbers of young people going to university has grown exponentially since the 1960s, with nearly one in two now going into higher education before they reach the age of thirty[69], including an increasing proportion of women[70].

In recent years there has been a drive to increase the numbers and proportions of 'disadvantaged students'[71] attending university. Alongside the introduction of tuition fees and loans there has been a record number of students[72], including an increase in the number and proportion of those from low-income families[73]. And, repaying loans falls more heavily on those who will earn the most during their careers[74]. While in 2006 one in ten from the lowest income families went to university, this is now one in five[75]; a significant improvement, but still very unsatisfactory considering that half of those from the least deprived areas are in higher education[76]. This huge gap demonstrates how far there still is to go. Unless the rate of progress rapidly accelerates in the next few years the target set by the government, of having twenty-eight per cent from the poorest backgrounds in higher education by 2020, will not be reached[77].

Disturbingly the vast majority of the increase in students from low-income families has come from the former polytechnics and colleges, and the contribution from the so called 'elite' universities has been very small[78]. This is something that has been spotted by the new university regulator, the Office for Students (OfS), which has formally warned Cambridge and Oxford Universities about their poor record in admitting disadvantaged students. In future, says the OfS, 'institutions will be judged on what they achieve, not how much they spend on trying to widen access' and those who 'fail could have their annual fees capped at £6,000, instead of £9,250, or be fined'[79]. Additionally there are high numbers of students not completing a large number of higher education courses[80], with retention rates of students from low-income families having 'scarcely improved in the last two decades'[81].

Over the years studying at university part-time has been a well-trodden route for those who hadn't gone down the traditional full-time higher education path on leaving school. In contrast to full-time students, most of those on part-time courses are mature students[82], from less affluent backgrounds, in employment[83], and one in four does not have qualifications beyond GCSE[84]. While the hike in tuition fees hasn't put off young people going to university full-time, this is not the case with part-time and mature students, whose numbers have declined dramatically in the last decade[85]. The UK also has a lower proportion of mature students in higher education than most other developed countries[86].

It is clear that the dramatic decline in the number of part-time and mature students is a massive setback in seeking to widen access to higher education. For this reason we strongly support the calls for a national inquiry to tackle the barriers to higher education for part-time and mature students[87], better financial support for part-time students generally[88], the restoration of maintenance grants and tuition fee loan write offs for mature students in shortage areas such as nursing[89], and more flexible organisation of courses to better meet the needs of mature students (such as work commitments and childcare).

Universities are required to use a 'significant proportion' of the additional funding they received when tuition fees were trebled[90] on widening student participation; in excess of £800 million nationally[91], supplemented by a £60 million National Collaborative Outreach Programme[92]. The main approach used by universities appears to be quite broad-brush, mainly working with schools in low-income areas, missing out young people from low-income families attending schools located in generally well-off areas. Also, the House of Commons Public Accounts Committee has concluded that the government hasn't a sufficient 'grip' on the actions needed to widen participation and is over-reliant on universities to do this[93]. There are programmes, run by some charities, which provide more intensive support to high-ability students from low-income backgrounds[94]. This way of working could be rolled out into a comprehensive programme by identifying all those school and college students who have the ability to enter higher education, but who may need extra support to do so. For such a programme to be successful would require close collaboration between schools, colleges, universities, voluntary and community organisations, and family support services.

Consideration needs to be given to whether bringing back maintenance grants for those from poorer families[95], scrapped in 2016/17, would encourage more disadvantaged students to apply for university. Along the same lines, a case has also been made for reintroducing lower or no fees for students from low-income households (a policy which ended in 2006)[96].

There are four other issues that have an indirect effect on higher education's contribution to promoting lifelong learning for all – quality of teaching, student and institutional funding, value for money and local community benefit.

It is not possible to objectively assess the standard of university teaching. The House of Commons Public Accounts Committee has debunked the government's premise that market forces would improve standards in universities, finding that 'the government can provide no evidence that competition between institutions will drive the quality of education they provide'[97]. Anecdotal feedback suggests that there is some good and exceptional teaching, but too much is poor and uninspiring, particularly in the first year of courses[98]. In 2016 the government introduced the Teaching Excellence Framework (TEF) where, using institutionally provided data, a panel[99] graded each participating university as gold, silver or bronze. There has to be doubt about how robust the TEF is, given that participation is voluntary, there is no observation of teaching, and all three ratings are described in highly positive terms[100]. How effective the new regulatory body, the Office for Students, will be in improving teaching quality remains to be seen[101]. As a condition of public funding each university should have a system for identifying the standard of teaching and academic support, and for improving this, especially where it is judged to be poor. It is interesting that when asked, students prefer to have lecturers with teaching qualifications and industry experience than being active researchers[102].

It is not surprising, then, that just over a third of students in England say they get value for money from higher education[103]. Spending on English higher education, particularly per student, is 'high by international standards'[104]. The trebling of tuition fees in 2012 increased funding for higher education[105] by twenty-eight per cent per student[106], and the university sector holds £44 billion. in reserves[107]. Prime Minister Teresa May, has said that this is 'one of the most expensive systems of university tuition in the world' and 'the level of fees charged do not relate to the cost or quality of the course'[108]. The National Audit Office found that universities were 'under very little competitive pressure to provide best value'[109]. Most students have around twenty-two weeks teaching and four weeks of examinations a year, and an average of twelve hours teaching contact per week[110].

One way of achieving better value for money is by shortening many three-year degrees to two years[111], and Masters programmes to three rather than four years[112]. The Higher Education and Research Act 2017 makes it easier to offer two-year degrees[113]. Although still very small, the number of students on two-year degrees in 2017/18 was the highest it has ever been[114]. Students on two-year programmes undertake the same number of units and have the same amount of teaching and supervision as they would on three-year courses, but pay £5,500 less in tuition fees and save one year's worth of living costs[115]. Universities routinely offering two-year degree courses would cut average student debt by £20,000 and free 100,000 rooms up for renting[116].

Although there has been a great deal of concern about the huge debts students accrue from their loans (£50,000 per student on average[117]), the most pressing issue with the current higher education funding system is its sustainability in the long term. With eight in ten students unlikely to repay their loans off in full, it is estimated that nearly half of the debt will be written off[118]. The total amount of debt has doubled in four years to more than £100 billion[119] and is projected to rise to £1 trillion by 2044, £1.2 trillion by 2049[120] and £1.5 trillion by the late 2050s[121]. An estimated 300,000 additional university students by 2030 will create an even larger debt[122]. Under current treasury accounting rules the student loan debt is not reflected in the public spending deficit[123], described by the independent Office for Budget Responsibility as a 'fiscal illusion'[124]. A ruling by the Office for National Statistics in December 2018 that unpaid student loans have be included in the government's deficit (adding £12 billion annually) will expose the true cost of the taxpayers' contribution to the funding of higher education[125].

The government review of 'post-18' education funding[126], currently under way, presents an opportunity to put higher education funding on a more sustainable footing. Abolishing fees, costing £11 billion a year[127] (if funded from increases in general taxation), or reducing the amount paid[128] would benefit high earning graduates[129] and would be regarded as 'regressive'. A graduate tax might be seen as more equitable as it could be levied on all those who have been to university or its equivalent, including those who prior to 1998 paid no tuition fees at all[130]. The administrative problems in designing a workable graduate tax are considerable[131]. We have neither the data nor expertise to assess whether such problems can be reasonably overcome. What is clear is that the government needs urgently to look at how the nation's growing student loan debt can be better controlled, either through reducing fees or through increased general or specific taxation, or a mix of some or all of these.

Given their extensive facilities and range of expertise, universities could do more to help local people get back into learning[132]. Some universities sponsor academies[133], others are active in their local communities, including working with disadvantaged young people[134]. We propose that either as a condition of their public funding or charitable status, all universities should be members of their local lifelong learning partnership, and work with teenagers and adults who have become disengaged from education.

In chapter 3 we reported that the large proportion of graduates the UK has compared to other countries[135] makes a major positive impact on the country's economic growth and productivity. There is strong evidence, however, that higher education could play an even more significant part in meeting the nation's skill requirements, and this is explored extensively in chapter 12.

Distance and e-Learning

Another well-established route for those who want to return to or extend their formal education is distance learning, which enables people to study in their homes rather than travel to a college or university building. Over time the core vehicle for distance learning has moved from correspondence (later on supported by radio and television) to the internet – online or e-learning. Using computers and the internet, and the ongoing technological advancements, have made distance learning easier, more accessible, faster and capable of delivering full study programmes at all levels. Distance learning is generally far less costly and is, therefore, financially more accessible. It is not for everyone, however, with many preferring and needing the face-to-face interaction with and support of tutors and fellow students that more traditional education courses bring. New technology has facilitated an explosion in the number of subjects and courses offered online by private training providers, businesses and education establishments, including practical subjects that in the past could only be accessed by attending a class[136].

The biggest provider of distance learning in the UK is the Open University (OU) [137], which currently has around 168,000 students[138]. The OU is being severely challenged as the premium provider of distance learning in the UK, by private learning companies and traditional universities offering 'massive open online courses' (MOOCs), which are free to anyone in the world with access to a computer[139]. Mainly as a consequence of considerable government funding reductions[140] and MOOCs, the OU has haemorrhaged student numbers, which have fallen by thirty-five per cent since 2009-10[141].

Given its enormous potential for opening up learning on a universal scale, we need a national e-learning strategy that supports the diversity of public and private provision and the innovation and choice this brings, ensures the right investments are made, and enhances accessibility, particularly for those who have become disengaged from furthering their education.

Learning organisations

The concept of the learning organisation is one which harnesses the knowledge, skills and creativity of all employees and other stakeholders as an integral and vital part of the organisation's business model[142]. Individual employees committed to their own lifelong learning are the foundation upon which a learning organisation is built[143]. In an increasingly knowledge-intensive economy, optimising learning at work is becoming more and more important, particularly in product development. It is extremely worrying, therefore, that in recent years the amount of workplace training has been declining. This is something that is explored in more detail in chapter 12.

While our emphasis so far has been on individuals learning, within organisations there is often more focus given to team learning. For a significant part of our lives we are involved in groups – at work, in our families and in our social lives, and so learning how to be a responsible and productive member of a team is critically important.

Positive culture needed for learning organisations

The effectiveness of learning, and how well this is applied to create business success, depends to a large extent on the culture of the organisation. The principal values and behaviours of a learning organisation's culture are trust and empowerment – that is, staff feel safe to engage in critical thinking and honestly challenge what is happening in the business. Staff also have to be self-reliant, able to use their initiative, but at the same time 'work together to pool their talents and energies for the good of the organisation'[144].

How well individuals and the organisation as a whole learn from mistakes and errors is also an important ingredient of a learning organisation. One sector that is diligent in learning from failure is the aviation industry, which has spent decades trying to understand why mistakes occur and how they can be spotted as fast as possible[145]. Professor Jan Hagen argues that all businesses can learn from this[146]. Learning organisations create working environments where people and teams see failure and mistakes as the chance to learn and make improvements[147]. It is a lesson we need to apply to all learning, particularly in schools and other education establishments.

Employers under no legal requirement to provide learning

Except for certain training for union and health and safety representatives, employers are under no specific legal obligation to provide or give time off for work-related education for their employees. Employees in organisations that employ 250 people or more have a statutory right to ask for time off work for training or study, although this is usually unpaid and employers have the discretion to turn the request down[148].

In reality sixteen and seventeen-year-olds in work do not have the right to paid leave for education purposes. From 1996 teenagers who left school without obtaining five 'good' GCSEs[149] had the right to paid time off work to acquire a 'relevant academic or vocational qualification'[150]. In 2008 this was overtaken by broader legislation[151] requiring that young people participate in education and training up to the age of 18. With the change of government in 2010, however, the duty on employers to accommodate education and training for employees under eighteen was not brought into force. This is something we believe should be changed. Certainly, the statutory requirement on employers to enable their teenage employees to participate meaningfully in education and training up to the age of eighteen needs to be made clearer and firmer. This should be particularly so for those who leave school with poor basic literacy, numeracy and personal skills.

Should organisations take any responsibility for their employees' personal learning?

We raise the question whether organisations, in addition to developing their workforce to improve business performance, should also take some responsibility for the personal learning of their employees, especially those whose basic skills are poor. The prime purpose of organisations is to serve their customers and shareholders, and in pursuance of this they need to have a workforce that has relevant, up-to-date knowledge and skills, and there will be an understandable reluctance to accept a wider obligation for meeting learning needs that do not directly benefit their business. There is an argument that it is the duty of the state to ensure a good general education for all, and not that of employers. More materially the costs of fulfilling this wider learning function may well impact on the financial health and even viability of businesses, particularly small and medium sized enterprises. These are valid points and call for careful consideration of what the role of organisations should be in promoting lifelong learning. Except for employees under the age of eighteen, it would not be sensible to place statutory duties on organisations to help meet the generic learning needs of their employees. That is not to say, however, that organisations should not make a more substantial contribution to the overall effort to improve the nation's learning.

We say this in the context that only a nationwide effort will be effective in stimulating the renaissance in learning that we need, and that this should include families, education establishments, businesses and the public sector. Organisations through their workforce development already make a significant contribution to this effort, and job-specific learning has wider benefits for people's overall personal development. The question is, however, whether with their substantial resources including premises and staff expertise, organisations (or at least some of them) could do more in supporting the wider learning of their staff and other people in the local community, particularly those with poor basic skills. We need to ask how these resources could be best put to use in helping people learn without impacting adversely on the organisation's core business. Organisations should be encouraged to participate in their local lifelong learning partnerships, both to ensure that the skills needs of their businesses are being met, as well as to see how they might contribute to learning generally within the local area.

Trade unions have much to offer lifelong learning

Trade unionism has much to offer lifelong learning in encouraging their members to take up learning programmes, in running courses for their officials and members, and making representation for more extensive and improved workplace training and learning opportunities. Where unions are recognised at a workplace they can appoint Union Learning Representatives to promote employee learning, and there are 26,000 such volunteer representatives[152]. The government-provided Union Learning Fund, established in 1998, supports unions in helping their members to 'explore learning, develop skills, achieve qualifications and promote lifelong learning opportunities within the workplace'[153]. With declining membership and competition for members, unions want to market themselves to workers through offering services and specific benefits including training and education courses. Unions are increasingly providing learning facilities and courses for their members, some in collaboration with colleges and universities.

Conclusion – government must lead in promoting lifelong learning

Releasing the untapped potential of lifelong learning is the key to tackling the country's gross levels of educational underachievement and skills shortages. In order for people to thrive in a future constantly being reshaped by advancing technology and science, they will need the wherewithal to continuously learn new ways of living and working. There has to be a clear message underpinning the promotion of lifelong learning – that learning throughout life is for everyone, not just for those who start school with the advantage of a stimulating family upbringing, and who go on to achieve good qualifications and a higher education. Another imperative is to put the fun and interest back into learning. This means moving away from the drudgery of the content-laden and exam-driven school curriculum that's been in place for the past thirty years.

It is imperative that the government take the lead in driving lifelong learning for all forward. Lifelong learning must be at the very heart of government's social and economic policy. It requires a holistic understanding of learning – that people learn in many different ways and through a variety of channels; those that are intentional and structured, as well as from life's day-to-day experiences that are incidental and unstructured. The overriding aim should be to increase and widen opportunities and participation in all aspects of lifelong learning – in families, schools, colleges and universities, e-learning, and at work. Out-of-school education, including supplementary schooling, has a part to play in enhancing children's learning. Such additional help is particularly needed for pupils struggling at school, and private schools, universities and businesses need to be encouraged to do more to support those children.

Central to any programme that will make a tangible difference to the country's overall learning capability must be measures that start to re-engage those who have been previously turned off formal learning. Unfortunately, since 2010 the government has de-prioritised those services that traditionally have been at the forefront of helping young people and adults get back into formal learning. Adult and further education, the careers and youth services, and the Open University have all suffered from large funding cuts, undermining their capacity to work with those who need the most support in getting their learning back on track. In contrast higher education, the sector serving the highest educational achievers, has had more than a twenty-five per cent increase per student. A change in national direction is clearly needed, with 'making lifelong learning real for everyone' at its core.

Recommendations

- *Promote lifelong learning* in an ongoing and high profile way, championing its benefits for both individuals and the nation as a whole, including campaigns to raise awareness about how people can best learn from their day-to-day experiences; access more formal learning opportunities, and the support they will receive.
- Statutorily establish *lifelong learning partnerships* in each local area[154] involving, amongst others[155], learning providers[156], employers, the voluntary sector and local authorities. The role of the partnerships would be to foster an inclusive and inspiring learning culture in their local area, including developing new learning opportunities, particularly for those who have previously 'missed out' on learning; to ensure provision matches need; and that there are clear pathways to enable learners to progress.

- A duty be placed on the government to ensure that the *formal learning system as a whole is fit for purpose*. This will require providing a clear national direction and adequate funding for those services that have a significant role in helping young people and adults back into learning, such as the youth and careers services, further and adult education, and the Open University. Out-of-school provision should be strengthened, to include enhancing supplementary schooling; incentivising private schools, universities and businesses to contribute to extra-curricular programmes for children needing additional educational support; and giving local authorities the power to monitor home education. New national pathways for adult learning are required, such as a 'Citizen Skills Entitlement', 'Personal Learning Accounts' and a 'Career Advancement Service', alongside innovative ways of attracting adults to learning (including short-term 'taster' events, targeting particular demographics[157], using non-conventional venues like cafes and pubs[158], and reading initiatives[159]). All universities should be required to have more targeted programmes to increase the numbers of disadvantaged students in higher education, and systematic approaches to improving the quality of teaching. There has to be a more sustainable alternative to funding higher education than the current tuition fees and student loans system.
- Government to explore how employers, especially small and medium enterprises, can be encouraged to *increase learning opportunities for* their *employees* by the possible use of subsidies, incentives (such as allowances for corporation tax) and regulation[160]. There should be an un-ambivalent statutory requirement for employers to give employees under the age of eighteen reasonable time off for education and training.
- Introduce and implement a national *e-Learning strategy* to support the development of e-Learning infrastructure and provision, guiding investment decisions in new technologies and their use, and maximising access to learning.

A number of recommendations for improvements in four other major aspects of the lifelong learning spectrum are made later on – learning in families (chapter 10), early years and childcare services (chapter 10), schools (chapter 11), and skills and apprenticeships (chapter 12).

10
BUILDING STRONG FAMILIES

It has to be recognized that closing the gap in outcomes between those from more and less disadvantaged backgrounds will only happen when what happens to children outside as well as inside school changes. This means changing how families and communities work, and enriching what they offer to children.
Professor Mel Ainscow[1]

It is fascinating being in a maternity ward wondering how the lives of the newly born babies you are surrounded by will work out. Each of the babies will have vastly different futures in front of them. A discussion about why this might be invariably centres on the nature versus nurture argument. There are characteristics that are passed on genetically, most obviously physical features, and some specific conditions impacting on people's learning and development, for example dyslexia and autism. By far the greatest influence on people's lives, however, is their experiences as children growing up in the family home.

Many children, unfortunately, have poor family experiences, don't engage positively with school and underachieve educationally. This perpetuates the cycle of disadvantage from one generation to the next, and contributes significantly to the country's social and economic divisions, and skill shortages. This chapter looks at what can be done to positively influence family life for these children who are disadvantaged from birth and most at risk of having poor learning outcomes. To this end there is a need for a national long-term family support strategy and high quality, well-resourced local services to deliver this. Nothing illustrates the imperative for such a strategy more than the fact that eight times more is spent on reacting to the 'problems of troubled families' than on delivering 'targeted interventions to turn around their lives'[2]. There is, however, no 'quick fix', which was the underlying reason for the failure of previous government initiatives such as the Troubled Families Programme. A sustained systemic approach is required.

Seeking to make a discernible impact on children's family experience in order to improve their life chances is extremely difficult and massively challenging. The multiple problems faced daily by many families are often deeply ingrained, going back to previous generations. While use of legal interventions (such as those for child protection, school attendance and offending) are absolutely necessary, the only sustainable way of creating more supportive home lives for children is influencing parents. That will require building trusting long-term relationships, which takes time and patience.

To improve the life chances of our vulnerable and disadvantaged children, then, family life needs to be at the heart of the government's policy and legislative programme, coupled with a sustained course of national and local action founded on strong partnerships between professionals and families. A core proposal of this book is the establishment of 'local family support services' that act as the main contact with families where support is needed, including co-ordinating the involvement of other public, private and voluntary sector services.

Give children the best life chances

It goes without saying that strong families give children love, identity and a secure base from which to explore and enjoy life as they grow up. The quality of a child's early relationship with parents is vital to their social and emotional development, and a huge determinant of how well they settle at school, work independently and co-operatively, and behave appropriately. Supporting parents in understanding and fulfilling their children's emotional needs can help to provide a secure base from which children grow into well-rounded, capable adults with robust mental health. In the last two decades there has been a diversification of family life covering heterosexual and same sex couples, single parents, fostered and adopted children, and blended and extended families with grown up children and grandparents. Services will need to be tailored to meet the particular needs of different families.

Whilst most children and young people are thriving, act responsibly and achieve well, there is a significant number, however, who experience problematic lives that stem from their family and home circumstances. There are particular circumstances that influence a child's overall quality of life. Enjoying good physical and mental health provides a child with the self-esteem, confidence and resilience to realise her/his potential. How safe and stable a child feels impacts greatly on her/his emotional well-being. Education provides the main pathway for the child's future achievement in life. The behaviours and attitudes exhibited by a child determine how well s/he relates to others and operates in groups, including at school. All of these feed into a child's preparedness for adult life, including their social and cognitive skills, and levels of maturity and independence.

There are some key behaviours and conditions within families that have a particular impact on children's physical, emotional, social and cognitive development. These include parenting, domestic abuse, housing, health, substance misuse, skills and employment. Above all else the quality and consistency of parenting is the most critical factor.

Domestic abuse, which unfortunately is growing[3], has a massively debilitating effect on family life, especially for children. Witnessing and/or directly experiencing domestic abuse traumatically effects children, and is the single largest cause of concern about child welfare. Half of all child protection investigations involve children caught up in domestic violence[4]. To improve family life for children growing up there is clearly a need to strengthen services aimed at reducing domestic abuse and supporting the victims of it. This includes more stringent enforcement of the law against such crimes, protection and therapeutic support for adult and child victims, and rehabilitative work with perpetrators.

There is a need for a strong system of family-based prevention work, supporting a good quality of life for all children and young people, and particularly for those who are vulnerable and at risk of poor outcomes. Preventing these vulnerabilities transferring from one generation to the next, as they do now, must be an overriding aim. National and local family support strategies should therefore be founded on:

• Identifying those families in need of support.
• Developing long-term non-judgemental trusting relationships with family

members, including building on the strengths that they already have, to positively influence the environment for children growing up.

- Supporting families in ways that meet their specific needs, including developing parenting skills.
- Building capacity within families so that they become more independent and less dependent on external support.

Support families to provide all children with loving and stable home lives

We propose the statutory establishment of local multi-agency family support services in all areas of the country. Unlike previous government family programmes, these would be permanent services committed to long-term working with families in helping develop home environments that are strongly supportive of children's social and cognitive development. Duties would need to be placed on key local agencies (for example local authorities, schools, NHS and police) to co-operate in the setting up and running of the family support services. Local joint multi-agency governance and management arrangements will be needed to ensure effective delivery and accountability.

To work productively with families in the most challenging circumstances, staff of the support services will require high-level personal and professional skills. Recruiting the right staff and giving them access to high quality professional development, therefore, will be vital. Listening to what children, young people and their families are saying in designing and delivering services is crucially important. There is a need to enable families to access good quality independent advice and guidance, and specific services and support to meet different family needs and ages of children, for example post-natal mothers, and teenagers. The overriding objective, however, must be to help families over time to become more self-sufficient and less dependent on external support and public services, so that they are able to exercise positive choices over their own lives.

Most families with complex needs have several different agencies involved with them[5], often in excess of twenty! It is rare that the work of these agencies is co-ordinated and there is inevitably a great deal of overlap, especially in assessing need and drawing up support plans. This generally leads to much replication of human and other resources, and highly fragmented services that have little positive impact on the life of the family members, and indeed the demands of all these different sets of professionals often causes more stress and anxiety. A main function of the family support services, therefore, will be to act as a single point of contact with families, and unite the efforts of agencies in early identification of needs and timely access to appropriate services.

The voluntary and community sector (for example *Home Start*[6]) has a vital role to play in the development and delivery of family support and needs to be encouraged to be actively involved in the local family services. These organisations are extensively involved in working with families, particularly in relation to legal, benefits and debt advice, domestic abuse, housing and childcare. Many voluntary organisations are community-based and have a good understanding of the characteristics and needs of local neighbourhoods. By their very nature it is often relatively easier for these organisations to gain the trust of families than for statutory bodies to do so.

Develop learning families

A major challenge for the local family support services will be how far they can help to create a culture of aspiration in every family so as to give all children the best chances in life. Family learning is key to developing high aspirations and can be defined as:

> *Any learning activity that involves both children and adult family members, where learning outcomes are intended for both, and that contributes to a culture of learning in the family[7].*

Learning in the family can happen in a number of different ways. It can simply be about providing the love, security, stability and boundaries that children need for healthy development. Creating such conditions provides the foundation for children to grow up with confidence and resilience and engage positively with learning. Most learning takes place informally, for example discussions around the dinner table, parents and older siblings reading to children, and watching and talking about television programmes. Children's cognitive, social and emotional development also benefits enormously from involvement in cultural, sporting and social experiences but, as explained in chapter 7, children from better-off families go to clubs and activities far more than those from poorer families[8]. One of the functions of family support services, therefore, will be to provide encouragement and practical help to families to enable their children to partake in social and cultural activities.

There are four particular ways of supporting parents that enriches their own and their children's learning - parents accessing adult learning courses; helping parents support their children in school; helping parents engage their children in reading; and improving parenting skills.

Children of parents with high levels of education are far more likely to engage positively with school and have good education outcomes[9]. There are, however, substantial numbers of parents who have difficulties with everyday English and numeracy[10].   Adults engaged in learning are more likely to be involved in school life, and improve their parenting skills, helping them to better communicate with their children and manage their behaviour[11]. Also, research evidences that parental involvement with their children's schooling has much more influence on their children's educational achievement than other factors such as social class[12]. There are opportunities for adults to engage in education courses at local colleges, adult education centres and online. A key role of the family support services will be encouraging, and where appropriate, facilitating parents' involvement in one or more of these different ways of learning. Given that participating in education helps parents to better support their children's learning, it is shameful that from a very low base, the number of adults participating in family learning, (predominantly women[13]), has declined significantly in recent years[14].

There is evidence that interventions tailored to helping parents support their children in school can improve learning for both the children and the adults; for example the SPOKES[15] programme...

Targets children who have just started primary school with the aim of improving their reading and behaviour. An evaluation found that in one year the children showed an average improvement equivalent to six months of reading age, on top of the development expected of children of this age; as well as improving their writing skills and behaviour. A major contribution to the positive impact of the programme was enhancing parents' confidence and ability to help their children's reading[16]. Despite the success of this programme, it does not appear to have been taken up widely[17].

The importance of parents reading to and listening to their children read cannot be over-emphasised. Children who interact with their parents from a young age in such activities as reading, tend to do well at school[18]. In fact reading books as a family has the greatest impact on children's academic performance[19]. It is sad, then, that nearly two in three parents never share books with their babies and more than half of families do not own a single baby book[20]. A central role of the local family support services will be encouraging and supporting families in engaging their children in reading. In carrying out this role, one organisation that family support services will need to work with is Bookstart, a national early intervention literacy programme offering free books and parental guidance materials to babies, toddlers and pre-school children to inspire a love of reading. Every year a million book packs are given out by health visitors at clinics and GP surgeries or are available from libraries. Unfortunately, the government's grant to Bookstart was halved in 2011[21].

Put parenting skills at heart of family support strategy

There is a clear link between the quality of children's parenting and their educational outcomes[22]. An overriding focus of the strategy to provide all children with a supportive home life, therefore, must be to improve parenting skills. For some this is a sensitive and controversial area. Those on the right of the political spectrum are generally opposed to too much state interference in people's lives[23], while the political left traditionally place responsibility for inequality and disadvantage on the injustices of society's economic and social systems. There are those who say that it is wrong to 'blame' struggling parents who themselves may well be 'victims' of poverty, poor housing, physical and mental ill-health, and domestic abuse.

In fact there is merit in all of these points. However, we are not suggesting that additional powers be given to agencies to intervene in families. There are currently very high statutory thresholds that govern local authorities' ability to use their legal powers to intervene in families in such areas as child protection and school attendance. We are not proposing altering these thresholds. To do so anyway would be counter-productive as the only way to help improve parenting skills is through services forming and developing trusting relationships with families. Making value judgements about parents is unfair, unnecessary and also not conducive to productively working with them.

Having said all of this, the evidence is clear. To stand any realistic chance of successfully combatting disadvantage and educational underachievement means facing up to the fact that it is improvements in parenting that will make the difference. There is no greater case for improving parenting skills than knowing that in the last ten years more than 2.5 million children in England 'had not reached the Government's definition of a good level of development at the age of five [which has] a lasting impact on children's outcomes'[24]. The consequence is that there are today hundreds of thousands of children at all stages of the school system who are struggling with their learning. As research by the Social Mobility Commission has concluded: 'to improve social mobility… it is important that public policy does not shy away from the issue of parenting and what the Government could do to support families'[25].

There is strong evidence that programmes for improving parenting skills can be successful, particularly where they develop a good understanding of child development and positively impact on parenting style, the home learning environment, relationships within the family, and parental stress and mental health.

Research[26] shows that evidence-based parenting programmes can be effective in improving parenting skills and parent mental well-being, which then help to reduce children's behaviour difficulties, and 'impact positively on educational attainment'[27]. An important part of the family support strategy, therefore, will be to provide such programmes and encourage parents to participate. Evaluations of parenting programmes conclude that they should be 'directed mainly at those in greatest need', but that there are 'also benefits in recruiting a broader spectrum of parents in order to optimise group dynamics and achieve better outcomes'[28].

In addition there is an imperative for a more systemic approach. The cycle of generational low aspiration, poor life choices and underachievement needs to be broken. That is why we are proposing that parenting skills are introduced as a core subject in schools[29]. This could start in primary schools at the age of seven, would need to be age appropriate as children move through school, and be more substantial and direct in the latter part of secondary education. Presently (through science, sex and relationships education) schools teach children about how babies are made, but not how they are cared for and nurtured once they are born!

Focus of childcare must be on the quality of children's development

Between birth and five years of age are the most formative in a person's life[30], and the quality of parenting has by far the most influence in these early stages[31]. Supporting families and children in the early years is an extensive and diverse range of childcare and education provision with over three million child places[32]. Parents in the UK spend a third of their income on childcare, making it the most expensive childcare in the developed world[33].

As explained in chapter 5, the most significant development in early years services in the last thirty years has been Sure Start, which evaluations show had some positive effects, including on parenting and some health indicators, but not on children's readiness for school. Nevertheless, an all-party parliamentary group[34] has recommended extending Sure Start children's centres into Family Hubs, similar to the local family support services we are proposing[35].

Fifteen hours per week free education for four-year-olds (for 38 weeks a year) regardless of parental income was introduced in 1997, extended to three-year-olds in 2004[36], and in 2010 to two-year-olds from the poorest homes[37]. In 2017 free education for three and four-year-olds was extended to 30 hours per week[38], where both parents are working and earning £120 or more a week (but less than £100,000 a year). There have been severe criticisms of this latest extension of early education provision, including that only a small proportion of the additional funding benefits the neediest families[39] (children whose parents are not in work, for example, are excluded), and that there is insufficient funding overall[40], resulting in nursery costs for families rising[41].

Research does show that early childhood education and care can bring significant benefits for children, but this is 'conditional' on the quality of the provision[42]. More importantly, 'if quality is low, it can have long-lasting detrimental effects on child development'. For example, the evidence is absolutely clear that while early years settings need a focus on emerging literacy and numeracy skills, it is play that is the 'most effective vehicle for young children's learning and development'. There are two other fundamental concerns about the extensive institutionally-based childcare provision in the UK.

Firstly, there is a question about whether it is in the best interests of very young children (i.e. under two years of age) to be cared for in institutional settings on any consistent basis. The staff-child ratios in institutionalised childcare[43] do not necessarily allow for the personal attention that very young children need. Childcare settings also find it difficult to follow the natural rhythms that infants have, such as eating when they are hungry and sleeping when they are tired. In childcare nurseries, for example, it is generally the case that all children eat together and take rest periods (including to sleep) at the same time. Another consideration is the well-established research findings about the intense distress caused to infants by separating them from their parents, particularly their mothers. Extensive research[44] shows that the distress of separation can lead to a lack of attachment (or bonding) between child and parent, and long-term emotional damage to the child. There are strong arguments that very young children should be cared for most of the time in the family home.

Many parents out of economic necessity, however, need to work or study (or simply to have some respite) and this means paying nurseries, crèches or childminders to look after their infant children. There are no easy solutions to this economic versus child development conflict faced by many families. Something that might help would be to give families the same funding for one parent to stay at home to look after their very young children, as is currently available for placing them with a registered provider[45]. This is a principle strongly supported by Frank Field MP who has made the case for the 'system of benefits for families with children [to] be reshaped by offering to frontload payments that parents would be free to draw down in the child's first years of life, to reflect the fact that it is often better for children and their parents to spend the first years together, building the foundations that will enable the child to flourish'[46]. The UK government could also consider the scheme operating in Finland, where after paid maternity and/or paternity leave[47], one parent can receive €450 a month to stay at home with the child[48].

Secondly, successive governments have built up education and childcare provision in the belief that it would close the achievement gap between those children who suffer disadvantage and their peers. There is no evidence, however, that extending institutional provision has made any discernible difference to the school-readiness or achievement of disadvantaged children. This is because the home lives of these children have largely remained unchanged. While the state has taken more and more responsibility for caring for young children, no obligations have been placed on parents to improve what they do, for example by taking part in parenting courses or attending joint sessions with their children at children's centres. Perhaps the time has come for there to be a national statement of intent to what a child growing up is entitled to in terms of love, security and support, and what the respective responsibilities of parents and the state are. In practical terms this might lead to certain aspects of 'free' childcare or family services (funded from public sources) being provided on condition that parents access particular support and/or work jointly with services on actions that will help their children's social and cognitive development.

Conclusion - Family life must be at the heart of the programme of government

For too long governments have neglected the critical part played by family life in people's learning. Where governments have run programmes aimed at enhancing the quality of family life they have done so in a way that aims to elicit short-term gains. As a result, initiatives such as the Troubled Families Programme have failed to deliver any short-term improvements, never mind the fundamental and lasting changes that are necessary to give far more children the chances in life they should have. Because of this we are calling for government to construct and action a family strategy aimed at providing children with the quality of family life they need for healthy social and emotional development. Such a strategy would have to be at the heart of the government's drive to improve educational standards and skills, and tackle social and economic inequality. It should give priority to prevention and to those children who, without improvements in their home life, are most likely to have poor social, education, employment and health outcomes. To achieve sustainable change, an overriding objective has to be developing parenting skills and enabling families to be independent, and cease their dependence on external support.

Towards this end we have to be open and explicit about the support children growing up should have – what is expected of parents on the one hand, and the state on the other.

Several Conservative parliamentarians have launched a 'families manifesto' because they believe that a 'comprehensive strategy to strengthen families [is] essential to tackle... social problems, from addiction and mental ill health to children having a poor start in life and educational underachievement'[49]. Set largely in the context of the adverse impacts of family breakdown on children, the manifesto urges government to prioritise supporting families and to establish local 'Family Hubs' (similar to our family support services). It also promotes active and positive fatherhood, financial incentives to help 'form lasting couple relationships', weekly 'stay and play' sessions for parents with their two-year-old children as a condition of state funded childcare, and relationship education[50]. It also argues for more vigorous efforts in tackling the 'mental health crisis'. This manifesto is the closest we have seen to national politicians understanding the importance of family life to social and economic policy, and lobbying for this to become a strong feature of the government's programme.

To support the delivery of the strategy we propose the statutory establishment of multi-agency family support services in all unitary authority[51] areas. These would be permanent multi-agency services, committed to long-term working with families, served by staff with appropriate skills for working with families in challenging circumstances. The underpinning modus operandi of these local services would be to support families by building non-judgemental trusting relationships with family members. From our professional experience this is the only sustainable way of influencing family members to positively change.

Alongside this, absolute priority must be given to the quality of childcare that helps young children develop positively, rather than the quantity of such provision. To complement this, parents should be given a real economic choice between caring for their very young children at home or by taking them to a childcare provider.

Recommendations

- Family life to be placed at the heart of government policy including a *national family support strategy* aimed at providing all children growing up with a stable, loving and stimulating family life. Part of this would be a statement of the respective responsibilities of parents and the state in supporting children growing up. The strategy to be implemented at a local level, building capacity within families (including developing parenting skills and accessing adult learning) to create greater independence and less dependency on external support.

- Statutorily establish *local family support services* to work with families long-term, particularly those where children's life chances are poor, to help parents in supporting their children's emotional and cognitive development. To be effective these services will need to involve all appropriate agencies including those in the voluntary and community sector, and work through establishing and developing trusting relationships with parents.

- Developing *parenting skills* to be at the centre of the family support strategy and service. Evidence-based parenting programmes to be expanded and parents encouraged to participate. Parenting skills to become a core subject in the revised national school curriculum.

- Policy on *childcare* must prioritise quality of care that will best help young children's social and cognitive development, rather than the quantity of the provision offered. As part of this the government to investigate how best to provide financial incentives for one parent to stay at home and care for their very young children, including reviewing statutory maternity, paternity and shared parental leave arrangements, and benefits equivalent to those available for families whose children are in registered childcare settings.

11
SUPPORTING SCHOOL IMPROVEMENT

A national education system belongs not to ministers and officials,
but to all of us.
Professor Robin Alexander[1]

Since the 1988 Education Reform Act national governments of different political colours have had a broadly consistent policy predilection towards schools. This political consensus has manifested in increasing government control over what schools do, including the detail of the curriculum, and a heavy system of mechanistic accountability. While during this time more young people have acquired good academic results and gone to university, there is a large proportion of people who underachieve, and a growing gap between the highest and lowest achievers. We have a restricted curriculum, neither suitable nor motivating for all pupils and which, because of its narrow 'academic' bias, does not meet the skill needs of the country. The workload pressures on teachers, caused by excessive and disproportionate accountability measures, which don't add value to pupils or teachers, have led to poor staff morale and major retention and recruitment problems.

To effectively tackle what is a quintet of education, economic and social scourges – children's mental ill-health, underachievement, gross inequality, skill and teacher shortages – a major shift in national policy is required. The starting point is to fundamentally change the conditions within which schools operate. Radically re-thinking the twin methods of exerting accountability – external testing and inspections – is a pre-requisite. The big question is whether it is possible to persuade our national politicians to move away from their instruments of command and coercion, and create supportive, but still challenging environments for schools, teachers and children to work in. If we can, then it may be possible to generate the means to actively engage all pupils with learning, and provide the skills that the country needs.

In this chapter, therefore, we put forward proposals for changing the assessment and inspection regimes, which then lay the foundations for modernising the curriculum, bringing about a better way of supporting and holding schools to account, and improving the retention and recruitment of teachers.

What do we want from schools?

Before examining how we might improve the current schools system, we should ask what the real purpose of schooling should be. We suggest that schools might have three broad aims, which need to be pursued in partnership with children and young people, parents, businesses and other public services.

Firstly, schools should be concerned with helping to develop individual children into independent, confident and resilient young people, well prepared for adult life including parenthood and the world of work. This involves helping children and young people to look after themselves, emotionally and physically, and to be self-improving with the desire and skills to continue learning throughout their lives so that they are able to adapt and innovate as the world changes. They should have respect for other people (including being respectful and understanding of people's diverse backgrounds – their gender, race, religion, sexuality and disability) and exhibit positive behaviour, so that they are able to work and co-operate with others in their families, workplaces and socially.

Secondly, schools should help children and young people to become good citizens, capable of making an ongoing positive contribution as parents and family members, to the economy and their community, including in the making of democratic decisions.

Thirdly, schools should help to equip young people for the world of work, enabling them to acquire the knowledge and the personal, cognitive and technical skills they need for employment throughout their working lives. In turn this provides the basis for the skilled workforce required to compete in domestic and global markets, and provide the services that people need.

Assessment should be used to improve learning

Assessment serves a number of purposes: giving pupils valuable feedback and informing teachers how to plan learning for individuals or groups of children (diagnostic assessment); assisting further and higher education, and employers with selecting entrants (e.g. A levels and their equivalents); and performance data for judging school effectiveness. As evidenced in chapter 6 the main purpose of nationally determined tests and examinations is to hold schools to account, rather than to benefit children's learning.

A review of the system for testing children in England is essential for four main reasons. While children in England are among the most tested in the developed world[2], there is no correlation between the amount of testing undertaken and a country's education achievement[3]. The increase in testing in English schools has contributed to rising stress and associated mental health problems amongst children and young people[4]. Tests and examinations take place predominately or solely for the purpose of judging and holding schools to account, and offer little or no diagnostic feedback to teachers or children to aid further learning. The high stakes nature of testing has led to a narrowing of the curriculum.

The government must face up to the damage that is being done to children's emotional well-being by the target-driven school system, by reviewing the extent and nature of the statutory tests and examinations that pupils have to endure. (In addition there should be an evidence-driven, long-term national child mental health strategy, adequately resourced, and vigorously implemented. Such a strategy should be preventative, covering the full spectrum of mental health conditions, as well as providing treatment for those with more serious mental health disorders).

To add value to pupils' learning the emphasis should be on assessment *for* learning (or formative assessment), as opposed to assessment *of* learning (or summative assessment). The former provides ongoing feedback to students about what they have achieved, areas of study that might need to be re-visited, and lessons learnt that can be applied to improve future learning. As education researchers Flórez and Sammons say, 'Assessment for learning helps to shape what lies ahead rather than simply to gauge and record past achievements'[5]. An important element of assessment for learning is building pupils' capacity to 'learn to learn' through developing their skills of reflection and self-assessment, essential for lifelong learning. The end result of successive governments' obsession with summative assessment, as Black and Wiliam so aptly articulate, is that 'the giving of marks and grades is overemphasised and the giving of useful advice and the learning function is underemphasised'[6].

There is a strong case for doing away with all the statutory national tests in primary schools, bringing the UK in line with the vast majority of other developed countries[7]. No evidence can be presented, for example, that Key Stage 2 SATs tests, taken at the end of primary education, accrue any benefit for children's learning.

Fewer than half of OECD countries have examinations at aged 16. Many of the highest performing countries have external examinations at aged 18 and not 16[8], and there is no other country in Europe other than the UK that has examinations at both 16 and 18[9]. Since statutory education has now been extended to 18, the age when over ninety per cent of young people are entering university or the workplace[10], it would make sense for the UK to follow suit and continue to have national examinations at 18 (i.e. A-levels and their equivalents) but not at 16 (i.e. GCSEs and their equivalents).

As suggested earlier, the emphasis should be on schools using assessment to gather information that will help them improve pupils' learning. Scarce resources should not be being squandered on the administration of tests that add little or nothing to the learning process. It would be far better to invest in supporting teachers to become highly skilled in the use of assessment for learning. In their self-evaluations and improvement plans, schools should be setting out their plans for strengthening assessment for learning. Ofsted should be evaluating and feeding back on the effectiveness of schools' use of assessment for learning.

Inspections should be used to continuously improve school effectiveness

The inspection system, as we know, is far more about holding schools to account than facilitating their improvement. How could inspections change to add greater value to schools and their pupils? Currently an inspection team has a brief passing involvement with a school (i.e. one or two days) but a long-lasting impact, which for some is wholly negative. It is possible, and would be much more beneficial, for inspectors to have a long-term relationship with a school, helping them on an ongoing basis to improve. This could include inspectors working with schools to assist them in drawing up their improvement plans and evaluating their impact on pupils' learning as they are implemented.

Another change that would give inspections more of an improvement focus would be to move away from the absolutism of Ofsted gradings, which distinguish in clear unequivocal terms between four types of schools – outstanding, good, requires improvement and inadequate. This practice is founded on a mistaken belief that you can, with precision, categorise each school into one of these four types. These labels are often unhelpful and misleading. We know from our own experience of working in and with schools that all schools, even those who are classified as outstanding, require improvement. If a school, however good it may be, is not pushing for further improvement it invariably goes backwards. Outstanding schools are never outstanding in everything they do, but that is the impression given by attaching that particular Ofsted moniker to them. And we know of no school judged inadequate at inspection that is inadequate throughout, although this is the distinct impression given to parents, pupils and the outside world. The vast majority of staff who work in such schools are dedicated, hardworking and effective professionals, but they have to constantly bear the ignominy of working in an 'inadequate' school. In fact it is generally the case in such schools that while a significant minority of what they do is unsatisfactory, most of what happens is of acceptable and good quality.

Inspection findings and reports could therefore be couched in a developmental context rather than judgmental terms. You could for example describe whether practices or standards in a school were 'emergent, established or advanced'[11]; or whether the key outcomes and drivers of school performance (such as pupils' achievement, work, behaviour, safety, and the quality of teaching, leadership and planning) should be 'prioritised, developed, maximised or sustained'[12]. Ofsted and a national system of inspection should continue, but have a fundamentally different focus. Later on in this chapter there is a plan to move away from the current coercive model for improving schools, replacing it with one that is much more supportive, but still challenging, which would operate through collaboration between schools working in local partnerships. Ofsted's role would be to evaluate the effectiveness of these local partnerships in adding value to schools and their pupils.

Laying the foundation for key school reforms

Assessment should be focused on helping pupils learn; the number of externally imposed tests and examinations substantially reduced; and inspection utilised to aid school development. These changes will provide the foundation for key reforms that need to be made to modernise the curriculum, tackle underachievement, support schools to improve, and have a strong and highly skilled teaching workforce.

Curriculum for all pupils to meet the skill needs of the country

The dominance of the national curriculum has resulted in an 'overcrowded' school curriculum, leaving schools with little discretion for improvisation and innovation. What is tested is taught, and the constant testing of pupils, has narrowed the curriculum, squeezing the more vocational and creative side. Probably because of the personal educational experiences of ministers and senior civil servants, there is a massive curriculum bias in favour of academic knowledge, and not enough emphasis on skills, and creative and vocationally-based studies. This bias is a cause of why so many pupils, particularly in their latter stages of secondary education, are turned off learning and underachieve, and why the UK has such large skills shortages. Overall, the school curriculum lacks modernity. According to a major study by the Edge Foundation[13], the curriculum for schools in England and Wales is 'still stuck in the Victorian era'[14]. The study finds that the contemporary education system continues 'to be dominated by 19th century concepts of merit and ability, which were based on abstract reasoning rather than the ability to design and make things or solve practical problems'[15], and suggests that 'it might be time to question the subject boundaries of the 19th and 20th centuries and their associated working methods'. Particularly in the context of our 21st century digital age, these are all very strong arguments for having a fundamental review of the national curriculum.

Review national curriculum, and set up a National Curriculum Council

In deliberating about the sort of school curriculum needed, we don't want to repeat the mistake made by successive governments of not meaningfully involving the key stakeholders such as teachers, employers, children and young people, and parents. With this in mind we offer four proposals:

- Re-statement of the principle, established in the 1988 Act, of having a national curriculum to provide all pupils with a learning entitlement and consistency across all state schools.
- The current law exempting academies from the requirements of the national curriculum should be changed, so that all state schools, irrespective of their governance status, have to operate within the parameters of the national curriculum.
- Create a national professional body for keeping the national curriculum under review; in effect re-establishing the National Curriculum Council (set up in 1988 and abolished in 1993).
- Through an evidence-based, highly engaging and transparent process, undertake a fundamental review of the national curriculum to make it fit for purpose for the 21st century and particularly the new digital age.

The National Curriculum Council (NCC) could have a similar remit to that of the body that operated previously i.e. to keep all aspects of the national curriculum under review; advise the Secretary of State; commission and publish the findings of research projects; and ensure proper consultation on changes to the national curriculum[16]. To provide democratic accountability the Secretary of State should continue to be the final decision maker. However, it must be legally obligatory that for all changes to the national curriculum, the advice of the NCC must have been sought, given and published. Membership of the NCC would include senior school leaders; teachers with experience and expertise in curriculum development, planning, implementation and evaluation; employers; and education academics.

The fundamental review of the national curriculum should be co-ordinated by the NCC with their recommendations to the Secretary of State made in public. The broad remit for the review might include having a revised national curriculum that:

- Is broad, with a balance of knowledge acquisition and skills development; and academic, creative, technical and vocational studies.
- Meets the skill needs of the country.
- Is capable of sustaining the interest of all pupils and tackling underachievement.
- Provides a 14-19 curriculum that integrates the academic and vocational curriculum including work experience, apprenticeships and pre-apprenticeships.
- Is less prescriptive than the current one, being more of a national framework comprising learning aims and objectives, with schools and teachers having discretion about how to meet these.

Need for broad and balanced curriculum

There is a very strong case for a 'broad and balanced' curriculum. As well as acquiring knowledge, children need the practical skills to apply this knowledge in real life. Getting the basics of reading, writing and numeracy right is absolutely critical, as they provide the foundation required for future learning. At the same time there is a need to cultivate children's natural inquisitiveness through activities that are relevant and interesting. Children also need to develop creativity and innovation, through the arts, drama, music and dance. They need to learn about the world they live in through the humanities and modern foreign languages. Acquiring scientific and technical knowledge and skills through the sciences, design and technology, and computing and information technology, is particularly important in giving youngsters employment opportunities and plugging the skill gaps. Activities such as citizenship, sex and relationship education (including parental skills), and sport and physical education, help young people develop positive behaviours and personal skills to become productive and responsible adults. Learning in one subject area can help people gain confidence and understanding in other areas; for example musical education can help develop mathematical concepts[17], and drama, verbal skills.

It is ironic that while the government recognises personal, social, health and economic (PSHE) education as 'an important and necessary part of all pupils' education[18'] it nonetheless is a non-statutory subject, which schools can choose not to include in their curriculum. The government also say that 'sex and relationship education (SRE) is an important part of PSHE[19']. Although statutory in schools maintained by the local authority, SRE is optional for academies. Why is understanding about sex and relationships important for youngsters attending one type of state school and not another? A revised national curriculum, including PSHE and SRE, would need to apply to all schools, irrespective of their governance status.

The curriculum for our very youngest children is in urgent need of major reform. Ofsted has concluded that the government's Early Years Foundation Stage framework (EYFS) 'leads to box-ticking rather than good teaching'. The chief inspector gives this as a major reason why a third of all young children and half of those from low-income families do 'not have the essential knowledge and understanding they needed to reach a good level of development by the age of five', resulting in 'many who fall behind never catch[ing] up'. Ofsted reports that the EYFS is 'burdensome' and that 'there is no clear curriculum in Reception [classes]'[20]. This tick box approach causes problems for children's learning when they get into year 1, and Ofsted has recommended that the government 'review the scope, content and breadth of the early years framework and streamline its assessment to reduce teachers' workload' [21].

We have seen how the use of Key Stage 2 SATs results as the main accountability measure has led to a narrowing of the primary school curriculum, with non-SATs subjects including technology, arts and humanities being squeezed. There has even been a narrowing of the primary school literacy curriculum due to the requirement for pupils to have command of a range of complex linguistic terminology, which has resulted in children being put off reading and writing, and losing a 'focus on composition and creativity' [22]. Ending statutory national testing in primary schools will provide the opportunity to design a primary school curriculum that is genuinely 'broad and balanced' but continues to have basic literacy and numeracy skills at the heart of it.

A more skills-orientated curriculum

As explained previously, one crucial way in which the current national curriculum lacks breadth and balance is that it is narrowly focused on pupils acquiring and regurgitating academic knowledge (which can be scored and graded in a relatively easy manner), and not on the development and application of skills. Possessing underpinning knowledge is obviously key to effective learning, but the knowledge has to be understood and have meaning (not just memorised parrot fashion) and people need the necessary skills to use and apply the knowledge productively. Skills are best learnt by practising them in real life or simulated situations.

In redesigning the national curriculum, thought will have to be given to the key cognitive, technical and interpersonal skills that young people need to properly prepare them for adult life and the world of work in the 21st century. These will then need to be translated into identifying the skills (and the level of skill) that should be learnt at each stage of schooling. Schools should be enabling their pupils to develop the skills that prepare them for their working lives. This will not be possible in any specific sense. Children starting school in September 2018 will enter the workforce in the mid-2030s and will still be working as the current century is ending (i.e. the 2090s). An estimated sixty-five per cent of children entering primary schools today will work in jobs that don't currently exist[23]. It is simply unrealistic therefore to believe that schools can provide young people with the specific skills they will need during the next seventy years or more. What is possible, and absolutely necessary, is to furnish youngsters with the generic personal skills that will help them become lifelong learners, and be able to adapt to the seismic social, scientific and technological changes that will take place in their lifetimes.

A look at what skills might be prized in the future may give us a guide to the generic skills we should be focusing on. The world is entering what is called the Fourth Industrial Revolution[24], bringing us advanced robotics, autonomous transport, artificial intelligence, machine learning, advanced materials, biotechnology and genomics, which will 'transform the way we live, and the way we work'[25]. According to the World Economic Forum the ten main skills we will need to meet the challenges and exploit the opportunities of this Fourth Industrial Revolution are complex problem solving, critical thinking, creativity, people management, co-ordinating with others, emotional intelligence, judgement and decision making, service orientation, negotiation and cognitive flexibility[26].

Looking closely at these 'skills of the future' it is clear that they cover two main sets of skills. Those concerned with problem solving, judgement and decision making combine rational processes (including science, technology, engineering and mathematics), with creativity and innovation. The other skills set is the ability to work with people – interpersonal skills (including emotional intelligence) to negotiate, collaborate and operate effectively in teams. We should be looking at a national curriculum, therefore, that develops children's logistical skills (particularly through STEM subjects) alongside their ability to think and act creatively, and to be able to form productive working relationships with others. Research commissioned by the Royal Academy of Engineering identifies problem solving as the most important skill in the future and recommends that schools should focus less on 'subjects' and more on teaching problem-solving skills through 'playful experimentation'. Evaluation of three practically-based pilot projects found there had been improvements in pupils' scientific, mathematical, artistic and communications skills, and that they were more able to tackle open-ended questions and generate creative solutions[27]. Such projects offer a possible way forward for re-designing the curriculum of the future.

A big shift in pedagogy will also be required, as much of the skills curriculum will need delivering through practical activities. Teachers will have to be freed up from the current requirements of imparting weighty subject content to their pupils, to provide time to engage them in 'real-life' experiments and exercises. There will be professional development needs for teachers as to how particular skills can best be taught and learnt, and how they will be assessed both formatively and summatively.

It goes without saying that basic literacy and numeracy skills lay the foundation for the development of the range of skills people need for life and work. These basics also continue to be the bedrock upon which other learning takes place, and need to be a constant in people's lifelong learning journey.

With the focus on synthetic phonics and learning linguistic terminology it is easy to forget that reading is the key to developing good literacy skills. Reading regularly for pleasure is the most effective way to improve literacy skills, as a child's breadth of vocabulary is related to the number of words s/he regularly comes into contact with. It is the key skill that opens up the door to learning. Conversely, in too many cases the learning door closes to those who struggle with reading. Daniel Rigney makes a similar point in saying that 'While good readers gain new skills very rapidly, and quickly move from learning to read to reading to learn, poor readers become increasingly frustrated with the act of reading, and try to avoid reading where possible'[28]. Unfortunately, half of year one pupils and more than four in ten year seven pupils have such a limited vocabulary (a 'word gap') that it adversely affects their learning. The main cause of the 'word gap' is too little reading for pleasure[29]. There are also some worrying signs that many young people find reading boring and don't read books regularly[30]. This is why an integral part of the school curriculum should be promoting reading for pleasure for all pupils, not just in primary, but in secondary schools as well.

Mathematics is the core subject where UK fifteen and sixteen-year-olds most lag behind their counterparts in other developed countries[31]. England is also one of the few developed countries where only a minority of pupils continue studying mathematics after the age of 16. Because of this the government is actively encouraging primary schools to adopt what is termed as the 'Shanghai maths method' or 'mastery maths' [32], which is credited with placing countries such as China, Hong Kong and Singapore at the top end of the international education performance tables[33]. A review by Professor Adrian Smith[34] came up with two particular recommendations that should be seriously considered in reviewing mathematics in a new national curriculum. One was that the government commission a study from 'pre-school onwards' into the 'root causes of negative attitudes to mathematics'. The other that 'there should be fresh consideration of appropriate curricula and qualifications' for those students who don't achieve at least a C grade in GCSE mathematics first time, rather than simply requiring them to re-sit the examination, a proposal supported by the Shadow Education Secretary, Angela Rayner[35].

Perhaps there is a need to go even further. People need differing levels of mathematical competence depending on the career path they follow. Everyone needs a firm grasp of basic quantitative skills – calculating, measuring, and understanding data and statistics. Such skills are necessary in everyday life and most jobs require us to make calculations, and use and interpret data. But is it really necessary for all sixteen-year-olds to master all parts of the GCSE mathematics curriculum[36] including, for example, some fairly complex algebraic formulae? Is there some differentiation needed – for example a high level of proficiency in functional mathematics for all, and then more advanced work for those who want to take their mathematical studies further and/or have ambitions to pursue careers in areas such as architecture, engineering, medicine and science? Former Education Secretary Lord Baker supports such a move, arguing for two separate qualifications – 'Core Mathematics', compulsory for all, and an optional 'Further Mathematics'[37].

We saw that the top skills needed for the future require a good grasp of science, technology, engineering and mathematics, combined with creativity and innovation. While the creative industries are growing twice as fast as the UK economy generally, there are substantial and increasing skill shortages in this sector[38]. Providing more and better opportunities across the curriculum for pupils to develop their creative skills, therefore, should be an integral part of a revised national curriculum.

A significant and growing shortage of skilled information technology professionals is putting the cybersecurity of UK businesses at risk, and holding back productivity[39]. A major source of this problem is the very small and declining number taking computer science GCSE – just over one in ten – with less than half of secondary schools offering the subject[40]. Fewer and fewer girls are taking computer studies at GCSE and A level, which seems to have worsened as a result of the phasing out of GCSE information and communication technology (ICT) and its replacement by a new computer science course[41]. A review by the Royal Society contrasts that while 'data and digital technologies promise revolutionary transformational changes across the full range of industry sectors and spheres of life [that] will impact everyone… computing education across the UK is patchy and fragile'[42]. The Royal Society has called for major changes to computer education in schools, including have a range of qualification pathways suitable for *all* pupils, research to investigate how to improve female participation, and initiatives to increase the supply of computing teachers.

Make learning fun

Freed from the straitjacket of an omnipresent exams regime, schools and teachers can explore how they make learning more relevant and interesting for their pupils. Science, vital to the country's economy and health service, and providing substantial opportunities to young people for quality employment, is an example of a subject that could be made much more engaging to pupils. There seems to be a good argument for making the science curriculum more practically-based, with the aim of stimulating and maintaining children's interest in the subject, rather than the current approach which makes it necessary for teachers to speedily go through every aspect of what is a heavy, wide-ranging school science curriculum. A powerful advocate of this is the chief executive of the British Science Society, Katherine Mathieson, who says:

> *Science practicals in schools are boring and irrelevant and children should instead conduct real experiments that relate to their lives. Science should become a part of everyday culture. People should hold opinions on scientific issues, similar to their beliefs about football or music, instead of feeling they are not qualified to comment. Schools should not perpetuate the myth that only brainy pupils with top grades are needed in science. [There should be] much more focus on children doing science. Science practicals that spend hours teaching children how to manage the beakers or bunsen burners, that's just recipe-following. Where's the creativity? I'd rather see a few years of genuine open-ended research by pupils, rather than fiddling around with beakers*[43].

Modernise secondary school curriculum, and introduce an integrated 14-19 curriculum

The narrowing of the curriculum is particularly evident in secondary schools because of the government's use of the EBacc as a school performance measure. As reported in chapter 6, most secondary schools have cut staff in non-EBacc subjects[44] and the number and proportion of students entering GCSE arts and vocational examinations has dropped dramatically[45]. Clearly the EBacc needs to be abandoned as a school performance measure in order to remove the pressure on schools to narrow the year 9, 10 and 11 curriculum. The evidence suggests that if we are serious about tackling underachievement and our chronic skills shortages, we need to go much further. Given that young people are expected to be in full-time education until they are aged eighteen, and that no other country in Europe requires its pupils to sit national examinations at both sixteen and eighteen, there has to be considerable doubt about the appropriateness and value of GCSEs. We, therefore, endorse the proposal put forward by former Education Secretary, Lord Baker, to only having national examinations at age eighteen and not sixteen.

Not having examinations at aged sixteen paves the way to look afresh at the 14-19 curriculum. Any objective look at what is happening in our schools system tells us that while around half of pupils are achieving well academically[46], it is 'letting down those unsuited to academic [studies] and exams'[47]. A levels, in many respects rightly, seen as the 'gold standard' and the passport to university and professional employment, are only taken by a third of the school population[48]. Too few young people are gaining A level or equivalent qualifications, and we spelt out in chapter 3 the economic consequences of the UK having a dearth of workers with vocational and technical qualifications at this level. Having suggested that the UK come in line with most other countries and not have public examinations at aged 16, we argue that this needs to be taken one step further by replacing both GCSEs and A levels with an integrated curriculum and set of qualifications for all 14 to 19-year-olds.

It is not a new idea. Arguments for such an approach first started to be made at least thirty years ago. In 2002 the then education secretary, Charles Clarke, grasped the nettle when he issued a white paper with the overriding aim of creating 'a clearer and more appropriate qualifications framework for the 14-19 phase' with a 'unified framework of qualifications'[49]. He commissioned former chief schools inspector, Sir Mike Tomlinson, to carry out a review along these lines. The Tomlinson report was published in 2004[50]. It recommended replacing GCSEs, A-levels and vocational qualifications with a single diploma, to be implemented over a period of ten years. The diploma would be awarded at four levels - entry (equivalent to pre-GCSEs), foundation (GCSEs at grade D-G[51]), intermediate (GCSE A*-C[52]) and advanced (A level). Extra 'stretch' could be added for advanced-level students with recognition through higher marks. The diploma would be made up of modules adapted from existing GCSE, A level and vocational programmes. Students would be able to study for an 'open diploma' where they would have some choice of the combination of modules, or one of the 20 'specialised diplomas'. There would be a compulsory 'core' for all students including functional mathematics, communication skills, information and communications technology, an extended essay, and 'wider activities' (covering such things as work experience, paid jobs, voluntary work and family responsibilities)[53].

We remember at the time that these proposals met with almost universal acclaim. 'Rarely has a government-commissioned inquiry done its job so thoroughly' said the BBC's education editor, Mike Baker. He wrote 'For two years, Sir Mike's working group sifted the evidence, took advice, cajoled and persuaded. By the end he had achieved the near impossible: a very broad consensus in favour of wholesale reform of the examination system. He had found a way of doing precisely what he was asked to do, specifically to recommend 'a unified framework of qualifications' to cover all types of learning.'[54] So why were these imaginative and practical changes, which 'were backed by the government's senior qualifications adviser, the head of Ofsted, the teacher and head teacher associations, most university leaders, and many employers' [55] killed off, and never resurrected? It is pertinent to explore the reasons briefly, because the fears that led to the decision then, are still alive and kicking today. Mike Baker explains that when the report was published (in October 2004) 'The prime minister's [Tony Blair] popularity had plummeted, the Tories were pinning their electoral flag to a defence of A-levels, and an election was looming'. On the very day the report came out, Tony Blair made clear that 'A levels and GCSEs would stay'. As Philip Collins, who was then one of Blair's closest advisers, pithily recalls 'When this idea reached Tony Blair he instantly worked out that abolishing A levels just before a general election was pretty poor politics'[56]. And with that 'the door... slammed in the face of wholesale reform' [57]. In the week in which the government formally rejected Tomlinson, Mike Baker asked 'will [it] now be another decade before an over-arching diploma is introduced?'[58]

It is salutary to re-visit the reasons given in the Tomlinson report for the reforms it put forward, as they echo the issues and concerns we have raised and remain highly relevant today. Tomlinson's proposals for reforming the 14-19 curriculum and qualifications were 'building on strengths within the current system while addressing its weaknesses' to:

• Raise participation and achievement – by tackling the educational causes of disengagement and underachievement.
• Get the basics right – ensuring that young people achieve specified levels

in functional mathematics, literacy and communication and ICT, and are equipped with the knowledge, skills and attributes needed to succeed in adult life, further learning and employment.

- Strengthen vocational routes – improving the quality and status of vocational programmes.
- Provide greater stretch and challenge – ensuring opportunities for greater breadth and depth of learning.
- Reduce the assessment burden for learners and teachers by reducing the number of times learners are examined, and by extending the role of teacher assessment.
- Make the system more transparent and easier to understand.[59]

There is a powerful case, therefore, for having an integrated 14-19 curriculum aimed at helping to re-engage disaffected students to learning, and improve skills and strengthen vocational education to fill skill gaps in the economy and public services. While the clear, detailed and pragmatic recommendations of the Tomlinson report are highly apposite to the current day situation, they will need updating. We suggest that the Tomlinson recommendations be taken as a basis for a further review that takes account of developments since 2004 (for example technological advancements, changes to curricula and examinations, the proposals for T-levels, and the growth in apprenticeships). The purpose of the review would be to set out the practical means by which an integrated 14-19 curriculum and related qualifications could be brought about.

Young people who have had work experience inevitably acquire employability skills and become more employable, for example pupils who have more contact with employers are far more likely to be in education, employment and training when they leave school[60]. The employers' organisation, the CBI, is 'calling for every young person to have at least four opportunities to see the world of work first-hand before they turn 16'[61]. And that is why work experience for all pupils should become a compulsory part of a new 14-19 curriculum.

Schools should be responsible for curriculum delivery, supported by research and sharing of good practice

How the school curriculum is organised and delivered should be left to school leaders and teachers to determine. The NCC would have a role in commissioning and distributing research findings, and Ofsted in evaluating and disseminating good professional practice. One of the main functions of local school improvement partnerships would be to identify and disseminate successful or particularly innovative practice to all schools in the partnerships (and beyond). Existing local, sub-regional, regional and national networks can also be built upon and, where necessary, extended to facilitate sharing of good practice on a much wider basis. Contacts and exchanges with other countries also need to be continued so that we can learn from what is happening in learning across the world.

Improve schools through collaboration not coercion

There is a cornucopia of evidence indicating that the national 'command and control' system holding schools to account by successive governments over the last thirty years is deeply flawed. When we look at 'real-life' measures, which directly affect the lives of people, there is powerful evidence to suggest that the current model isn't working, with growing children's mental health problems, acute skills shortages, and increasing difficulties retaining and recruiting teachers and school leaders. Alongside this, at a time when the UK's prosperity depends more than ever on how successful we are in global markets, we languish in the mid-table of developed countries educationally, a position that has been stagnant for nearly twenty years.

There is also a need to ask whether the current national infrastructure is sufficiently robust to support schools in an effectually sustainable way. The attempts by governments over the last thirty years to marketise the education system has meant that schools generally see themselves as competitors for pupils rather than collaborators in pursuing the best educational outcomes for all children, irrespective of which school they attend. We have seen the pursuit by successive governments of an ideology that 'independent state schools, free of local authority control' will in themselves raise educational standards, resulting in the substantial growth of academies, and multi-academy trusts[62]. These academies are directly accountable to central government through Regional Schools Commissioners, who are civil servants, arbitrarily exercising enormous statutory powers, without any link or answerability to the local communities that schools serve. As evidenced in chapter 6, academy schools overall do no better than those remaining with local government, and government reforms, particularly since 2010, 'have created a structural mess, opening up profound gaps in accountability and governance'[63]. It is clear also that there simply aren't enough multi-academy trusts, especially of sufficient quality, to take on the increasing numbers of schools that the government are compelling to be academies[64].

Optimise sharing good practice and school-to-school support

There is, we believe, a more effective way of supporting schools to continue improving; one that is collaborative, predicated on sharing good practice and school-to-school support. At the centre of this proposed alternative is the setting up of local school improvement partnerships to provide all schools with ongoing, consistent support and challenge. These partnerships would involve all schools (including academies), academy trusts, local authorities and diocesan boards of education. Other key players, including private schools, further education colleges, universities, businesses and voluntary sector organisations, could also be part of the local partnerships. There are already several successful partnerships (exemplified later on); we want to see this practice in operation across the whole country. How the partnerships work should be a matter for the schools, academy trusts and local authorities to agree on and operate. National guidance would be needed to ensure that the partnerships' work is robust and leads to real improvements. Key elements of the guidance could include partnerships:

- Informing their work through *annual self-evaluations* carried out *by each school* that would be *moderated by the partnership*, providing the basis for improvement plans for each school. An example of this type of process operating at the moment is the National Association of Headteachers' *Instead* programme, organised around a small group of schools, involving each school being reviewed over two or more days by some leaders and teachers from the other schools, plus an external independent lead reviewer. The school undertakes a self-review, which then informs the external review[65].
- Based on schools' self-evaluation and improvement plans, agreeing and implementing an *annual plan for school-to-school support* (including schools

being partnered with each other); *external support for schools* (where this is necessary); and *joint work* including continuing professional development, inter-school activities on developments prioritised by a number of schools, teacher exchanges, and collaboration on *initial teacher training* (building on the work of local teaching schools).
* Identifying *good and innovative practice* and disseminating across all schools.
* *Evaluating the impact of the partnership* programmes on individual schools and on pupil attainment.

In order to establish and run the partnerships, a duty would be placed on all schools, academies, academy trusts, and diocesan boards and local authorities to co-operate and actively engage. The work of the partnerships would be informed by and build upon the very good inter-school work that is currently being undertaken in 'clusters' within local authority areas and many academy chains. Some of the best evidence of effective inter-school work comes from the London, Greater Manchester and Black Country Challenges. Independent evaluations of these major school improvement programmes show significant improvements in school performance. 'During the period of the London Challenge, secondary school performance in London saw a dramatic improvement, and local authorities in inner London went from the worst-performing to the best-performing nationally'[66]. All three City Challenges according to independent evaluation showed that 'schools which initially had low and average attainment improved significantly more than those schools with similar initial attainment outside Challenge areas…attainment of pupils eligible for FSM [free school meals] improved by more than the national figure… [and that] the most plausible explanation for the greater improvement in Challenge areas is that the City Challenge programme was responsible'[67]. Each local partnership could decide to join together regionally or sub-regionally so that the benefits of inter-school working could be shared across a wider area.

From his experiences as chief adviser to the Greater Manchester Challenge and an extensive education research record, Professor Mel Ainscow makes a strong case for locally-based collaborative approaches to school improvement. Professor Ainscow says that 'national policy makers would be naive to overlook the influence of what happens at the local level… where local history, inter-connections between schools and established relationships are always significant'. Together with evidence about the limits of school improvement based on individual schools, Professor Ainscow's account of the Greater Manchester Challenge suggests that 'a national education strategy for raising standards for all students, in all schools, requires the systematic and locally organised redistribution of available resources and expertise through a contextually sensitive strategy for collaboration.'[68] In addition to the City Challenges there are many other successful examples of partnership-based approaches to school improvement; two examples are given below:

> Duncan Spalding, head of a high school in Norfolk, which chose not to become an academy and works within a local co-operative foundation trust:
>
> *We achieve a lot on very limited funds and without creating expensive central bureaucracies or needing a CEO. Every school retains its legal status and unique identity and understands its collective responsibility for all of our children. All this without a multi-academy trust, which could serve to undermine rather than strengthen our collaborative work*[69].
>
> *Nottingham Schools Trust is a formal trust of thirty primary and special schools. The trust focuses on school improvement and generates efficiencies for schools through economies of scale. Each school retains its independence with 'discrete identities' and the trust has a strong relationship with the local authority*[70].

Renew and re-invigorate role for local authorities

We envisage a renewed and re-invigorated role for local authorities in the school improvement partnerships. This certainly must not be a return to the pre-1988 Act days when local education authorities (as they were then) controlled the staffing and budgets of schools. The emancipation of schools to run their own affairs brought about in 1990 must continue. Local authorities, however, would have a major co-ordinating role within the partnership and retain the duties and powers they currently have for supporting, challenging and intervening in schools[71], along with their other statutory responsibilities[72].

With the agreement of the other partners, local authorities might contribute to the administration and education advisory work of the partnership. These local authority functions, however, will need to be exercised as an integral part of the work of the partnerships.

Ofsted to be central to school improvement, not just inspection

The role of Ofsted would change so that its prime responsibility would be for evaluating the effectiveness of each of the local partnerships and making recommendations for improvement. In this way they would contribute to strengthening a systemic approach to improving school performance and pupil achievement. As part of their inspections of partnerships, Ofsted would still need to evaluate the work of schools, but this would be in the context of how effectively each partnership was contributing to improving individual schools. Such a change in Ofsted's role is supported by a range of major research into the effectiveness of school inspections.

The research reflects that in many countries (but not the UK) 'the limited and sometimes negative impact of centralized reforms and accountability structures' is leading to a move away from 'standard-based centralized improvement to strengthening decentralized local networks of schools that exchange knowledge about effective practices and support each other in finding and developing innovative solutions for complex educational problems'[73]. The purpose of these local networks is 'to enhance innovation and generate system-wide improvement'[74]. In contrast, the 'accountability framework in England [including Ofsted inspections] is focused on individual schools'. International research into inspection effectiveness carried out by Ehren et al[75] found that centralised inspections 'enhance and legitimize a "one size fits all" strategy for success to national standards, [and] encourage risk averse behaviour in schools and window dressing of successful rituals. In performing for inspectors, management and staff become adept at disguising the real problems and issues that face the school which means they do not get the attention and support they require'.

Former headteacher, council director of education and chief executive, and head of Ofsted, Christine Gilbert, champions 'localized processes of change and innovation where stakeholders work together in strong supportive and high-trust networks to define the problems they need to solve (e.g. low student achievement in a particular area), and trial and test solutions for these problems with all stakeholders involved'[76]. A review of the research[77] suggests that key changes need to be made to the system of school inspections in the UK. These changes include: Ofsted's role, inspection framework and working methods being revised so that they 'encourage localized decision-making and local structures and networks for improvement'; inspections evaluating how well a school uses partnership working to improve learning; inspecting all schools in an improvement partnership at the same time; and evaluating the 'quality and functioning' of partnerships 'with the purpose of validating and supporting improvement at the local level'. There are examples of such school inspections operating and being tested 'in small scale settings' in the Netherlands and Northern Ireland[78].

School places planning and admissions best managed by local authorities

We are enthusiastic advocates of delegating decision-making powers, strategic and operational, to those who are best placed to make them – headteachers and governing bodies. There are, however, two responsibilities that the local authority is best able to exercise – school place planning and admissions. Local authorities traditionally have had the duty of ensuring that there are sufficient school places in their area. The laissez-faire way in which free schools have been allowed to be set up, and the local authorities' lack of powers now to commission or establish new schools, have fundamentally undermined their ability to fulfil this important function.

Because of this it is extremely difficult for local authorities to meet the growing demand for school places. Without change, it is estimated that by 2022/23 half of local authorities will be unable to meet increasing demand, leaving 125,000 youngsters without secondary school places[79]. As the law stands at present there is a clear disconnect between local authorities' duty to secure sufficient school places and their powers to meet this duty. To address this anomaly, powers should be restored to councils to commission, establish and build new schools; and ministers, in considering applications for new free schools, should have to take into account how these new schools would meet the demand for school places.

Previously we described the practice whereby many academies were using their role as admissions authorities to deny access to children with special needs, low prior attainment, and learning and behavioural difficulties[80]. Local authorities have a long-standing record of administering school admissions in a legally compliant, objective and fair manner. For these reasons we propose that admissions to all state schools should be administered by each local authority. Faith schools would set their own admissions arrangements, but these would be managed by the local authority. Local authorities would need to fully involve their school improvement partnerships when setting and reviewing school places and admissions arrangements.

Neither fully academised system, nor a return to local authority control

For the Conservative-led governments since 2010, academies have become an 'ideological crusade'. Forcing 'schools causing concern' to be run by multi-academy trusts has become the government's single intervention vehicle. The evidence strongly indicates, however, that having academies as the main or sole driver for school improvement is not working. While converting local authority schools to academies costs around £106,000 per school[81], there is overall no real difference in performance (as measured by test and inspection results) between the two types of institutions. A number of cross-party parliamentary reports have highlighted fundamental weaknesses in the academy system. We have shown also that the claim that academies enjoy greater autonomy is illusory, with establishments within multi-academy trusts often having far less independence than they did in the local authority. Due to poor standards and/or weak financial management, several academy trusts have had to cease responsibility for their schools. It is clear that there are insufficient academy trusts of good enough quality to meet current and future demand to manage schools judged 'inadequate' by Ofsted. The ad-hoc nature of approving new free schools results in there being additional schools 'where there is no demographic need[82]' creating surplus places, at the same time as there are shortages of school places in other areas.

What place is there then for academies and academy trusts within our partnership-based approach to school improvement? A pragmatic rather than an ideological or structural view needs to be taken. The academy system has been running for fifteen years, has major fault lines, and is not suitable to be the main or single vehicle for school improvement. There are, however, many strong academies and academy trusts (as there are local authorities) that have proven records in improving schools and raising educational standards. Abolishing academy status and returning academies to the bosom of local authorities would have major consequences. Precious energy would be wasted in managing the legal and administrative processes involved in dismantling academies and their trusts. More importantly the experience and expertise of school improvement built up by academy trusts would be lost to the whole school system going forward. For these reasons we agree with the research findings of the Education Policy Institute (EPI) following their extensive research into the respective performances of local authorities and academy chains:

> *Our findings continue to demonstrate the wide range of outcomes that are being achieved in different academy chains and local authorities. It remains the case that what matters most is being in a high performing school group, not being in an academy rather than a local authority maintained school or vice-versa. This means, consistent with our research at system level, neither a move to a fully academised system, nor a return to a system of local authority oversight (for the vast majority of schools), is likely to lead to an increase in school standards by itself*[83].

We are proposing, therefore, that academies and academy trusts should continue, but like all other state schools and local authorities they would have a statutory duty to be actively involved and fully co-operate with local school partnerships. Local authority schools would still be able to convert to academies or become part of academy chains. Yet it should not be an irrevocable act, as it is presently, and it should be possible for academies to go back within the local authority umbrella. It should be for school improvement partnerships to make judgements about what will be the most effective governance arrangements for those schools that consistently underperform, using local authority intervention powers, and subject to final approval by the Education Secretary.

Act to generate sufficient numbers of highly skilled and motivated teachers

It is self-evident that to have good schools and learning outcomes for all children and young people requires there to be a sufficient number of highly skilled and motivated teachers. The excessive workload pressures that teachers endure, and their correct perception that governments don't take any real notice of their legitimate concerns, have created a workforce which feels battered and bruised. As detailed in chapter 6, therefore, there have been increasing numbers of teachers leaving the profession over the last decade due to 'heavy workload and poor morale' [84]. These retention problems, together with growing pupil numbers and a year-on-year failure to train the number of teachers needed, has caused major shortages in schools. These shortages mean higher pupil-teacher ratios; increased spend by schools on recruitment and supply staff; and vacancies being filled by temporary, unqualified and inexperienced staff, or not being covered at all.

Government's response to teacher retention 'sluggish and incoherent'

The government (and individual schools, local authorities and academy trusts) have put a great deal of effort and money into improving teacher recruitment, with limited success. Fifteen times more has been spent on recruitment initiatives[85] than on measures to retain teachers[86], but they have 'done little to prevent a mass exodus from the profession'[87], and, despite substantial bursaries to incentivise graduates to train as teachers in shortage subjects, numbers on these courses have fallen[88]. Moreover, tens of millions of pounds is being spent on such bursaries for graduates who don't go on to teach in state schools[89]!

But the current government (and its predecessors) have refused to face up to the central problem – that overbearing workload, caused largely by the undue and unnecessary pressures of the government-imposed school accountability regime, is resulting in record numbers of teachers leaving the profession. Heavy criticism has been levied at the government for its ineffective response to the teacher retention and recruitment crisis, for example by the House of Commons Public Accounts Committee[90], whose chair, Meg Hillier MP, has warned that

'A crisis is brewing in English classrooms but government action to address it has been sluggish and incoherent'[91].

Like in several other areas of concern, the government has made positive noises about teacher workload, with plenty of surveys, reviews, working groups, reports and protocols. In October 2014, for example, the coalition government introduced the 'Workload Challenge', asking teachers for ways to reduce workload. Flowing from this was a protocol concerned with 'accountability, curriculum and qualifications'. Funding was allocated in January 2017 for eleven schools to undertake research projects. Another survey of teacher workload took place in early 2016 with a report in February 2017. Three workload review groups were formed with a report published in March 2016. The Conservative manifesto proposed that teachers would not repay tuition fees while they remained in teaching, but following the 2017 general election this seems to have bitten the dust[92]. At the 2017 Conservative party conference the then Education Secretary, Justine Greening, announced that the government would pilot a scheme of loan reimbursements for new teachers in subjects and regions with shortages[93]. Yet another government initiative was announced in January 2018 when the schools minister wrote to teacher training providers to urge them to 'maximise recruitment' onto courses – that is reject fewer applicants! [94] A 'Workload Advisory Group' was set up in May 2018 to report in summer of that year[95].

Justine Greening's successor, Damien Hinds, has recognised that 'one of the biggest threats to retention, and... recruitment, is workload'. He says that 'Too many of our teachers and our school leaders are working too long hours... on... tasks that are not helping children to learn'. The Education Secretary promised to tackle the teacher shortage as a 'top priority' and to cut teachers' workload. Unfortunately Mr. Hinds didn't specify how he was going to do this. He proposed that in the life time of the current parliament (up to 2022) there would be no more changes (to testing and examinations arrangements) other than those already in the pipeline. But this at best will not increase workload any more than had already been planned[96]. Chief inspector, Amanda Spielman, has said that Ofsted wants to help reduce teacher workload. The consequences of not doing so, she says, is that improvements in schools will not be sustained because 'the people, who make them run so well, are burning out and leaving the profession'. But as with the education secretary, the Ofsted chief puts forward no practical measures for making positive impacts on the undue pressure that teachers are under. Mrs. Spielman's comments that schools shouldn't prepare as they do for inspections, what she calls 'entirely unnecessary work', seems well intentioned, but naive[97].

The remarks of these two most powerful individuals in the English education system go to the heart of the teacher and school leader retention and recruitment crisis. At long last there is recognition from the very top that teacher workload is a major cause of the retention and recruitment difficulties (the evidence suggests that it is by far the biggest single cause). What the government doesn't or won't recognise is that it is the high stakes scrutiny and accountability system, that they and their predecessors have created and intensified, which is the main reason why teachers are under so much pressure and have to work such long hours.

Preparing children for the incessant statutory tests, which are used to hold schools to account, and ensuring that there is an 'audit trail' to provide the evidence when Ofsted calls, adds enormously to teachers' workload. As does preparing for an inspection, where to minimise the risk of failure, schools plan for all eventualities as they may be asked for evidence (which usually means in a written form) to justify what they are doing in any aspect of school life. It is common for inspectors to select individual pupils as case studies and require written evidence on each of these to evaluate whether the school's actions are appropriate. It is pointless advising schools not to make such preparations, when a poor inspection outcome might end a headteacher's career and mean the school being directed into the control of a multi-academy trust, with its staff, pupils and parents having to endure the stigma of being at a 'failing school'. The difference between an 'outstanding' and 'good' Ofsted judgement may mean a loss or gain of several pupils for a school, equating to an increased or reduced budget of tens or hundreds of thousands of pounds (and the increase in or loss of staff).

Despite the government's warm words and their cascade of initiatives, they are either oblivious to the true causes of excessive workload, or simply do not want to face up to the reality that it is their own policies on testing and inspections that bear by far the major responsibility for the enormous stress placed on teachers.

End retention and recruitment crisis by reducing teacher
workload and raising morale

It is clear then that the main solution to ending the retention and recruitment
crisis is reducing teacher workload and raising their morale. Our proposals go to
the heart of the problem, reducing the number of statutory national tests, and re-
focusing the role of inspections and Ofsted more towards school development
than making absolutist judgements. These steps, we believe, will create the
conditions within schools where senior leaders can start to reduce their stress
and workload and that of their staff.

Alongside this it is vitally important to ensure that teachers feel trusted and
valued for the crucial job they do. International evidence suggests that a common
ingredient of all high performing education systems is that teachers are held in
high regard. It is not simply about 'leaving education to the professionals'.
There has to be public and democratic accountability, ensuring schools and
teachers are doing the right things, enabling continuous improvement in schools
and pupil achievement. Also, teachers cannot deliver all on their own: they need
to be part of a productive partnership with children and families, providing the
strongest platform for individual young people to succeed. Central and local
government can do a great deal to demonstrate the value that society places on
teachers. The rhetoric used by elected representatives, particular senior ones,
as we have shown previously, has an enormous impact on how well teachers
feel they are valued.

Yet a more fundamental re-defining of the role of teachers as valued
professionals, and the context within which they work, is needed. In this regard
we are attracted to the proposition put forward by former Home and Education
Secretary, Charles Clarke, in reviewing how best to achieve public service reform,
that the government should be 'reopening dialogue with the professions to seek
agreement on their modern role'[98]. This could be the start of a government approach
that saw teachers as valued and trusted partners in the process of continuing to
improve knowledge and skills of all young people. It would be a 'partnership
model' – democratically elected national and local politicians working together
with the professionals tasked with making the improvements. It contrasts with
the 'top down' and 'structural' models that we have seen in recent times that have
failed to use the energy and talents of all stakeholders.

Whilst by far the best way to retain and recruit more teachers is to reform the testing and inspection regimes (in order to provide teachers with reasonable workloads), other initiatives are also likely to be necessary. These measures include continuing to provide financial incentives, including bursaries, to attract students into teacher training for subjects where there are particular shortages such as science and mathematics.

There is an array of pathways to becoming a qualified teacher. As there have been for many years, there are separate full-time routes for those who have a degree (a one-year post-graduate certificate in education) and for those who haven't (a three or four-year degree) along with their part-time equivalents. While universities are still the largest provider of initial teacher training, an innovation in recent years has been for students to do the bulk of their training in schools, often being employed as unqualified teachers or teaching assistants[99]. Part of the current campaign is supporting people moving from established careers who want to train to be teachers. This has been the specific remit of one recruiter, *Now Teach*, and has been taken up by another, *Teach First*. Numbers on these programmes are increasing, but from a very low base[100].

Teachers being trained in schools have all the advantages of apprenticeships. From the students' point of view, they are being paid and won't be accruing large debts through taking out loans for tuition fees. Schools are able to recruit newly qualified teachers who should have good practical pedagogic skills because of the on-the-job nature of their training. But there are restrictions in the numbers you can train through schools and the costs are much higher than the traditional university route[101]. It would not be financially realistic, therefore, to suggest that all teacher training should be organised through this apprenticeship-type vehicle. There perhaps are too many separate teacher training routes, which can be quite confusing when people are considering teaching as a career choice. Some simplification might be needed without losing the need to have differentiation and to attract people from a diverse range of backgrounds into the profession.

Conclusion - collaborative approaches needed to engage all children productively in quality learning

No one objects in principle to testing, inspection of schools or intervening in some schools where things are not good and can't be retrieved other than through outside help. Most parents and those working in schools want government to work in partnership with school leaders and staff rather than impose decree after decree on them. They also want less pressurised and bureaucratic environments for school staff and pupils to work in.

It is clear that to tackle underachievement, child mental health problems, the national skills gap, and to have sufficient numbers of quality teachers for our schools, there is a need to move away from the 'command and control' system of accountability that has intensified over the last thirty years. This means making fundamental changes to the curriculum, testing and examinations, national inspections and how schools are supported and held to account. Most importantly, these coercive measures need to be replaced by a collaborative partnership approach, both nationally and locally.

Making these changes will provide the different conditions in schools that are necessary to engage all children productively in learning, and to provide the country and individuals with the skills that are needed for them to flourish and move into the future with confidence.

Recommendations

- In order to modernise the curriculum, tackle underachievement and have a strong teacher workforce, *fundamentally change the conditions under which schools operate* by reforming national testing and inspection arrangements. End all national statutory tests in primary and secondary schools (up to the age of eighteen) and replace GCSEs, A levels and vocational qualifications with a 14-19 integrated curriculum. Equip teachers with high-level assessment for learning skills. Re-focus inspections and the work of Ofsted from holding schools to account, to helping them to continuously improve, including replacing absolutist inspection grades with conclusions that are expressed in developmental terms.
- *Modernise the school curriculum* through a root and branch review aimed at achieving the right balance between knowledge and skills, and academic, vocational and technical studies; and providing for greater flexibility for schools to meet the needs of all pupils; and re-engage young people with learning. Set up a National Curriculum Council to initially oversee the

revision of the national curriculum and then keep it under review. Introduce an integrated 14-19 curriculum, with compulsory work experience, based on the work of the Tomlinson report.

• *Create new school improvement and governance structures* through statutorily establishing local school improvement partnerships to provide schools with ongoing support and challenge. Duties to be placed on all state schools, academy trusts, and local and diocesan authorities to actively participate in the partnerships. As its principal role, Ofsted to evaluate and report on the effectiveness of the local school improvement partnerships. Local authorities to retain their current duties and powers for intervening in individual schools (including academies), and to be given (restored) powers to commission, establish and build new schools. Free schools to be approved only where extra places are needed. Admissions arrangements for all schools to be determined and administered by local authorities. Local authority schools to continue to be able to become academies, and academies able to become local authority schools. Where a school is consistently underperforming, the school improvement partnership to determine whether different governance arrangements are needed.

• *Improve retention and recruitment of teachers* by substantially reducing their workload, principally by ending statutory national tests, and making school development and improvement Ofsted's primary role. Continue and review the financial incentives and other initiatives used to attract more people into teaching. Government to develop a new productive partnership with teachers.

• Reduce the pressure of testing and examinations, and develop well-funded preventative and specialist services to *tackle the growing child mental health problem.*

12
SKILLING UP THE NATION

*In the 21st century, our natural resource is our people — and their potential
is both untapped and vast. Skills will unlock that potential. The prize will be
enormous — higher productivity, the creation of wealth and social justice.*
Lord Sandy Leitch

One of the biggest challenges facing the country is to tackle our skills shortage,
which is acting as a drag on the economy and limiting employment opportunities
for large numbers of people. Consequently we have a higher proportion of
low-skilled, poorly paid and insecure jobs than most other developed countries,
contributing to weak productivity and declining living standards. There is no
short-term fix to what is a long-term national problem. A systemic, long-term
approach is needed, which reaches deep into the main institutions of our society
- families, schools, colleges, universities, businesses and public services. Major
cultural change will be required. In this chapter we examine the main factors
that contribute to the UK's skills problem. From this we will suggest a number
of ways that the skills gap can start to be filled.

Why has the UK a skills crisis?

There are a multiplicity of reasons why the country has skill shortages. It starts
with *children's home life*. Chapter 5 demonstrated that children who are not
well supported at home often have poor learning outcomes, including in basic
skills. The nature of the *school curriculum*, particularly as it is impacted on
by high stakes testing, contributes to the skills crisis in three specific ways
– firstly in helping to turn too many young people off learning; secondly its

lack of focus on skills development; and thirdly its academic bias, which has marginalised creative and vocational education. This dominant 'academic education culture', where vocational and technical education has low parity of esteem, permeates the whole education system. While more young people are doing well academically and entering university, there is significant *underachievement*, with too many leaving school every year without marketable skills and qualifications. As a result a substantial proportion of young people and adults lack adequate *basic skills* and *employability skills*. There is a dearth of young people studying science, technology, engineering and mathematics (*STEM*) after the age of sixteen.

While demand for specialist and generic *digital skills* is growing rapidly, a significant proportion of the adult population don't have basic digital skills. Severe public spending cuts since 2010 have eviscerated the capacity of *further education* to deliver the medium to higher skills that the country is so short of. Traditionally colleges have been the major supplier of this crucial range of skills. Neither do we have sufficient of the type and quality of *apprenticeships* that the economy requires. Although the massive expansion of *higher education* in recent years has provided many of the higher skills that are needed, both generically and in specialised areas, there is a dearth of STEM graduates. Furthermore, employers express concern that too many leave university without the skills required for employment, and large numbers of graduates are in jobs not requiring a degree. There appears also to be disquiet at the quality and relevance of much of the *careers* advice for school leavers, adult learners and graduates. In addition, while demand for skills seems to be rising exponentially, the amount of *workplace training* has reduced.

Systemic, long-term approach to skilling up the nation

The UK skills crisis is severe and the causes culturally embedded in many families, government, education establishments and businesses. Only a systemic, long-term strategy that permeates all dimensions of our society, as depicted below, has any realistic chance of providing the full range of skills the nation needs.

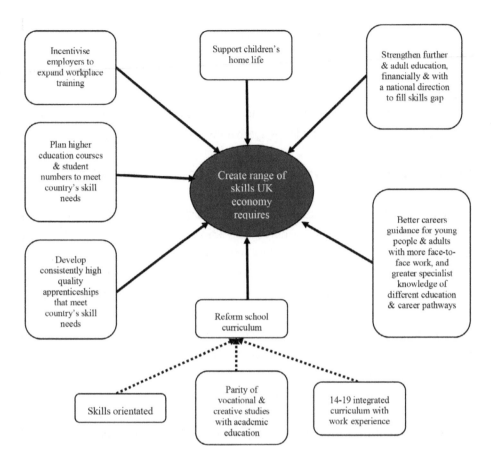

In previous chapters we made proposals that we believe will significantly contribute to improving skills:

- A national strategy and dedicated local services supporting families so that all children have the quality of home life that will enable them to develop the personal and cognitive skills to prosper in school and in employment (chapter 10).
- A broader school curriculum that is more skills and vocationally orientated, and engaging of all students, including a new 14-19 curriculum integrating academic, vocational and apprenticeship programme, and including substantial mandatory work experience for all students (chapter 11).
- Greater recognition of the critical role played by adult education in re-engaging adults with learning, and equipping people with much needed skills (chapter 9).

In this chapter we focus on the need to give much greater priority to further education; higher education that better contributes to the country's skill needs; improving careers guidance; meeting the growing demand for STEM and digital skills; getting the apprenticeship system right; and enhancing workplace training. Firstly, though, we need to face up to the core reason why the UK has a skills shortage – the ingrained bias against vocational and technical education.

Cultural bias against vocational and technical education

There is an acute and long-standing cultural bias in the UK towards 'academic' courses, with vocational and technical education lacking parity of esteem and being considered as an option for 'less-able' young people. This is embedded deep in the school curriculum and examinations system. In the UK there are less than a third of young people following vocational qualifications, contrasting with an average of a half in most other developed countries[1].

This dominant academic education culture bears a great deal of responsibility for the poor state of the University Technical College (UTC) sector in England, comprising of forty-nine non-selective free schools that offer technically orientated courses of study combined with the national curriculum requirements for students aged between fourteen and nineteen. UTCs have struggled since they first opened in 2010[2]. Several have closed due to low student numbers [3] and others have significant spare capacity[4]. They have not generally done well in inspections[5] or in pupils' progress measures[6], but have a good record of students going into universities and apprenticeships[7]. By comparison, in Finland more than four in ten sixteen-year-olds go to upper vocational schools[8]. Former education secretary, Lord Baker, believes that 'there has always been a snobbery against technical colleges'. He accuses one of his successors, Michael Gove, of 'squeeze[ing] the technical subjects by excluding them from the core curriculum [EBacc]'[9]. The EBacc is another example of the bias against vocational education which, as reported in chapter 11, has resulted in far fewer pupils taking vocational courses.

The Labour government missed a golden opportunity in 2004 to end this cultural bias when it didn't accept the recommendation of the Tomlinson review[10] to bring academic and vocational education together into a unified curriculum and qualifications system for fourteen to nineteen-year-olds. We might by now be seeing far more young people studying high quality vocational programmes and have fewer skill shortages, but the sad fact is that we've gone backwards. Lord Willetts, an education minister from 2010-15, said that he 'regretted not changing the narrow structure of sixth-form education when he was in government'. He says that the current 16-19 curriculum is 'a policy disaster'[11]. By comparison Germany has a strong vocational culture. Demand for vocational education is high and there are clear vocational pathways, including for trainees to attend technical universities and gain Meister (masters) qualifications in such areas as electrical or plumbing. School leavers can opt for an occupational route with an apprenticeship of between two and three and a half years that can lead to higher level courses at Berufsakademien (vocational colleges) or Fachhochschule (technical universities). Vocational courses have the same parity of esteem as the academic routes[12].

Further education must be given higher political profile

As we illustrated in chapter 9, further education is extremely diverse, with up to four million full and part-time learners of all ages post-sixteen[13], studying for around 15,000 different qualifications[14], ranging from programmes of a few hours to two years or more[15]. Three-quarters of further education learners are over the age of nineteen[16], and most live in the local area[17]. The overall governance arrangements for the sector are complex. The Department for Education provides the overall regulatory framework and policy, the Education and Skills Funding Agency monitors financial health and management, Ofsted inspects the quality of provision, and there is a Further Education Commissioner who 'intervenes in the most poorly performing colleges'[18]. The House of Commons Public Accounts Committee, understandably, sees these governance arrangements as being 'overly complex'[19].

Further education treated as Cinderella service

Despite their immense and diverse coverage, further education colleges have in reality been treated as the 'Cinderella' of the education service, squeezed between their politically more influential school and university counterparts. For example, can it be right that a 'home' university undergraduate is funded at a rate that is at least four times greater than a full-time FE college student?[20] In reviewing the sector in 1997, Helena Kennedy QC summed up the political status of further education very aptly:

> *Despite the formidable role played by further education, it is the least understood and celebrated part of the learning tapestry. Further education suffers because of prevailing British attitudes. Not only does there remain a very carefully calibrated hierarchy of worthwhile achievement, which has clearly established routes and which privileges academic success well above any other accomplishment, but there is also an appalling ignorance amongst decision-makers and opinion-formers about what goes on in further education. It is so alien to their experience*[21].

Twenty years on, nothing much seems to have changed. Sir Vince Cable says that when he was the Secretary of State in the 2010-15 coalition government responsible for further education, 'government officials wanted to axe all further education colleges in England and Wales to save money' and advised him that 'nobody will really notice'[22]! Fortunately Sir Vince did not act on the advice. Those of us who have studied or worked in colleges will be outraged and alarmed at the proposal put forward by these officials, but given that the vast majority of senior civil servants will not have gone anywhere near a further education establishment, it is not surprising.

Massive cuts to further education funding

The relatively low political profile of further education is probably the reason it has suffered more from budget cuts than other sectors. Between 2010 and 2015, while school budgets were largely protected and university funding increased by over twenty-five per cent[23], further education college budgets were cut by fourteen per cent[24], resulting in a loss of around one million adult learners including those studying English and mathematics, and reductions in the number of students aged 19 to 24 taking courses such as construction, engineering and creative arts. The House of Commons Public Accounts Committee found that 'the declining financial health of many further education colleges has potentially serious consequences for learners and local economies, but the bodies responsible for funding and oversight have been slow to address the problem. Too often, they have taken decisions without understanding the cumulative impact that these decisions have on colleges and their learners'[25].

Thankfully, a decision in 2015 to reduce further education funding by another quarter was reversed[26], but, no allowance was made for inflation, and thus cuts in provision have continued. Since 2010 further education colleges have overall lost almost a third of their income, particularly affecting adult learners with numbers of students over the age of twenty-five down from over five million to less than two million, including in major skill shortage areas such as construction, engineering and information technology[27].

These cuts have meant that colleges have closed courses, had problems retaining and recruiting staff, and not properly invested in facilities for students such as buildings, technology and online learning[28]. There are now several colleges in severe financial difficulties[29]. These substantially reduced budgets have led to thirty-seven 'area-based reviews', which the government expect will result in 'fewer, larger, more resilient and efficient' colleges. Between 50 and 80 college mergers are expected to result from the reviews[30]. There are concerns that the reviews are driven by financial rather than educational considerations or student interests, and that the resultant enlarged colleges[31] may impact adversely on student participation rates[32].

Strengthen further education to play an even greater part in tackling skill shortages and underachievement

With a view to enabling the further education sector to play an even greater part in tackling skill shortages and underachievement, and helping young people and adults to re-engage with learning, we propose:

- That government demonstrate a greater understanding of and empathy with the further education sector. Efforts should be made to recruit senior civil servants to relevant departments and agencies that have a background in further education.
- Continuing cuts to further education be halted, through the government providing additional funding up to 2020 to cover inflationary cost pressures.

- Following consultation, a national strategy setting out the role of and priorities for further education (including sixteen to nineteen-year-olds, apprenticeships, adult returners and basic skills), backed up by local delivery plans.
- A re-vamped careers advice service for school leavers, which presents them with all post-16 and post-18 education and employment options in an informed and impartial way.
- Specific programmes for re-engaging school leavers, young people and adults with learning, supported by national and local campaigns targeted at encouraging participation in post-16 learning of those from 'hard to reach' groups.
- Simplified governance arrangements with one overriding national body (such as the Further Education Funding Council was[33]) to provide strong and cohesive leadership to the further education sector.

Getting apprenticeship system right is key to tackling country's skills shortages

The single biggest thing that most employers are looking for when recruiting new staff is work experience, followed by vocational qualifications, and finally academic qualifications[34]. There could be no stronger case for apprenticeships, which are paid jobs combining work experience and training, culminating in vocational qualifications. But, as explained in chapter 3, there are major weaknesses with the current apprenticeship system. Numbers have plummeted since the introduction of the funding levy in 2017, and there are serious concerns about quality and whether apprenticeships overall are meeting the country's skill needs.

This chapter examines the reasons for these weaknesses. There are four main ones – recruitment difficulties, the type of apprenticeships being offered, their quality, and the funding levy and its administration

Negative image and low pay constrain apprenticeship recruitment

One of the main obstacles to recruiting apprentices, particularly onto advanced and higher programmes, is the negative image that many young people and those who influence them (including parents, teachers and careers officers) have of apprenticeships. Many parents, for example, especially those who might be considered as having high aspirations for their children 'think an apprenticeship is a step down from university'[35]. As one business leader puts it, 'The idea that university is the right route is fairly ingrained with some parents'[36]. Parents, who often have gone down the higher education route themselves, may fear that their children's opportunities in life will be limited if they don't have a 'normal degree'[37]. Schools and colleges add to this bias with eighty-five per cent of teenagers being advised to go to university and only eight per cent to start a work-based apprenticeship[38]. These attitudes result in only 8,000 young people being on higher and degree-level apprenticeships, compared to the 300,000 starting university courses[39]. In contrast industry is increasingly choosing to recruit apprentices rather than university graduates[40].

While it is relatively easy, to apply for university through UCAS, there is no overall system for applying for the maze of different apprenticeship programmes[41]. It is also the case that young people from low and moderate-income backgrounds are much less likely than those from better-off families to take up high quality apprenticeships[42].

Low pay is probably the biggest issue[43] deterring young people from starting apprenticeships. The statutory minimum wage for apprentices in their first year and under nineteen years of age is £3.70 an hour[44]. Many young people end up paying more in travelling to work and other expenses than they earn. Some employers 'exploit' apprentices on the minimum wage by requiring them to do 'the same work and [and take on the same] responsibilities as non-trainee workers' [45]. Most MPs do not believe the minimum wage for these apprentices is enough to live on[46]. It is no wonder, therefore, that there is such a low take up of apprenticeships by young people.

Not enough of the right type of apprenticeships

Chapter 3 explained that while the government's focus was on increasing the overall number of apprenticeships, the major flaw in the system is that there is not enough of the skill-type and quality of apprentices needed to meet the nation's requirements. There are good numbers of adults in apprenticeships, yet not sufficient numbers of young people. Most apprenticeships are in the services sector, when far more are needed for technical and scientific occupations[47]. There is too large a proportion of apprenticeships at the lower end of the skills spectrum, and not enough at middle and higher skill levels, with half of all apprenticeships at level two or below[48]. Progression from level two to three is not automatic and apprentices wishing to do this often have to start a new programme[49].

While most German apprenticeships are at level 3 or above, in the UK most are below level 3[50]. One of the main causes of not having enough advanced-level apprenticeships is that many businesses, mainly in retail, are converting low-skilled jobs, such as fast food and café front of house roles, to apprenticeships and claiming funding for them. These 'apprenticeships' add little or anything to the country's overall skills base. Research shows that forty per cent of government-approved apprenticeships do not meet the traditional or the international definition of what constitutes an apprenticeship[51].

Quantity of apprenticeships being sacrificed for quality

Businesses are rightly concerned about the 'patchy training standards' in our apprenticeship system and have 'accused ministers of putting quantity... before quality'[52]. The chair of the parliamentary Education Select Committee, Robert Halfon MP, has called for an 'urgent reassessment of the whole sector to ensure that quality [is] not being sacrificed for quantity'[53]. There are three main concerns about the quality of the national apprenticeship programme – too many training providers judged at inspection to be not good enough, the lack of jobs at the end of apprenticeships, and significant numbers of schemes that have little or no training.

As many new apprenticeships start each year in the UK as they do in Germany, but while the German system is of consistent high quality, the British have too many schemes of a poor standard. In 2017 more than half of apprenticeship training providers inspected by Ofsted were judged as requiring improvement or inadequate[54], meaning that a fifth of apprentices were with training providers deemed to be inadequate[55]. Additionally Ofsted report 'an over-emphasis on simply ticking the box to show that the next part of the qualification ha[d] been achieved' with not 'enough focus on the actual skills, knowledge and behaviours learned'. Ofsted said that most providers inspected 'found it difficult to demonstrate what actual progress their apprentices were really making'[56]. Twelve training providers have been barred by the Education and Skills Funding Agency from taking on new trainees[57]. The experiences of trainees on apprenticeship programmes is of equal concern. One in 10 apprentices are not aware that they are on an apprenticeship[58]! Forty per cent of level two and three apprentices receive fewer than the required six hours a week training[59], and three per cent receive no training at all[60]. Just over half of apprentices get jobs at the end of their apprenticeships[61].

Since the introduction of the levy there has been a dramatic increase in the number of apprenticeship training providers[62], and now three-quarters of apprenticeships are delivered by independent providers[63]. It is clear that Ofsted simply do not have the resources to inspect this increased number of training providers on a regular basis[64]. The scandal of *Learndirect*[65] (responsible for 75,000 learners[66] and in receipt of £600 million of government funding since 2011[67], and deemed to have inadequate standards and poor financial management by Ofsted) highlights a major problem with the current system of apprenticeships in this country – the contracting out of training to hundreds of different, mainly commercial, organisations with little regard to their quality, nor any meaningful monitoring of their performance.

Bureaucratic implementation of levy causes downturn in apprenticeship numbers

In April 2017 the government introduced a levy on large companies as the principal way of funding apprenticeships. Employers can draw on the levy funding to help cover the cost of training (up to £27,000 a year for each apprentice). They can also use up to a tenth of their fund for use by their suppliers and subcontractors[68]. Organisations with wage bills under £3 million, but who employ between 50 and 200 staff, are compelled to release apprentices for one day a week for training, and contribute a tenth of the total training costs. It is argued that this 'has made apprenticeships less popular'[69]. For those organisations with fewer than fifty employees the government meets the full cost of training for 16 and 17 year old apprentices[70]. Apprenticeships have to be a minimum duration of twelve months, and off-the-job training must constitute a fifth of the total apprenticeship programme[71].

Some employers, such as small accounting firms[72], are happy with the apprenticeship system, but most have serious concerns about the levy[73]. Since the levy's introduction there has been a major downturn in the number of apprenticeships, the largest drop being 16 to18- year-olds[74]. Four main reasons are cited for this reduction - the levy's implementation, its use for training existing employees rather than taking on new apprentices, costs, and restrictions on large companies transferring levy funds to suppliers and subcontractors.

Amongst employers there is a mixture of indifference to and confusion about apprenticeships and the levy. Unfortunately, most employers don't offer apprenticeships[75]. Far more organisations appear to be paying the levy than the government initially indicated[76]. Some are unaware of the levy's existence[77] and just over a fifth do not know whether or not they have to pay the levy![78] Others 'don't understand' how it works[79]. Most concerning, forty per cent of employers say the levy won't make a difference to the amount of training they offer[80], a fifth plan to write off the levy as a stealth tax and 'not use it to fund apprenticeships' [81], and only a third are developing new apprenticeship programmes[82]. Many employers blame the dramatic decline in apprenticeship numbers on the overly complex and bureaucratic implementation of the levy by the civil service[83]. The manufacturers' organisation, the EEF, say that many of its member firms have 'struggled to get their heads around the complex rules and restrictions in accessing funds' and as a result have been unable to offer apprenticeships[84]. Some have not been able to get existing schemes accredited to access funding[85] and there have been considerable delays in obtaining certification for training programmes[86]. Three-quarters of manufacturers have reported that they have not been able to access the funding[87]. The bureaucracy has especially affected smaller companies[88].

To draw down funding many companies have found it easier to re-brand current training programmes, benefitting existing and usually older employees, rather than take on new apprentices, including school leavers. Such re-branding neither raises the overall level of workplace skills nor increases the number of apprenticeships [89]. For example, there are many organisations using the levy to sponsor senior staff on external management courses, including MBAs[90]. Mainly due to the expansion of these expensive management apprenticeships, and even though the overall number of apprentices has dramatically declined, the apprenticeship budget in 2017/18 was overspent by £0.5 billion[91].

A significant part of the cost of having apprenticeships is not met from the levy funding, which can only be used to cover formal training costs[92]. This means organisations incur considerable costs including salaries, recruitment and mentoring, releasing apprentices for one day a week, and meeting part of the training fees. Prior to the introduction of the levy the costs of apprenticeships for 16 to 18-year-olds were wholly funded by the government (but only fifty per cent for other apprentices). Now all but the smallest companies have to contribute ten per cent to the cost of apprenticeship training. This has acted as a disincentive for some employers taking on the youngest apprentices[93]. In response to this, in his autumn budget the Chancellor announced that the contribution that 'smaller firms' make to training costs will be reduced to five per cent[94]. The maximum allowance of £27,000 per apprentice does not cover the cost of all high-level apprenticeships[95], nor much high-level technology and engineering training[96]. And, while there has been a rise in higher and degree apprenticeship starts, numbers are still very small, particularly school leavers[97].

There is concern about a lack of flexibility in the mechanism that allows large firms to transfer ten per cent of their levy funding to smaller companies in their supply chain, resulting in this not being fully used. Such inflexibility particularly hits the construction and car industries[98].

Opportunity for government to fundamentally strengthen apprenticeship system

The review into post-18 education, initially driven by the concern about student debt, presents a golden opportunity for the government to take a fundamental look at apprenticeships. In widening the remit of the review, the Prime Minister rightly said that 'the route into further technical and vocational training is hard to navigate' and that 'standards… too varied and the funding… patchy'[99]. The Prime Minister and her colleagues should make the most of the chance they have created to instigate the fundamental improvements that are necessary to strengthen apprenticeships, and vocational and technical education generally. We have identified five main areas that might provide the basis for the significant improvement that's required – improving recruitment; designing a national programme that meets the country's skill needs; ensuring consistent quality; reforming the levy; and strengthening national leadership.

Promote benefits of apprenticeships and introduce UCAS style applications process

Persuading parents (their children and teachers) that doing a degree should not be the 'default option' and that an apprenticeship can have as much merit (if not more, in many cases) as a university place, will be crucial in driving up the numbers of higher apprentices[100]. There are some obvious advantages to apprenticeships that should make them attractive propositions to both employers and those wishing to pursue a career. Employers are able to recruit talented people, train them up in the way they want, and enhance the overall skills of their workforces. For school leavers at the age of 16 there are opportunities for 'learning a trade' with either an intermediate or advanced programme, with prospects to progress to apprenticeships at a higher level. Degree or higher apprenticeships are a good alternative to university, being paid while you learn, becoming more employable, and generally being paid better once in employment[101].

Much more needs to be done to persuade parents, young people, teachers and careers advisers of the benefits of apprenticeships, in order that students see these as credible and worthwhile alternatives to university. There need to be more initiatives such as that taken by accountancy firm, EY, in setting up 'Parentaship', a campaign and workshop to help parents understand what modern apprenticeships are all about, and that they offer an excellent route to a professional career[102]. There should be an ongoing promotional campaign highlighting the benefits of apprenticeships to sixteen and eighteen-year-olds school leavers, and adults, and providing clear up-to-date information to teachers, careers advisers and parents.

One measure that would help in the recruitment of apprentices would be to simplify the process for applying for apprenticeships. While applicants for university have a single point of entry – UCAS, those thinking about the apprenticeship route have to navigate each of the thousands of apprenticeship vacancies separately. A UCAS-style process[103], which could be administered by the national apprenticeship body (we are proposing is set up), would hold all apprenticeship vacancies, and enable potential trainees to complete one application form on which they would express their preferences. The process would then facilitate liaison between employers and trainees to arrange interviews and appointments. A portal listing 3,000 higher and degree apprenticeships has been set up by the government[104], and although a good start, it doesn't go far enough. It simply lists the different higher apprenticeship programmes accompanied by a link to the particular employer's website. It is interesting that while students applying for university courses get a full service from UCAS, in contrast those applying for higher apprenticeships receive a very limited service. Also, the portal excludes the vast majority of apprenticeships i.e. those at intermediate and advanced levels.

Match types and numbers of apprenticeships to needs of economy and public services

Apprenticeships as a whole need to be making a more direct contribution to tackling the country's skills deficit. Over half of all apprentices are on intermediate programmes, only four in ten on advanced, and only seven in a hundred on higher. Sixty per cent of apprenticeship starts are in just four sectors – health, public services and care, business administration, and law[105]. Two main measures are needed to radically shift the balance of the current apprenticeship system. Firstly, the national apprenticeship programme should be more directly geared to meeting the specific short and medium-term occupational skill requirements of business and the public sector. Secondly, a substantially increase in the numbers of young people (particularly 16-19-year-olds) are needed, and far more technical and scientific, level 3 and higher level apprenticeships. To achieve this better balance some national and regional planning will be required, informed by analyses of need and demand. Such measures, together with the improved recruitment process (described above), should help in moving towards an apprenticeship programme that better meets the country's skill needs.

Commit to quality even if it leads to short-term decline in apprentice numbers

There has to be a determined focus on building consistent quality into the national apprenticeship system.

The production of the standards, the responsibility of the Institute for Apprenticeships (IfA), has been very slow and skewed towards higher apprenticeships[106]. It appears that some organisations, including those that have only just been established, with no track record whatsoever, can be successful in getting on the government's register as approved training providers, without having to evidence their credentials for delivering quality[107]. We know from Ofsted inspections that too many apprenticeship and training providers are not good enough.

There are some doubts as to whether the IfA and Ofsted have the capacity to fully undertake their critical regulatory roles[108]. Chief inspector Amanda Spielman recognises that there is a capacity problem[109]. While the Education and Skills Funding Agency (ESFA) has the responsibility and the powers to intervene in 'failing' training organisations, it is not clear who, if anyone, is doing the external development work with the employers and training providers where significant improvement is needed. Added to this, the Public Accounts Committee recommended that the government should better understand companies that have multiple public contracts and how the government then manages the inherent risks[110]. Undoubtedly more resources are needed, but is there also a case for rationalising the number of national organisations for apprenticeships? a matter we look at later on.

To summarise, the government needs to strongly commit to quality even if in the short term this means a decline or slower increase in overall numbers of apprenticeships; on this basis we make the following proposals:

- Additional resources to be put into speeding up work on developing apprenticeship standards, ensuring that they meet the requirements of the different occupational sectors[111].
- Develop a more rigorous process for accrediting apprenticeship and training providers. Ofsted's recent initiative to make 'early monitoring visits' to new providers has to continue and be properly resourced. The public accounts committee has also recommended that Ofsted 're-visit' how it prioritises its resources in regard to the risk involved with private sector training contracts[112].
- Allocate adequate resources to ensure there is an ongoing systematic evaluation of apprenticeship provision, and enable there to be immediate follow-up development work with those providers where significant improvement is needed.

Make levy less bureaucratic, easier to access and cover full costs of training

Most businesses seem to be of the view that the apprenticeship levy is 'not fit for purpose' and needs to be more flexible, or be replaced[113]. More than half of employers want the levy converting into a 'broader training tariff'[114]. One argument for a levy with a broader purpose is that it would 'prompt greater employer investment in skills, including apprenticeships, but in a way that is much more responsive to employers' needs'[115]. There are concerns, however, about moving to a training levy that is too broad and flexible.

Many employers are committed to quality training to skill up their workforce, and willing and able to make short-term sacrifices for medium to long-term gains in productivity. There are others, however, who are not. Examples are those organisations who convert existing training schemes in order to draw down levy funding, which defeats the main objective of the levy of increasing the skills base. There are others who use the apprenticeship programme as a source of subsidised cheap labour, taking on young people under the age of nineteen, paying them the minimum wage (of £3.70 an hour), giving them little or no training, dismissing them at the end of the 'apprenticeship', and then bringing on another batch of low-paid and poorly trained apprentices. Although it seems within the rules, these practices are a serious abuse of the system, do not improve skills for the economy, and bring the apprenticeship system into disrepute, contributing to the poor image it already suffers from.

The concept of the levy is a good one – that employers, particular the larger ones, make a major contribution to the funding of apprenticeships, sharing the overall cost with the general taxpayer. We believe the levy should continue to be dedicated to funding and promoting apprenticeships, as the main, targeted way of plugging the nation's skills gap, rather than become a broader training fund. We also need some clear conditions for accessing levy funding that are firmly and consistently applied, to ensure high quality programmes that meet the country's skill requirements. There are legitimate concerns about bureaucracy, costs incurred by employers, the mechanism for large employers transferring access to the funding within their supply chain, and the two-year limit for accessing funding. With all this in mind we make the following suggestions about how the funding of apprenticeships could be improved.

- The government in conjunction with employers should review how the levy fund is administered, with a view to making it less bureaucratic and easier to access.
- The government should consider the financial feasibility of funding the full costs of off-the-job training of all apprenticeships (including such costs as travel, books, and examination fees) from the levy[116]. This may mean the government putting a greater contribution into the levy fund or funding fewer, but better quality apprenticeship schemes.
- Increase the proportion of levy funding that large companies can transfer to smaller companies in their supply chain. Employer organisations including the CBI, the Federation of Small Businesses, and the Science, Engineering and Manufacturing Technologies Alliance, are in favour of such a move[117]. The government should consult with employers about whether the proportion of the levy fund that can be transferred should be increased, and if so by how much.
- Give greater support to small businesses. Employers have called for more funding 'to help small businesses to respond to the apprenticeship levy'[118], and the Education Secretary is to release £80 million to help small businesses take on apprentices[119]. The Labour Party goes much further, arguing for £440 million of the apprenticeship levy to be specifically ring-fenced to support small and medium-sized businesses[120].
- Extend the two-year time limit for employers to access the levy. It would make sense to extend the time limit to four years, the average duration of an apprenticeship, and to allow new programmes to be developed and existing programmes to be re-vamped and accredited[121].

Single powerful national body to drive apprenticeships forward with devolved powers to sub-regions

The national apprenticeship system is currently centrally administered and there is a growing plethora of training providers. There are presently four national bodies with responsibility for apprenticeships. The Department for Education and its ministers has the overall policy brief. Implementation is in the hands of the Education and Skills Funding Agency (ESFA) and the Institute for Apprenticeships (IfA). ESFA funds and has some regulatory responsibilities for training providers, 'intervening where there is risk of failure or where there is evidence of mismanagement of public funds'[122]. IfA's remit is to regulate the quality of apprenticeships, including approving standards and assessment plans, and maintaining quality criteria[123]. Ofsted seem to be a third arm of the regulatory structure in that they inspect training providers and publish reports on their findings.

The government should look at whether some integration of the functions of the national bodies that have responsibility for apprenticeships might help improve the quality of the apprenticeship system as well as delivering some administrative efficiencies. One option could be to bring together the apprenticeship functions of the ESFA with the IfA. A step further would be to include Ofsted's inspectoral functions (for training providers) creating a single national body responsible for implementing the government's policy on apprenticeships, and ensuring that they are meeting the country's skill requirements and are consistently of high quality. Such an organisation, well-resourced and appropriately skilled, could become a powerful national body that is able to grasp the apprenticeship agenda and drive it forward.

To enhance capacity, and enable regional skill and business needs to be better met, consideration should be given to devolving some planning and delivery functions to the sub-regions (for example Greater London, Merseyside and Greater Manchester). There are a growing number of sub-regional bodies such as the Local Enterprise Partnerships (LEPs) [124], sub-regional Mayors and combined authorities that could take on these responsibilities. The national apprenticeship body could have responsibility for needs analysis and planning for the whole of the country; and for standards, provider accreditation, contracting, funding and improvement work for programmes that are nationwide or running across more than one sub-region. Sub-regional bodies could take on responsibilities for needs analysis and planning for the sub-region, and for contracting, funding and improvement work for programmes that are contained within the sub-region[125].

Higher education – core purpose needed to meet nation's skill requirements

UK higher education has many strengths, with four of the world's top 10 universities[126]. The great majority of university students seem 'content with their degree courses'[127], and graduates generally, compared to non-graduates, earn more[128], enjoy better health, and their children are more likely to be well-educated[129]. A quarter of adults in the UK now have a degree, one of the highest proportions in the developed world, and this provides the country with an abundant supply of generic higher level skills, which has positively contributed to economic growth and productivity.

When you look deeper into British higher education, however, you discover that it is not meeting the skill requirements of the country as fully as it should and could be[130]. There is a substantial and growing shortage of STEM graduates[131]. Too many students leave university without essential employability skills[132], and a high proportion of graduates are doing jobs that don't require a degree. The UK has a laissez-faire higher education system. Universities run whatever courses they like and recruit as many students as they can[133], without necessarily having to take account of the country's skill requirements or whether there are appropriate jobs for their graduates to go to. Such laissez-faire is defended by government as a market that will deliver what the students and the country want. Yet, as the House of Commons Public Accounts Committee reports, it is not a market 'that works in the interests of students or taxpayers'[134]. Students, say the committee, have 'limited redress' if they are dissatisfied with their higher education experience, dropping out rather than switching to another university[135]. A destabilising effect of this 'marketisation' is that some universities have expanded massively whilst others have seen a dramatic decline in student numbers, to a point where their future viability is being questioned[136]. The rush for students has also seen the university sector's debts treble to £10.8 billion over the last decade[137].

Too many graduates doing non-graduate jobs

As many as half of recent graduates are doing jobs that you don't need a degree for, one of the highest rates in Europe[138], prompting the question as to whether the UK has too many university students. Many graduates, well qualified in their chosen subject, do not have the necessary employability skills[139]. For example, a significant number of those who have degrees in STEM, an area of acute skill shortage, find themselves unemployed six months after graduating[140], a main factor being that they do not have 'the "soft" employability skills, such as critical thinking, problem solving and working in teams, that employers are looking for'[141]. At the same time there is evidence that graduate over-qualification is squeezing lower qualified workers out of jobs[142].

Research also shows that students (including a third of male students) graduating from some courses and from some universities earn no more or 'earn less at the age of 29, on average, than their peers who opted to avoid higher education altogether'[143]. In fact, nearly one in five graduates are no better off five years after leaving higher education than those who took a non-university route[144]. It is interesting to note that while the UK has the fifth highest proportion of adults educated to degree level in the OECD, it only ranks seventeenth in terms of productivity[145].

Chair of the Education Select Committee and former Skills Minister, Robert Halfon MP, says that the 'labour market does not need an ever-growing supply of academic degrees' when 'there are skills shortages in several sectors' and a strong need for intermediate and higher technical skills[146]. The professional human resources organisation, CIPD, has thoroughly researched this 'over-qualification' and has concluded that:

> *There may be more cost-effective ways (for both government and individuals) of preparing many of our young people for entry into the labour market. Policy-makers need to scrutinise the range of courses offered by the HE sector and seriously consider the social and private returns to them. We conjecture that they will conclude that, in many cases, public funds could more usefully be deployed elsewhere in the education and training system. Our findings suggest that the presence of a large HE sector will not necessarily lead to the attainment of the knowledge economy so beloved by successive UK governments[147].*

Planned, needs-led approach to courses and student numbers

We believe that going forward UK higher education needs a core purpose of meeting the broad skill needs of the country. The practical manifestation of this would be a nationally planned, needs-led approach to courses and student numbers.

Meeting the 'broad skill needs of the country' can only be realised through a diverse higher education curriculum offer. We are not arguing for a narrowly-based curriculum, consisting only or mainly of specific vocational courses. We do, however, take a utilitarian approach. While we hold the view that learning is beneficial in its own right, we do not believe that 'education for its own sake' should be the underpinning philosophy of a higher education system that is so critical to the nation's economic and social well-being, and costs the taxpayer, students and businesses in the region of £35 billion a year[148]. Meeting the country's broad skill requirements will provide graduates with the best opportunities to find high quality, well-paid employment, benefitting graduates directly as well as the wider population.

Bringing greater diversity to university life is critical, both in terms of the student population as well as the type of courses on offer. There needs to be, for example, a significant increase in the number of higher level apprenticeships[149], degree apprenticeships[150] and employer-sponsored degrees[151]. An expansion of such programmes would help tackle skill shortages[152], create more diverse qualification routes, and reduce the overall cost of higher education. The government should explore how employers can be incentivised to sponsor or run their own higher level programmes, through direct funding, the apprenticeship levy, or corporation tax allowances.

Fulfilling a core purpose of meeting the country's skill needs will require a move away from the current unplanned, demand-led higher education system, to one that is more planned and needs-led in regard to courses offered and student numbers. Two main things will need to be put in place to achieve this – a system for collecting and analysing information, and consulting with stakeholders, including universities and employers; and an independent competent body to assess the evidence, and make decisions and/or recommendations to government.

STEM the problem

As explained, there are insufficient graduates in STEM subjects to meet the growing number of STEM jobs being generated in the economy. The source of this difficulty is that far too many pupils, especially girls, disengage from mathematics and science during secondary school[153]. This leads to only one in 11 leaving sixth form with mathematics and physics A levels[154], and England's 16 to 19-year-olds having amongst the poorest numeracy skills in the developed world[155].

One cause cited for this disengagement is the pressure placed on pupils and schools to achieve the highest grades, with science and mathematics perceived as being 'hard' subjects[156]. Removing high stakes testing and reforming the national curriculum (see chapter 11) offer the potential for pupils to learn mathematics and science in a much more practical and relevant way, and therefore sustain their enthusiasm for these two key subjects throughout their time at school.

Another reason for the STEM shortage is that although girls get better mathematics and science results at GCSE[157], far fewer girls than boys go on to take these subjects at A level[158]. This carries through to university[159] and the workplace[160]. Only fifteen per cent of the STEM workforce[161] and just eight per cent of engineers are women[162], the lowest in Europe[163]. Increasing the number of girls and women pursuing mathematics and science post-16, therefore, would be one of the main vehicles for improving the supply of STEM graduates. There is some promise here, with a slight increase in the overall numbers taking STEM A levels[164], and a fifth more girls since 2010[165] (albeit from a very small base). One radically innovative approach to training engineers is the UK's first specialist engineering university to be opened in Hereford in 2020, and which will admit students without mathematics and physics A-levels, particularly aimed at attracting more young women. Students will not specialise, but train as generalist engineers, working on real projects rather than attending lectures[166].

The problem is exacerbated by many science, technology, engineering and mathematics graduates not being appointed to STEM jobs[167], particularly because they lack the necessary employability skills[168]. Our proposals for a more skills-based school curriculum, and for having an integrated academic and vocational curriculum, with compulsory work experience, for 14-19-year-olds, would substantially help to address this deficit in employability skills. It is also an issue that universities themselves need to tackle in better preparing their graduates for the world of work.

Overall it seems that a more active, sharper partnership effort is needed to increase the supply of STEM skills to meet the accelerating needs of the economy. Such an effort has to be led by the government in a way that involves schools, higher education and industry working together much more closely in promoting the study of STEM subjects and STEM jobs. It needs to be informed by a clearer understanding of why science and mathematics are such a turn-off for so many young people, and especially why those girls who do so well in these subjects at GCSE don't continue with them into A level and beyond.

Pipeline of digitally skilled talent needed

Earlier in this chapter we explained the substantial vacancies there are in specialist digital roles and the growing demand for these jobs. Some of the vacancies and additional jobs might well be suited to 'digitally native' young people who may currently be unemployed or in low-skilled occupations, who with training could help to plug the digital skills gap[169]. The Chief Executive of mobile network operator O2, Ronan Dunne, says that such 'young people possess valuable skills that will be the future fuel of our economy, but not enough is being done to harness them'[170].

From 2020 adults without basic digital skills will be able to undertake a course and obtain a digital skills qualification free of charge[171], but funding will have to come out of the existing adult education budget. To accompany this in October 2018 the government launched a consultation on new national standards on digital skills involving qualifications at levels one ('beginners') and two ('essential')[172]. Only the level one course will be free of charge. The government has also made an extra £64 million available to retrain people in digital and construction skills in the building industry[173]. In addition, the UK is to have an Institute of Coding to 'produce courses better aligned to industry needs'[174]. However, the government is being pressed 'to accelerate the attainment of digital literacy across the population' with 'action at all levels of the 'talent pipeline' – primary, secondary, further and higher level education' [175]. The following very insightful findings of major reviews carried out by a House of Lords Select Committee[176], Vodafone[177] and the UK chief executive of Siemens[178] provide a sound basis for systemically tackling the country's digital skills shortages:

• Engaging girls 'in all education phases'.
• Digital skills becoming a core subject in the school curriculum.
• Increasing the numbers of   specialist information technology teachers, and

ensuring they have up-to-date and industrially-relevant knowledge.

- Stronger partnerships between industry and further education colleges.
- More digital apprenticeships for specific occupations being offered, including to those returning to work after a career break, and digital training becoming a significant feature of all other apprenticeships.
- Through working more directly with employers, universities better aligning their computer science courses with industry needs, including making graduates 'work-ready'. (There is evidence that a significant proportion of computer science graduates are not in related employment or are unemployed, and that universities find it a challenge to keep up with rapidly changing technologies[179])
- Universities ensuring that all their graduates, irrespective of their subject, are digitally competent.
- Establishment of a new national body[180] to include representatives from industry, government and academia, to put Britain at the forefront of the new digital technologies including the upskilling of one million industrial workers[181].

Multiplicity of disjointed careers provision

Employers, employees and students stress the importance of having good careers services to help people access the right education, training and employment opportunities, but the evidence suggests that poor careers advice is contributing to skill shortages. In recent years careers advice for school leavers, adult learners and for those in work, has been marginalised.

National Careers Service not making positive impact

The coalition government set up the National Careers Service (NCS)[182] in 2012 (for all those aged thirteen and over), bringing together the previous services for young people (Connexions) and adults (Next Step). The record of the NCS has been particularly unimpressive. An advisory body to the government on careers provision, the National Careers Council (NCC)[183], in 2013 and 2014 issued two highly critical reports on the NCS[184], finding that 'the growing careers market is crowded, confused and complex with a multiplicity of disjointed careers provision. Progress [of the NCS] has been slow. Not enough action has been taken towards achieving a genuinely relevant all-age careers system'[185].

Since producing these reports the National Careers Council has been closed down. Another government-commissioned evaluation of the NCS was unable to identify any positive impact of the service helping its users into employment. Those who had used the service spent less time in employment than people in similar circumstances who hadn't used the service[186].

Careers advice for young people turned into 'ghost services'

Research[187] shows that good careers advice in schools can help pupils remain engaged with education and improve their education attainment. Statutory responsibility for careers guidance for teenagers transferred from local authorities to schools in 2012[188]. A review into the impact of this transfer by the House of Commons Education Committee[189] expressed concern 'about the consistency, quality, independence and impartiality of careers guidance now being offered to young people'. There had been, said the committee 'a worrying deterioration in the overall level of provision for young people. Too many schools lack the skills, incentives or capacity to fulfil the duty put upon [them]'. Only one in six schools' spending on careers is at the level that pertained prior to the transfer[190].

When they took on responsibility for careers, schools received 'weak statutory guidance and little help or support', resulting in a poor service and 'a postcode lottery where some young people have access to much better career guidance than others'[191]. Large numbers of pupils feel that current careers advice in schools is 'irrelevant'[192]. Research by Barnardo's[193] found that the transfer had resulted in 'a much-reduced and underfunded service which limits the choices and opportunities for young people to pursue their aspirations and gain meaningful, sustainable employment. In particular, the paucity of guidance and lack of funding for schools to deliver careers guidance leaves pupils with below average achievement, attainment and attendance without the necessary support to develop their ambitions'.

Because of substantial government funding cuts[194] Connexions, which ran careers guidance on behalf of local authorities, has been emasculated, becoming largely 'a phone and online service'. One of the authors of the Barnardo's research, Jonathan Rallings, says these changes 'risk squandering young futures by failing to guarantee sufficient vital face-to-face support for people who need it. Ghost services [are] being offered in place of meaningful advice'[195]. Other research finds that young and adult learners are often making poor choices in choosing which further education course to choose, and casts serious doubt on whether 'young people at school have access to impartial advice'[196]. Alongside this the House of Commons Public Accounts Committee found that school leavers are making critical choices about university 'on the basis of too little information', due 'in large part to insufficient and inconsistent careers advice'[197].

Notwithstanding these warnings of poor and deteriorating services, very little seems to have improved since the responsibility for careers transferred to schools and the NCS was set up six years ago. Most of those leaving school in 2018 say they didn't receive sufficient careers advice[198], never used a careers adviser[199], nor had they heard of the National Careers Service[200]. In December 2018, Chair of the House of Commons Education Select Committee, Robert Halfon, was scathing in his evaluation of the careers service saying that 'millions of children are missing out because careers support is in a dire state'. Mr. Halfon concluded that careers guidance for young people was 'far too fragmented... a confused mish-mash of offerings with different agencies providing bits here and uncoordinated pieces there. For the student it must be like trying to negotiate through Spaghetti Junction with all the signs pointing the wrong way.'[201]

The advice provided also seems to be skewed, with more than seven in ten young people having knowledge of university entrance, but less than four in ten of apprenticeships[202]. This is despite the government launching a careers strategy in December 2017 including £4 million to enable each secondary school and college to have a careers leader, and £5 million funding to develop 20 'careers hubs'[203]. This latter initiative is being led by the Careers and Enterprise Company that has been the subject of severe criticism by the House of Commons Education Select Committee for 'spending almost £1 million on research and not on frontline guidance for learners', calling the publicly-funded private company an 'overbloated quango'[204]. Adults seem equally ill-served by the current careers system. As we reported in chapter 9, adult learners see careers guidance as absolutely vital, but the majority were not fully aware of the services being offered by the National Careers Service[205].

Weak careers service impacts directly on skills

The weak system of careers advice has a direct impact on the effort to tackle the country's skills crisis. For example, the vast majority of teenagers would consider a career in a STEM related industry, but many don't know what jobs are available. This is not surprising, given that most science and mathematics teachers are unaware of the job opportunities for school leavers in these subject areas[206]. A parliamentary committee reviewing digital skills concluded that careers guidance is 'outdated and does not support the needs of the future digitally-skilled workforce'[207]. Carolyn Fairbairn, Director General of the employers' organisation the CBI, expresses similar misgivings, saying that 'The UK is facing a skills emergency. Careers advice in schools needs to be transformed if Britain is to prepare pupils for the jobs of the future'[208].

Better informed, more face-to-face careers advice for teenagers and adults needed

A review commissioned by the Sutton Trust[209] proposed that the NCS should provide schools with professional careers advisers, incentives to encourage schools and colleges to prioritise and invest in careers, Ofsted giving 'greater prominence' to inspections of careers services, and new statutory guidance informed by benchmarks of what constitutes good careers guidance. The review stressed the need for schools to have access to careers advisers who had expertise in vocational options and entry to universities. Research establishes that schools that have good careers advice have commitment from senior leadership, well-resourced and high quality careers staff, programmes starting at aged eleven or twelve, involvement of employers and post-school education and training providers, and provision of one-to-one career guidance. An all-party parliamentary group concluded that there was a need to 'improve awareness of and access to careers information, advice and guidance' for adult learners, and for them to have 'better informed careers guidance provision on progression pathways, including those in work'[210].

These findings lead us to make two suggestions for improving careers advice for all age groups. Firstly, based on the research evidence and good practice the government, after consultation, should issue statutory guidance that sets out minimum standards and provision for the careers guidance service that teenagers, graduates and adult learners should expect to receive. Secondly, the statutory guidance would be used to benchmark the adequacy and quality of services provided by schools, colleges, universities, the NCS and other careers providers. The outcomes from this benchmarking exercise would then inform a national plan for developing a 'fit for purpose' national careers service, including 'its structure, management, service provision and funding.

Promote more workplace training

Countries with high productivity have greater levels of on-the-job training and better management[211]. It is concerning, therefore, that the amount of training being undertaken in the workplace has declined in the last decade[212]. Only one in four employees now receives any form of work-based training, down from one in three 10 years ago; lower than any other country in the European Union[213]. The duration of training sessions has also fallen, as has the proportion of workers studying for a qualification[214], and most managers don't receive any training[215].

The best organisations carry out regular skills audits to tell them what they need and what they've presently got. Outcomes from these audits then inform workforce planning and development, which is about getting the right staff (recruitment), keeping staff (retention) and developing staff competence (training). Providing good training for staff can help organisations to recruit and retain employees, improve their employees' motivation and performance and improve their business' productivity, return on investment and competitiveness. There are four main vehicles through which organisations can provide their staff with the specific skills they will need to be effective in the workplace – on-the-job training, 'in-house' programmes, apprenticeships and sponsoring employees to undertake external courses.

There are two possible courses of action aimed at boosting workplace training. Firstly, the government could more actively promote work-based training to employers and provide a service to support organisations to get started or develop what they are already doing. Secondly, the government could explore what incentives there might be (including corporation tax allowances) to encourage organisations, particularly smaller ones, to initiate or extend in-house training. Complementary to this the government is consulting on extending current tax relief to support self-employed people and employees who are funding their own training[216], especially as the number of self-employed people continues to grow.

Conclusion – systemic long-term strategic drive is needed to solve skills crisis

The UK undoubtedly has a major skills problem, impacting on economic growth and productivity, and resulting in too many poor-quality jobs. There are multiple causes of this skills crisis, which means that there is no quick fix and that a long-term strategy is needed. None of the recent initiatives or ministerial announcements, however, have come anywhere close to what is needed.

In his first public speech on becoming Education Secretary, Damien Hinds struck some optimistic chords about skills. Schools said Mr. Hinds 'needed a mix of traditional academic subjects and a sense of "resilience" and skills'. He placed a big emphasis on digital skills and called for 'improvements in vocational training for adults'. All of this said Mr. Hinds was 'to prepare people for a shifting jobs market'[217]. But what was the new Education Secretary's first major decision – making skill development an integral part of the national curriculum; or perhaps having digital skills as a core subject; or maybe reversing some of the cuts to further and adult education to help adults retrain? No, it was to fund the expansion of grammar school places![218]

This vividly illustrates the single biggest obstacle in the way of creating the skills revolution that this country so desperately needs. It is cultural, deeply ingrained in the psyche of those who make the decisions on these critical matters – senior government ministers and civil servants. Virtually to a person they have one thing in common; they have travelled a path from grammar school or private school, through A levels, on to university, having never experienced a college of further education, an adult education centre or an apprenticeship. Despite their rhetoric about the importance of skills, in their heart of hearts they believe that the traditional academic education route is the best, and that is why for so long skills, vocational and technical education have been so marginalised, and the main reason we have a growing skills crisis.

Lord Sandy Leitch's review of skills, commissioned by Gordon Brown when he was Chancellor and published in 2006, set out the skills challenge the country faced in clear and stark terms[219]. It was ambitious, talking about the UK 'becoming a world leader in skills by 2020', and spelling out that this meant 'doubling attainment at most levels', improving 'functional literacy and numeracy' and the numbers of those with qualifications at levels 2, 3 and 4+ and apprenticeships. Significantly Lord Leitch argued that 'shifting the balance of... skills from level 2 to level 3' was vital. 'Employers, individuals and the Government' he said, 'must increase action and investment'. Workplace training needed to increase and 'a new universal adult careers service' be developed. Lord Leitch was emphatic that 'the new 14-19 Diplomas must succeed'. Of course, by the time the Leitch report was published the 14-19 diplomas (the major recommendation of the Tomlinson report) were already truly dead and buried.

The year 2020 is fast approaching and we can see that we haven't travelled a great deal from the position that Lord Leitch described over twelve years ago. In 2030 (in another twelve years' time) will we be looking back at another period of wasted opportunity because successive governments have failed to grasp the necessity of having a comprehensive skills strategy? To be successful such a strategy has to tackle all the main causes of the skills problem we have – too many children raised in unstimulating home environments; a school curriculum that marginalises skill development and vocational education; poorly funded further and adult education; unplanned higher education with shortages of STEM graduates; inadequate careers guidance; and a demise in workplace training. If we don't tackle these issues in a systematic, determined and sustained way we are likely, as Lord Leitch put it, to 'condemn ourselves to a lingering decline in competitiveness, diminishing economic growth and a bleaker future for all'.

Recommendations

- *National long-term strategy* aimed at generating the range of skills that the nation needs, including basic skills, employability and occupationally specific skills.
- Strengthen *further education* by having a financial settlement that provides

sufficient resources to deliver the national priorities, including programmes for school leavers without good qualifications, adult returners, basic skills and apprenticeships. Establish a single national body to provide strong and cohesive leadership, funding and quality oversight.

- Institute a major renewal of the national *apprenticeships* programme. Improve recruitment by promoting the benefits of apprenticeships, introduce a UCAS-style process for applications and appointments, and make the remuneration of apprentices far more attractive. Revise the apprenticeship levy fund, making it less bureaucratic and easier to access, by: paying the full cost of training for all apprenticeships; increasing the proportion of the levy fund that can be transferred by large companies to smaller companies in their supply chain; providing more financial support to small businesses; and extending the time limit for employers to access funding from two to four years. Develop consistent quality apprenticeships through: speeding up the development and publication of the apprenticeship standards; instituting more robust procedures for accrediting training providers; having a more systematic evaluation of apprenticeship programmes, including early monitoring visits to new providers, regular inspections of training providers, and intensive development work for those providers that require major improvement. Create a powerful single national body to lead and deliver apprenticeships, with devolvement of certain planning and delivery functions to sub-regions.

- Establish a core purpose for *higher education* to meet both the broad and specific skill needs of the country, including skill gaps. Replace the current 'laissez-faire' way of determining university courses and student numbers with one that is more needs-led and nationally planned.

- Establish a partnership of schools, higher education and industry to develop and implement a more targeted strategy to increase the supply of *STEM* skills, informed by a better understanding of why so many pupils, particularly girls, disengage from science and mathematics.

- Produce and implement a national *digital skills* strategy. Identify digitally aware young people to be trained to take up specialist digital roles. Make digital skills a core subject of the school national curriculum. Launch a campaign to specifically encourage girls to develop their digital skills. Promote different routes for training specialist information technology teachers and ensuring they have up-to-date industry-relevant knowledge.

Offer more digital apprenticeships for specific occupations. Universities to ensure that their computer science courses are aligned with employer needs, that their graduates are 'work-ready', and that graduates in all subject areas are digitally competent.

- Develop a fit-for-purpose *careers* service. Draw up statutory guidance with minimum standards and service that teenagers, graduates and adult learners should be entitled to. The current careers service to be reviewed against the statutory guidance benchmarks, from which a national plan for improving careers advice for all age groups can be prepared and implemented.

- Government to actively promote *workplace training* by providing a high quality advice service to employers, and exploring what further financial incentives might be offered to encourage employers to start or expand their in-house training.

Previous chapters contain recommendations that will contribute to enhancing the nation's skills base – family support (chapter 10); and greater emphasis on skills, vocational and creative studies in a revised school national curriculum (chapter 11).

13
TACKLING UNDERACHIEVEMENT

Optimism is the faith that leads to achievement.
Nothing can be done without hope and confidence.
Helen Keller

Whilst the education performance of our highest achievers compares well with other countries, the UK has one of the largest proportions of young people and adults with poor education attainment and skills in the developed world. This underachievement is the major cause of why the UK has such high levels of social and economic exclusion, and major skill shortages.

Long tail of underperformance: Half our future

One of the most influential educational texts of the 1960s and 70s was the report of a review colloquially known after its main author, Sir John Newsom, entitled *Half Our Future*[1]. This report vividly expressed a major national concern of the time that substantial numbers of young people were leaving school not well prepared for adulthood and the world of work. The title of the report was inspired by Benjamin Disraeli's[2] comment that 'Upon the education of the people of this country the fate of this country depends'[3]. Given the transformative scientific and technological changes of the intervening years, Disraeli's words ring even truer today than when he uttered them nearly a century and a half ago. Equally the concerns highlighted by the Newsom report (of significant numbers of young people underachieving) are still present today, albeit in greatly different circumstances than pertained over fifty years ago.

Given the currency that five good GCSEs including English and mathematics have today, and that just over half achieve these, 'half our future' may still be an appropriate catchphrase for the burning educational issue of underachievement we face in the current age. The Newsom report's clarion call of 1963 is highly applicable to the challenge we face today.

> *Our pupils constitute, approximately, half the pupils of our secondary schools; they will eventually become half the citizens of this country, half the workers, half the mothers and fathers and half the consumers. We are concerned that there should be a change of attitude towards these young people not only among many of those who control their education but among the public at large and this cannot be achieved solely, if at all, by administrative action. It involves a change of thinking and even more a change of heart. But there is no time to waste. Half our future is in their hands. We must see that it is in good hands[4].*

Newsom's main recommendation was to raise the school leaving age from fifteen to sixteen (which came into effect in 1972). But the report also emphasised issues that continue to be highly pertinent today including strengthening vocational education, the arts, personal and social development, careers advice, further education and the youth service[5]. How, then, do we go about tackling the modern equivalent of 'half our future'? Firstly we need to define what is meant by the 'long tail of underperformance'. We do so by delving into two measures – school attainment, and what might be considered as the more 'real-life' measure of workplace skills.

Large minority underachieve – an unacceptable waste of human potential

Five good GCSEs (grades A*-C/4-9) including English and mathematics, achieved by just over half of sixteen year-olds[6], is the main passport to advanced apprenticeships, employment in the professions, A levels and higher education. Only a third are on A-level courses[7]. The significant numbers of youngsters not obtaining good GCSEs contributes to one in seven young adults not being in education, employment and training[8]; an apprenticeship system skewed towards the over twenty-fives, low-level qualifications and poor-quality training; major skills shortages; and large numbers of low-skilled, low-paid, insecure jobs. There is an ability gap between children from low-income families and those from better-off homes when they start school, and this widens as they go through school[9], a gap which is one of the highest in the developed world[10]. As we saw in chapter 7, there are lower levels of educational achievement amongst those from low-income families, black Caribbean and white backgrounds (especially boys), and in the north and Midlands of England.

A significant proportion of teenagers then leave school each year without the qualifications and skills needed to progress well educationally or obtain quality employment. Many of these youngsters lack 'work-readiness' skills - a mixture of low-level basic cognitive skills[11], poor social and communication skills, and negative attitudes and behaviours. A significant barrier to tackling such underachievement is the rigidity of our age-determined qualifications system; the belief, for example, that if you don't get good GCSEs at age 16 you have failed and cannot progress any further. For the vast majority of youngsters who don't do well in their GCSEs this turns out to be the case i.e. what they do at this stage in their life determines the rest of it. It is more cultural than real, but in reality young people in this situation feel that there is no route back into education[12]. As Helena Kennedy QC pithily says 'If at first you don't succeed... you don't succeed'[13]. This is re-enforced by a testing culture that constantly tells significant numbers of children that they are 'failing'.

There are fundamental consequences of this underachievement, most importantly for the individuals concerned. The sense of 'failure' is tangible for those young people who leave school without the qualifications and skills to further their education, or secure jobs that offer quality training, a career and the prospects of decent remuneration. For many who 'underachieve' there are significant personal effects including low self-esteem, confidence and ambition, which can be lifelong. For example, it is estimated that there are over five million adults in England who are functionally illiterate[14]. The societal consequences are also evident – deep inequality and social division, and a failure to provide the economy and public services with the skills they need to prosper and grow. If nothing changes, and as scientific and technological change accelerates, these skill shortages and the economic exclusion of 'underachieving' individuals, will worsen. Former chief inspector, Sir Michael Wilshaw, summed this up succinctly when he said 'A large minority of children still do not succeed at school or college, becoming increasingly less visible as they progress through the system. This unseen body of children and young people that underachieve throughout our education system represents an unacceptable waste of human potential and incurs huge subsequent costs for all of us'[15].

Having defined the nature and scale of underachievement, we now put forward some ways of tackling this phenomenon through addressing the main causes as well as suggesting some specific initiatives. By far the most significant cause of underachievement is children experiencing negative and unstimulating home lives. Alongside this, a school curriculum skewed by a narrow range of national tests and examinations and school performance measures, helps to turn many children off learning. We will also explore how excluding pupils from school contributes to the levels of underachievement, and the role that private tutoring might have in tackling underachievement. Finally, we examine how well children with special educational needs are being supported.

Family support to tackle underachievement that starts in the home

We know that the quality of a child's home environment has the most influence on their future life chances including their engagement with and outcomes from school[16]. This is illustrated in blunt terms by former chief inspector, Sir Michael Wilshaw, saying that the country is 'not doing enough about the long tail of underachievement, which is one of the worst in the OECD, made up mainly of poor children, mainly made up of white British children from low-income backgrounds'[17]. Sir Michaels's successor, Amanda Spielman, is clear that from the evidence collected by her inspectors, white working-class children have fallen behind because their families often 'lack the aspiration and drive seen in many migrant communities'[18]. Ofsted's judgement is backed up by the results of phonics testing that shows that white children have poorer reading skills at the age of five than those from other ethnic groups[19].

Previously we proposed that a national family strategy aimed at improving children's life chances should be at the heart of the programme of government. Local multi-agency family support services would be established across the country with a primary purpose of promoting a culture of learning in all families. The relationship of these services with families would be a long-term one, prioritising those households where children are most at risk of not achieving good educational and other quality of life outcomes. We envisage that over time this strategy would mean that more and more children would start school with the social and cognitive skills needed to fully benefit from the opportunities that school offers. Alongside this, increasing numbers of parents would positively engage with their children's schools, creating the productive partnerships between home and school that is so vital to children's progress and achievement.

Develop a curriculum for all

The overwhelming majority of pupils start secondary school with 'initial enthusiasm' as to how they feel about school, and their attitudes to teachers and school attendance, but this substantially diminishes during the first two years. A third of year 9 pupils report that they are bored with school[20]. Ofsted found that in 'too many schools' Key Stage 3 represented 'wasted years' for a large number of pupils[21], with the 'quality of teaching [which failed to challenge and engage pupils] and the rate of pupils' progress and achievement not [being] good enough'. A major cause of these 'wasted years' was a 'lack of priority given to Key Stage 3 by many secondary school leaders' who gave preference to Key Stage 4 in all major aspects of policy and decision making, including the timetabling of teachers, building on prior learning, monitoring pupils' progress, homework and use of pupil premium for disadvantaged pupils. This reinforces the pernicious influence of the overwhelming pressure put on schools by the high stakes nature of GCSEs.

Ofsted also found that many secondary schools do not have a productive enough working arrangement with primary schools and as a result don't have a good understanding of pupils' prior learning. Alarmingly Ofsted report that 'some secondary leaders simply accepted that pupils would repeat what they had already done in primary school during the early part of Key Stage 3'.

Too many young people are leaving school having been turned off learning, with low attainment levels, lacking confidence and not wishing to return to education[22]. The reasons given by young people for their disengagement are that they don't receive the personal attention they feel they need, and are bored in lessons. According to the young people, boredom is due to the heavy use of repetitive worksheets, listening, reading and copying; and the speed that teachers go through the curriculum, placing greater importance on completing the lesson as planned, more than meeting the needs of individual students, causing many of them to be 'left behind'. This is a product of an over-prescriptive national curriculum and a 'high stakes' examinations system, where schools and teachers are pressurised into covering the curriculum in a timely manner and focusing on those pupils who are most likely to get good results. Many disaffected young people also feel that the highly structured (didactic) way that they were taught (listening to the teacher and recording what they said) didn't suit them, and that they would have done better from 'learning while doing'[23].

The key to engaging all pupils in meaningful learning and enabling them to achieve positive outcomes is having a school curriculum that stimulates and sustains their interest. That is why we have proposed ending statutory testing in schools (up to the age of eighteen), and radically revising the national curriculum, including a curriculum and qualifications for 14 to 19-year-olds that integrate academic and vocational studies. These measures would remove the perverse incentive for schools to narrow the curriculum and make policy decisions that disadvantage non-examination year groups and classes.

The proposal to set up local school improvement partnerships would facilitate the more productive cross-phase partnerships to improve the transition of pupils from Key Stages two to three that Ofsted is calling for[24]. Maybe, however, there is a need to go further than this. Primary and secondary schools are radically different in a number of ways. Secondary schools are far larger institutions, both in terms of buildings and pupil numbers (they have on average five times more pupils than primaries[25]), and pupils in secondary schools are organised in an acutely different manner than in primary schools. While in primary schools a pupil's principal relationship is with the one teacher, who teaches her/him the vast majority of lessons, in secondary s/he will be taught each subject by a specialist teacher, usually ten or more different teachers each week.

Vulnerable children are usually managed well in primary schools. Most youngsters adapt successfully to their new secondary school environment, but for many vulnerable children, going from a small primary school to a large secondary school can be a big shock. Moving from one class to many throughout the school day, and not having the security and stability of a single class teacher, can be highly disruptive and traumatic for such children, and something they often don't recover from. These pupils can become withdrawn, school refusers, poorly behaved and be excluded, and as a result their learning suffers. We would suggest that some specific research is commissioned to identify the reasons why some children find the transition into secondary school so difficult, what the impact of this is on the rest of their education; and what measures could be introduced to improve the experiences of these pupils (for example in terms of transition planning, how secondary schools organise their pupils, and pastoral care).

Strengthen in-school behaviour support and cease permanent exclusions

Poor behaviour by pupils and their exclusion from school have a major impact on achievement levels. Persistent poor behaviour not only badly affects the learning of pupils who perpetrate it, but also that of other children[26]. Only one per cent of young people permanently excluded from school get five good GCSEs[27], and their long-term quality of life outcomes tend to be poor. For example, former excluded pupils make up half the UK prison population[28].

In the last five years there have been substantial increases in the number of pupils being excluded from school, both on a permanent and fixed-term basis[29]. More than eight in ten exclusions are from secondary schools[30], the majority made in the run-up to GCSEs[31]. While official data shows that around 6,500 are permanently excluded each year, there are 48,000 in alternative provision[32] for excluded pupils[33]. The main explanation for this anomaly is that alternative provision includes tens of thousands of pupils who have been excluded from school, but without going through the statutory procedures, and are, therefore, not included in the government statistics. In addition parents choose, often with the complicity of, or persuasion from schools, to electively home educate their children in order to avoid recording a permanent exclusion[34].

A number of reasons are cited why exclusions, both official and unofficial, are rising, but a major one is the pressure on schools to deliver good GCSE results. This pressure is such that there is an incentive for schools to permanently exclude those who are poorly behaved, who are unlikely to get decent GCSE outcomes, and who may well be disrupting the education of other examination pupils[35]. Another reason is the growing numbers of pupils with complex and demanding needs including mental ill-health and emotional trauma caused by parental neglect and family circumstances[36], who find it difficult to cope with the pressure of school life.

Young people permanently excluded are largely from the poorest families[37], with three times more boys than girls[38], and a significantly disproportionate number from black Caribbean backgrounds[39]. Half of those excluded have a recognised mental health need[40] and eight out of ten have special education needs or a disability[41]. Children under the age of five, some as young as two years old, are excluded from nurseries and schools, and sent to alternative provision[42]. Permanently excluded pupils tend to end up in 'alternative provision' and are twice as likely as pupils in schools to be taught by unqualified staff[43].

The House of Commons Education Committee[44] raised some serious concerns about exclusions. These included 'zero-tolerance' behaviour practices leading to exclusions of pupils that 'could and should be managed within the mainstream school environment'; schools 'off-rolling' pupils who are not making required progress into alternative provision, home education or other schools; disproportionate numbers of disadvantaged pupils being excluded; and a lack of clarity about where responsibility for excluded pupils lay, resulting in many 'falling through the net'. In its report the committee concluded that 'an unfortunate and unintended consequence of the Government's strong focus on school standards has led to school environments and practices that have resulted in disadvantaged children being disproportionately excluded, which includes a curriculum with a lack of focus on developing pupils' social and economic capital'[45].

Education secretary, Damien Hinds, has set up a review of exclusions[46]. His comments that pupils should only be permanently excluded as a 'last resort', are to be welcomed, as is his wish to 'see the number of children who are excluded from school coming down'[47]. We believe there is a need to go much further. There is a place for fixed-term exclusions, especially in enabling a 'cooling off period' for children who have behaved badly, and to give time to put plans and programmes in place for when the pupil returns to school. The rules around fixed-term exclusions need to be reviewed as some children can be excluded for excessive amounts of time and on a persistent basis, but we suggest that the government should give serious consideration to doing away altogether with permanent exclusions. We take what many might see as a bold and risky step, because of the evidence of what happens to youngsters once they are permanently excluded in terms of their education outcomes and future social and economic lives. As one headteacher poignantly puts it, 'Permanent exclusions are consigning certain children to the dumpster'[48].

We propose that pupils who previously would have been permanently excluded stay on school rolls, and headteachers exercise their powers to exclude them 'internally', either into a school facility or to a joint provision run by a consortium of schools (both of which already exist). The aim of this 'internally excluded' provision would be to support the pupil to return to the mainstream of the school once it was assessed that his/her behaviour was positive enough for this to be beneficial both to the individual pupil and the school as a whole. This would allow for youngsters to be 'phased' back into mainstream classes on a carefully planned and supported basis. There will be exceptions – individual young people, for example, who have developed serious mental health problems causing such extreme behaviour that cannot reasonably be accommodated in mainstream settings. Special arrangements will need to be made for such pupils, as there are now.

Make private tutoring available for 'underachieving' pupils

Support that children receive outside of school, including private tutoring (usually organised by parents), can be a significant factor in helping them to progress their learning. The use of this type of additional educational support for children is quite extensive and on the increase, with more than a quarter of pupils receiving private tuition, an increase of fifty per cent since 2005[49]. Pupils have private tuition to prepare them for entrance examinations for private or grammar schools, specific GCSE exams and school work in general[50]. As you might expect, the take-up is uneven with private tuition used more in London than elsewhere[51], by affluent families more than poorer households[52], by those from ethnic minorities more than white pupils[53], and by two-parent families more than single parents[54]. Private tutoring, therefore, plays a part in creating and accentuating educational advantage and disadvantage.

Having researched private tuition, the Sutton Trust makes two main recommendations for improving access to this additional educational support for school pupils - a means-tested voucher scheme for tuition funded from schools' pupil premium monies, and expanding the free private tutoring for low-income pupils provided by charities and tuition agencies[55]. While a voucher system along the lines proposed by the Sutton Trust[56] could make an important contribution to tackling underachievement, we do not believe it is right for this to be funded from the pupil premium allocations that schools receive for their most needy pupils. How the free tutoring provided by charities and tuition agencies can be extended to more young people needs to be actively explored. We believe, however, that a more radical step is required, and we are proposing that the government bring in a national volunteer home tutoring scheme for those children and young people most in need of additional educational support.

Thousands of children with special needs missing out on support

In 2014 the government boldly announced that its major changes for providing support to children with special educational needs and disabilities (SEND)[57] would 'offer simpler, improved and consistent help' to these youngsters. The then Children and Families Minister, Edward Timpson, heralded it as 'a landmark moment'. According to Mr. Timpson school budgets would be protected, and children and parents would be at the heart of the system'[58]. Just over four years later the Chief Inspector, Amanda Spielman, describes SEND provision in England as a 'bleak picture' of too many children 'failed by the education system'[59].

SEND broadly covers children that have 'significantly greater difficulty in learning than the majority of others of the same age' or 'a disability which prevents or hinders [children] from making use of facilities of a kind generally provided for others of the same age'[60]. In England one in five children has SEND[61]; 1.3 million pupils have been identified as having special education needs[62]. How well children with SEND are supported, therefore, is a significant factor in tackling educational underachievement.

Detailed and specific duties are placed on local authorities, health trusts, schools and others by the SEND Code of Practice[63]. The Code requires schools to identify those children who may have SEND, assess their needs and put individual support plans in place to enable these pupils to achieve the best possible educational outcomes. Parents, young people aged sixteen or over, or schools can request that the local authority consider carrying out a multi-agency education, health and care (EHC) assessment. This is usually for more acute or complex cases, and/or where the pupil is not making 'expected progress'[64]. In such circumstances an assessment may result in the issuing of an Education, Health and Care Plan (EHCP)[65] setting out the child's needs and the specific support required to meet these, which is statutorily binding on all agencies.

There are serious concerns about the provision for children with SEND. The needs of many children with the most challenging conditions are not being met. Demand for EHC assessments has risen by a half since 2015. In 2017/18, while 45,200 children were assessed, 14,600 were refused an assessment, a third more than in 2015. Ofsted suggest that 'Often the worst hand is dealt to those who do not quite meet the threshold for an EHC plan'. Between 2010 and 2016/17, the number of children with an EHCP who received no provision increased from around 800 to more than 4,000. By 2017/18 this had been reduced to 2,060, still more than double what it was eight years previously[66].

A consequence of the growing demand for support at the higher end of the SEND spectrum, are moves to 'reduce the number of children diagnosed with lower levels of special needs' and shift the cost of supporting more pupils with SEND to schools. These moves add further pressure on schools struggling with budget cuts. Furthermore, Ofsted report that the special needs of too many children are 'inaccurately' assessed or identified too late, which 'exacerbates [these] children's needs and put[s] even greater strain on the need for services'. Ofsted also describe SEND provision as 'disjointed and inconsistent'. Finally it is extremely perturbing that in secondary schools, over a quarter of pupils with SEND receive fixed-term exclusions and are five times more likely to have been permanently excluded than their peers. With 6,000 SEND pupils leaving their school between years 10 and 11, there are strong reasons to believe that many of these have been 'illegally' removed because they are difficult to teach and would damage schools' GCSE results[67].

There are clearly some fundamental weaknesses in the system for identifying and supporting children with SEND, cutting across the lofty ambitions of the government when they launched their reforms in 2014. Insufficient resources are certainly a cause of the problem. In response, at the end of 2018 the Education Secretary announced an extra £350 million over the next two years for SEND[68];

but will this be enough, given the enormous demand that is evident? While it will be necessary to look again at providing adequate funding to meet need and demand, there are clearly other, more qualitative, issues to tackle. Given the inherent deficiencies, and being eight years on from the introduction of the current SEND system, is it not time to have an independent review of how well the needs of children and young people with SEND are being provided for?

Conclusion: Determined effort needed to tackle 'long tail of underperformance'

The high levels of educational underachievement represent the single biggest failing of the UK's system of learning, blighting millions of lives, and creating great inequality and major skill shortages. As there are multiple causes, only a determined multi-pronged effort can be successful in starting to reduce the 'long tail of underperformance'. There are four areas that should be the focus of this effort.

Firstly, implementing the plans for *family* support that are detailed in chapter 10. The main objective of the local family support services will be to enable all children to be 'school-ready', providing them with the personal skills to positively engage with school and achieve their learning potential.

Secondly, reforms are needed to allow *schools* to prioritise the learning and achievement of all pupils and not just those who are likely to acquire the prescribed national attainment targets. For schools to be able to do this they have to be freed up from the current pernicious accountability regime. This means reducing the number of statutory examinations and tests, re-focusing the inspection system, and having a genuinely broad and balanced curriculum, with teachers empowered to implement it in a way that engages all pupils. While local school improvement partnerships will provide a vehicle for improving children's transition between primary and secondary school, there is a need to better understand why some children find these moves especially traumatic, so that these problems can be addressed. Changes are also needed to the regulations and practice relating to school exclusions including stopping children being permanently excluded from school, as this leads to all but a handful leaving compulsory education without qualifications, adversely impacting the rest of their lives.

Thirdly, there should be encouragement and incentives (and possibly legislation and funding) for schools to establish '*compacts*' with colleges, universities and employers to give pupils, particularly those who potentially will underachieve, clear routes to quality apprenticeships, and further and higher education courses. Employers, colleges and universities would offer the schools specific pathways for named students into apprenticeships or onto courses, subject to those students meeting certain pre-determined requirements along the way. These requirements could be qualifications or/and demonstrating other attributes such as working hard, positive behaviour, school attendance and punctuality, and helping and working well with others. Managed effectively these pathways could provide students with clear achievable goals, giving them a direction in life and including those who may otherwise become disaffected.

Fourthly, *supplementary* (extra-school) *learning* has an important part to play in combatting underachievement. Greater support for supplementary schools, as well as better utilising the array of resources in private schools, universities and businesses to help children and young people with their learning, are needed. In addition we propose setting up a national mentoring and personal tutoring scheme, made up of volunteers, to be recruited and managed at a local level. Core personnel would be employed to recruit, train, deploy and manage tens of thousands of volunteers to work with young people and adults with poor basic skills. Volunteers could include the growing army of retired people, higher education students and those in work.

Finally, far more funding is required to enable local authorities and schools to effectively support all children with *SEND*. It is also vital for there is an independent review of the needs of, and provision for, SEND to ensure that the right resources, procedures, and professional expertise and practice are put in place.

Recommendations

- The government to commission research to establish the reasons why the *transition from primary to secondary school* impacts adversely on the learning of many vulnerable children, in order to identify what steps can be taken to improve the experiences of these pupils.
- Promote and support schools in establishing '*compacts*' with colleges,

universities and employers to provide pupils, particularly those at risk of underachieving, with clear routes to quality apprenticeships, and further and higher education courses.

• *End permanent school exclusions* and strengthen provision within individual schools and groups of schools for managing the education of poorly behaved children.

• Set up a *national mentoring and personal tutoring scheme* of volunteers, to be recruited and co-ordinated at a local level.

• Institute an *independent review of SEND*; the government to act on its findings.

Previous chapters make other recommendations that will significantly contribute to combatting underachievement – supplementary schools (chapter 9); family support (chapter 10); tests, examinations and curriculum (chapter 11).

14
CONCLUSION: A MANIFESTO FOR LEARNING

The case for building a strong learning nation is an overwhelming one. The extent to which that mission is achieved will determine what kind of country we, our children and grandchildren will in the future be living in. Much will depend on the country's capacity to learn, both individually and collectively, and how well that learning is applied to improve the quality of people's lives, be that to do with health, the environment, economic prosperity or how people work and live together.

Strong case for fundamentally reviewing our system of learning

In the thirty years since the passing of the 1988 Act we have seen substantial increases in the number of young people in England and the UK leaving school with good academic qualifications[1] and going to university[2]. However, this shows only one side of the coin; on the other is a country with one of the highest levels of underachievement in the developed world. It shows the deep divisions within our society, between those who have benefitted from our academically driven, pass/fail learning system, and those who have been left increasingly behind without marketable skills and quality employment. Successive governments have used the provisions of the 1988 Act to take an ever tightening grip on the running of schools. In doing so, governments have used their main instruments of control - testing and inspections – to mechanistically hold schools to account, more than to benefit children's learning. Unintended, but extremely concerning consequences of this excessive controlling culture have been the increases in child mental ill-health, significant numbers of pupils underachieving, and major difficulties in retaining and recruiting teachers and school leaders.

The country as a whole has therefore suffered. Governments' obsession with testing and examinations has led to a narrowing of the school curriculum and the marginalisation of creative, vocational and technical education. This restriction of the curriculum, combined with the underperformance of a great minority of young people, have been the main causes of the substantial skill shortages across key areas of the British economy and public services. The skills crisis, together with the UK's poor education performance compared to other countries, places the UK at a distinct disadvantage in competing successfully in global markets, particularly at a time when we are about to leave the European Union.

Alongside this, governments have failed to back lifelong learning. Governments since 2010, for example, have cut the funds of those services that traditionally have re-engaged young people and adults – the youth service, adult and further education and the Open University – by over a quarter. At the same time funding for higher education (for those already on a successful education path) has been increased by a similar proportion. Most critically family life, the single most important influence on a child's ability to learn, has been largely ignored in shaping national education policy.

Underachievement and skills shortages – main failings of our system of learning

Reflecting on the mass of research, reviews and other evidence used for this book, we have come to the conclusion that there are two main ways in which our system of learning is failing. Firstly, significant numbers of young people and adults are underachieving. These levels of underachievement are amongst the highest in the developed world, and are the principal contributory factor to the second failing – the country's major skills shortage. The scale of these deficiencies has a debilitating effect on individuals (in terms of the quality of their work and social lives) as well as on the country's economic health. Alongside this, the undue stress of testing and inspections on pupils and staff is a significant factor in growing child mental ill-health, and the main cause of the teacher retention and recruitment crisis we have.

By changing nothing, nothing changes[3]

Nothing will change unless this or a future government can be persuaded to do so. There are some small signs for optimism. The current government and other national leaders at least recognise that some aspects of the current system are not working well.

Mental health has been championed by the Prime Minister. Some additional funding has been provided and school-based initiatives announced seeking to improve children's mental health. There is an awareness of the chronic skills shortages, an ambition to have more apprenticeships, and plans for new vocational qualifications (T-levels). Education Secretary Damien Hinds has warned that we have become a nation of 'technical education snobs' because 'opinion formers, commentators and... politicians' see vocational courses as being 'for other people's children'[4]. Attempts have been made, including the Troubled Families Programme, to create better home lives for children. Damien Hinds, in response to the poor vocabulary of many children in their early years of schooling, has called an education summit of businesses, charities, technology companies and media groups to 'encourage more parents to read and learn new words with their children'[5]. Mr. Hinds has acknowledged that workload is the main cause of the teacher retention and recruitment problems. He has also implied that skills should be a more important part of the school curriculum. Theresa May, on the steps of 10 Downing Street on the day she became prime minister, spoke passionately about 'fighting against... burning injustice'. 'If you're a white, working-class boy' she said 'you're less likely than anybody else in Britain to go to university', and 'If you're at a state school, you're less likely to reach the top professions than if you're educated privately[6].

Chief inspector, Amanda Spielman, has highlighted how the pressure of examinations and testing has created a 'tick box' culture in early years, narrowed the school curriculum, and led to some schools excluding pupils with learning and behavioural difficulties. Ofsted says that a revised inspection framework (to be introduced from September 2019) will be place less emphasis on examination results and more on the 'quality of education', focusing on the richness and breadth of the curriculum[7]. Ms. Spielman has also exposed the poor quality of many apprenticeship programmes. Children's Commissioner, Anne Longfield, has reported on what she describes as the 'shocking' situation in regard to growing child mental ill-health. Various cross-party parliamentary committees have produced well-researched reviews that have heavily criticised key aspects of government policy and practice including SATs, apprenticeships, digital skills, child mental health, family support, higher education, teacher and school leader retention and recruitment, and careers guidance.

These tiny glimmers of hope, however, fade rapidly when you closely examine the government's record in responding to these major areas of concern. There seems to be a huge chasm between the government's sentiments and their understanding of what needs to be done to make the step changes that are necessary, as we now illustrate.

The government seem unwilling to face up to the fact that its intensive 'high stakes' testing of young people is a major cause of the increasing mental health problems that children are experiencing. Nor to the adverse impact on tackling mental illness of the savage cuts made to preventative services. Nor to the reality that specialist mental health services are grossly under-resourced. There is a naïveté also in believing that schools are the main vehicles for solving growing mental ill-health amongst children.

Ministers show little sign that they understand the nature of the skills crisis, and that it has multiple causes. Government policies strengthen the cultural bias against vocational and technical education, which is at the heart of the skills problem we have. There have been massive reductions in college budgets, an emphasis on the quantity and not the quality of apprenticeships, the move to an unplanned higher education system, and the dismantling of decent careers guidance services. Above all else the narrowing of the secondary school curriculum, particularly with the introduction of the EBacc school performance measure, has further marginalised technical, vocational, creative and skill-based studies. All of these have contributed to the worsening skills situation we have in this country. At first sight T-levels appear to be a step in the right direction. Like many other government initiatives, it seems they are being rushed in without adequate preparation[8]. More fundamentally it is highly unlikely that T-levels will do anything to challenge the lack of parity between academic and vocational qualifications, which is at the heart of the country's skills problems. They are likely to go the same way as the other distinct vocational qualifications (such as BTECs) popularly seen as second class alternatives to A levels.

The quick fix 'payment by fast results' attitude that underpinned the Troubled Families Programme (TFP) led, hundreds of millions of pounds later, to it having no effect on the quality of the families that it was meant to help. Most significantly, however, the failure of TFP can be attributed to the government's own failure to recognise the generational nature of the problems many families have, and that only a patient long-term approach will have any chance of working.

Damian Hinds accepts that teachers 'are being overwhelmed by excessive workloads' that are 'pushing [them] out of the classroom', although he mistakenly puts the responsibility for this on schools, teachers and parents, rather than the government's high stakes testing and inspection policies, introducing a toolkit 'showing school staff how to ditch time-consuming issues such as onerous marking policies and demanding parents'. He has 'rebuked primary schools that put pressure on young pupils to do well in their national assessments or Sats', when the future of schools, their leaders and teachers depend on getting positive outcomes from these tests[9].

Four key principles vital to building a strong learning nation

Although there are many well-presented and valid criticisms of the current system, we have not seen any overall alternative being articulated. The system of learning in this country should and can be run in a different and better way. At the end of each of the last four chapters we put forward a comprehensive list of recommendations. We have done so to illustrate that there is substance behind the alternative we are putting forward, not to offer up a set of hard-and-fast, must-do changes. If we are to be successful in tackling the nation's 'long tail of underperformance' and skills crisis, however, a fundamental sea change in thinking and action is required. There are four key principles needed to guide us. These principles centre on the importance of:

1. *Looking holistically at learning, seeing it as continuous and inclusive, not a once in a lifetime chance to succeed or fail.* In a world of continuous change, the need for lifelong learning is axiomatic. All the key elements of learning including family life, learning from day-to-day experiences, school, and pre- and post-school education, need to be embraced and

developed. The government has to take the lead in creating the conditions within which lifelong learning for all can thrive – raising awareness of the importance and benefits of continuous learning, and helping people to have the motivation and good basic skills needed to progress through the learning system. In particular, services that traditionally have helped young people and adults re-engage with learning (including the youth service, further and adult education, and careers service) need to be substantially strengthened. Being inclusive means tackling underachievement head-on through a comprehensive multi-faceted strategy, vigorously implemented, nationally and locally, through support for families, school reforms, ending permanent exclusions, supporting supplementary education, strengthening provision for children with SEND, and setting up a nationwide personal tutoring and mentoring scheme.

2. *Supporting families*. While most children grow up in stable, loving and stimulating families, a substantial number do not, and this is the main source of underachievement. For this reason we contend that family life should be at the heart of the programme of government, including in the pursuit of building a strong learning nation. There needs to be a national families' strategy, with services in each local area that work with households where children are at serious risk of underachieving. Such a strategy needs to be underpinned by a clear understanding of what children growing up are entitled to, with the respective responsibilities of parents and the state made explicit. Parents should be given a realistic economic choice of looking after their very young children at home as opposed to using a care provider. Major investment is needed in the grossly under-resourced preventative and specialist child mental health services.

3. *Changing the cultural bias against technical and vocational education* including having a more skills and vocationally orientated school curriculum. An important element of this reform would be a 14-19 curriculum integrating academic and vocational studies, with mandatory work experience for all students. There should be a systematic approach to tackling the multiple causes of the country's substantial skills deficit including supporting families, reforming the school curriculum, strengthening further and adult education,

and better aligning higher education to the broad skill requirements of the economy. A major cultural shift is needed so that apprenticeships become a real option of choice for school leavers and adults. The national apprenticeship programme needs to be of consistent high quality and meet the nation's specific skill requirements. Careers guidance services need to be made fit for purpose, and encouragement and support given to businesses to expand workplace training.

4. *Changing the conditions within which schools operate* to create more positive places for pupils to learn and teachers to teach. Central to this would be not having statutory tests in schools (up to the age of eighteen) and having a broader, balanced and skills-orientated curriculum. There would also be a radically different approach to school improvement and accountability. Schools would be actively and positively supported to improve via local school improvement partnerships. Ofsted would re-focus on practically helping schools improve.

What we are proposing is an ambitious and long-term programme of cultural transformation, which we believe will take at least ten years to fully implement. Sufficient time and care will have to be taken for the changes to be made in a way that is effective and sustainable. Practical actions will be needed – legislation, funding, strategies and campaigns. A number of national and local bodies will need to be set up to provide the leadership, drive and co-ordination to take the changes forward. Most importantly, building a strong learning nation will require mobilising the energy, skills and ideas of the whole country. To do so will necessitate a radical change in government's way of working, moving from a command and control style to one that truly works in partnership with others.

Our purpose in writing this book has been to influence thinking about the future of learning and education in our country. The significant shortcomings we have evidenced make a strong case, at the very least, for having the fundamental review of our system of learning that we called for at the beginning of the book. Such a review needs to be underpinned by evidence, open-mindedness and the meaningful inclusion of everyone who wants to be involved. We believe there are better alternatives to what we have now, and have put forward a particular example of one to illustrate what might be possible. At the heart of this alternative is championing lifelong learning for all; supporting families; having a better balance of academic, creative, vocational and technical studies, and skill development, in our learning system; and taking a radically different approach to how schools are supported to improve and held to account. In the introduction we suggested that a 'great learning debate' might be organised across the country as a means (or one of the means) of conducting a review of our system of learning. We hope that in some way what we have set out in this book will make a contribution to helping to create an impetus for this 'great learning debate'.

NOTES

Introduction

[1] Eric Hoffer, *Vanguard Management*, 1989 – quoted in Warren Bennis, *On Becoming a Leader* (Century Business, London, 1992) p. 189

[2] Labour Prime Minister, James Callaghan, gave a speech in Ruskin College, Oxford on 18 October 1976, which was widely regarded as having begun 'The Great Debate' about the nature and purpose of public education.

Chapter 1: What is learning and why is it so important?

[1] Yuval Noah Harari, *Sapiens, A Brief History of Humankind* (Vintage, London, 2012) p. 4

[2] Ibid, pgs. ix & 1-69

[3] From The Campaign for Learning's definition of learning, Campaign for Learning website, http://www.campaign-for-learning.org.uk/cfl/yourlearning/why_is_learning_important.asp

[4] Yuval Noah Harari, *Homo Deus, A Brief History of Tomorrow* (Harvill Seeker, London, 2015) p. 212

Chapter 2: Mental health

[1] Sarah Marsh, *Exam stress creating 'troubled generation', says ex-civil service chief*, Guardian, 27 December 2018, https://www.theguardian.com/society/2018/dec/27/exam-stress-creating-troubled-generation-ex-civil-service-chief-gus-odonnell

[2] World Health Organisation website, *Mental health: a state of well-being*, http://www.who.int/features/factfiles/mental_health/en/

[3] David Johnston, Carol Propper, Stephen Pudney & Michael Shields, *Child mental health and educational attainment: multiple observers and the measurement error problem*, No. 2011-20, Institute for Social and Economic Research, and Economic and Social Research Council, August 2011, https://www.iser.essex.ac.uk/research/publications/working-papers/iser/2011-20.pdf

[4] Martin Knapp, Derek King, Andrew Healey & Cicely Thomas, *Economic outcomes in adulthood and their associations with antisocial conduct, attention deficit and anxiety problems in childhood*, Journal of mental health policy and economics, 2011, 14 (3), pgs. 137-147, http://eprints.lse.ac.uk/38200/. Francesca Cornaglia, Elena Crivellaro & Sandra McNally, CEE DP 136, *Mental Health and Education Decisions* (Centre for the

222

Economics of Education, London School of Economics, February 2012), http://cee.lse.ac.uk/ceedps/ceedp136.pdf

[5] Francesca Cornaglia, Elena Crivellaro & Sandra McNally, CEE DP 136, *Mental Health and Education Decisions* (Centre for the Economics of Education, London School of Economics, February 2012), http://cee.lse.ac.uk/ceedps/ceedp136.pdf

[6] 'Children who are unhappy at school are more likely to be late in the mornings and to skip classes': Organisation for Economic Co-operation and Development (OECD) questionnaire of 540,000 15-year-olds in 72 countries: OECD, *PISA 2015 Results (Volume III): Students' Well-Being*, (OECD Publishing, Paris, 2017), http://dx.doi.org/10.1787/9789264273856-en. Half of children permanently excluded from school have a recognised mental health problem: Kiran Gill, with Harry Quilter-Pinner & Danny Swift, *Making the Difference, Breaking the Link between School Exclusion and Social Exclusion*, Institute for Public Policy Research, London, October 2017, https://www.ippr.org/files/2017-10/making-the-difference-report-october-2017.pdf

[7] NASUWT: Nicola Woolcock & Greg Hurst, *Most teachers have pupils with mental health issues*, The Times, 14 April 2017, https://www.thetimes.co.uk/edition/news/most-teachers-have-pupils-with-mental-health-issues-r2tdzvmhd

[8] Place2Be website, *Results of survey of 705 pupils in their final year of primary school*, February 2017, https://www.place2be.org.uk/media/587987/childrens-survey-factsheet.pdf

[9] A third of parents say their child is stressed by examinations. Two in five parents of pupils aged between 5 and 11 report that there is too much pressure on their children to perform well in tests - Survey by OnePoll, on behalf of Oxford Home Learning: Nicola Woolcock, *Primary pupils facing five hours of homework a week*, The Times, 25 October 2018, https://www.thetimes.co.uk/article/primary-pupils-facing-five-hours-of-homework-a-week-pbfg9qhbp. Survey of teachers by the Key: Sally Weale, *More primary school children suffering stress from Sats, survey finds*, Guardian, 1 May 2017, https://www.theguardian.com/education/2017/may/01/sats-primary-school-children-suffering-stress-exam-time

[10] House of Commons Education Committee, *Primary assessment,* 1 May 2017, House of Commons, https://publications.parliament.uk/pa/cm201617/cmselect/cmeduc/682/682.pdf

[11] Survey of families by OnePoll, on behalf of Oxford Home Learning: Nicola Woolcock, *Primary pupils facing five hours of homework a week*, The Times, 25 October 2018, https://www.thetimes.co.uk/article/primary-pupils-facing-five-hours-of-homework-a-week-pbfg9qhbp

[12] Around 1 in 6 fifteen year-olds say they are unhappy at school; girls particularly feel 'they do not fit in at school' OECD, *PISA 2015 Results (Volume III): Students' Well-Being*, PISA, OECD Publishing, Paris, 2017, https://doi.org/10.1787/9789264273856-en. Anxiety about school was cited as one of the two main causes of why children in the UK are amongst the unhappiest in the developed world - Study by the Varkey Foundation, February 2017: Sian Griffiths & Nicholas Hellen, *Eight-year-olds to get lessons in happiness*, The Sunday Times, 12 March 2017, http://www.thetimes.co.uk/edition/news/eight-year-olds-to-get-lessons-in-happiness-bkpbj7tc5

[13] Poll of 500 secondary school pupils for the teenage mental health charity, stem4: Rachel Ellis, *Mental health problems rife among teenagers but teachers lack skills to help*, Observer, 26 March 2017, https://www.theguardian.com/society/2017/mar/26/mental-health-teenagers-teachers. 69% of girls identify school exams as the key cause of stress; more than any other factor: Girlguiding, *We see the big picture, Girls' Attitudes Survey 2018*, September 2018, https://www.girlguiding.org.uk/globalassets/docs-and-resources/research-and-campaigns/girls-attitudes-survey-2018.pdf

[14] Merryn Hutchings, *'Exam factories? The impact of accountability measures on children and young people*, Research commissioned by the National Union of Teachers, London Metropolitan University, July 2015, https://www.teachers.org.uk/files/exam-factories.pdf. Survey of 1,200 teachers by the Key, a national school support service: Sally Weale, *More primary school children suffering stress from Sats, survey finds*, Guardian, 1 May 2017, https://www.theguardian.com/education/2017/may/01/sats-primary-school-children-suffering-stress-exam-time. More than 7 in 10 fifteen-year-olds feel very anxious about tests, even when they say they are well-prepared for them, compared to the OECD average of just over half of children: Organisation for Economic Co-operation and Development (OECD) questionnaire of 540,000 15-year-olds in 72 countries: OECD, *PISA 2015 Results (Volume III): Students' Well-Being*, (OECD Publishing, Paris, 2017), http://dx.doi.org/10.1787/9789264273856-en

[15] Between 2015-16 and 2016-17 the number of Childline's counselling sessions on examination stress increased by 11%, with those children and young people attending citing 'excessive workloads' and feeling unprepared as the main reasons for their stress: Daniel Sanderson, *Exam fears drive rise in calls to Childline*, The Times Scotland, 12 May 2017, https://www.thetimes.co.uk/edition/scotland/exam-fears-drive-rise-in-calls-to-childline-6p30tghwg

[16] Two-thirds of British adults have experienced mental ill-health at some point in their lives, compared to 1 in 4 globally: NatCen, Surviving or Thriving, The state of the

UK's mental health, Mental Health Foundation, London, May 2017, p.5, https://www. mentalhealth.org.uk/sites/default/files/surviving-or-thriving-state-uk-mental-health.pdf

[17] 1 in 4 people experience mental health problems every year and three quarters of these start in childhood: The Times, *Mental Health Matters*, Leading Article, 22 September 2016, http://www.thetimes.co.uk/edition/comment/mental-health-matters-7gxn5lz5c

[18] Ibid

[19] On a 'life-satisfaction scale' of 0 to 10, teenagers in the UK scored 6.98 compared to the average of 7.3; ranking 23rd out of 28 countries. 28% in the UK felt very satisfied with life, compared with the average of 34%: OECD, *PISA 2015 Results (Volume III): Students' Well-Being*, (OECD Publishing, Paris, 2017), http://dx.doi. org/10.1787/9789264273856-en. A Study by the Varkey Foundation, published in February 2017, found that British children were among the unhappiest in the developed world, behind only Japan, with school and money cited as the biggest causes of anxiety: Sian Griffiths & Nicholas Hellen, *Eight-year-olds to get lessons in happiness*, The Sunday Times, 12 March 2017, http://www.thetimes.co.uk/edition/news/eight-year-olds-to-get-lessons-in-happiness-bkpbj7tc5.

[20] 30% of 10 and 11-year-olds said that once they started worrying they couldn't stop; 21% did not know what to do when they were worried; and two-thirds that they were 'worried all the time': Place2Be website, *Results of survey of 705 pupils in their final year of primary school*, February 2017, https://www.place2be.org.uk/media/587987/childrens-survey-factsheet.pdf

[21] 11% of 11 to 16-year-olds described being 'unhappy overall': ComRes, BBC School Report- 11-16 Year-Olds Mental Health Survey, 16 March 2017, http://www. comresglobal.com/wp-content/uploads/2017/05/BBC-School-Report-Mental-Health-Survey-11-16-Year-Olds-Data-Tables.pdf

[22] 27% of university students say that they are suffering from a mental health problem including depression, anxiety and eating disorders: YouGov survey in 2016 of a sample of 1061 students: YouGovUK, *One in four students suffer from mental health problems*, https://yougov.co.uk/news/2016/08/09/quarter-britains-students-are-afflicted-mental-hea/

[23] 20% of 16 to 24 year olds 'evidence... depression or anxiety' - Study on the wellbeing and mental health of 7.5 million young people in the UK aged 16 to 24, Office for National Statistics, October 2015: Sean Coughlan, *One-fifth of youngsters suffer from 'high anxiety'*, BBC News, 20 October 2015, http://www.bbc.co.uk/news/education-34586032

[24] Of 5,555 13 and 15-year-olds surveyed from across the UK, Action for Children

assessed 1,840 of them as requiring treatment for depression: Denis Campbell, *One in three young people suffering mental health troubles, survey finds*, Guardian, 18 October 2018, https://www.theguardian.com/society/2018/oct/18/one-in-three-young-people-suffering-mental-health-troubles-survey-finds

[25] Diagnosable mental health disorders, including depression, anxiety and conduct disorder, affect about 1 in 10 children and young people in England (around 720,000): Health and Social Care Information Centre: Mental Health Foundation website, Children and Young People, https://www.mentalhealth.org.uk/a-to-z/c/children-and-young-people

[26] In a YouGov poll 1,009 people aged 16-25, were asked 'have you ever self-harmed?' 45% of women and 27% of men said yes: Chris Smyth, *Nearly half of girls have self-harmed*, The Times, 1 March 2018, https://www.thetimes.co.uk/article/74ef16b0-1cd8-11e8-95c3-8b5a448e6e58

[27] Rates of depression and anxiety among teenagers have increased by 70% in the past 25 years: Carli Lessof, Andy Ross, Richard Brind, Emily Bell & Sarah Newton, *Longitudinal Study of Young People in England cohort 2: health and wellbeing at wave 2, Research report*, Department for Education, London, July 2016, https://assets.publishing.service.gov.uk/government/uploads/system/uploads/attachment_data/file/599871/LSYPE2_w2-research_report.pdf. Between 1995 and 2014 the proportion of children and young people aged 4-24 in England reporting a long-standing mental health condition increased six fold: Research by University College London, Imperial College London, Exeter University and the Nuffield Trust, *Psychological Medicine* journal, 11 September 2018, University of Exeter website, Research News, *Striking increase in mental health conditions in children and young people*, http://www.exeter.ac.uk/news/research/title_681014_en.html

[28] In 2017 24% of girls and 9% cent of boys were depressed compared to 12% and 5.5% respectively, ten years previously - Research by University College London Institute of Education: *Quarter of girls are depressed at 14 in mental health crisis*, Chris Smyth, The Times, 20 September 2017, https://www.thetimes.co.uk/article/41a465d2-9d7e-11e7-a7be-33f2196a0804. Five times as many university students (15,000) in 2015-16 disclosed mental health problems as did in 2006 (3,000) - Institute of Public Policy Research analysis: Judith Burns, *'Sharp rise' in student mental illness tests universities*, BBC News, 4 September 2017, http://www.bbc.co.uk/news/education-41148704. The number of referrals to child and adolescent mental health services in England for under-18s increased from 157,000 in 2013-14 to 198,280 in 2017-18; a 26% rise: Whitney

Crenna-Jennings & Jo Hutchinson, Access to children and young people's mental health services – 2018, Education Policy Institute, October 2018, https://epi.org.uk/publications-and-research/access-to-camhs-2018/. The number of incidents of self-harming of pupils recorded by schools has more than doubled between 2012 and 2018 – Freedom of information request by The Times: Nicola Woolcock, Sam Joiner & Ryan Watts, *Schools buckle under 70,000 self-harm cases*, The Times, 9 June 2018, https://www.thetimes.co.uk/article/schools-buckle-under-70-000-self-harm-cases-nbfxpg5h7

[29] Survey of Headteachers and Deputy Headteachers by Association of School and College Leaders with the National Children Bureau: Greg Hurst, *Anxiety and self-harm on the rise in schools*, The Times, 5 March 2016, p. 26, https://www.thetimes.co.uk/article/anxiety-and-self-harm-on-the-rise-in-schools-b8zgs9dcf

[30] There were a total of 389,727 'active referrals' to NHS specialist mental health services for people aged 18 or younger in April 2018, a third higher than the same month two years previously - NHS Digital statistics: Denis Campbell, *Sharp rise in under-19s being treated by NHS mental health services*, Guardian, 12 July 2018, https://www.theguardian.com/society/2018/jul/12/sharp-rise-in-under-19s-being-treated-by-nhs-mental-health-services

[31] Care Quality Commission: BBC News, *Child mental health: Camhs 'not fit for purpose'*, 24 September 2018, https://www.bbc.co.uk/news/health-45607313

[32] There were 948 child psychiatrists in 2017 compared to 1,015 in 2013: Royal College of Psychiatrists analysis of NHS Digital's workforce breakdown: Denis Campbell, *Falling number of NHS child psychiatrists provokes 'deep concern'*, Observer, 24 September 2017, https://www.theguardian.com/society/2017/sep/24/falling-number-of-nhs-child-psychiatrists-provokes-deep-concern. In January 2018 the King's Fund reported that 10% of specialist posts in mental health services were vacant and the number of full-time mental health staff had fallen by 13% since 2010. In February 2018 the British Medical Association reported that half of Clinical Commissioning Groups planned to decrease their proportion of mental health spending: Greg Hurst, *Mental health services for young fail to live up to the promise*, The Times, 10 October 2018, https://www.thetimes.co.uk/article/mental-health-services-for-young-fail-to-live-up-to-the-promise-fqkph5xcf. A poll of UK GPs found that 99% feared that under-18s would come to harm as a direct result of facing long delays to see a specialist and vital care being rationed. 90% said health and social care services for young people who have anxiety, depression, eating disorders and other conditions were either 'extremely inadequate' or 'very inadequate'. 88% say it is impossible or very difficult for young

people to get help with anxiety: stem4 news release, *99% of GP's fear that young patients will come to harm while on the waiting list for mental health services*, 31 December 2018, https://stem4.org.uk/wp-content/uploads/2018/12/FINAL-PRESS-RELEASE-Stem4-GP-survey-CYP-MH-18-12-18-PL.pdf

[33] Research by Centre-Forum: Lucy Bannerman, *Young denied mental health care*, Times, 11 April 2016, p. 18

[34] Of more than 338,000 children referred to CAMHS in 2017/18, 31% received treatment within the year. Another 37% were not accepted into treatment or discharged after an assessment, and 32% were still on waiting lists at the end of the year: Martin Lennon, *Children's Mental Health briefing*, Office of the Children's Commissioner for England, 22 November 2018, https://www.childrenscommissioner.gov.uk/wp-content/uploads/2018/11/childrens-mental-health-briefing-nov-2018.pdf.   Whitney Crenna-Jennings & Jo Hutchinson, Access to children and young people's mental health services – 2018, Education Policy Institute, October 2018, https://epi.org.uk/publications-and-research/access-to-camhs-2018/

[35] Care Quality Commission, *Review of children and young people's mental health services, Phase One Report, CQC*, Newcastle, UK, October 2017, https://www.cqc.org.uk/sites/default/files/20171103_cypmhphase1_report.pdf, p. 13

[36] 1,039 children and young people in England were admitted to a non-local bed in 2017-18, in many cases more than 100 miles from home - Analysis of data provided by NHS England following a Freedom of Information request from Barbara Keeley MP: Denis Campbell, *Children forced to travel hundreds of miles for NHS mental health treatment*, Guardian, 29 August 2018, https://www.theguardian.com/society/2018/aug/29/children-forced-to-travel-hundreds-of-miles-for-nhs-mental-health-treatment

[37] Care Quality Commission, *Review of children and young people's mental health services Phase one report*, October 2017, http://www.cqc.org.uk/sites/default/files/20171103_cypmhphase1_report.pdf

[38] Daniel Boffey, *Gove school reforms 'ignored' rise in pupils' mental illness*, The Observer, 4 July 2015, https://www.theguardian.com/education/2015/jul/04/michael-gove-ignored-school-pupils-mental-illness

[39] Survey of NHS child and adolescent child psychotherapists by the Association of Child Psychotherapists: Caroline Davies, *Mental health services for the young is NHS's 'silent catastrophe'*, Guardian, 25 June 2018, https://www.theguardian.com/society/2018/jun/25/mental-health-services-young-nhs-silent-catastrophe-survey-chronic-underfunding

[40] 70% of children and young people who experience mental health problems have not had appropriate support early enough: Mental Health Foundation website, Children and Young People, https://www.mentalhealth.org.uk/a-to-z/c/children-and-young-people

[41] Alice Ross, *Schools are cutting back on mental health services, MPs warn*, Guardian, 2 May 2017, p. 4, https://www.theguardian.com/society/2017/may/02/schools-mental-health-services-funding-gaps-mps-report

[42] Between 2010 and 2016 the early intervention budget was reduced by 92% – from £3.2b. to £250m: The Times, *Ofsted inspection for mental health services in schools*, 16 May 2016, p. 6, https://www.thetimes.co.uk/article/ofsted-inspection-for-mental-health-services-at-schools-rcnm0hpbh. 27 out of the 111 local authorities who responded to a Freedom of Information request from Education Policy Institute reported that in the last 8 years they had abolished mental health and wellbeing services for children including community-based early intervention services, family counselling and mental health support for looked-after children, and school-based programmes to support children with mild to moderate mental health difficulties: Whitney Crenna-Jennings & Jo Hutchinson, Access to children and young people's mental health services – 2018, Education Policy Institute, October 2018, https://epi.org.uk/publications-and-research/access-to-camhs-2018/

[43] House of Commons Education and Health Committees, *Children and young people's mental health — the role of education,* 2 May 2017, House of Commons, https://publications.parliament.uk/pa/cm201617/cmselect/cmhealth/849/849.pdf

[44] The Times, *Mind the Gap, Promises to improve mental healthcare for young people are not being kept,* Leading Article, 28 May 2016, p. 29, https://www.thetimes.co.uk/article/mind-the-gap-mntqvfqd2

[45] Lucy Bannerman, *Young denied mental health care*, Times, 11 April 2016, p. 18, https://www.thetimes.co.uk/article/young-denied-mental-healthcare-k97rlcw5j

[46] BBC News, *Child mental health money not making frontline – report*, 15 November 2016, http://www.bbc.co.uk/news/health-37983593

[47] Of the additional £1.5b. funding announced in 2015 for children's mental health, by the end of 2016 only £75m. had been used for child mental health: Emily Frith, *Children and Young People's Mental Health: Time to Deliver, The report of the Independent Commission on Children and Young People's Mental Health*, Education Policy Institute, November 2016, https://epi.org.uk/publications-and-research/children-young-peoples-mental-health-time-deliver/. Between 2015-16 and 2016-17 48% of clinical commissioning groups in England spending on child mental health services

reduced in real terms, in some areas of the country by as much as a third: Kat Lay, *Funding falls for young people's mental health*, The Times, 18 September 2017, https://www.thetimes.co.uk/article/e4c02bee-9be8-11e7-a7be-33f2196a0804. 'NHS England cannot be certain all the additional £1.4 billion funding to date was spent as intended, and does not have strong levers to ensure that CCGs [Clinical Commissioning Groups] increase spending in line with their intentions': Sir Amyas Morse KCB, Comptroller and Auditor General, *Improving children and young people's mental health services*, National Audit Office, 9 October 2018, p.7, https://www.nao.org.uk/wp-content/uploads/2018/10/Improving-children-and-young-peoples-mental-health-services.pdf

[48] Michael Savage, *May calls for revolution in child mental health care*, The Times, 9 January 2017, http://www.thetimes.co.uk/edition/news/may-calls-for-revolution-in-child-mental-health-care-9cxwgsw6l

[49] Department for Health and Department for Education: *Transforming Children and Young People's Mental Health Provision*: a Green Paper Presented to Parliament by the Secretary of State for Health and Secretary of State for Education, December 2017, https://assets.publishing.service.gov.uk/government/uploads/system/uploads/attachment_data/file/664855/Transforming_children_and_young_people_s_mental_health_provision.pdf

[50] The current average waiting time for children to access CAMHS is 11 weeks.

[51] The target is to have specialist mental health teams for 1 in 4 schools in place by 2022.

[52] Nicola Woolcock, *£300m boost for children with mental health issues*, The Times, 4 December 2017, https://www.thetimes.co.uk/article/83c4e574-d85a-11e7-aacd-025601055216

[53] The government's pledge to have 100 child psychiatrists more is aimed at providing treatment for just 35% of young people with a mental illness. The Association of Child Psychotherapists (ACP) has criticised the government's plans as 'inadequate', based on 'false assumptions' that will produce 'adverse consequences and failures'. Their main concern is that there are insufficient specialist staff to meet current service need, and that this will get worse as demand continues to grow. The government's plan for CAMHS to supervise the new mental health support teams will add enormously to the pressure, and the net result say the ACP will be that fewer and fewer children with serious mental health problems will be treated: Denis Campbell, *Troubled children at risk from mental health proposals, warn therapists*, Observer, 28 January 2018, https://www.theguardian.com/society/2018/jan/27/troubled-children-at-risk-mental-health-green-paper-schools

[54] Now called *Future in Mind*. Sir Amyas Morse KCB, Comptroller and Auditor General, *Improving children and young people's mental health services*, National Audit Office,

9 October 2018, p.7, https://www.nao.org.uk/wp-content/uploads/2018/10/Improving-children-and-young-peoples-mental-health-services.pdf

[55] House of Commons Education and Health & Social Care Committees, *The Government's Green Paper on mental health: failing a generation*, House of Commons, 9 May 2018, https://publications.parliament.uk/pa/cm201719/cmselect/cmhealth/642/642.pdf

[56] The Times, *Ofsted inspection for mental health services in schools*, 16 May 2016, p. 6, https://www.thetimes.co.uk/article/ofsted-inspection-for-mental-health-services-at-schools-rcnm0hpbh

[57] 45% of 655 school leaders surveyed said they were 'struggling to get mental health support for their pupils'; 44% of head teachers said not knowing what type of support was needed was a barrier to them providing mental health support for pupils. 37% said they did not feel confident in commissioning a counsellor or therapist. 34% of 1,198 counsellors and psychotherapists currently working in schools that were surveyed said that providing services in schools was 'difficult': research by the children's mental health charity Place2Be: Katherine Sellgren, *Schools struggle to get mental health help*, BBC News, 9 February 2018, http://www.bbc.co.uk/news/education-42962273

[58] 54% of primary school teachers surveyed said that they 'do not feel adequately trained in supporting pupils with mental health problems' – YouGov poll: Niall McGourty, *Teachers identify training gap in mental health*, 21 September 2017, Anna Freud National Centre for Children and Young People, https://www.annafreud.org/insights/news/2017/09/teachers-identify-training-gap-in-mental-health/

[59] Poll of 500 secondary school pupils for the teenage mental health charity, stem4 - Only 1 in 20 say they would turn to a teacher for help if they felt depressed, anxious, stressed or unable to cope. A third of young people think mental health first aid training for teachers is a good idea, and 36% say the initiative is 'woefully inadequate', because one teacher in a school of over 1,000 would make no difference. 1 in 5 teenagers would prefer to see properly trained mental health professionals in school rather than a teacher, and a third want to see the creation of dedicated young people's health hubs – away from school – where they can seek help anonymously: Rachel Ellis, *Mental health problems rife among teenagers but teachers lack skills to help*, Observer, 26 March 2017, https://www.theguardian.com/society/2017/mar/26/mental-health-teenagers-teachers

Chapter 3: Skills

[1] Decca Aitkenhead, *Keir Starmer interview: 'Winning elections is all I'm here for, that's why I came into it'*, Guardian, 24 March 2017, https://www.theguardian.com/politics/2017/mar/24/keir-starmer-labour-brexit-interview?

[2] The number of students in full time university education increased from around 330,000 in 1996 to 1.1 million in 1996, with a further 500,000 studying part-time. In 2008, full and part-time university numbers had risen to 1.96 million: Tejvan Pettinger, *Number of students at university in UK*, Economics website, 14 September 2011, http://www.economicshelp.org/blog/3190/education/number-of-students-at-university-in-uk/. By 2016 there were 2.28 million university students – 1.7 million full-time and 540,285 part-time: Universities UK, *Higher education in numbers*, http://www.universitiesuk.ac.uk/facts-and-stats/Pages/higher-education-data.aspx.

[3] 27% of adults now have a degree compared to 8% in 2004: Allison Dickinson, *Online learning: not just for jobs*, Guardian Education, 10 January 2017, p. 36

[4] Ana Rincón Aznar, John Forth, Geoff Mason, Mary O'Mahony & Michele Bernini, *UK skills and productivity in an international context, BIS Research Paper Number 262*, Department for Business, Innovation and Skills/National Institute of Economic and Social Research (NIESR), December 2015, p. 6 https://assets.publishing.service.gov.uk/government/uploads/system/uploads/attachment_data/file/486500/BIS-15-704-UK-skills-and-productivity-in-an-international_context.pdf

[5] Ibid, p. 88

[6] Speech by Andreas Schleicher, the Organisation for Economic Co-operation and Development's Director of Education, at the Education World Forum in London, 2124 January 2018: Sean Coughlan, *Hinds says schools face digital challenge*, BBC News, 22 January 2018, http://www.bbc.co.uk/news/education-42781375

[7] The proportion of 18-24 year-olds Not in Education, Employment or Training (NEET) between January and March 2018 was 13.2%: Office for National Statistics, *Dataset: Young people not in education, employment or training (NEET)*, 23 May 2018, https://www.ons.gov.uk/employmentandlabourmarket/peoplenotinwork/unemployment/datasets/youngpeoplenotineducationemploymentortrainingneettable1

[8] Małgorzata Kuczera, Simon Field & Hendrickje Catriona Windisch, *OECD Skills Studies Building Skills for All: A Review of England Policy Insights from the Survey of Adult Skills*, OECD Publishing, Paris, January 2016, http://www.oecd.org/unitedkingdom/building-skills-for-all-review-of-england.pdf

[9] *Building Skills for All: A Review of England – Policy Insight from the Survey of Adult*

Skills, Organisation for Economic Co-operation and Development, Paris, 2016, https://www.oecd.org/unitedkingdom/building-skills-for-all-review-ofengland. Philippa Stroud & Stephen Brien, *The Maker Generation Post-Millennials and the future they are fashioning*, The Legatum Institute, London, July 2018, https://lif.blob.core.windows.net/lif/docs/default-source/default-library/maker_generation.pdf?sfvrsn=0

[10] More than two thirds of businesses feel that school leavers are not effectively prepared for employment: Sherry Coutu, *Let's give a new generation the work skills they need*, Daily Telegraph, 13 September 2017, http://www.telegraph.co.uk/business/2017/09/13/give-new-generation-work-skills-need/

[11] Organisation for Economic Cooperation and Development, *OECD Skills Outlook 2015: Youth, Skills and Employability*, OECD Publishing, Paris, 2015, http://www.oecd.org/education/oecd-skills-outlook-2015-9789264234178-en.htm

[12] House of Commons Business, Innovation and Skills Committee, and Education Committee, *Education, skills and productivity: commissioned research*, The Stationery Office Limited, 5 November 2015, https://publications.parliament.uk/pa/cm201516/cmselect/cmbis/565/565.pdf, pgs. 23- 27

[13] BBC News, *Graduates aren't skilled enough, say employers*, 15 March 2017, http://www.bbc.co.uk/newsbeat/article/39268144/graduates-arent-skilled-enough-say-employers

[14] Sunday Times Business, *Students will learn more by getting a job*, 3 January 2016, p. 10. 29,498 child employment permits were issued in 2012 and 23,071 in 2016: Elisabeth Mahy, *Are Saturday jobs less popular among teenagers now?* BBC News, 4 December 2017 http://www.bbc.co.uk/news/business-41989185

[15] Over the last 10 to 15 years the proportion of those employed in the UK with 'upper-intermediate and lower-intermediate vocational qualifications' has stayed roughly static at 35%: Ana Rincón Aznar, John Forth, Geoff Mason, Mary O'Mahony & Michele Bernini, *UK skills and productivity in an international context, BIS Research Paper Number 262*, prepared for the Department for Business, Innovation and Skills by the National Institute of Economic and Social Research (NIESR), December 2015, p.7, https://assets.publishing.service.gov.uk/government/uploads/system/uploads/attachment_data/file/486500/BIS-15-704-UK-skills-and-productivity-in-an-international_context.pdf

[16] The UK has a much smaller proportion of those with upper-intermediate and lower-intermediate vocational qualifications than other countries such as Germany and France: Ibid, p. 6

[17] House of Commons Business, Innovation & Skills Committee, *Education, skills and*

productivity: commissioned research, The Stationery Office Limited, 5 November 2015, https://publications.parliament.uk/pa/cm201516/cmselect/cmbis/565/565.pdf, pgs. 23- 27

[18] Only 10% of 20 to 45 year-olds have a technical subject as their highest qualification; ranking the UK 16th out of the top OECD 20 countries: Sunday Times, *'T-levels' to launch technical careers*, 5 March 2017, http://www.thetimes.co.uk/edition/news/t-levels-to-launch-technical-careers-gj6mn6v5t

[19] Ana Rincón Aznar, John Forth, Geoff Mason, Mary O'Mahony & Michele Bernini, *UK skills and productivity in an international context, BIS Research Paper Number 262*, prepared for the Department for Business, Innovation and Skills by the National Institute of Economic and Social Research (NIESR), December 2015, pgs. 88 & 89, https://assets.publishing.service.gov.uk/government/uploads/system/uploads/attachment_data/file/486500/BIS-15-704-UK-skills-and-productivity-in-an-international_context.pdf,

[20] College budgets have been cut by 7% in the last 5 years: Newsnight, BBC, 3 March 2017. Sally Hunt, *The neglectful bias against vocational training*, Guardian, Letters, 20 February 2017, https://www.theguardian.com/education/2017/feb/20/the-neglectful-bias-against-vocational-training

[21] Nick Boles MP, *Technical and professional education revolution continues*, Press release from the Department for Education, Skills Minister, 4 March 2017, https://www.gov.uk/government/news/technical-and-professional-education-revolution-continues

[22] Sunday Times, *'T-levels' to launch technical careers*, 5 March 2017, http://www.thetimes.co.uk/edition/news/t-levels-to-launch-technical-careers-gj6mn6v5t

[23] Billy Camden, *DfE to consult on level 4 and 5 T-levels for introduction from* 2022, FE Week, 6 December 2018, https://feweek.co.uk/2018/12/06/dfe-to-develop-new-suite-of-higher-technical-qualifications/

[24] Rosemary Bennett, *Change 'outdated' views of technical training*, The Times, 21 September 2018, https://www.thetimes.co.uk/article/change-outdated-views-of-technical-training-bb08c635b

[25] Alice Thomson, *Snobbery is killing the apprenticeship dream*, The Times, 24 January 2018, https://www.thetimes.co.uk/article/a9e88cd6-0075-11e8-a2b0-4e5c7848ab02

[26] Alice Thomson, *The rise and fall and rise again of apprenticeships since 1563*, The Times, 25 January 2017, http://www.thetimes.co.uk/past-six-days/2017-01-25/elite-apprenticeships/the-rise-and-fall-and-rise-again-of-apprenticeships-since-1563-kfkxcpkqj

[27] Companies with a payroll of £3m. or more.

[28] Tom Knowles, *Apprentice levy 'could sacrifice quality for quantity'*, The Times, 31 January 2017, http://www.thetimes.co.uk/edition/business/apprentice-levy-could-sacrifice-quantity-for-quantity-9lmtjh2mc

[29] Josephine Moulds, *Are apprentices now the luxury small companies cannot afford?* The Times, 26 September 2016, http://www.thetimes.co.uk/past-six-days/2016-09-26/business/are-apprentices-now-the-luxury-small-companies-cannot-afford-zbm76tjbr

[30] Department for Education: May-October 2017 - 162,000 apprenticeship starts, 41% down on 273,000 in 2016; October-December 2017 - 43,600 starts, 61% down on 113,000 in 2016; November 2017-January 2018 - 27% down on 2016/17. 375,800 new apprentices during June 2017 to July 2018, compared to 494,400 during June 2016-July 2017; a 24.1% reduction.

[31] Philip Aldrick, *Apprenticeship levy 'must be revised or it will miss targets'*, The Times, 13 July 2018, https://www.thetimes.co.uk/article/apprenticeship-levy-must-be-revised-or-it-will-miss-targets-qgdwj8jx0

[32] Alice Thomson, *Snobbery is killing the apprenticeship dream*, The Times, 24 January 2018, https://www.thetimes.co.uk/article/a9e88cd6-0075-11e8-a2b0-4e5c7848ab02

[33] Almost half of 1,640 business managers surveyed do not believe that the government's 2020 target of having 3m. apprentices will be met, and less than a fifth expressed confidence that target will be met: Chartered Management Institute, *Making Waves with the Levy*, CMI, March 2018, https://www.managers.org.uk/~/media/Files/Reports/making-waves-infographic.pdf

[34] Alison Fuller, Lorna Unwin, Chiara Cavaglia, Sandra McNally & Guglielmo Ventura, *Better Apprenticeships*, UCL Institute for Education, Centre for Vocational Education Research, & The Sutton Trust, November 2017, https://www.suttontrust.com/wp-content/uploads/2017/11/Better-Apprenticeships-1.pdf

[35] 44% (224,100) apprentices were over the age of 25; 30% (153,860) aged 19-24; and 26% (131,420) 16-18 year-olds: James Mirza-Davies, *2016 Apprenticeship Statistics*, House of Commons, 21 November 2016. Under 25s accounted for less than three-fifths of level 2 apprenticeships, just over half at level 3, and less than 1 in 3 of higher and degree level apprenticeship starts. Currently, only 6.9% of 17 year-olds are on apprenticeships: Press release from the Department of Education and Nick Boles MP, Skills Minister, *Technical and professional education revolution continues*, 4 March 2017, https://www.gov.uk/government/news/technical-and-professional-education-revolution-continues

[36] As in previous years, in 2015/16 the large majority of apprenticeship starts were in

the service rather than technical sectors; 71% in 3 sectors: business, administration and law; health, public services and care; and retail and commercial enterprise: James Mirza-Davies, *2016 Apprenticeship Statistics*, House of Commons, 21 November 2016

[37] The highest number of starts was for Intermediate Level 2 apprenticeships (291,330); 190,870 at Advanced Level 3 and 27,160 at Higher Level 4 and above: James Mirza-Davies, *2016 Apprenticeship Statistics*, House of Commons, 21 November 2016

[38] Geoff Mason & Ana Rincon-Aznar, *Skills and Productivity in the UK, US, France and Germany: a Literature Review, Report to the Business, Innovation and Skills and Education Select Committees*, House of Commons, 26 October 2015, https://publications.parliament.uk/pa/cm201516/cmselect/cmbis/565/56504.htm.   James Mirza-Davies, *2016 Apprenticeship Statistics*, House of Commons, 21 November 2016

[39] Alison Fuller, Lorna Unwin, Chiara Cavaglia, Sandra McNally & Guglielmo Ventura, *Better Apprenticeships*, UCL Institute for Education, Centre for Vocational Education Research, & The Sutton Trust, November 2017, https://www.suttontrust.com/wp-content/uploads/2017/11/Better-Apprenticeships-1.pdf

[40] BBC News, *Apprenticeships 'failing young people', says commission*, 21 March 2016, http://www.bbc.co.uk/news/education-35847191

[41] More women have started apprenticeships than men every year since 2010/11 including in 2015/16 with 268,730 females and 240,630 males: James Mirza-Davies, *2016 Apprenticeship Statistics*, House of Commons, 21 November 2016

[42] Men who have been on level 3 apprenticeships tend to work in highly paid sectors such as engineering and construction, and, therefore, earn far more than their female counterparts, who are more likely to be in low paid jobs such as hairdressing and childcare: Alison Fuller, Lorna Unwin, Chiara Cavaglia, Sandra McNally & Guglielmo Ventura, *Better Apprenticeships*, UCL Institute for Education, Centre for Vocational Education Research, & The Sutton Trust, November 2017, https://www.suttontrust.com/wp-content/uploads/2017/11/Better-Apprenticeships-1.pdf

[43] There were 27,160 higher level apprenticeship starters in 2016: Greg Hurst, *More high-level apprenticeships are on their way*, The Times, http://www.thetimes.co.uk/past-six-days/2017-01-25/elite-apprenticeships/more-high-level-apprenticeships-are-on-their-way-pg0q0j6j5

[44] James Hurley, *How to avoid debt and start your career in engineering*, The Times, 25 January 2017, http://www.thetimes.co.uk/past-six-days/2017-01-25/elite-apprenticeships/how-to-avoid-debt-and-start-your-career-in-engineering-82jvv0s2n

[45] 1,800 higher apprentices were 18 year-old school-leavers compared to the 235,000

who started a full-time university course: Greg Hurst, *More high-level apprenticeships are on their way*, The Times, http://www.thetimes.co.uk/past-six-days/2017-01-25/elite-apprenticeships/more-high-level-apprenticeships-are-on-their-way-pg0q0j6j5

[46] More than half of the 1 in 4 small businesses that have at least one apprentice, say that their biggest challenge is the quality of applicants they have to select from - Research by the Federation of Small Businesses: Josephine Moulds, The Times, *Are apprentices now the luxury small companies cannot afford?* 26 September 2016, http://www.thetimes.co.uk/past-six-days/2016-09-26/business/are-apprentices-now-the-luxury-small-companies-cannot-afford-zbm76tjbr

[47] Ofsted inspected 189 apprenticeship training providers (responsible for a total of 187,000 apprentices) in 2017 and assessed that 6% were outstanding, 43% good, 40% required improvement and 11% inadequate: Oliver Wright & Rosemary Bennett, *Scandal of inadequate apprenticeships*, The Times, 23 January 2018, https://www.thetimes.co.uk/article/afd9f4b0-ffbf-11e7-a2b0-4e5c7848ab02

[48] The average drop-out rate from apprenticeships is 27%: Greg Hurst, *More high-level apprenticeships are on their way*, The Times, http://www.thetimes.co.uk/past-six-days/2017-01-25/elite-apprenticeships/more-high-level-apprenticeships-are-on-their-way-pg0q0j6j5

[49] National Audit Office report, September 2016: Hannah Richardson, *Apprenticeships plan 'needs to be linked to economy'*, BBC News, 6 September 2016,Top of Form http://www.bbc.co.uk/news/education-37278545

[50] House of Commons Business, Energy and Industrial Strategy and Education Committees Sub-Committee on Education, Skills and the Economy, *Apprenticeships*, House of Commons, 28 March 2017, https://publications.parliament.uk/pa/cm201617/cmselect/cmese/206/206.pdf

[51] House of Commons Business, Innovation and Skills, and Education Select Committees, *Education, skills and productivity: commissioned research*, The Stationery Office Limited, 5 November 2015, pgs. 23 - 27 https://publications.parliament.uk/pa/cm201516/cmselect/cmbis/565/56502.htm

[52] Lorraine Candy, *Family: how to help teens choose their GCSE and A-level subjects*, The Sunday Times, 4 March 2018, https://www.thetimes.co.uk/article/07afb632-1c7d-11e8-8523-de565c87c927

[53] House of Commons Business, Innovation and Skills, and Education Committees, *Education, skills and productivity: commissioned research*, The Stationery Office Limited, London, October 2015, pgs. 23 - 27, https://publications.parliament.uk/pa/

cm201516/cmselect/cmbis/565/56502.htm. The cost of STEM vacancies to UK gross domestic product is estimated to be around £63m. a year: House of Commons Science and Technology Committee, *Digital skills crisis,* House of Commons, 13 June 2016, https://www.publications.parliament.uk/pa/cm201617/cmselect/cmsctech/270/270.pdf.

[54] 78% of job openings in STEM over the next six years will be to replace retiring workers: Social Market Foundation, *Jobs of the future Research*, EDF Energy, August 2017, https://www.edfenergy.com/sites/default/files/jobs-of-the-future.pdf

[55] Ibid

[56] Three-quarters of manufacturing employers surveyed had in the previous 3 years found difficulties in finding people with the right skills to fill their job vacancies. Two-thirds of manufacturers cited lack of technical skills amongst applicants and insufficient candidates as the reasons for not appointing. 35% of vacancies in manufacturing are 'hard-to-fill'. 72% of manufacturers say that they are 'worried about the skills their business will need in the next three years': Katie Allen, *Manufacturers press ministers to help fill skills gap*, Guardian Financial, 29 March 2016, p. 24

[57] Lack of skilled information technology professionals is putting cybersecurity for businesses at risk. 81% of agencies recruiting for this industry expect demand for information technology specialists to increase, but only 16% of them believe that this demand will be met: Mike Pattenden, *Lack of IT staff leaving companies exposed to hacker attacks*, Guardian, 25 December 2017, https://www.theguardian.com/technology/2017/dec/25/lack-of-it-staff-leaving-companies-exposed-to-hacker-attacks. The number of unfilled positions in the information and communication technology sector increased by 24.3% in the third quarter of 2018 compared to the same period in 2017 – National Office for Statistics: Emma Yeomans, *Skills shortage 'poses threat to technology growth'*, The Times, 17 December 2018, https://www.thetimes.co.uk/article/skills-shortage-poses-threat-to-technology-growth-zvjp2wzsg

[58] There are 42,000 nursing vacancies in the NHS: Royal College of Nursing: Toby Helm, *Fears for NHS as apprenticeships fail to plug gaps left by Brexit brain drain*, Guardian, 4 August 2018, https://www.theguardian.com/society/2018/aug/04/nursing-shortfall-apprenticeships-brexit-nhs-eu

[59] The Economist web-site, *A lack of skilled workers and managers drags the country down*, 11 April 2015, http://www.economist.com/news/britain/21648003-lack-skilled-workers-and-managers-drags-country-down-mind-gap

[60] 30% of companies that build boats and repair and maintain them, have 'identified critical skills gaps with technical skills being the biggest obstacle to recruitment'. These

skills shortages are 'holding back growth' in this sector of the economy: All at Sea magazine, *UK boat builders face a skills gap*, October 2016 edition. *Boaty McBoatface builders import workers to fill the skills gap*, Will Humphries, The Times, 21 November 2017, https://www.thetimes.co.uk/article/95518200-ce39-11e7-a505-dffc08ac33de

[61] The British Council estimate that the UK's 'linguistic shortfalls' result in losses of up to £50 billion a year in international trade: Bernadette O'Rourke, *Language skills are critical to success in a post-Brexit world, says Heriot-Watt professor*, The Times Scotland, 9 June 2017, https://www.thetimes.co.uk/edition/scotland/language-skills-are-critical-to-success-in-a-post-brexit-world-says-heriot-watt-professor-h7v8m3v6z

[62] In excess of half of organisations in a survey of the creative sector (which includes architecture, art, design, fashion, film and music) indicated that they had skills shortages and 80% of these were not confident that such shortages would be 'resolved any time soon'. The creative industries are growing at nearly twice the rate of the UK economy as a whole, and offer substantial job opportunities for British people, but many of these are filled by recruits from overseas: John Kampfner, *Britain's got talent but we are not providing the skills*, The Times, Comment, 5 June 2017, https://www.thetimes.co.uk/past-six-days/2017-06-05/business/britains-got-talent-but-we-are-not-providing-the-skills-lgt5rqf09

[63] Research by Teach First: The Times, *Plug the Skills Gap*, Letters to Editor, 6 March 2017, http://www.thetimes.co.uk/edition/comment/tackling-the-rising-tide-of-obesity-in-the-uk-tw3qvbpvx

[64] In 2018 40% of employers found it more difficult to fill vacancies than in 2017: Chartered Institute of Personnel and Development, *Labour Market Outlook, Views From Employers, Summer 2018*, CIPD, London, August 2018, https://www.cipd.co.uk/Images/lmo-summer2018-report_tcm18-45850.pdf. 80% of companies surveyed said they would be increasing the number of highly skilled positions in the next few years, but 66% expected that they would have difficulties in finding suitable candidates: Confederation of British Industry/Pearson, *Educating for the Modern World, CBI/Pearson Education and Skills Annual Report*, Pearson, November 2018, http://www.cbi.org.uk/index.cfm/_api/render/file/?method=inline&fileID=12087B3C-FD5F-497B-908E5285EA942928

[65] David Smith, *We must act now to prevent the skills gap becoming unbridgeable*, The Times, Comment, 24 January 2018, https://www.thetimes.co.uk/article/b4a7b8b6-004a-11e8-9de1-e6776d524215

[66] Katie Allen, *Manufacturers press ministers to help fill skills gap*, Guardian Financial,

29 March 2016, p. 24

[67] James Hurley, *Dyson heads overseas for engineers*, Times, 14 February 2017, http://www.thetimes.co.uk/article/dyson-heads-overseas-for-engineers-3vjds023b?shareToken=cf53eb891edb1d399d80855a8f1fa07f. *Dyson students will clean up with salaries and free tuition*, Greg Hurst, Times, 4 November 2016, p. 4

[68] Tim Wallace, *Skills shortage holding back building work, surveyors warn*, Telegraph Business, 16 November 2017, p. 5

[69] 78% of job openings in STEM over the next six years will be to replace retiring workers: Social Market Foundation, *Jobs of the future Research*, EDF Energy, August 2017, https://www.edfenergy.com/sites/default/files/jobs-of-the-future.pdf. It is projected that in the next 5 years 700,000 people more will need to be recruited into the construction workforce to replace those who are leaving - Construction consultancy Arcadis: Isabelle Fraser, *The stark warning for builders: change or die*, Daily Telegraph, 17 October 2016, p. 4

[70] Klaus Schwab, Founder and Executive Chairman, World Economic Forum, *The Fourth Industrial Revolution: what it means, how to respond*, World Economic Forum website, 14 January 2016, https://www.weforum.org/agenda/2016/01/the-fourth-industrial-revolution-what-it-means-and-how-to-respond/

[71] House of Lords Select Committee on Digital Skills, *Make or Break: The UK's Digital Future*, The Stationery Office Limited, London, 17 February 2015, https://publications.parliament.uk/pa/ld201415/ldselect/lddigital/111/111.pdf

[72] The government estimated that the digital sector alone was worth an estimated £105b. in gross value added to the UK in 2011. A report by the National Institute of Economic and Social Research in 2013 found that the size of the digital economy was almost double official estimates: House of Lords Select Committee on Digital Skills, *Make or Break: The UK's Digital Future*, The Stationery Office Limited, 17 February 2015, https://publications.parliament.uk/pa/ld201415/ldselect/lddigital/111/111.pdf

[73] Skills You Need website, *The Importance of Digital Skills in the Modern Workplace*, https://www.skillsyouneed.com/rhubarb/digital-skills-modern-workplace.html

[74] Development Economics, *The Future Digital Skills Needs of the UK Economy*, O2, September 2013, http://cdn.news.o2.co.uk.s3.amazonaws.com/wp-content/uploads/2013/09/The-Future-Digital-Skills-Needs-of-the-UK-Economy1.pdf

[75] Mark Bridge, *Degree apprenticeships could plug tech skills gap*, The Times, 24 January 2018, https://www.thetimes.co.uk/edition/elite-apprenticeships/degree-apprenticeships-could-plug-tech-skills-gap-3hft9h0sp

[76] Harry de Quetteville, *Teaching tech*, Daily Telegraph, 19 March 2018, https://www.telegraph.co.uk/technology/teaching-tech/

[77] Tech Nation 2017 survey, *Talent supply remains the number one challenge facing digital tech businesses in the UK*, Tech City UK website, https://technation.techcityuk.com/digital-skills-jobs/digital-skills-shortage/. Mark Bridge, *Degree apprenticeships could plug tech skills gap*, The Times, 24 January 2018, https://www.thetimes.co.uk/edition/elite-apprenticeships/degree-apprenticeships-could-plug-tech-skills-gap-3hft9h0sp

[78] Euan Blair, *Providing the digital skills that companies seek*, The Times, 24 January 2018, https://www.thetimes.co.uk/edition/elite-apprenticeships/providing-the-digital-skills-that-companies-seek-tkc6f92rz

[79] 23% of the UK adult population, 12.6 million, do not have the required level of Basic Digital Skills. The digital skills level starts to decline amongst the 45+ age group with the 65+ groups having a Basic Digital Skills level of 43%. The Basic Digital Skills level amongst social groups ABC1s is 87%, and 65% for the C2DE social groups: Go ON UK & Lloyds Banking Group, *Basic Digital Skills, UK Report 2015*, http://s3-eu-west-1.amazonaws.com/digitalbirmingham/resources/Basic-Digital-Skills_UK-Report-2015_131015_FINAL.pdf

[80] Office for National Statistics, *UK productivity research summary: February 2018, Main findings from official statistics and analysis of UK productivity to present a summary of recent developments*, https://www.ons.gov.uk/economy/economicoutputandproductivity/productivitymeasures/articles/ukproductivityanalyticalrelease/february2018#main-points. Richard Partington, *Worker productivity in north grew twice as fast as London in 2016*, Guardian, 7 February 2018, https://www.theguardian.com/uk-news/2018/feb/07/worker-productivity-in-north-grew-twice-as-fast-as-london-in-2016. Sherry Coutu, *Let's give a new generation the work skills they need*, Daily Telegraph, 13 September 2017, http://www.telegraph.co.uk/business/2017/09/13/give-new-generation-work-skills-need/

[81] The CBI report that more manufacturing companies cite skills shortages as a factor restricting output than at any time over the past four decades: David Smith, *We must act now to prevent the skills gap becoming unbridgeable*, The Times, Comment, 24 January 2018, https://www.thetimes.co.uk/article/b4a7b8b6-004a-11e8-9de1-e6776d524215

[82] The long-term trend in the UK prior to 2008 was productivity growth averaging nearly 2% per annum. Productivity growth in 2017 quarter 1 -0.4%. Q2 -0.2%, Q3 +0.8%, Q4 +0.7%, 2018 Q1 -0.4%; Q2 +1.45; Q3 +0.1%: Office for National Statistics:

Statistical bulletin, Labour productivity, UK, January to March 2018, https://www. ons.gov.uk/employmentandlabourmarket/peopleinwork/labourproductivity/bulletins/ labourproductivity/januarytomarch2018.

[83] Ana Rincón Aznar, John Forth, Geoff Mason, Mary O'Mahony & Michele Bernini, *UK skills and productivity in an international context, BIS Research Paper Number 262*, Department for Business, Innovation and Skills/ National Institute of Economic and Social Research (NIESR), December 2015, p. 88. The US, France and Germany produce a third more goods and services than the UK in the same amount of time: Philip Aldrick, *Could do better; Britain lags rivals in school report*, Times, 18 January 2016, https://www.thetimes.co.uk/article/could-do-better-britain-trails-rivals-in-school-report-dzv69cfbh6d, p. 40

[84] Ana Rincón Aznar, John Forth, Geoff Mason, Mary O'Mahony & Michele Bernini, *UK skills and productivity in an international context, BIS Research Paper Number 262*, Department for Business, Innovation and Skills/National Institute of Economic and Social Research (NIESR), December 2015, p. 88 https://assets.publishing.service. gov.uk/government/uploads/system/uploads/attachment_data/file/486500/BIS-15-704-UK-skills-and-productivity-in-an-international_context.pdf,. The UK's level of productivity is further behind that of other advanced economies than at any time since records started to be kept in 1991: Tom Knowles, *Productivity of British workers falls to new low*, Times Business, 19 February 2016, p. 45

[85] Speech made by Philip Hammond, Chancellor of the Exchequer, to the Conservative Party Conference on 3 October 2016: Philip Aldrick, *We're all paying for Brexit now*, Times, 24 November 2016, *http://www.thetimes.co.uk/edition/autumn-statement/were-all-paying-for-brexit-now-t2j7v6bx8*

[86] Philip Aldrick, *Could do better; Britain lags rivals in school report*, The Times, 18 January 2016, p. 40, https://www.thetimes.co.uk/article/could-do-better-britain-trails-rivals-in-school-report-dzv69cfbh6d

[87] Ibid

[88] Louise Woodruff, *It's time to give Britain a pay rise and improve our low-wage economy*, Joseph Rowntree Foundation website, 11 February 2015, https://www.jrf. org.uk/blog/it%E2%80%99s-time-give-britain-pay-rise-and-improve-our-low-wage-economy

[89] The Living Wage is calculated by the Living Wage Foundation and is non-statutory. The current UK Living Wage is £8.75 an hour, and for London Living Wage is £10.20 an hour. The Minimum Wage, which from 1 April 2018 is £7.83 for employees age

twenty-five and over, is statutory: Living Wage Foundation website, *Explaining UK wage rates*, https://www.livingwage.org.uk/what-real-living-wage

[90] Katie Jacobs, *Job quality in an hourglass labour market*, HR magazine website, 16 February 2015, http://www.hrmagazine.co.uk/article-details/job-quality-in-an-hourglass-labour-market

[91] Ibid

[92] Between 2000 and 2016 the number of people on zero-hours contracts increased from 200,000 to 920,000: Angela Monaghan, *Record 910,000 UK workers on zero-hours contracts*, Guardian, 3 March 2017, https://www.theguardian.com/business/2017/mar/03/zero-hours-contracts-uk-record-high. By October-December 2017 4,000 fewer people were on zero-hours contracts. But, the total number of zero-hours contracts (individuals have more than one contract) was 1.8m. compared to 1.7m. in November 2016 - Office for National Statistics: Tom Knowles, *Number of zero-hours contracts hits 1.8m*, The Times, 24 April 2018, https://www.thetimes.co.uk/article/number-of-zero-hours-contracts-hits-1-8m-7968wsg6x

Chapter 4: International comparisons

[1] Greg Hurst, *Schools fail to raise their game in global league table*, The Times, 6 December 2016, http://www.thetimes.co.uk/edition/news/schools-fail-to-raise-their-game-in-global-league-table-0qh2rxd90

[2] Ibid

[3] The UK moved to 15th place in the PISA rankings in science. Its average test score of 509 points was lower than in 2012.

[4] In reading the UK moved up one place to 22nd equal in 2015 PISA rankings, with an average test score of 498, 4 points more than in 2012.

[5] In mathematics the average PISA score for the UK fell from 499 to 492 points, as did the ranking, one place to 27th equal.

[6] Sian Griffiths, *Tigers extend lead over UK pupils*, The Sunday Times, 4 December 2016, http://www.thetimes.co.uk/edition/news/tigers-extend-lead-over-uk-pupils-70nxp3sr2

[7] Greg Hurst, *Schools fail to raise their game in global league table*, The Times, 6 December 2016, http://www.thetimes.co.uk/edition/news/schools-fail-to-raise-their-game-in-global-league-table-0qh2rxd90

[8] In England the achievement gaps in mathematics and science are the equivalent of eight school years. In reading while the top 10% of students compared well to other

countries' high performing students, this was not so with the lowest achieving students and when average scores were compared: Greg Hurst, *Schools fail to raise their game in global league table*, The Times, 6 December 2016, http://www.thetimes.co.uk/edition/news/schools-fail-to-raise-their-game-in-global-league-table-0qh2rxd90

[9] Analysis by University College London's Institute of Education of the performance of London school students in international sample tests sat by 15-year-olds in 65 developed countries run by the OECD (Pisa): The Times, *London pupils trail their foreign peers*, 21 February 2016, p. 16

[10] Greg Hurst, *Must do better: British schools fail to impress in world ranking*, The Times, 7 December 7 2016, http://www.thetimes.co.uk/edition/news/must-do-better-british-schools-fail-to-impress-in-world-ranking-k3pd8nm6k

[11] Progress in International Reading Literacy Study (PIRLS)

[12] IEA, TIMSS & PIRLS, International Study Centre, Lynch School of Education, Boston College, US, *PIRLS 2016 International Results in Reading*, http://timssandpirls.bc.edu/pirls2016/international-results/pirls/student-achievement/. Joshua McGrane, Jamie Stiff, Jo-Anne Baird, Jenny Lenkeit & Therese Hopfenbeck, *Progress in International Reading Literacy Study (PIRLS): National Report for England*, Department for Education/Government Social Research/Pearson, December 2017, https://assets.publishing.service.gov.uk/government/uploads/system/uploads/attachment_data/file/664562/PIRLS_2016_National_Report_for_England-_BRANDED.pdf

[13] Trends in International Mathematics and Science Study (TIMSS)

[14] IEA, TIMSS & PIRLS, International Study Centre, Lynch School of Education, Boston College, US, *TIMSS 2015 International Results in Mathematics*, http://timssandpirls.bc.edu/timss2015/international-results/timss-2015/mathematics/student-achievement/

[15] Report by the University College London's Institute of Education based on analysis of the Trends in International Mathematics and Science Study (TIMSS): Nicola Woolcock, *England's maths attainment gap 'among largest in world'*, The Times, 13 December 2017, https://www.thetimes.co.uk/article/85f0732e-df6f-11e7-872d-4b5e82b139be

[16] Sunday Times, *Two-thirds of pupils will miss global standard*, 17 January 2016, p. 5. Sean Coughlan, *GCSEs 'need tougher pass mark to catch international rivals'*, BBC News, 23 August 2017, http://www.bbc.co.uk/news/education-41014624

[17] Małgorzata Kuczera, Simon Field & Hendrickje Catriona Windisch, *OECD Skills Studies, Building Skills For All: A Review of England Policy Insights from the Survey of Adult Skills*, OECD, 2016, http://www.oecd.org/unitedkingdom/building-skills-for-all-review-of-england.pdf

[18] Ibid

[19] 7% of graduates aged 20 to 34 in England had numeracy skills below level 2, with skills ranked from 0 to 5. Some 3.4% had literacy skills below this level, meaning that they struggled to estimate how much petrol was left in a tank from looking at the gauge or had difficulty understanding instructions on an aspirin bottle. About 1 in 5 young university graduates could manage basic tasks, but struggled with more complex problems - OECD: The Times, *Students in crisis over poor maths and English*, 29 January 2016, p. 1, https://www.thetimes.co.uk/article/students-in-crisis-over-poor-maths-and-english-0mn5pr7rjhh

[20] Ibid

[21] Lucy Crehan has written about her experiences of working in schools in five areas of the world that are high up in the PISA rankings including Finland and Canada: Lucy Crehan, *Cleverlands, The secrets behind the success of the world's education superpowers* (Unbound, London, 2016). Dr. Pasi Sahlberg is a Harvard professor, who has written extensively about the Finnish education system: Pasi Sahlberg, *Finnish Lessons 2.0, What can the world learn from educational change in Finland* (Teachers College Press, New York, 2015). Tim Walker is an American teacher who taught in Finland: Timothy D. Walker, *Teach Like Finland, 33 Simple Strategies for Joyful Classrooms* (W.W. Norton & Company, London, 2017). In 2014 Allison had the benefit of going on a visit to Finland to experience their schools system, and talk to teachers, and school and political leaders. We both then participated in a follow-up seminar the year after and heard feedback from three of the schools (including Allison's) that visited Finland, and presentations from two professors from the University of Helsinki, about developments that are under way in Finnish education. The Times' education editor, Greg Hurst, observes that Canada 'may have more lessons for British policy-makers than Asian schools systems with [their] cultures of rote learning, high stakes exams, long school days and high levels of private tuition'. The OECD attributes Canada's success to personalised learning, strong results for poor children and effective assimilation of immigrants. Greg Hurst, *Must do better: British schools fail to impress in world ranking*, The Times, 7 December 7 2016, http://www.thetimes.co.uk/edition/news/must-do-better-british-schools-fail-to-impress-in-world-ranking-k3pd8nm6k. Rhonda Evans made a documentary about the education system in the Canadian state of Alberta, and wrote a newspaper article about her experiences: Rhonda Evans, *Is the Canadian model right for UK schools?* Guardian, 4 January 2011, https://www.theguardian.com/education/2011/jan/04/education-policy-canadian-model

[22] Pupils' engagement with mathematics and science declines during secondary school – 74% amongst girls and 56% amongst boys: Edwina Dunn, *UK skills shortage: Misconception about STEM subjects are failing young people*, CITY A.M. website, 5 February 2016, http://www.cityam.com/233916/uk-skills-shortage-misconception-about-stem-subjects-are-failing-young-people.

[23] Research indicates that there is a strong link between a country having a well-regarded teaching profession and high educational standards in that country: Peter Dolton, Oscar Marcenaro, Robert De Vries & Po-Wen She, *Global Teacher Status Index 2018*, Varkey Foundation, November 2018, https://www.varkeyfoundation.org/media/4790/gts-index-9-11-2018.pdf

[24] Pasi Sahlberg, *Finnish Lessons 2.0, What can the world learn from educational change in Finland* (Teachers College Press, New York, 2015) p. 47

Chapter 5: Families

[1] National Institute of Adult Continuing Education, *Family Learning Works, The Inquiry into Family Learning in England and Wales*, 2013, p. 7, http://shop.niace.org.uk/media/catalog/product/n/i/niace_family_learning_report_web_version_final.pdf

[2] The Times, *Improving mental health 'starts at home' not schools*, 19 February 2016, p. 20

[3] Students whose parents spend time just talking to them, and discussing how well they are doing at school every day or almost every day, score higher in PISA tests, and are more likely to have high levels of life satisfaction: Organisation for Economic Co-operation and Development (OECD) questionnaire of 540,000 15-year-olds in 72 countries: OECD, *PISA 2015 Results (Volume III): Students' Well-Being*, (OECD Publishing, Paris, 2017), page 156, http://dx.doi.org/10.1787/9789264273856-en. Reading to children when they are young, engaging in discussions that promote critical thinking and setting a good example are strongly related to cognitive and non-cognitive student outcomes: Francesca Borgonovi & Guillermo Montt, *Parental involvement in selected PISA countries and economies*, OECD Education Working Papers, No. 73, OECD Publishing, Paris, 2012, https://www.oecd-ilibrary.org/docserver/5k990rk0jsjj-enpdf?expires=1532946368&id=id&accname=guest&checksum=92639C77A16D57 87E26B2B382CE22EB1. 'The role of parents plays a large part in performance at school, as the more they engage, the better their children do': Research by LKMco and Education Datalab, for the Social Mobility Commission: BBC News, *Social mobility promise 'broken' for ethnic minority children*, 28 December 2016, http://www.bbc.

co.uk/news/uk-38447933

[4] John Ermisch, *Origins of social immobility and inequality: parenting and early child development* (National Institute Economic Review, volume 205, issue 1, 2008), pgs. 62 – 71

[5] The Economic and Social Research Council, *Evidence Briefing, Parenting style influences child development and social mobility*, 2007, http://www.esrc.ac.uk/_images/parenting-style-social-mobility_tcm8-20071.pdf

[6] Parenting, Economic and Social Research Council, *Parenting style influences child development and social mobility*, Evidence Briefing - Social Mobility – 2012, http://www.esrc.ac.uk/files/news-events-and-publications/evidence-briefings/parenting-style-influences-child-development-and-social-mobility/

[7] OECD questionnaire of 540,000 15-year-olds in 72 countries: OECD, *PISA 2015 Results (Volume III): Students' Well-Being* (OECD Publishing, Paris, 2017), http://dx.doi.org/10.1787/9789264273856-en

[8] John Ermisch, *Origins of social immobility and inequality: parenting and early child development* (National Institute Economic Review, volume 205, issue 1, 2008) pgs. 62 – 71

[9] Richard Wilkinson & Kate Pickett, *The Spirit Level, Why Equality is Better for Everyone* (Penguin Books, London, 2010) p.106

[10] Professor Michael Martin, executive director of the TIMSS and PIRLS International Study Center at Boston College, US, reporting on the 2016 Progress in International Reading Literacy Study: BBC News, *Northern Ireland and England schools in global top 10 for reading*, Sean Coughlan, 5 December 2017, http://www.bbc.co.uk/news/education-42222488

[11] Research by Oxford University: Katherine Sellgren, *Babies with involved fathers learn faster, study finds*, BBC News, 10 May 2017, http://www.bbc.co.uk/news/education-39869512

[12] Children whose mothers ranked in the top 25% of the internal locus of control scale tend to obtain total GCSE scores about 12% higher than children whose mothers in the bottom 25%: Warn N. Lekfuangfu, Nattavudh Powdthavee, Nele Warrinnier & Francesca Cornaglia, *Locus of Control and its Intergenerational Implications for Early Childhood Skill Formation*, The Economic Journal, 128 (February), pgs. 298–329, 6 August 2016, https://www.onlinelibrary.wiley.com/doi/epdf/10.1111/ecoj.12414

[13] John Ermisch, *Origins of social immobility and inequality: parenting and early child development* (National Institute Economic Review, volume 205, issue 1, 2008) pgs. 62 – 71, http://journals.sagepub.com/doi/abs/10.1177/0027950108096589

[14] Research by Oxford University: Katherine Sellgren, *Babies with involved fathers learn faster, study finds*, BBC News, 10 May 2017, http://www.bbc.co.uk/news/education-39869512

[15] Michael Rosen, *Letter from a curious parent*, Guardian Education, 28 February 2017, p. 32, https://www.theguardian.com/education/2017/feb/28/justine-greening-homework-rich-poor-children-michael-rosen

[16] 11% of UK parents spend an hour per day helping their children with their homework, one of the lowest percentages of 29 countries surveyed - Survey of 27,830 parents in 29 countries commissioned by the Varkey Foundation: Sean Coughlan, *UK parents help less with homework*, BBC News, 9 March 2018, http://www.bbc.co.uk/news/education-43316741

[17] Sarah Marsh, *Vulnerable children in England 'falling through cracks' in social services*, Guardian, 14 August 2017, https://www.theguardian.com/society/2017/aug/14/vulnerable-children-england-falling-through-cracks-social-services-charity-warns

[18] Anne Longfield OBE , Children's Commissioner for England, *On measuring the number of vulnerable children in England*, Office for Children's Commissioner for England, July 2017, https://www.childrenscommissioner.gov.uk/wp-content/uploads/2017/07/CCO-On-vulnerability-Overveiw-2.pdf

[19] BBC News, *Too many new pupils not school ready, say head teachers*, 6 September 2017, http://www.bbc.co.uk/news/education-41160919

[20] Primary school headteachers report that 194,000 four-year-olds, a third, are not ready to start school because of poor speech, language and communication skills: Carey Oppenheim, *To support children, focus early on parents*, Guardian Society, 13 April 2016, p. 36, https://www.theguardian.com/society/2016/apr/12/helping-parents-improve-relationship-best-early-intervention-for-children

[21] Ofsted, *Bold beginnings: The Reception curriculum in a sample of good and outstanding primary schools*, November 2017, https://assets.publishing.service.gov.uk/government/uploads/system/uploads/attachment_data/file/663560/28933_Ofsted_-_Early_Years_Curriculum_Report_-_Accessible.pdf

[22] Comment from a Headteacher in *State of Education report* by Fergal Roche of The Key: Metro, *1 in 3 pupils 'not ready for school'*, 9 May 2016, p. 2

[23] 70% of primary school teachers noticed an increase in the number of children aged 3 to 7 wetting or soiling themselves during the school day compared with 5 years ago: Sian Griffiths, *Teachers driven potty as more parents fail to toilet-train children*, The Sunday

Times, 4 September 2016, http://www.thetimes.co.uk/past-six-days/2016-09-04/news/
teachers-driven-potty-as-more-parents-fail-to-toilet-train-children-w0fpg0sg2. 70% of
primary schools report an increase in the number of four-years-olds starting school
wearing nappies: Amanda Spielman, *The Annual Report of Her Majesty's Chief
Inspector of Education, Children's Services and Skills 2017/18*, Ofsted, 4 December
2018,   https://assets.publishing.service.gov.uk/government/uploads/system/uploads/
attachment_data/file/760991/29523_Ofsted_Annual_Report_2017-18_WEB.pdf

[24] In 2018 almost 2.4m. people contacted children's services because they were
worried about a child - a 78% increase since 2008. Investigations by social workers
into concerns of significant harm of children increased from 77,000 in 2008 to almost
200,000 in 2017 - a rise of 159%: Carole Brooks Associates Limited, *Research
Report Safeguarding Pressures Phase 6*, The Association of Directors of Children's
Services Ltd, 6 November 2018, http://adcs.org.uk/assets/documentation/ADCS_
SAFEGUARDING_PRESSURES_PHASE_6_FINAL.pdf.   The annual number of
referrals to children's social care has increased by 100,000 children in the last 10 years:
Michael Savage, *Revealed: cash crisis pushing child services to tipping point*, Observer,
1 September 2018, https://www.theguardian.com/society/2018/sep/01/children-social-
care-services-councils-austerity

[25] Numbers of children on child protection plans increased from 40,000 in 2009/10 to
nearly 60,000 in 2017/18 – Department for Education: Alison Holt, *Child protection
services near crisis as demand rises*, BBC News, 6 November 2018, https://www.bbc.
co.uk/news/education-46049154

[26] At 31 March 2018, there were 75,420 children in care in England, compared to under
50,000 in 1995. There have been increases in every year since 2012: Department for
Education/National Statistics, *Children looked after in England (including adoption),
year ending 31 March 2018*, 15 November 2018, https://assets.publishing.service.
gov.uk/government/uploads/system/uploads/attachment_data/file/756232/Children_
looked_after_in_England_2018_Text.pdf

[27] Jess Staufenberg, *New DfE research shows 'lasting negative impact' on attainment
of children in need*, Schools Week, 10 December 2018, https://schoolsweek.co.uk/new-
dfe-research-shows-lasting-negative-impact-on-attainment-of-children-in-need/

[28] Between 2010 and 2016 central government funding for early intervention fell by
£1.7bn, a 40% reduction; cuts in the poorest areas were six times worse than in the
richest: Children's Society, Action for Children and the National Children's Bureau,
Turning the tide, Reversing the move to late intervention spending in children and young

people's services, November 2017, https://www.childrenssociety.org.uk/sites/default/files/turning-the-tide.pdf. A further £183m. will be cut from the early intervention budget by 2020: Sarah Marsh, *Vulnerable children in England 'falling through cracks' in social services*, Guardian, 14 August 2017, https://www.theguardian.com/society/2017/aug/14/vulnerable-children-england-falling-through-cracks-social-services-charity-warns

[29] Taking inflation into account, overall spending on children's services in England from 2010 to 2017 reduced by 16%; in the poorest areas by 27% and in the wealthiest areas by 4% - Analysis of Department for Education data by researchers at Huddersfield and Sheffield Universities: Alison Holt, Sophie Woodcock & Judith Burns, *Poorest areas face biggest cuts to children's services*, BBC News, 6 February 2018, http://www.bbc.co.uk/news/education-42891705. Children services' spending per child reduced from £850 in 2009-10 to £700 in 2018-19 – Institute of Fiscal Studies: Alison Holt, *Child protection services near crisis as demand rises*, BBC News, 6 November 2018, https://www.bbc.co.uk/news/education-46049154

[30] Councils have had to increase spending on children's social care by almost 10% in 4 years. In 2017/18 councils in England had to spend £816m. more on children's social care than they had budgeted for. Spending on children's social care has increased at a faster rate than any other council service: Michael Savage, *Revealed: cash crisis pushing child services to tipping point*, Observer, 1 September 2018, https://www.theguardian.com/society/2018/sep/01/children-social-care-services-councils-austerity

[31] The Local Government Association forecast that because of rising demand and cuts in government grants to children services there will be a shortfall in the funding of children's services of £2b. by 2020: Judith Burns, *Funding shortfall 'threatens support for vulnerable children'*, BBC News, 11 May 2017, http://www.bbc.co.uk/news/education-39849120.

[32] Elaine Kelly, Tom Lee, Luke Sibieta & Tom Waters, *Public Spending on Children in England: 2000 to 2020*, Children's Commissioner for England, London, June 2018, https://www.childrenscommissioner.gov.uk/wp-content/uploads/2018/06/Public-Spending-on-Children-in-England-CCO-JUNE-2018.pdf

[33] All Party Parliamentary Group for Children, *Storing Up Trouble, A postcode lottery of children's social care*, National Children's Bureau, July 2018, London, https://www.ncb.org.uk/sites/default/files/field/attachment/report/APPGC_NCB_storing%20up%20trouble_final_0.pdf

[34] Such as severe mental health problems and domestic violence in the household.

[35] Anne Longfield OBE, Children's Commissioner for England: BBC Radio 4's

Today programme on 4 August 2018: Press Association, *Council funding crisis could be 'catastrophic' for vulnerable children*, Guardian, 4 August 2018, https://www.theguardian.com/society/2018/aug/04/council-funding-crisis-could-be-catastrophic-for-vulnerable-children

[36] A study by Ofsted in 2015 found that if children do not get help early their problems get worse and they are often re-referred to social services: Sarah Marsh, *Charity says 140,000 youngsters considered in need of help because of neglect or abuse are not being offered any*, Guardian, 14 August 2017, https://www.theguardian.com/society/2017/aug/14/vulnerable-children-england-falling-through-cracks-social-services-charity-warns

[37] In the cabinet reshuffle in January 2018 the role of children's minister was downgraded from minister of state to parliamentary under-secretary: Louise Tickle, *Don't blame social workers. It's the system that's broken*, Guardian, 18 January 2018, https://www.theguardian.com/commentisfree/2018/jan/17/social-workers-child-protection adoption?utm_source=esp&utm_medium=Email&utm_campaign=GU+Today+main+NEW+H+categories&utm_term=260850&subid=21534152&CMP=EMCNEWEML6619I2

[38] Rachel Williams, *The evolution of Sure Start: the challenges and the successes*, Guardian, 19 October 2011, https://www.theguardian.com/society/2011/oct/19/evolution-of-sure-start-success

[39] Actual cash spent on Sure Start was 46% lower in 2015/16 than it was in 2010/11; a 47% reduction in real terms. The Conservative government elected in 2015 cut the grant that mainly funded Sure Start by nearly a quarter from £1.58bn. to £1.21bn. in 2017/18, with plans to reduce it further to £1.0 billion in 2019/20. By June 2017 the number of children's centres had further reduced to 2,443 (plus 731 subsidiary sites): Alex Bate & David Foster, *Briefing Paper, Number 7257, Sure Start (England)*, House of Commons Library, 9 June 2017, http://researchbriefings.parliament.uk/ResearchBriefing/Summary/CBP-7257

[40] Multi-year, longitudinal studies commissioned by the Labour government (National Evaluation of Sure Start co-ordinated by Birkbeck, University of London, which reported every year from 2002-2012) and the coalition government (Evaluation of Children's Centres in England) – research carried out by NatCen Social Research, University of Oxford and Frontier Economics, producing 11 publications between 2012 and 2016; and a 2010 quantitative study by the Audit Commission. The National Evaluation of Sure Start (NESS) Team, Institute for the Study of Children, Families and Social Issues,

Birkbeck, University of London, *The impact of Sure Start Local Programmes on seven year olds and their families, Research Report DFE-RR220*, Department for Education, 2010, http://www.ness.bbk.ac.uk/impact/documents/DFE-RR220.pdf

[41] Alex Bate & David Foster, *Briefing Paper, Number 7257, Sure Start (England)*, House of Commons Library, 9 June 2017, http://researchbriefings.parliament.uk/ResearchBriefing/Summary/CBP-7257.

[42] Department for Children, Schools and Families, *Think Family Toolkit Improving support for families at risk, Strategic overview*, 2009

[43] The independent evaluation of the Think Family pathfinder programmes concluded that there were significant improvements in outcomes for 46% of families supported by the Family Pathfinders and 'savings to local partners, so that for every £1 spent, the Family Pathfinders generated a financial return of £1.90': York Consulting, *Turning around the lives of families with multiple problems - an evaluation of the Family and Young Carer Pathfinders Programme* (York Consulting, 2011), https://assets.publishing.service.gov.uk/government/uploads/system/uploads/attachment_data/file/197376/DFE-RB154.pdf

[44] Ibid

[45] DCLG (Press release), *Troubled Families Programme on track at half way stage* https://www.gov.uk/government/news/troubled-families-programme-on-track-at-half-way-stage

[46] BBC News, *Eric Pickles: 105,000 troubled families' lives turned round*, 10 March 2015, http://www.bbc.co.uk/news/uk-politics-31819172

[47] Ibid

[48] Laurie Day, Caroline Bryson, Clarissa White, Susan Purdon, Helen Bewley, Laura Kirchner Sala & Jonathan Portes, *National Evaluation of the Troubled Families Programme Final Synthesis Report*, Department for Communities and Local Government, October 2016, https://assets.publishing.service.gov.uk/government/uploads/system/uploads/attachment_data/file/560499/Troubled_Families_Evaluation_Synthesis_Report.pdf

[49] Professor Ruth Levitas, *'Troubled Families' in a Spin*, March 2014, http://www.poverty.ac.uk/sites/default/files/attachments/Troubled%20Families%20in%20a%20Spin.pdf

[50] Michael Savage, *Failed troubled families scheme gets a reboot*, The Times, 17 February 2017, http://www.thetimes.co.uk/edition/news/failed-troubled-families-scheme-gets-a-reboot-zwswqw95n. Chris Cook, *Troubled Families report 'suppressed'*, BBC News,

8 August 2016, http://www.bbc.co.uk/news/uk-politics-37010486. One stark example of the lack of impact of TFP was that after interventions only 3.8% (4,555 families) were in continuous employment; a result that would have been expected without any intervention anyway, given the overall reductions in unemployment that there had been: Troubled Families Update, Adfam discussion paper, 2014, http://www.adfam. org.uk/cms/docs/adfam_troubledfamilies.pdf

[51] Each local authority received a payment of £3,200 for each family that was enrolled onto TFP. The success criteria were vague – for example, families could be ticked off as being 'turned around' even if children were continuing to truant or commit crime, as long as there were fewer of these incidences than before. Local authorities were then provided with a further £800 for each family they claimed they had 'turned around'. Some local authorities claimed to have 'turned around' 100% of the families they were working with: Chris Cook, *Troubled Families report 'suppressed'*, , BBC News, 8 August 2016, http://www.bbc.co.uk/news/uk-politics-37010486

[52] House of Commons Committee of Public Accounts, *Troubled families: progress review*, House of Commons, London, 20 December 2016, https://publications. parliament.uk/pa/cm201617/cmselect/cmpubacc/711/711.pdf

[53] Jonathan Portas blog, *Troubled Families - anatomy of a policy disaster*, 17 October 2016, http://notthetreasuryview.blogspot.com/2016/10/troubled-families-anatomy-of-policy.html

Chapter 6: Schools

[1] Michael Bassey, *Political impact: from the least state-controlled to the most in 24 years*, Free schools from government control.com website, http://www.free-school-from-government-control.com/political.html

[2] Alan Smithers, *Education Policy, In The Blair Effect*, edited by Anthony Seldon (Little Brown, London, 2001) pgs. 405-426

[3] David Weisbloom, *Rupert Murdoch 'a great man' – Michael Gove*, Channel 4 News website, 3 October 2011, https://www.channel4.com/news/rupert-murdoch-a-great-man-michael-gove

[4] George Eaton, *Gove's "hero" Andrew Adonis attacks decision not to reappoint Ofsted head*, New Statesman, 3 February 2014, http://www.newstatesman.com/politics/2014/02/goves-hero-andrew-adonis-attacks-decision-not-reappoint-ofsted-head

[5] Under the Labour government (2010-15) primary school spending per pupil increased

by 114% in real terms and secondary school spending by 90%: John Blake, *Schools cry wolf when claiming they are underfunded*, The Times, 16 November 2017, https://www.thetimes.co.uk/edition/comment/schools-cry-wolf-when-claiming-they-are-underfunded-9vt55dmll

[6] Total school spending per pupil has fallen by 8% in real terms between 2009–10 and 2017–18. This was mainly driven by a 55% cut to local authority spending on services and cuts of over 20% to school sixth-form funding: Chris Belfield, Christine Farquharson & Luke Sibieta, *2018 annual report on education spending in England*, Institute of Fiscal Studies, 17 September 2018, https://www.ifs.org.uk/uploads/publications/comms/R150.pdf

[7] Rowena Mason & Sally Weale, *Justine Greening raids free schools budget for £1.3bn education bailout*, Guardian, 18 July 2017, https://www.theguardian.com/education/2017/jul/17/justine-greening-raids-free-schools-budget-for-education-bailout

[8] OECD, Education at a Glance 2018: OECD Indicators, United Kingdom country notes, OECD Publishing, https://read.oecd-ilibrary.org/education/education-at-a-glance-2018/united-kingdom_eag-2018-70-en#page1

[9] BBC News, *'Historic' schools funding change confirmed*, 14 September 2017, http://www.bbc.co.uk/news/uk-politics-41269926

[10] Mike Baker, *Can naming and shaming help schools?* BBC News, Friday 13 June 2008, http://news.bbc.co.uk/1/hi/education/7453301.stm

[11] The Guardian, *Headteachers at 'coasting' schools face threat of sack*, 17 May 2015, http://www.theguardian.com/education/2015/may/17/headteachers-at-coasting-schools-face-threat-of-sack

[12] In 2016 Ofsted named the East Midlands as the worst performing region; Leicester the worst for early years; and Northamptonshire the worst for disadvantaged children: Guardian, *East Midlands schools 'worst in England'*, says Ofsted chief, 8 June 2016, p. 11, https://www.theguardian.com/uk-news/2016/jun/07/east-midlands-schools-worst-performing-ofsted-michael-wilshaw-gcse

[13] Sian Griffiths, *Children at risk in 'rotten borough' Birmingham*, The Sunday Times, 11 December 2016, http://www.thetimes.co.uk/edition/news/children-at-risk-in-rotten-borough-birmingham-fl5f00pkb

[14] Greg Hurst, *Failing schools fuelled Brexit, says Ofsted head*, The Times, 2 December 2016, http://www.thetimes.co.uk/edition/news/failing-schools-fuelled-brexit-says-ofsted-head-mk3ngpwpp

[15] Out of the 35 OECD countries only 4 have national tests for primary school

children. Fewer than half have exams at 16; the standard being exams at 18: OECD, *How are schools held accountable?"* Education at a Glance: OECD Indicators, OECD Publishing, http://www.oecd.org/edu/skills-beyond-school/48631582.pdf)

[16] In 2016, for example, primary schools were deemed to be 'underperforming' if they had fewer than 65% of pupils achieving the 'expected standard' in key stage 2 SATs; and secondary schools if fewer than 40% of students had acquired at least five GCSEs at grade C or more including English and mathematics. From 2018 secondary schools are judged on their EBacc average points score. EBacc refers to a combination of subjects that has to include English language and literature, mathematics, science, geography or history, and a language: GOV.UK website, Department for Education, Policy paper, English Baccalaureate (EBacc), Updated 18 December 2017, https://www.gov.uk/government/publications/english-baccalaureate-ebacc/english-baccalaureate-ebacc

[17] Nine documents in total; see https://www.gov.uk/government/publications/primary-school-accountability, and https://www.gov.uk/government/publications/progress-8-school-performance-measure

[18] Information obtained by the Times Education Supplement from freedom of information requests made to the Department for Education: Camilla Turner, *Pupils sit GCSEs twice 'to boost school results'*, Daily Telegraph, 26 September 2017, p. 2

[19] OECD, *How are schools held accountable?*, Education at a Glance: OECD Indicators, OECD Publishing, http://www.oecd.org/edu/skills-beyond-school/48631582.pdf)

[20] In 2013/14, for the first time, school and education problems appeared in the top ten concerns raised by children with ChildLine, representing a 13% rise from the previous year. 58% of counselling sessions in relation to school and education problems were about exam stress, a 200% rise on the previous year: Childline, *Under pressure, ChildLine Review, What's affected children in April 2013 – March 2014*, NSPCC, 2014, https://www.nspcc.org.uk/globalassets/documents/annual-reports/childline-review-under-pressure.pdf

[21] Harvey Goldstein, Gemma Moss, Pamela Sammons, Gwen Sinnott & Gordon Stobart, *A baseline without basis, The validity and utility of the proposed reception baseline assessment in England*, British Educational Research Association, 4 July 2018, p.6, https://www.bera.ac.uk/wp-content/uploads/2018/07/A-baseline-without-basis_BERA-report_July2018.pdf?noredirect=1

[22] The evaluation explains that the baseline assessment 'is an untried experiment that cannot be properly evaluated until at least 2027, when the first cohort tested at reception has taken key stage 2 tests'. The assessment according to the evaluation 'is

likely to produce results with little predictive power and dubious validity' for a number of reasons including differences in age in the early years that produces pronounced developmental differences; statistically insignificant pupil cohorts; pupil mobility; teacher and headteacher turnover; and a range of contextual factors: Ibid

[23] Standard Assessment Tests are compulsory for all 7 year olds (end of Key Stage 1) and 11 year olds (end of Key Stage 2), testing what they have learnt in areas of the national curriculum. Key Stage 1 is teacher-assessed, externally moderated, covering speaking and listening, reading and writing, mathematics and science. Key Stage 2 involves externally set and marked written tests in reading, writing (including handwriting), spelling, mathematics, mental arithmetic and science. There are different levels that pupils are graded at, level 2 being the standard at Key Stage 1 and level 4 at Key Stage 2.

[24] Nicola Woolcock, *Don't stress about Sats, urges minister*, The Times, 11 July 2018, https://www.thetimes.co.uk/article/don-t-stress-about-sats-urges-minister-vrxmphpzw

[25] Sean Coughlan, *Tory resit plan for pupils with poor Sats results*, BBC News, 8 April 2015, https://www.bbc.co.uk/news/education-32204578

[26] NAHT News, *Plan for optional SATs resits in year seven scrapped*, November 2018, Issue 322, National Association of Headteachers

[27] Ofqual issued 890 penalties to school staff for exam malpractice in 2017 compared with 360 in 2016 - Hannah Richardson, *More students found cheating in GCSE and A-level exams*, BBC News, 5 January 2018, http://www.bbc.co.uk/news/education-42578874. For England, Wales and Northern Ireland, Ofqual issued 388 penalties in 2016 compared to 97 in 2013 - Research by the Royal Society of Arts: Rosemary Bennett, *Big rise in teachers caught cheating to boost exam results*, The Times, 16 November 2017, https://www.thetimes.co.uk/article/3cf6bb7e-ca3e-11e7-9ee9-e45ae7e1cdd4

[28] Amanda Spielman, *The Annual Report of Her Majesty's Chief Inspector of Education, Children's Services and Skills 2016/17*, House of Commons, 13 December, 2017, p.19, https://assets.publishing.service.gov.uk/government/uploads/system/uploads/attachment_data/file/666871/Ofsted_Annual_Report_2016-17_Accessible.pdf

[29] Katherine Sellgren, *Times table check trialled ahead of rollout*, BBC News, 14 February 2018, http://www.bbc.co.uk/news/education-43046142

[30] Ofsted's full title is 'Office for Standards in Education, Children's Services and Skills'

[31] In addition to schools, Ofsted inspect and regulate early years provision, schools, sixth form colleges, further education, work-based learning and skills training, adult and community learning, initial teacher education, local authorities' education role,

children's social care services, the Children and Family Court Advisory Support Service (Cafcass), and prison education. Ofsted has a budget of £135 million and 1,500 employees.

[32] A school that requires improvement will have another full inspection within two years. Inadequate schools are subject to termly monitoring by Ofsted.

[33] Robert Colvile, *Ofsted is failing, so give parents access to data on schools*, Times, 18 April 2017, https://www.thetimes.co.uk/edition/comment/ofsted-is-failing-so-give-parents-access-to-data-on-schools-w5hlzxpdg

[34] Jo Hutchinson, *School Inspection in England: Is There Room to Improve?* Education Policy Institute, November 2016, https://epi.org.uk/publications-and-research/school-inspection-england-room-improve/

[35] BBC news, *Ofsted inspectors 'lack key skills' required for job*, 17 March 2014, http://www.bbc.co.uk/news/education-26580679. *Ofsted announces plans to bring management of all school and further education inspections in-house*, 29 May 2014, Ofsted, https://www.gov.uk/government/news/plans-to-manage-school-and-further-education-inspections-in-house

[36] Hannah Richardson, *Ofsted purges 1,200 'not good enough' inspectors*, BBC News, 19 June 2015, http://www.bbc.co.uk/news/education-33198707

[37] Will Ryan, *Leadership with a Moral Purpose, Turning Your School Inside Out* (Crown House Publishing Limited, 2008) p. 160

[38] Sean Coughlan, *How many good schools are there really?* BBC News, 9 December 2014, http://www.bbc.co.uk/news/education-30319949

[39] 579,000 pupils attend schools that are rated as good or outstanding that have not been inspected since at least 2010, and 124,000 pupils in schools that have not been inspected in the last 10 years: Jon Andrews, *Does the claim of '1.9 million more children in good or outstanding schools' stack up?* Education Policy Institute, July 2018, https://epi.org.uk/publications-and-research/does-1-9m-claim-stack-up/. In excess of 1,600 schools judged 'outstanding' by Ofsted have not been inspected for at least six years and 300 for more than ten years: Sir Amyas Morse KCB, Comptroller and Auditor General, *Ofsted's inspection of schools*, National Audit Office, 21 May 2018, https://www.nao.org.uk/wp-content/uploads/2018/05/Ofsteds-inspection-of-schools.pdf

[40] Of the schools inspected in 2017/18, 54% were rated good (47%) or outstanding (7%); 37% require improvement; 9% were inadequate: Amanda Spielman, *The Annual Report of Her Majesty's Chief Inspector of Education, Children's Services and Skills 2017/18*, Ofsted, 4 December 2018, https://assets.publishing.service.gov.

uk/government/uploads/system/uploads/attachment_data/file/760991/29523_Ofsted_ Annual_Report_2017-18_WEB.pdf. All schools good or outstanding inspected in Autumn 2014 - 75%; All schools good or outstanding inspected in Autumn 2015 - 64%; Secondary schools good or outstanding inspected in Autumn 2015 - 45%: Sophie Scott, *'How many schools did Ofsted rate last term? (And what did they get)'*, Schools Week, 8 January 2016, http://schoolsweek.co.uk/who-got-the-good-grades/

[41] Sophie Scott, *'How many schools did Ofsted rate last term? (And what did they get)'*, Schools Week, 8 January 2016, http://schoolsweek.co.uk/who-got-the-good-grades/

[42] Jon Andrews, *Does the claim of '1.9 million more children in good or outstanding schools' stack up?* Education Policy Institute, July 2018, https://epi.org.uk/publications-and-research/does-1-9m-claim-stack-up/

[43] Melanie Ehren, Jane Perryman & Ken Spours, *Accountability and school inspections*, June 2014, Institute of Education, University of London, http://doc.utwente.nl/93511/1/ Ehren_et_al_-_FINAL.pdf

[44] I. Shaw, D. P. Newton, M. Aitkin & R. Darnell, *Do OFSTED Inspections of Secondary Schools Make a Difference to GCSE Results?* British Education Research Journal, 29 (1), February 2003 p. 63

[45] Ibid. A. Harris & C. Chapman, *Improving Schools in Difficult Contexts: towards a differentiated approach*, British Journal of Educational Studies, 52 (4), pgs. 417-431, 2004. L. Rosenthal, *Do School Inspections Improve School Quality? Ofsted Inspections and School Examination Results in the UK*, Economics of Education Review, 23 (2), pgs. 143-151, 2004: all quoted in Melanie Ehren, Jane Perryman & Ken Spours, *Accountability and school inspections*, June 2014, Institute of Education, University of London, http://doc.utwente.nl/93511/1/Ehren_et_al_-_FINAL.pdf

[46] Melanie Ehren, Jane Perryman & Ken Spours, *Accountability and school inspections*, June 2014, Institute of Education, University of London, http://doc.utwente.nl/93511/1/ Ehren_et_al_-_FINAL.pdf

[47] K. Jones & P. Tymms, *Ofsted's role in promoting school improvement: The mechanisms of the school inspection system in England*, Oxford Review of Education – quoted in Melanie Ehren, Jane Perryman & Ken Spours, *Accountability and school inspections*, June 2014, Institute of Education, University of London, http://doc. utwente.nl/93511/1/Ehren_et_al_-_FINAL.pdf

[48] Royal Society of Arts *(Un)satisfactory? Enhancing life chances by improving 'satisfactory' schools*, RSA, London, 2012. Melanie Ehren, Jane Perryman & Ken Spours, *Accountability and school inspections*, June 2014, Institute of Education,

University of London, http://doc.utwente.nl/93511/1/Ehren_et_al_-_FINAL.pdf

[49] S.J. Courtney, *Ofsted's revised school inspection framework: experiences and implications*, Paper presented at BERA conference, Manchester, 2012 - quoted in Melanie Ehren, Jane Perryman & Ken Spours, *Accountability and school inspections*, June 2014, Institute of Education, University of London, http://doc.utwente.nl/93511/1/Ehren_et_al_-_FINAL.pdf

[50] Royal Society of Arts *(Un)satisfactory? Enhancing life chances by improving 'satisfactory' schools*, RSA, London, 2012 - quoted in Melanie Ehren, Jane Perryman and Ken Spours, *Accountability and school inspections*, June 2014, Institute of Education, University of London, http://doc.utwente.nl/93511/1/Ehren_et_al_-_FINAL.pdf

[51] Ofsted, *The education inspection framework, Draft for consultation*, January 2019, https://assets.publishing.service.gov.uk/government/uploads/system/uploads/attachment_data/file/770924/Proposed_education_inspection_framework_draft_for_consultation_140119.pdf.pdf

[52] Researchers analysed Ofsted data over a 10-year period and the impact of multi-academy trusts; and conducted 47 detailed school case studies and a survey of almost 700 school leaders: Toby Greany & Rob Higham, *Hierarchy, Markets and Networks, Analysing the 'self-improving school-led system' agenda in England and the implications for schools*, (UCL Institute of Education Press, London, July 2018), https://www.ucl-ioe-press.com/ioe-content/uploads/2018/08/Hierarchy-Markets-and-Networks.pdf, pgs.11 &12

[53] Research by Durham University's Centre for Evaluation and Monitoring found no significant evidence that effective schools were reducing the gap in attainment: Peter Tymms, Christine Merrell & Katharine Bailey, *The long-term impact of effective teaching*, School Effectiveness and School Improvement, 29:2, published online 14 December 2017, pgs. 242-261, https://www.tandfonline.com/doi/full/10.1080/09243453.2017.1404478?scroll=top&needAccess=true

[54] GOV.UK website, *Find and compare schools in England*, https://www.gov.uk/school-performance-tables

[55] Examples of school attainment league tables include the Daily Telegraph's 'Top 1000 primary schools in England'; the Sunday Times's 'Top 500 English state primary and secondary schools', the Independent's '100 best-performing state [secondary] schools', and the Sun's top ten English primary schools and best regions.

[56] The Cumberland News, *Cumbrian school plunged into special measures after failing inspection*, 3 March 2017, http://www.cumberlandnews.co.uk/learning/Cumbrian-school-plunged-into-special-measures-after-failing-inspection-ea116074-c5f6-4da3-

8185-c123d2617f89-ds

[57] K. Whitby, *School inspections: recent experiences in high performing education systems*, CfBT Education Trust, Reading, 2010. A. Wiggins & P. Tymms, *Dysfunctional effects of league tables: a comparison between English and Scottish primary schools*, Public Money and Management, 22 (1), 2002, pgs. 43-48. M. Ehren & M. Swanborn, *Strategic Data Use of Schools in Accountability Systems*, School Effectiveness and School Improvement, 23 (2), 2012, pages 257-280: all quoted in Melanie Ehren, Jane Perryman & Ken Spours, *Accountability and school inspections*, June 2014, Institute of Education, University of London, http://doc.utwente.nl/93511/1/Ehren_et_al_-_FINAL.pdf

[58] At some primary schools only 7% of applicants received a place. Half of secondary schools were oversubscribed in 2018, compared with 43% in 2015. Catchment areas at some primary schools are less than 100 metres, with up to 14 children competing for each place, according to an audit: Nicola Woolcock, *PE cuts raise fears for pupil health*, The Times, 1 September 2018, https://www.thetimes.co.uk/article/schools-slash-pe-and-welfare-to-focus-on-core-subjects-9s3rlqp6w. Nearly 25,000 more students applied for admission to secondary schools in Year 7 places in England for the 2018/19 academic year than for 2017/18, making it the highest number of applications for 20 years: Rosemary Bennett, *Demand for school places reaches 20-year high*, The Times, 17 October 2018, https://www.thetimes.co.uk/article/demand-for-school-places-reaches-20-year-high-6kczj28fv

[59] Department for Education, *Schools causing concern, Intervening in failing, underperforming and coasting schools, Guidance for local authorities and RSCs*, March 2016, https://www.gov.uk/government/consultations/intervening-in-failing-underperforming-and-coasting-schools

[60] The Education and Adoption Act 2016

[61] Department for Education, *Schools causing concern, Intervening in failing, underperforming and coasting schools, Guidance for local authorities and RSCs*, March 2016, https://www.gov.uk/government/consultations/intervening-in-failing-underperforming-and-coasting-schools

[62] GOV.UK, *Open academies and academy projects in development, Information on all academies open in England, and those in the process of becoming academies*, 17 May 2018, Department for Education, https://www.gov.uk/government/publications/open-academies-and-academy-projects-in-development

[63] Sir Amyas Morse KCB, Comptroller and Auditor General, *Converting maintained schools to academies*, National Audit Office, 20 February 2018, https://www.nao.org.

uk/wp-content/uploads/2018/02/Converting-maintained-schools-to-academies.pdf

[64] Greg Hurst, *Cameron ditches plans to impose academy status*, The Times, 7 May 2016, p. 6, https://www.thetimes.co.uk/edition/news/cameron-ditches-plans-to-impose-academy-status-5p9tlpdgv

[65] Louise McEvoy, *Campaign mounted in bid to stop Stevenage school becoming an academy*, The Comet, 23 November 2018, https://www.thecomet.net/news/education/campaign-to-stop-stevenage-s-barclay-school-becoming-academy-1-5789020

[66] Department for Education and Skills, *Higher Standards, Better Schools For All, More choice for parents and pupils* (Schools White Paper), HM Government, October 2005

[67] OECD, *PISA in Focus 7, Private schools: Who benefits?* 2011, https://www.oecd-ilibrary.org/docserver/5k9h362mhtkd-enpdf?expires=1535641595&id=id&accname=guest&checksum=66226545421A59AFDA3E2213F0AED592

[68] Alex Bryson & Francis Green, *Do private schools manage better?* National Institute Economic Review, Issue 243, Sage Publications, London, 7 February 2018, https://www.niesr.ac.uk/publications/do-private-schools-manage-better

[69] The research measures how each local authority and academy chain ('group') fares with pupil improvement and takes into account characteristics such as pupil prior attainment, levels of disadvantage and historic performance of a school. The Education Policy Institute state that 'this allows for a clear measure of performance, undistorted by schools' differing pupil intakes'. At Key Stage 2 local authorities made up 15 of the top 20 school groups; only 1 academy chain was in the top 10; 11 academy chains are in the bottom 20 groups. At Key Stage 4, 14 academy chains are in the top 20: Jon Andrews, *School performance in academy chains and local authorities – 2017*, Education Policy Institute, June 2018, https://epi.org.uk/publications-and-research/performance-academy-local-authorities-2017/

[70] In the 2017 Key Stage 1 SATs 76% of pupils in academies achieved the expected standard of level 2 or above, and 77% of pupils from local authority schools achieved this level: Nicola Woolcock, *Free schools outperform state schools and academies in SATs*, The Times, 29 September 2017, https://www.thetimes.co.uk/article/7f6a6de6-a439-11e7-8955-1ad2a9a7928d. Local authority-maintained schools did slightly better than those with academy status in Key Stage 2 tests of literacy and maths taken 2018: Richard Adams, *KS2 results show widening gulf between strongest and weakest primary schools*, Guardian, 4 September 2018, https://www.theguardian.com/education/2018/sep/04/ks2-results-primary-schools-performance

[71] Only three multi-academy trusts (those with at least 5 schools) out of 20 had a value added score that was above the national average. 85% of academy chains underperformed on this measure: Department of Education, *Measuring the performance of schools within academy chains and local authorities*, Statistical Working Paper, 19 March 2015

[72] Researchers examined 58 multi-academy academy trusts over five years and found that 38 of them disadvantaged pupils performed below the national average for all state schools: Merryn Hutchings & Becky Francis, *Chain Effects 2018, The impact of academy chains on low-income pupils*, Sutton Trust, December 2018, https://www.suttontrust.com/wp-content/uploads/2018/12/Chain-Effects-2018.pdf

[73] Ofsted found that 38% of 'converter' academies were worse and 48% no better than they had been as local authority schools: Ofsted, *The Annual Report of Her Majesty's Chief Inspector of Education, Children's Services and Skills 2013/14*, Controller of Her Majesty's Stationery Office, 10 December 2014, https://assets.publishing.service.gov.uk/government/uploads/system/uploads/attachment_data/file/384699/Ofsted_Annual_Report_201314_HMCI_commentary.pdf. In terms of Ofsted grades received by schools 'at their most recent inspection', as at March 2015, there was the same proportion (83%) of good or outstanding local authority (LA) maintained as academy primary schools; and in the secondary sector, slightly more LA schools (67%) than academies (67%): Helen Ward, *Ofsted: good and outstanding schools at record high*, Times Education Supplement, 16 June 2015, https://www.tes.com/news/school-news/breaking-news/ofsted-good-and-outstanding-schools-record-high. At April 2016 86% of local authority schools were rated good or outstanding, compared with 82% of academies and 79% of free schools. Based on Ofsted's more 'rigorous' inspections (introduced in 2012) 81% of local authority schools were good or outstanding compared with 73% of academies and 79% of free schools. 90% of local authority schools improved in their first inspection after being rated 'inadequate' compared to 80% of academies: Sally Weale, *Council-run schools 'beat academies in Ofsted inspections'*, Guardian, 26 April 2016, p. 18. 'Evidence on the performance of academies compared to local authority schools is mixed, but on the whole suggests there is no substantial difference in performance': Full Fact website, *Academies and maintained schools: what do we know?* 26th May 2017, https://fullfact.org/education/academies-and-maintained-schools-what-do-we-know/

[74] Researchers, Angel Solutions, on behalf of the Local Government Association, analysed the inspection histories of 429 council maintained schools that had been

judged by Ofsted inspections to be inadequate in 2013. Of these 152 had stayed with their local authority and 212 had become sponsored academies. Most of the remaining 65 either closed or were taken over by other schools. By December 2017 all 152 of the local authority schools had been re-inspected and 115 (75%) were rated good or outstanding; and 155 of the sponsored academies had been re-inspected, and 92 of these (59.4%) rated good or outstanding: Judith Burns, *'Councils beat academy trusts at boosting failing schools'*, BBC News, 5 July 2018, https://www.bbc.co.uk/news/education-44698272

[75] Nicola Woolcock, *Failing academies 'pay to offload difficult children'*, The Times, 14 March 2016, p. 4, https://www.thetimes.co.uk/article/failing-academies-pay-to-offload-difficult-children-g2xrkpf5m

[76] Rowena Mason, *Cameron – our aim is for every school to become an academy*, The Guardian, 15 August 2015, p. 2, https://www.theguardian.com/education/2015/aug/15/david-cameron-i-want-every-school-to-become-an-academy

[77] Estelle Morris, *The gaping hole between ministers' rhetoric and reality*, Guardian Education, 24 May 2016, p. 34, www.theguardian.com/education/2016/may/24/schools-ministers-education-dictate-policy

[78] Toby Greany & Rob Higham, *Hierarchy, Markets and Networks, Analysing the 'self-improving school-led system' agenda in England and the implications for schools*, UCL Institute of Education Press, London, July 2018, p.11, https://www.ucl-ioe-press.com/ioe-content/uploads/2018/08/Hierarchy-Markets-and-Networks.pdf

[79] Sally Weale, *Ofsted say academy chain is failing pupils*, Guardian, 5 February 2016, p. 12. Nicola Woolcock, *Thousands 'let down' by academy school*, The Times, 11 March 2016, p. 8, https://www.thetimes.co.uk/article/thousands-let-down-by-academy-schools-qxnt80h0v

[80] Greg Hurst, *First academy trust to lose its schools over poor standards*, The Times, 10 March 2017, http://www.thetimes.co.uk/edition/news/first-academy-trust-to-lose-its-schools-over-poor-standards-rz67nqpf0. Richard Adams, *Lauded academy chain to lose schools after inquiry highlights financial failings*, Guardian, 29 April 2016, p. 4. Martin George, *Number of closing academy trusts quadruples*, Times Education Supplement, 7 November 2018, https://www.tes.com/news/number-closing-academy-trusts-quadruples. Freddie Whittaker, *DfE 'minded to terminate' funding of four academies*, Schools Week, 15 November 2018, https://schoolsweek.co.uk/dfe-minded-to-terminate-funding-of-four-academies/

[81] Amanda Spielman, *The Annual Report of Her Majesty's Chief Inspector of Education,*

Children's Services and Skills 2017/18, Ofsted, 4 December 2018, https://assets. publishing.service.gov.uk/government/uploads/system/uploads/attachment_data/ file/760991/29523_Ofsted_Annual_Report_2017-18_WEB.pdf

[82] Examples include Park View academy chain in Birmingham (Lee Donaghy, *Academy over-expansion was the real Trojan horse scandal*, Guardian Education, 16 June 2015, p. 35, https://www.theguardian.com/education/2015/jun/16/academy-schools-trojan-horse-extremism-park-view); School Company Trust (Pippa Allen-Kinross, *Schools Company: Board minutes reveal extent of failure at doomed academy trust*, School Week, 13 July 2018, https://schoolsweek.co.uk/schools-company-board-minutes-reveal-extent-of-failure-at-doomed-academy-trust/); Wakefield City Academies Trust (BBC News, *Wakefield City Academies Trust pulls out of 21 schools*, 8 September 2017, http://www.bbc.co.uk/news/uk-england-leeds-41198403; Bright Tribe Trust (Pippa Allen-Kinross, *Embattled Bright Tribe academy trust to close*, Schools Week, 16 July 2018, https://schoolsweek.co.uk/embattled-bright-tribe-academy-trust-to-close/); and AET Academy Trust (Martin George, *Biggest academy trust AET to lose two more schools*, Times Education Supplement, 14 November 2018, https://www.tes.com/news/ biggest-academy-trust-aet-lose-two-more-schools)

[83] House of Commons Committee of Public Accounts, *School oversight and intervention*, House of Commons, 15 January 2015, https://publications.parliament.uk/pa/cm201415/ cmselect/cmpubacc/735/735.pdf. House of Commons Education Committee, *Academies and Free School*, House of Commons, 21 January 2015, https://publications. parliament.uk/pa/cm201415/cmselect/cmeduc/258/258.pdf. House of Commons Education Committee, *Multi-academy trusts*, House of Commons, 22 February 2017, https://publications.parliament.uk/pa/cm201617/cmselect/cmeduc/204/204.pdf. House of Commons Committee of Public Accounts, *Converting schools to academies*, House of Commons, 11 July 2018, https://publications.parliament.uk/pa/cm201719/ cmselect/cmpubacc/697/697.pdf

[84] House of Commons Education Committee, *Academies and Free Schools, Fourth Report*, House of Commons, 21 January 2015, https://publications.parliament.uk/pa/ cm201415/cmselect/cmeduc/258/258.pdf

[85] House of Commons Education Committee, *Multi-academy trusts*, House of Commons, 22 February 2017, https://publications.parliament.uk/pa/cm201617/ cmselect/cmeduc/204/204.pdf

[86] House of Commons Committee of Public Accounts, *Converting schools to academies*, House of Commons, 11 July 2018, https://publications.parliament.uk/pa/cm201719/

cmselect/cmpubacc/697/697.pdf

[87] Schools Week reporter, *DfE slammed for 48-hour 'fire sale' of troubled Durand academy*, Schools Week, 19 November 2018, https://schoolsweek.co.uk/dfe-slammed-for-48-hour-fire-sale-of-troubled-durand-academy/

[88] Sally Weale, *Business chiefs urged to set up academies amid talk of shortfall*, The Guardian, 8 September 2015, p. 6

[89] Of the 277 academies rated as inadequate between 2010 and 2015, by October 2016 new academy sponsors had only been found for 84 of them: Hannah Richardson, *Failing academies 'not being taken over fast enough'*, BBC News, 12 October 2016, http://www.bbc.co.uk/news/education-37631472. As at January 2018 more than 35,000 children were being taught in schools that were rated inadequate almost a year previously and have still not been converted into academies - National Audit Office report: Nicola Woolcock, *Failing schools turned into academies at a cost of £745m*, The Times, 22 February 2018, https://www.thetimes.co.uk/article/3e17892a-175f-11e8-9d2e-0477b9927049. At the end of 2017, 64 academy schools with approximately 40,000 pupils, were waiting to 'find a new sponsor after being abandoned by, or stripped from, the trust originally managing them': Frances Perraudin, *40,000 children trapped in 'zombie' academy schools*, Guardian, 3 December 2017, https://www.theguardian.com/education/2017/dec/03/thousand-pupils-trapped-in-zombie-academyschools. One academy trust that in March 2017 agreed to cease responsibility for 12 schools due to 'unacceptably poor standards and an unsustainable financial position', continues to run them because 'ministers cannot find an alternative sponsor to take them on': Rosemary Bennett & Geraldine Hackett, *Failed academy trust still runs a dozen schools*, The Times, 13 November 2017, https://www.thetimes.co.uk/article/4fcd92fa-c7ea-11e7-9ee9-e45ae7e1cdd4

[90] Sir Amyas Morse KCB, Comptroller and Auditor General, *Converting maintained schools to academies*, National Audit Office, 20 February 2018, p.13, https://www.nao.org.uk/wp-content/uploads/2018/02/Converting-maintained-schools-to-academies.pdf

[91] Amanda Spielman, *The Annual Report of Her Majesty's Chief Inspector of Education, Children's Services and Skills 2017/18*, Ofsted, 4 December 2018, https://assets.publishing.service.gov.uk/government/uploads/system/uploads/attachment_data/file/760991/29523_Ofsted_Annual_Report_2017-18_WEB.pdf

[92] Sir Amyas Morse KCB, Comptroller and Auditor General, *Converting maintained schools to academies*, National Audit Office, 20 February 2018, pgs. 12, 13 & 42, https://www.nao.org.uk/wp-content/uploads/2018/02/Converting-maintained-schools-to-academies.pdf

[93] Ibid

[94] Amanda Spielman, *The Annual Report of Her Majesty's Chief Inspector of Education, Children's Services and Skills 2017/18,* Ofsted, 4 December 2018, https://assets. publishing.service.gov.uk/government/uploads/system/uploads/attachment_data/ file/760991/29523_Ofsted_Annual_Report_2017-18_WEB.pdf

[95] Nicola Woolcock, *Academy acclaimed by Gove is stripped of state funding*, The Times, 12 October 2016, http://www.thetimes.co.uk/edition/news/academy-acclaimed-by-gove-is-stripped-of-state-funding-cvf2q99fx. Greg Hurst, *Academy charity faces closure*, The Times, 5 July 2016, p. 20, https://www.thetimes.co.uk/article/academy-charity-faces-closure-after-funding-threat-ccv58qvtw. Adrian Goldberg, *England's academy trusts 'run up debts of £25m'*, BBC News, 9 October 2016, http://www.bbc. co.uk/news/uk-37589921. Sally Weale, *Academy chain gives up control of school after campaign by parents*, Guardian Education, 30 November 2017, https://www. theguardian.com/education/2017/nov/30/academy-chain-gives-up-control-of-school-after-campaign-by-parents. Freddie Whittaker, *Academy trust bailed out by government over pensions delay*, Schools Week, 25 November 2018, https://schoolsweek.co.uk/ academy-trust-bailed-out-by-government-over-pensions-delay/. Pippa Allen-Kinross, *Single-academy trust rapped over £60k undeclared pay-offs*, Schools Week, 30 November 2018, https://schoolsweek.co.uk/single-academy-trust-rapped-over-60k-undeclared-pay-offs/

[96] Judith Burns, *Councils 'should monitor academy cash'*, BBC News, 26 August 2016, http://www.bbc.co.uk/news/education-37190840. Greg Hurst, *First academy trust to lose its schools over poor standards*, The Times, 10 March 2017, http:// www.thetimes.co.uk/edition/news/first-academy-trust-to-lose-its-schools-over-poor-standards-rz67nqpf0. Warwick Mansell, *Harris Federation biggest spender as golden goodbyes by academy chains soar to £1.6m*, Guardian Education, 15 March 2016, p. 36, https://www.theguardian.com/education/2016/mar/15/golden-goodbye-payments-academy-soar-harris. John Roberts, *School warned over its finances*, Yorkshire Evening Post, 6 July 2016, p. 12. Frances Perraudin, *Collapsing academy trust 'asset-stripped its schools of millions'*, Guardian, 21 October 2017, https://www. theguardian.com/education/2017/oct/21/collapsing-wakefield-city-academies-trust-asset-stripped-schools-millions-say-furious-parents. Nicola Woolcock, *Academy trusts generate surplus of £500m*, The Times, 27 October 2017, https://www.thetimes.co.uk/ edition/news/academy-trusts-generate-surplus-of-500m-b8x7q6xdt. The Observer, *The Observer view on the Tories starving schools of funding,* Editorial, 27 January

2018, https://www.theguardian.com/commentisfree/2018/jan/27/observer-view-how-tories-starving-schools-funding. Bronagh Munro, *Academy chain accused of misusing government funds*, BBC Panorama, 10 September 2018, https://www.bbc.co.uk/news/education-45472189; and BBC iPlayer, *'Profits Before Pupils? The Academies Scandal'*, https://www.bbc.co.uk/programmes/b0bk5q99. Sally Weale, *MPs criticise failure to tackle excessive salaries in academies*, Guardian, 30 March 2018, https://www.theguardian.com/education/2018/mar/30/mps-criticise-government-oversight-of-academy-school-finances. Sally Weale, *Former academy head given £850,000 payoff*, Guardian, 19 November 2018, https://www.theguardian.com/education/2018/nov/19/former-academy-head-given-850000-payoff. Freddie Whittaker & Pippa Allen-Kinross, *DfE troubleshooter 'hugely embarrassed' by Bright Tribe scandal*, School Week, 19 November 2018, https://schoolsweek.co.uk/dfe-troubleshooter-hugely-embarrassed-by-bright-tribe-scandal/

[97] Marc Ashdown, *Green Spring Academy: Intimidation and exam-fixing claims*, BBC News, 10 March 2017, http://www.bbc.co.uk/news/uk-england-london-39194587. Greg Hurst, *Leading head suspended in exams inquiry*, The Times, 11 February 2017, http://www.thetimes.co.uk/edition/news/leading-head-suspended-in-exams-inquiry-w58r83fws. Rosemary Bennett, *School bars underachieving year group from taking GCSEs*, The Times, 27 July 2017, p. 5, https://www.thetimes.co.uk/article/route-39-academy-in-higher-clovelly-bars-underachieving-year-group-from-taking-gcses-7vj7fszcm. Richard Adams, *Headteacher leaves primary school after tests investigation*, Guardian, 4 December 2018, https://www.theguardian.com/education/2018/dec/04/headteacher-leaves-primary-school-after-tests-investigation

[98] The Times, *Schools accused of illegally cherry-picking pupils*, 27 January 2017, http://www.thetimes.co.uk/edition/news/schools-accused-of-illegally-cherry-picking-pupils-lww32nlt0. Fiona Millar, *School admissions; why there's nowhere to go*, Guardian Education, 11 July 2017, p. 35. Hannah Richardson, *The children in care left without a school place*, BBC News, 23 October 2017, http://www.bbc.co.uk/news/education-41664460

[99] Nicola Woolcock, *Failing academies 'pay to offload difficult children'*, The Times, 14 March 2016, p. 4, https://www.thetimes.co.uk/article/failing-academies-pay-to-offload-difficult-children-g2xrkpf5m

[100] Greg Hurst, *Academy heads given £50,000 rises*, The Times, 14 January 2017, http://www.thetimes.co.uk/edition/news/academy-heads-given-50-000-rises-stwpm2j0j. Nicola Woolcock, *One in four academy heads gets 10% rise*, The Times, 18 November 2017, https://www.thetimes.co.uk/article/c15950a0-cbd5-11e7-b529-

95e3fc05f40f. 102 academy trusts paid some senior staff over £150,000 a year: House of Commons Committee of Public Accounts, *Academy schools' finances*, House of Commons, 30 March 2018, https://publications.parliament.uk/pa/cm201719/cmselect/cmpubacc/760/760.pdf

[101] Sir Amyas Morse KCB, Comptroller and Auditor General, *Converting maintained schools to academies*, National Audit Office, 20 February 2018, https://www.nao.org.uk/wp-content/uploads/2018/02/Converting-maintained-schools-to-academies.pdf

[102] Jen Garry, Chloe Rush, Jude Hillary, Carl Cullinane & Rebecca Montacute, *Free For All? Analysing free schools in England, 2018*, National Foundation for Education Research & Sutton Trust, 31 May 2018, p.2, https://www.suttontrust.com/wp-content/uploads/2018/05/FreeForAll-SuttonTrustNFER-1.pdf

[103] Sir Amyas Morse KCB Comptroller and Auditor General, *Capital funding for schools*, National Audit Office, 20 February 2017, https://www.nao.org.uk/wp-content/uploads/2017/02/Capital-funding-for-schools.pdf

[104] The Times, *Two in five secondary schools are overcrowded*, 20 September 2017, https://www.thetimes.co.uk/article/bd025ca0-9d7b-11e7-a7be-33f2196a0804

[105] The government is on average spending 19% above the market value for land to accommodate free schools (and on 20 sites, 60% or more): Sir Amyas Morse KCB, Comptroller and Auditor General, *Capital funding for schools*, National Audit Office, 20 February 2017, https://www.nao.org.uk/wp-content/uploads/2017/02/Capital-funding-for-schools.pdf

[106] Almost £140 million was spent on 62 free schools, university technical colleges and studio schools which either closed, partially closed or did not open - National Union of Teachers: Hannah Richardson, *Scrapped free schools 'wasted' nearly £140m, says NUT*, BBC News, 16 April 2017, http://www.bbc.co.uk/news/education-39608489. Alix Robertson, *DfE pays £260,000 for a school building to sit empty*, SCHOOLS WEEK, 5 November 2018, https://schoolsweek.co.uk/dfe-pays-260000-for-a-school-building-to-sit-empty/

[107] Sir Amyas Morse KCB Comptroller and Auditor General, *Capital funding for schools*, National Audit Office, 20 February 2017, https://www.nao.org.uk/wp-content/uploads/2017/02/Capital-funding-for-schools.pdf

[108] Sally Weale, £3.5bn cut for school buildings leaves pupils in crumbling classrooms – *Labour*, Guardian, 26 October 2018, https://www.theguardian.com/education/2018/oct/26/35bn-cut-for-school-buildings-leaves-pupils-in-crumbling-classrooms-labour

[109] In areas where free schools are located there are on average 32% of children on free school meals, but only 24% of children on free school meals attend these schools:

Jon Andrews & Rebecca Johnes, *Free Schools in England*, Education Policy Institute, November 2017, https://epi.org.uk/publications-and-research/free-schools-england/. Jen Garry, Chloe Rush, Jude Hillary, Carl Cullinane & Rebecca Montacute, *Free For All? Analysing free schools in England, 2018*, National Foundation for Education Research & Sutton Trust, 31 May 2018, p.2, https://www.suttontrust.com/wp-content/uploads/2018/05/FreeForAll-SuttonTrustNFER-1.pdf

[110] John Jerrim & Sam Sims, *The association between attending a grammar school and children's socio-emotional outcomes. New evidence from the Millennium Cohort Study*, UCL Institute of Education & Education Datalab, May 2018, http://www.nuffieldfoundation.org/archive/all/2018/5. Stephen Gorard & Nadia Siddiqui, *Grammar schools in England: a new analysis of social segregation and academic outcomes*, British Journal of Sociology of Education, volume 39, 2018, issue 7, pgs. 909-924, published online 26 March 2018, https://www.tandfonline.com/doi/pdf/10.1080/01425692.2018.1443432?needAccess=true

[111] Sam Coates, *May plans school selection at 14 and 16 as well as 11*, The Times, 9 September 2016, http://www.thetimes.co.uk/edition/news/may-plans-school-selection-at-14-and-16-as-well-as-11-5krzlvbwv

[112] Gordon Rayner, *Grammar school expansion will create up to 16,000 new places, Education Secretary reveals*, Daily Telegraph, 11 May 2018, https://www.telegraph.co.uk/politics/2018/05/10/grammar-school-expansion-will-create-16000-new-places-educationsecretary/

[113] Branwen Jeffreys, *Grammar schools: Thousands of new places created*, BBC News, 1 August 2018, https://www.bbc.co.uk/news/education-44727857

[114] 'Welfare' is concerned with children's security and safety, and the quality of the learning environment; and 'developmental' based on six areas of learning - personal, social and emotional; communication, language and literacy; problem solving and reasoning; understanding the world; and physical and creative development. Government guidance says that these 'will mostly be taught through games and play'. All childcare providers excluding parent and toddler groups, nannies and short-term crèches, have to be registered by Ofsted, who inspect providers based on the EYFS: GOV.UK WEBSITE, https://www.gov.uk/early-years-foundation-stage

[115] Judith Judd, *Ministers accused of subverting school curriculum*, Independent, 13 October 1992, http://www.independent.co.uk/news/uk/politics/ministers-accused-of-subverting-school-curriculum-1557241.html

[116] Duncan Graham & David Tytler, *A Lesson for All - the Making of the National*

Curriculum, (Routledge, London, 1992)

[117] Judith Judd, *Ministers accused of subverting school curriculum*, Independent, 13 October 1992, http://www.independent.co.uk/news/uk/politics/ministers-accused-of-subverting-school-curriculum-1557241.html

[118] Warwick Mansell, *Experts on the frontline in fight over 'fronted adverbials'*, Guardian Education, 9 May 2017, page 12, https://www.theguardian.com/education/2017/may/09/fronted-adverbials-sats-grammar-test-primary

[119] Ibid. Viv Apple, *Teaching basics at an early age frees children*, Times, Letters to the Editor, 3 May 2016, p. 26. Gaby Hinsliff, *Pity our children – they're being turned into grammar robots at school*, Guardian, 10 May 2017, https://www.theguardian.com/commentisfree/2017/may/10/bad-grammar-gove-english-killing-children-love-language-adverbials-digraphs

[120] House of Commons Education Committee, *Primary assessment*, House of Commons, 1 May 2017, https://publications.parliament.uk/pa/cm201617/cmselect/cmeduc/682/682.pdf

[121] Warwick Mansell, *Experts on the frontline in fight over 'fronted adverbials'*, Guardian Education, 9 May 2017, p. 12, https://www.theguardian.com/education/2017/may/09/fronted-adverbials-sats-grammar-test-primary

[122] Ibid

[123] Ibid

[124] Gaby Hinsliff, *Pity our children – they're being turned into grammar robots at school*, Guardian, 10 May 2017, https://www.theguardian.com/commentisfree/2017/may/10/bad-grammar-gove-english-killing-children-love-language-adverbials-digraphs

[125] Judith Judd, *Ministers accused of subverting school curriculum*, Independent, 13 October 1992, http://www.independent.co.uk/news/uk/politics/ministers-accused-of-subverting-school-curriculum-1557241.html

[126] House of Commons Education Committee, *Primary assessment*, House of Commons, 1 May 2017, https://publications.parliament.uk/pa/cm201617/cmselect/cmeduc/682/682.pdf

[127] Nicola Woolcock, *New tests leave children unable to write a story*, The Times, 8 May 2017, https://www.thetimes.co.uk/edition/news/new-tests-leave-children-unable-to-write-a-story-883htzcrn

[128] Amanda Spielman, *Authored article, HMCI commentary: curriculum and the new education inspection framework*, Ofsted website, published 18 September 2018, https://www.gov.uk/government/speeches/hmci-commentary-curriculum-and-the-new-

education-inspection-framework

[129] Subjects excluded from EBacc include art, business studies, classics, design and technology, drama, health and social care, information and communications technology, law, media studies, music, physical education, politics, psychology, religious studies, information and communications technology, and vocational subjects.

[130] Survey of 1,200 members of the teaching unions, ATL and NUT, carried out in February 2017: Judith Burns, *School budget squeeze 'is reducing pupils' subject choice'*, BBC News, http://www.bbc.co.uk/news/education-39527183

[131] Four-fifths of secondary school headteachers say that the EBacc performance indicator is 'limiting opportunities for pupils with vocational or technical aptitude'. A survey by Ipsos of secondary school Headteachers: Nicola Woolcock, *Students with vocational skills failed by exam system*, The Times, 22 May 2017, https://www.thetimes.co.uk/edition/news/students-with-vocational-skills-failed-by-exam-system-fn22m2th7

[132] Compared to 2014, entries for non-EBacc GCSE subjects in 2017 dropped in design & technology (by 23%), drama (14%), home economics (29%), media (27%), music (9%), performing arts (27%) & religious education (18%): GOV.UK, *Ofqual, Summer 2017 exam entries GCSEs AS and A levels in England*, 15 June 2017, https://www.gov.uk/government/statistics/summer-2017-exam-entries-gcses-level-1-2-certificates-as-and-a-levels-in-england.   Entries for GCSE creative subjects fell by more than 17% between 2016 and 2018: Deborah Annetts, *Creative block over arts GCSEs*, The Sunday Times, Letters to the Editor, 9 September 2018, https://www.thetimes.co.uk/article/letters-to-the-editor-aid-harms-africa-and-thetories-8tb3p602n.   Between 2016 and 2018 there was a 10% reduction in GCSE music entries: Dr. Ally Daubney & Duncan Mackrill, *Changes in Secondary Music Curriculum Provision over time 2016-18/19*, University of Sussex, October 2018, https://www.ism.org/news/new-uni-of-sussex-research-music-risk-disappearing.   Between 2010 and 2018 entries to GCSEs design technology dropped by 42%; and art, music, drama and dance by 19%: Kenneth Baker, *Lord Baker: 10 things wrong with our education system*, The Sunday Times, 19 August 2018, https://www.thetimes.co.uk/article/lord-baker-10-things-wrong-with-our-education-system-q2q9qtrbn

[133] Schools are reducing time spent on physical education (PE) lessons because of examination pressures. On average pupils in Key Stage 4 have 21% less time in PE than they did in Key Stage 3: Youth Sport Trust, *PE provision in secondary schools 2018, Survey Research Report*, February 2018, https://www.youthsporttrust.org/system/files/resources/documents/PE%20provision%20in%20secondary%20schools%202018%20

-%20Survey%20Research%20Report_0.pdf. Between 2011 and 2017 the number of hours dedicated to PE in state-funded secondary schools fell by 5% in years 7, 8 and 9 and by 21% in Years 10 and 11. Teaching hours devoted to PSHE lessons are down by 33% in in years 7, 8 and 9 ,and 47% in Years 9 and 10 - Analysis by *TES* of Department for Education data: Nicola Woolcock, *PE cuts raise fears for pupil health*, The Times, 1 September 2018, https://www.thetimes.co.uk/article/schools-slash-pe-and-welfare-to-focus-on-core-subjects-9s3rlqp6w

[134] Richard Adams, *English baccalaureate 'creates problems for motivation and behaviour'*, Guardian, 14 November 2016, https://www.theguardian.com/education/2016/nov/14/english-baccalaureate-creates-problems-motivation-behaviour

[135] John Kampfner, chief executive of the Creative Industries Federation (John Kampfner, *Britain's got talent but we are not providing the skills*, The Times, Comment, 5 June 2017, https://www.thetimes.co.uk/past-six-days/2017-06-05/business/britains-got-talent-but-we-are-not-providing-the-skills-lgt5rqf09). Paul Thompson, Vice Chancellor of the Royal College of Art (Paul Thompson, Letter to the Editor, The Times, 9 October 2017, https://www.thetimes.co.uk/edition/comment/investigation-into-allegations-against-heath-qv06rgv78). Robert Wise, chairman of The Music Sales Group (Robert Wise, Letter to the Editor, The Times, *Music Education 'Is Being Edged Out'*, 18 January 2018, https://www.thetimes.co.uk/edition/comment/equality-of-justice-for-men-and-women-q88h2f8tl). Dr. Tony Breslin, chair of Industry Qualifications (Dr. Tony Breslin, Letter to the Editor, The Times, *Core creativity*, 11 August 2017, p. 28). Rufus Norris, director of the National Theatre (Rufus Norris, *Creativity can be taught to anyone. So why are we leaving it to private schools?* Guardian, 17 January 2018, https://www.theguardian.com/commentisfree/2018/jan/17/creativity-private-schools-uk-creative-industries-state). David Ainley, Artist, teacher and university lecturer (Guardian Letters, *UK education is eroded by the Ebacc, academies and tuition fees*, 14 August 2017, www.theguardian.com/politics/2017/aug/14/uk-education-is-eroded-by-the-ebacc-academies-and-tuition-fees). Alice Barnard, Chief Executive, Edge Foundation (Alice Barnard, *The neglectful bias against vocational training*, Guardian Letters, 21 February 2017, p. 28). Tracey Emin, Rachel Whiteread, Phyllida Barlow, Anish Kapoor, Jeremy Deller, Antony Gormley, Grayson Perry & more than 100 other professional artists (Letters, *British artists: Ebacc will damage creativity and self-expression*, Guardian, 8 May 2018, https://www.theguardian.com/culture/2018/may/08/british-artists-ebacc-will-damage-creativity-and-self-expression)

[136] 76% of teachers and 60% of parents believe that schools have offered a more restricted

curriculum from an earlier age over the past three years than they did previously, with large majorities (92% of teachers and 76% of parents) saying the pressure placed on schools to deliver good exam results is to blame. This means some schools teaching a GCSE syllabus as soon as pupils arrive in Year 7 rather than the recommended Year 10. Teachers believe the problem is widespread. Nine in ten of them (90%) think too many schools are pressuring teachers to concentrate on an exam-driven syllabus to the exclusion of the wider curriculum – Survey of parents and teachers carried out by YouGov in October 2018: YouGov, *Obsession with exams is forcing schools to restrict curriculum and leading to damaging consequences, teachers and parents say*, GL Assessment, 15 November 2018, https://www.gl-assessment.co.uk/news-hub/press-releases/obsession-with-exams-is-forcing-schools-to-restrict-curriculum-and-leading-to-damaging-consequences-teachers-and-parents-say/

[137] At least three examination boards have designed tests for use in the first three years of secondary school - Research by Times Education Supplement: Nicola Woolcock, *Children drilled for exams from age of 11*, The Times, 22 August 2018, https://www.thetimes.co.uk/article/children-drilled-for-exams-from-age-of-11-says-ofsted-chief-amanda-spielman-wgm55w5p5

[138] Survey by Ofsted: Rosemary Bennett, *Longer GCSE courses force pupils to drop key subjects such as history and languages*, The Times, 8 September 2017, https://www.thetimes.co.uk/edition/news/longer-gcse-courses-force-pupils-to-drop-key-subjects-such-as-history-and-languages-amanda-spielman-kmtshvj2w

[139] Ibid

[140] Amanda Spielman, *Authored article, HMCI commentary: curriculum and the new education inspection framework*, Ofsted website, published 18 September 2018, https://www.gov.uk/government/speeches/hmci-commentary-curriculum-and-the-new-education-inspection-framework

[141] Amanda Spielman, *Speech to the Schools Northeast Summit*, Transcript, Ofsted, 11 October 2018, https://www.gov.uk/government/speeches/amanda-spielman-speech-to-the-schools-northeast-summit

[142] Rosemary Bennett, *A level results day 2018: Exam changes have narrowed pupils' focus*, The Times, 16 August 2018, https://www.thetimes.co.uk/article/a-level-results-day-2018-narrowing-of-subject-focus-is-the-unintended-consequence-of-exam-changes-5vplkdvdq

[143] Since 2013 entries in A level arts subjects has fallen by 14,000, nearly 15%; 8% in modern languages; and 10% in social sciences: Reality Check team, *Reality Check:*

Are exam changes affecting what students study? BBC News, 22 August 2018, https://www.bbc.co.uk/news/uk-45171371

[144] Entries for design and technology A-levels have declined from 16,000 in 2010 to 10,000 in 2018; a reduction of nearly 40%: Kenneth Baker, *Lord Baker: 10 things wrong with our education system*, The Sunday Times, 19 August 2018, https://www.thetimes.co.uk/article/lord-baker-10-things-wrong-with-our-education-system-q2q9qtrbn

[145] Katherine Sellgren, *Teaching to the test gives 'hollow understanding'*, BBC News, 11 October 2017, http://www.bbc.co.uk/news/education-41580550

[146] Peter Jones, *Brexit Britain and the education of children*, The Times, Letters to the Editor, 9 December 2016, http://www.thetimes.co.uk/edition/comment/brexit-britain-and-the-education-of-children-rkfb9h8k8

[147] Department for Education and Skills, *14-19 Curriculum and Qualifications Reform Final Report of the Working Group on 14-19 Reform*, DfES Publications, October 2004

[148] Peter Finegold *The neglectful bias against vocational training*, Guardian, Letters, 20 February 2017, https://www.theguardian.com/education/2017/feb/20/the-neglectful-bias-against-vocational-training?

[149] R. Pring, G. Hayward, A. Hodgson, J. Johnson, E. Keep, A. Oancea, G. Rees, K. Spours & S. Wilde, *The Nuffield Review of 14–19 Education and Training: Final report Education for All: the Future of Education and Training for 14–19 year-olds* (Routledge, 2009)

[150] Laura McLarty & Rhetta Moran, *Equality and Human Rights Commission Research Report Series 26: Engaging all young people in meaningful learning after 16: A qualitative study*, Equality and Human Rights Commission, 2009

[151] The 41 acts relating to education since 1979 have covered matters such as pupil discipline, school places and admissions, functions and membership of governing bodies, inspections, special educational needs, initial and in-service teacher training, early years and nursery education, public examinations, testing, qualifications, careers education, school milk and meals, relationships with parents, teaching, school administration, grants for specific initiatives, teachers' remuneration and conditions, safeguarding, pupil attendance at school, school budgets, definition of compulsory education, staff appointments and dismissal, political indoctrination, teacher appraisal, charges, targets, transport, and government and local government intervention in schools.

[152] Apprenticeships, Skills, Children and Learning Act 2009

[153] 1. To promote the education of the people of England and Wales; 2. To promote

the progressive development of schools and colleges; and 3. To secure that local authorities execute the national policy for providing a very comprehensive educational service: *Education in England: a brief history*, Dereck Gillard, 2016, http://www. educationengland.org.uk/history/

[154] Education Act 1944

[155] House of Lords Merits of Statutory Instruments Committee, *9th Report of Session 2008-09, The cumulative impact of statutory instruments on schools, Report with evidence*, published 13 March 2009, London : The Stationery Office Limited

[156] Dereck Gillard, *Education in England: a brief history*, 2016, http://www. educationengland.org.uk/history/

[157] Between 2012 and 2015 just under 150,000 teachers left England's schools, 1 in 10 teachers each year, the highest rate on record: Department for Education, *School workforce in England: November 2013, Statistics on the size and characteristics of the schools' workforce in state-funded schools*, 10 April 2014 (updated 22 January 2015), https://www.gov.uk/government/statistics/school-workforce-in-england-november-2013. 50,110 qualified teachers left the state-funded sector in the 12 months to November 2016, a 'wastage rate' of 10.5%, an increase from 9.9% in 2011: David Foster, *Briefing Paper Number 7222, Teacher recruitment and retention in England*, House of Commons Library, 4 June 2018, p. 10, http://researchbriefings.parliament.uk/ResearchBriefing/Summary/CBP-7222#fullreport

[158] In 2016/17 about 8% of teachers (34,910) left teaching for 'reasons other than retirement': Press Association web-site *Half of teachers 'thinking of quitting' by 2017, union warns*, 4 October 2015, http://www.msn.com/en-gb/news/national/half-of-teachers-thinking-of-quitting-by-2017-union-warns/ar-AAf581A. 'Among leavers, the proportion leaving for reasons other than retirement rose from 64% to 75%': Sir Amyas Morse KCB, Comptroller and Auditor General, *Training new teachers*, National Audit Office, 9 February 2016, p.14, https://www.nao.org.uk/wp-content/uploads/2016/02/Training-new-teachers.pdf. The proportion of teachers quitting teaching, excluding those retiring, rose from 6% to 8% between 2011 and 2016: House of Commons Committee of Public Accounts, *Retaining and developing the teaching workforce,* House of Commons, 24 January 2018, https://publications.parliament.uk/pa/cm201719/cmselect/cmpubacc/460/460.pdf

[159] Of the 24,100 newly qualified teachers taking up appointments in English schools in 2010, only 87% remained after one year: Written parliamentary answer from Schools Minister, Nick Gibb, to a question from the Liberal Democrat MP, Greg Mulholland:

BBC News, *New teachers: 30% of 2010 intake quit within five years*, 24 October 2016, http://www.bbc.co.uk/news/education-37750489

160 Ibid

161 Only 60% of teachers remained in state-funded schools five years after starting: Luke Sibieta, *The teacher labour market in England: shortages, subject expertise and incentives*, Education Policy Institute, London, 30 August 2018, https://epi.org.uk/publications-and-research/the-teacher-labour-market-in-england/

162 Only 50% of teachers in subjects like physics and mathematics remained in schools 5 years after starting: Ibid.

163 Rosemary Bennett, *Bored bankers sought for maths teacher shortage*, The Times, 19 November 2018, https://www.thetimes.co.uk/article/bored-bankers-sought-for-maths-teacher-shortage-lmpxqt790

164 79% of schools are experiencing major difficulties in recruiting and/or retaining teachers, 88% per cent believe this will get worse: Survey by the Guardian newspaper of 4,450 teachers: Liz Lightfoot, *Nearly half of teachers plan to leave in next five years*, Guardian, 22 March 2016, p. 34

165 Rosemary Bennett, *MPs condemn 'sluggish' response to teacher exodus*, The Times, 31 January 2018, https://www.thetimes.co.uk/article/eb80ac16-0609-11e8-8e80-008642e5faa1

166 In a survey by the teachers union, the Association of Teachers and Lecturers, the top reasons for teachers considering leaving teaching were heavy workloads, teacher bashing in the press, constant changes, challenging student behaviour, and Ofsted inspections: The Guardian website, *5 top reasons people become teachers – and why they quit*, 27 January 2015, http://www.theguardian.com/teacher-network/2015/jan/27/five-top-reasons-teachers-join-and-quit. The most common reasons given for leaving teaching were the long hours and heavy workload: House of Commons Education Committee, *Recruitment and retention of teachers,* House of Commons, 21 February 2017, https://publications.parliament.uk/pa/cm201617/cmselect/cmeduc/199/199.pdf. 1 in 2 newly qualified teachers planning to leave teaching give workload pressures and mental health concerns as the main reason - National Union of Teachers survey of 3,000 recently-qualified young teachers: Hannah Richardson, *Workload 'pushing young teachers to the brink'*, BBC News, 10 April 2017, http://www.bbc.co.uk/news/education-39592567. 73% of teachers say that excessive workload is affecting their physical health, and 75% their mental health: Liz Lightfoot, *Nearly half of teachers plan to leave in next five years*, Guardian, 22 March 2016, p. 34. Compared to 2015-16,

in 2016-17 there was a 5% increase in the numbers of teachers on long-term sick due to work pressure, anxiety or mental illness: Nicola Woolcock, *Thousands of teachers off sick in 'stress epidemic'*, The Times, 11 January 2018, https://www.thetimes.co.uk/article/039f95c2-f6c0-11e7-9cfd-f28094b4d5ce

[167] 76% of teachers cited high workload as the most common reason for considering leaving the profession: Loic Menzies, Dr Meenakshi Parameshwaran, Anna Trethewey, Bart Shaw, Dr Sam Baars & Charleen Chiong, *Why teach?* Pearson & LKMCo, October 2015, p. 19, http://whyteach.lkmco.org/wp-content/uploads/2015/10/Embargoed-until-Friday-23-October-2015-Why-Teach.pdf. '76% of NQT respondents say they have considered leaving teaching because their workload is too high': Written evidence submitted by the Association of Teachers and Lecturers to the House of Commons Education Committee, November 2015, http://data.parliament.uk/writtenevidence/committeeevidence.svc/evidencedocument/education-committee/supply-of-teachers/written/24671.pdf. 90% of teachers say they are under increasing pressure; 82% say their workload in unmanageable: Liz Lightfoot, *Nearly half of teachers plan to leave in next five years*, Guardian, 22 March 2016, p. 34

[168] John Higton, Sarah Leonardi, Neil Richards, Arifa Choudhoury, Dr Nicholas Sofroniou & Dr David Owen, *Teacher Workload Survey 2016 Research report*, Department for Education, Government Social Research, February 2017, https://assets.publishing.service.gov.uk/government/uploads/system/uploads/attachment_data/file/592499/TWS_2016_FINAL_Research_report_Feb_2017.pdf

[169] Teachers in England work longer hours than those in 34 out of 36 countries surveyed by the OECD: Research by the Education Policy Institute and Organisation for Economic Co-operation and Development: Hannah Richardson, *Many teachers 'working 60-hour week'*, BBC News, 10 October 2016, http://www.bbc.co.uk/news/education-37585982

[170] John Higton, Sarah Leonardi, Neil Richards, Arifa Choudhoury, Dr Nicholas Sofroniou & Dr David Owen, *Teacher Workload Survey 2016 Research report*, Department for Education, Government Social Research, February 2017, https://assets.publishing.service.gov.uk/government/uploads/system/uploads/attachment_data/file/592499/TWS_2016_FINAL_Research_report_Feb_2017.pdf

[171] Research by the Education Policy Institute and Organisation for Economic Co-operation and Development: Hannah Richardson, *Many teachers 'working 60-hour week'*, BBC News, 10 October 2016, http://www.bbc.co.uk/news/education-37585982

[172] 'Inspection and policy change were key drivers for increased workload, which then

led to [teachers'] poor health and feeling undervalued': Sarah Lynch, Jack Worth, Susan Bamford & Karen Wespieser, *Engaging Teachers: NFER Analysis of Teacher Retention*, National Foundation for Educational Research, Slough, UK, published September 2016, p. 15, https://www.nfer.ac.uk/media/1925/lfsb01.pdf. 'A series of changes to curriculum, assessment and the accountability system, as well as uncertainty about changes to school structures… have led to increased workload and pressure as schools implement the changes': House of Commons Education Committee, *Recruitment and retention of teachers,* House of Commons, published on 21 February 2017, p.15, https://publications.parliament.uk/pa/cm201617/cmselect/cmeduc/199/199.pdf

[173] Alice Thomson, *Exodus of teachers is a lesson for politicians*, The Times, 26 September 2018, https://www.thetimes.co.uk/article/exodus-of-teachers-is-a-lesson-for-politicians-9php59q67

[174] The number of teachers calling the crisis helpline of the Education Support Partnership over the 12 months up to September 2018 rose by 35% to more than 8,500 cases: Ibid

[175] 15 of 22 countries had 'much higher' teacher job satisfaction than England. All English-speaking countries (USA, New Zealand, Canada and Australia) had higher teacher job satisfaction than England - Researchers analysed data from over 100,000 teachers who had taken part in the Teaching and Learning International Survey (TALIS) survey, including nearly 2,500 teachers from England: Laura Zieger, John Jerrim & Sam Sims, *Comparing teachers' job satisfaction across countries. A multiple-pairwise measurement invariance approach*, UCL Institute of Education, London, September 2018, https://samsimseducation.files.wordpress.com/2018/09/comparing-teachers_-job-satisfaction-across-countries-working-paper1.pdf

[176] Sir Amyas Morse KCB, Comptroller and Auditor General, *Retaining and developing the teaching workforce,* National Audit Office, House of Commons, 11 September 2017, https://www.nao.org.uk/wp-content/uploads/2017/09/Retaining-and-developing-the-teaching-workforce.pdf

[177] House of Commons Education Committee, *Recruitment and retention of teachers,* 21 February 2017, https://publications.parliament.uk/pa/cm201617/cmselect/cmeduc/199/199.pdf

[178] The pupil-teacher ratio has risen from around 15.5 in 2010 to nearly 17 in 2018: Luke Sibieta, *The teacher labour market in England: shortages, subject expertise and incentives*, Education Policy Institute, London, 30 August 2018, https://epi.org.uk/publications-and-research/the-teacher-labour-market-in-england/. David Foster,

Briefing Paper Number 7222, Teacher recruitment and retention in England, House of Commons Library, 4 June 2018, p. 6, http://researchbriefings.parliament.uk/ ResearchBriefing/Summary/CBP-7222#fullreport Pupil numbers fell in 2015-16, but a greater decline in the number of teachers caused there to be a higher teacher-pupil ratio: House of Commons Committee of Public Accounts, *Retaining and developing the teaching workforce,* House of Commons, 24 January 2018, https://publications. parliament.uk/pa/cm201719/cmselect/cmpubacc/460/460.pdf

[179] In the year to November 2016, 2,620 more teachers left the profession than joined: Department for Education, *School workforce in England: November 2016*, last updated 20 July 2017, table 7a, https://www.gov.uk/government/statistics/school-workforce-in-england-november-2016

[180] In 2017 teacher numbers in state-funded schools in England were at their lowest level since 2013. In 2017, 451,900 full time equivalent teachers were working in schools, compared with 457,000 in 2016: Department for Education, School Workforce in England: November 2017, 28 June 2018, https://assets.publishing.service.gov.uk/ government/uploads/system/uploads/attachment_data/file/719772/SWFC_MainText.pdf

[181] In September 2017 teacher recruitment agency, Eteach, reported that compared to two years previously there had been a 24% increase in the number of teaching vacancies. Another agency, Teach Vac, reported a 15% increase in vacancies: Hannah Richardson, *Schools open doors to 'more unfilled teacher posts'*, BBC News, 6 September 2017, http://www.bbc.co.uk/news/education-41125279

[182] Paul Howells, Chief Executive, Eteach: Hannah Richardson, *Schools open doors to 'more unfilled teacher posts'*, BBC News, 6 September 2017, http://www.bbc.co.uk/ news/education-41125279

[183] Alice Thomson, *Exodus of teachers is a lesson for politicians*, The Times, 26 September 2018, https://www.thetimes.co.uk/article/exodus-of-teachers-is-a-lesson-for-politicians-9php59q67

[184] Sir Amyas Morse KCB, Comptroller and Auditor General, *Retaining and developing the teaching workforce*, National Audit Office, 11 September 2017, https://www. nao.org.uk/wp-content/uploads/2017/09/Retaining-and-developing-the-teaching-workforce.pdf

[185] David Foster, *Briefing Paper Number 7222, Teacher recruitment and retention in England*, House of Commons Library, 4 June 2018, http://researchbriefings.parliament. uk/ResearchBriefing/Summary/CBP-7222#fullreport

[186] Sir Amyas Morse KCB, Comptroller and Auditor General, *Retaining and developing*

the teaching workforce, National Audit Office, 11 September 2017, https://www.nao.org.uk/wp-content/uploads/2017/09/Retaining-and-developing-the-teaching-workforce.pdf. House of Commons Committee of Public Accounts, *Retaining and developing the teaching workforce,* House of Commons, 24 January 2018, https://publications.parliament.uk/pa/cm201719/cmselect/cmpubacc/460/460.pdf. The number of unqualified teachers has increased by almost 20% between 2015 and 2017. More than a fifth of secondary maths teachers and a third of physics teachers are not qualified in these subjects beyond A level: Nicola Woolcock, *Schools plug gaps with unqualified teachers*, The Times, 6 January 2018, https://www.thetimes.co.uk/edition/news/schools-plug-gaps-with-unqualified-teachers-dnlqmvn3h

[187] Two thirds of secondary schools are struggling to recruit mathematics teachers; half of schools physics teachers; and two fifths of schools chemistry teachers: Survey by the National Governance Association and Times Education Supplement: Nicola Woolcock, *Two thirds of schools finding it hard to recruit maths teachers,* The Times, 5 October 2018, https://www.thetimes.co.uk/article/most-schools-finding-it-hard-to-recruit-maths-teachers-38rbdtxp8

[188] David Foster, *Briefing Paper Number 7222, Teacher recruitment and retention in England*, House of Commons Library, 4 June 2018, http://researchbriefings.parliament.uk/ResearchBriefing/Summary/CBP-7222#fullreport

[189] Hannah Richardson, *Teacher training target missed for fifth year in a row in England*, BBC News, 30 November 2017, http://www.bbc.co.uk/news/education-42181703

[190] As of mid-December 2017, 12,820 had applied for graduate teaching training places (for starting in autumn 2018). In 2016 the number applying was 19,330 and in 2015 20,330. The decrease of 6,510 between 2017 and 2016 equates to 33%. Applications to teach science fell by 23%, English by 25% and mathematics by 28%: Nicola Woolcock, *Crisis in teacher recruitment as applications fall by a third*, The Times, 5 January 2018, https://www.thetimes.co.uk/article/crisis-in-teacher-recruitment-as-applications-fall-by-a-third-2fkp0p8xz

[191] 27,590 were recruited onto primary school teacher courses for 2018 compared to 16,870 in 2017; a 48% decrease: Nicola Woolcock, *Crisis in teacher recruitment as applications fall by a third*, The Times, 5 January 2018, https://www.thetimes.co.uk/article/fec7715a-f1b0-11e7-a480-969f697997ea

[192] Between 2010 and 2018 pupil numbers increased by around 10%: Luke Sibieta, *The teacher labour market in England: shortages, subject expertise and incentives*, Education Policy Institute, London, 30 August 2018, https://epi.org.uk/publications-

and-research/the-teacher-labour-market-in-england/

[193] Department for Education, *Schools, pupils and their characteristics: January 2018*, 28 June 2018, https://assets.publishing.service.gov.uk/government/uploads/system/uploads/attachment_data/file/719226/Schools_Pupils_and_their_Characteristics_2018_Main_Text.pdf

[194] Numbers of pupils of compulsory school age are forecast to increase from 7.24m. (in 2015) to 7.85m. in 2020, an increase of 615,000: Sally Weale, *Teacher shortage and surge in pupils creating 'perfect storm' in schools*, Guardian, 6 October 2015, p. 4, https://www.theguardian.com/education/2015/oct/05/teacher-shortage-pupils-perfect-storm-uk-schools

[195] Compared to 2015, by 2024, there will be 8% more pupils in primary schools, and 20% more in secondary schools: Branwen Jeffreys, *How can schools recruit, and keep, more teachers?* BBC News, 30 May 2017, http://www.bbc.co.uk/news/education-40088691. Secondary school pupil numbers are to increase by more than 500,000 to 3.3 m. by 2025: Rosemary Bennett, *Science and maths teachers quit in their thousands*, The Times, 17 May 2017, https://www.thetimes.co.uk/edition/news/science-and-maths-teachers-quit-in-their-thousands-0qz0rqnzw. Secondary school pupil numbers in England are forecast to be 3.3m. in 2027 - 418,000 higher than in 2018: BBC News, *Number of secondary pupils in England to rise 15% by 2027*, 13 July 2018, https://www.bbc.co.uk/news/education-44809258

[196] Nicola Woolcock, *Two thirds of schools finding it hard to recruit maths teachers*, The Times, 5 October 2018, https://www.thetimes.co.uk/article/most-schools-finding-it-hard-to-recruit-maths-teachers-38rbdtxp8

[197] Sean Coughlan, *Damian Hinds to cut workload to tackle teacher shortage*, BBC News, 10 March 2018, http://www.bbc.co.uk/news/education-43345857

[198] Incentives offered by schools to help recruit teachers include 'duvet days', 'golden hellos', gym membership and shopping vouchers: Julie Henry & Sian Griffiths, *Desperate schools woo teachers with duvet days and £1,000*, The Sunday Times, 2 April 2017, http://www.thetimes.co.uk/edition/news/desperate-schools-woo-teachers-with-duvet-days-and-1-000-wlj5ct03x

[199] Research by the National Association of Head Teachers: *Schools crisis as hundreds of heads quit*, Nicola Woolcock, The Times, 31 December 2016, http://www.thetimes.co.uk/edition/news/schools-crisis-as-hundreds-of-heads-quit-fj9dc6v7s

[200] Czech Republic, Germany, Poland and the United States of America

[201] Julie Henry & Sian Griffiths, *Desperate schools woo teachers with duvet days*

and £1,000, The Sunday Times, 2 April 2017, http://www.thetimes.co.uk/edition/news/desperate-schools-woo-teachers-with-duvet-days-and-1-000-wlj5ct03x. Camilla Turner, *Drive to hire foreign teachers*, Daily Telegraph, 15 July 2017, p. 1

[202] In some schools fees paid to agencies for recruiting teachers have increased tenfold in four years, for example from £400 per applicant to £5,500: *'Uber for teachers' to tackle hiring crisis*, Nicola Woolcock, The Times, 3 April 2017, http://www.thetimes.co.uk/edition/news/uber-for-teachers-to-tackle-hiring-crisis-hr2dcb2p6

[203] Sally Weale, *Teachers' pay in England down by 12% in 10 years, influential study reveals*, Guardian, 12 September 2017, https://www.theguardian.com/education/2017/sep/12/teachers-pay-in-england-down-12-per-cent-10-years-influential-study-reveals. Between 2010 and 2018 teacher pay declined by about 10% in real-terms; while pay rises of up to 3.5 % from September 2018 will halt this real-terms decline: Luke Sibieta, *The teacher labour market in England: shortages, subject expertise and incentives*, Education Policy Institute, London, 30 August 2018, https://epi.org.uk/publications-and-research/the-teacher-labour-market-in-england/

[204] Toby Helm, Kaif Siddiqui & Rebecca Ratcliffe, *Teachers '£5,000 a year worse off under Tories'*, Guardian 2 September 2017, https://www.theguardian.com/education/2017/sep/02/teachers-5000-pounds-a-year-worse-off-under-tories-claims-labour

[205] Guardian, *At £50,000 for the full service it's costly finding a new headteacher*, 23 June 2015, p. 34

[206] 86.8% of headteachers believe that headship is 'less attractive than it was a year ago': Survey of school leaders by The Key, a national information service for school leaders: Sally Weale, *Headteacher shortage looms as role loses appeal,* Guardian, 26 January 2016, p. 9, https://www.theguardian.com/education/2016/jan/26/english-schools-struggling-to-recruit-headteachers-research-finds

[207] Excluding those who retire at normal age, around 90% of headteachers are retained in the system from year to year. Retention rates are higher in primary schools than secondary schools. 7% of primary school heads and 10% of secondary school heads are leaving headship each year before retirement age. Retention rates have fallen between 2012 and 2015: from 94% to 92% in primary schools, and 91% to 87% in secondary schools: Sarah Lynch, Bobbie Mills, Katy Theobald & Jack Worth, *Keeping Your Head: NFER Analysis of Headteacher Retention*, National Foundation for Educational Research, Slough, April 2017, https://www.nfer.ac.uk/publications/LFSC01/LFSC01.pdf

[208] Sarah Lynch, Bobbie Mills, Katy Theobald & Jack Worth, *Keeping Your Head:*

NFER Analysis of Headteacher Retention, National Foundation for Educational Research, Slough, April 2017, https://www.nfer.ac.uk/publications/LFSC01/LFSC01.pdf

[209] 3 in 10 headteachers say that they plan to leave within 5 years: *Not enough young teachers are applying to run schools*, The Times, Leading Article, 11 November 2016, http://www.thetimes.co.uk/past-six-days/2016-11-11/comment/heads-up-tz6m5rd32. 1 in 2 of those in school leadership roles are expected to leave in the next 6 years. Report of an England-wide view of retention and recruitment of school leaders: Teach First, Future Leaders Trust and Teaching Leaders, *The School Leadership Challenge: 2022*, November 2016, https://www.ambitionschoolleadership.org.uk/school-leadership-challenge-2022/

[210] 26% of headteachers of academies resigned from their jobs in 2013-14; 25% of primary headteacher jobs advertised in January 2013 were not filled within 60 days, compared to 15% in 2012; and 44% of headteacher posts in London were re-advertised in 2013, compared to 20% in 2012: UHY Hacker Young and Education Data Survey/BBC: Guardian, *At £50,000 for the full service it's costly finding a new headteacher*, 23 June 2015, p. 34

[211] There were no applications for 30% of headteacher posts advertised: Research by the National Association of Head Teachers: Nicola Woolcock, *Schools crisis as hundreds of heads quit*, The Times, 31 December 2016, http://www.thetimes.co.uk/edition/news/schools-crisis-as-hundreds-of-heads-quit-fj9dc6v7s

[212] Survey of school governors by the National Governors' Association: Sally Weale, *Headteacher shortage looms as role loses appeal*, Guardian, 26 January 2016, p. 9, https://www.theguardian.com/education/2016/jan/26/english-schools-struggling-to-recruit-headteachers-research-finds

[213] The Times, *Not enough young teachers are applying to run schools*, Leading Article, 11 November 2016, http://www.thetimes.co.uk/past-six-days/2016-11-11/comment/heads-up-tz6m5rd32.

[214] 86% of senior teachers consider being a head teacher less attractive than they did 5 years ago: The Times, *Not enough young teachers are applying to run schools*, Leading Article, 11 November 2016, http://www.thetimes.co.uk/past-six-days/2016-11-11/comment/heads-up-tz6m5rd32

[215] Report of an England-wide view of retention and recruitment of school leaders - Teach First, Future Leaders Trust and Teaching Leaders, *The School Leadership Challenge: 2022*, November 2016, https://www.ambitionschoolleadership.org.uk/

school-leadership-challenge-2022/

[216] Fiona Millar, *Teacher recruitment 'a mess' as every school slugs it out for themselves*, Guardian Education, 19 January 2016, p. 34

[217] Will Hutton, *Doctors, teachers, the police: our public servants are demoralised*, Observer, 18 October 2015, p. 38

[218] OECD, *Education Policy Outlook 2015, Making Reform Happen*, OECD Publishing, https://read.oecd-ilibrary.org/education/education-policy-outlook-2015_9789264225442-en#page1

Chapter 7: Equality

[1] Richard Wilkinson & Kate Pickett, *The Spirit Level, Why Equality is Better for Everyone* (Penguin Books, London, 2010) pgs. 19 & 20

[2] Ibid, pgs. 66 & 67

[3] Ibid, p. 82

[4] As measured by the United Nations Children's Fund (UNICEF) index of child wellbeing (a combination of forty different indicators): Richard Wilkinson & Kate Pickett, *The Spirit Level, Why Equality is Better for Everyone* (Penguin Books, London, 2010) pgs. 23 and 24

[5] Ibid, p.106

[6] Ibid, pgs. 15-17

[7] Middle class parents spend 240 hours more than less well-off parents playing and reading with their young children: Libby Purves, *Tackling inequality must start in the cradle*, The Times, 13 June 2016, p. 29, https://www.thetimes.co.uk/article/tackling-inequality-must-start-in-the-cradle-q60hmxm98. Bart Shaw, Sam Baars, Loic Menzies, Meena Parameshwaran & Rebecca Allen, *Low income pupils' progress at secondary school*, Social Mobility Commission, 27 February 2017, pgs. 25-29, https://assets.publishing.service.gov.uk/government/uploads/system/uploads/attachment_data/file/594363/Progress_at_Secondary_School_report_final.pdf

[8] Libby Purves, *Tackling inequality must start in the cradle*, The Times, 13 June 2016, p. 29, https://www.thetimes.co.uk/article/tackling-inequality-must-start-in-the-cradle-q60hmxm98

[9] Ibid

[10] Dr. Philip Kirby, *Shadow Schooling, Private tuition and social mobility in the UK*, Sutton Trust, September 2016, https://www.suttontrust.com/wp-content/uploads/2016/09/Shadow-Schooling-formatted-report_FINAL.pdf

[11] 14% of children looked-after get 5 good GCSEs; the national average is 55%: Matthew Oakley, Guy Miscampbell & Raphael Gregorian, *Looked-after Children, The Silent Crisis*, Social Market Foundation, August 2018, http://www.smf.co.uk/publications/looked-after-children/. Only 6% of children in care go to university: Rachel Sylvester & Alice Thomson, *Neglected children never get to learn about 'normal' life*, The Times, 26 June 2018, https://www.thetimes.co.uk/article/neglected-children-never-get-to-learn-about-normal-life-h6vp2m9lc

[12] The proportion of care leavers between the ages of 19 and 21 not in education or training was approximately 40% in 2017: Matthew Oakley, Guy Miscampbell & Raphael Gregorian, *Looked-after Children, The Silent Crisis*, Social Market Foundation, August 2018, http://www.smf.co.uk/publications/looked-after-children/

[13] Nearly half of all children in care had a diagnosable mental health issue in 2015: Matthew Oakley, Guy Miscampbell & Raphael Gregorian, *Looked-after Children, The Silent Crisis*, Social Market Foundation, August 2018, http://www.smf.co.uk/publications/looked-after-children/

[14] Looked-after children are five times more likely to be excluded from school: Yago Zayed & Rachael Harker, *Children in Care in England: Statistics*, House of Commons Library, 5 October 2015, p. 6, https://researchbriefings.parliament.uk/ResearchBriefing/Summary/SN04470; and Matthew Oakley, Guy Miscampbell & Raphael Gregorian, *Looked-after Children, The Silent Crisis*, Social Market Foundation, August 2018, http://www.smf.co.uk/publications/looked-after-children/

[15] Yago Zayed & Rachael Harker, *Children in Care in England: Statistics*, House of Commons Library, 5 October 2015, p. 6, https://researchbriefings.parliament.uk/ResearchBriefing/Summary/SN04470

[16] In 2015-2016 approximately 39% of the young people in youth offending institutions had been in care. Almost 25% of the adult prison population has previously been in care, and children who have been in care reoffend at roughly twice the rate of children who have never been looked after: Matthew Oakley, Guy Miscampbell & Raphael Gregorian, *Looked-after Children, The Silent Crisis*, Social Market Foundation, August 2018, http://www.smf.co.uk/publications/looked-after-children/

[17] Proportionally more children who have been in care die in early adulthood (i.e. aged 19 to 21) than other young people – Data gained from BBC Freedom of Information request: George Greenwood, *Early deaths among care leavers revealed*, BBC News, 15 February 2017, http://www.bbc.co.uk/news/uk-38961818

[18] Anne Longfield OBE, *Stability Index Overview and Initial Findings*, Children's

Commissioner, April 2017, https://www.childrenscommissioner.gov.uk/wp-content/uploads/2017/06/Childrens-Commissioners-Stability-Index-2017-Overview-Document-1.3.pdf

[19] Children who are adopted on average do far worse in GCSE examinations than their peers. This is because of the long-term and often lasting effect of the abuse and neglect that they suffered prior to being adopted. In 2016 22.8% of adopted children achieved 5 or more A*-C grades at GCSE, including English and mathematics, compared to the England average of 57.1% - Statistics published by the Department for Education: Sam Coates, *Tough start means adopted children perform only half as well in GCSEs*, The Times, 20 August 2016, p. 14, https://www.thetimes.co.uk/article/tough-start-means-children-who-are-adopted-do-half-as-well-in-exams-v93jxnbgm. Adopted children are 20 times more likely to be excluded from school than other pupils and are more likely to leave education without any qualifications: Adoption UK, *Schools & Exclusions Report*, November 2017, https://www.adoptionuk.org/Handlers/Download.ashx?IDMF=e6616ae3-7b0a-449c-b037-070a92428495. 'Adopted children are barely surviving in the current high-pressure school environment and are falling behind in their studies because they are struggling to cope emotionally with the demands of the current education system which prizes exam results at the expense of wellbeing': Adoption UK, *Bridging the Gap, Giving adopted children an equal chance in school*, June 2018, https://www.adoptionuk.org/Handlers/Download.ashx?IDMF=e460b99a-4ebb-4348-bd23-64a50d747901

[20] The top 10% of households on average have a disposable income of £83,875, for the bottom 10% this is nine times less at £9,644: The Equality Trust website, https://www.equalitytrust.org.uk/scale-economic-inequality-uk

[21] The UK is the 7th most unequal of the 30 OECD countries, and the 4th most unequal amongst the European OECD countries: The Equality Trust website, https://www.equalitytrust.org.uk/scale-economic-inequality-uk

[22] Ibid

[23] Total net household wealth in the UK – including property, cash savings and shares, pensions and possessions such as cars and antiques – increased by 15% to £12.8tr. in the two-year period ending in June 2016. The top 10% of households owned almost half of all total wealth, while those in the top 1% owned assets worth at least £3.2m. Those in the bottom 10% had £14,100 or less: Office for National Statistics, *Statistical bulletin: Wealth in Great Britain Wave 5: 2014 to 2016, Main results from the fifth wave of the Wealth and Assets Survey covering the period*

July 2014 to June 2016, published 16 January 2018, https://www.ons.gov.uk/peoplepopulationandcommunity/personalandhouseholdfinances/incomeandwealth/bulletins/wealthingreatbritainwave5/2014to2016

[24] Rosemary Bennett, *Poverty forces children to keep moving*, The Times, 27 March 2017, p. 12, https://www.thetimes.co.uk/article/poverty-forces-children-to-keep-moving-b08ct86k5

[25] At around 21%, the UK has one of the highest proportions of low paid people of the OECD nations: http://www.theworkfoundation.com/Datalab/Average-incidence-of-low-pay-in-the-OECD---2011-12; and The Centre for Social Justice, *The Future of Work Part I: State of the Nation*, CSE, June 2018, https://www.centreforsocialjustice.org.uk/core/wp-content/uploads/2018/06/CSJJ6291-Future-of-Work-WEB-180604.pdf

[26] The Minimum Income Standard (MIS) is calculated by Loughborough University based on what members of the public think is a reasonable income to live on. Examples are a single person renting a flat outside London - £17,300 a year; and a working couple with two children, living in social housing, each need to earn £18,900 a year. In 2014-15 19m. people were living on less than the Minimum Income Standard (MIS), including 6m. (45% of) children; a 25% increase from six years previously: JRF Analysis Unit UK, *Poverty 2017, A comprehensive analysis of poverty trends and figures*, Joseph Rowntree Trust, December 2017, https://www.jrf.org.uk/report/uk-poverty-2017

[27] Relative poverty is defined as a family having an income of less than 60% of median income for their family type, after housing costs: for example couples with no children less than £248 a week; single person with no children less than £144; couple with two children, aged five and 14, less than £401; single parent with children, aged five and 14, less than £297 per week.

[28] Almost 400,000 more children were living in relative poverty in 2016 than there were in 2013, 'the first sustained increases in child and pensioner poverty for 20 years': JRF Analysis Unit UK, *Poverty 2017, A comprehensive analysis of poverty trends and figures*, Joseph Rowntree Trust, published December 2017, https://www.jrf.org.uk/report/uk-poverty-2017. More than 14m. people, including 4.5m. children, are living in poverty according to a new measure developed by the Social Metrics Commission aimed at providing a more sophisticated analysis of material disadvantage in the UK: Patrick Butler, *New study finds 4.5 million UK children living in poverty*, Observer, 16 September 2018, https://www.theguardian.com/society/2018/sep/16/new-study-finds-45-million-uk-children-living-in-poverty

[29] It is estimated that the number of children living in relative poverty will rise from 4m.

presently to 5.2m.by 2022: Andrew Hood & Tom Waters, *Living standards, poverty and inequality in the UK: 2017–18 to 2021–22*, The Institute for Fiscal Studies, November 2017, https://www.ifs.org.uk/publications/10029

[30] Press Association, *Number of homeless children in temporary accommodation rises 37%*, Guardian, 22 July 2017, ttps://www.theguardian.com/uk-news/2017/jul/22/number-of-homeless-children-in-temporary-accommodation-rises-37

[31] As at July 2017 local authorities were providing temporary housing for around 120,540 children with their families - a net increase of 32,650 or 37% since the second quarter of 2014 - Local Government Association: Press Association, *Number of homeless children in temporary accommodation rises 37%*, Guardian, 22 July 2017, ttps://www.theguardian.com/uk-news/2017/jul/22/number-of-homeless-children-in-temporary-accommodation-rises-37

[32] Research by the Social Mobility Commission: Sean Coughlan, *Half of teenagers 'never been in a theatre'*, BBC News, 5 April 2017, http://www.bbc.co.uk/news/education-39479035

[33] Ibid

[34] In key stage 1 tests the gap between the results of those from the wealthier families and the poorest is widening: Nicola Woolcock, *Free schools outperform state schools and academies in SATs*, The Times, 29 September 2017, https://www.thetimes.co.uk/article/7f6a6de6-a439-11e7-8955-1ad2a9a7928d. Children from low income families tend to fall further behind at secondary school: Bart Shaw, Sam Baars, Loic Menzies, Meena Parameshwaran & Rebecca Allen, *Low income pupils' progress at secondary school*, Social Mobility Commission, 27 February 2017, https://assets.publishing.service.gov.uk/government/uploads/system/uploads/attachment_data/file/594363/Progress_at_Secondary_School_report_final.pdf

[35] Previously A*–C grades, now 9-4.

[36] While 63% of all pupils achieve a GCSE A*–C grade in English and mathematics, only 36.8% of those from poorer backgrounds do: Department for Education, Data, Research and Statistics, 2011–12 GCSE results

[37] Bart Shaw, Sam Baars, Loic Menzies, Meena Parameshwaran & Rebecca Allen, *Low income pupils' progress at secondary school*, Social Mobility Commission, 27 February 2017, https://assets.publishing.service.gov.uk/government/uploads/system/uploads/attachment_data/file/594363/Progress_at_Secondary_School_report_final.pdf. Jon Andrews, David Robinson & Jo Hutchinson, *Closing the Gap? Trends in Education Attainment and Disadvantage*, Education Policy Institute, August 2017,

https://epi.org.uk/wp-content/uploads/2017/08/Closing-the-Gap_EPI-.pdf

[38] Passing GCSEs in English, maths, the sciences, a language and history or geography at grade 4 or above.

[39] Research by Teach First found that 10.3% of pupils on free school meals 'passed' the English baccalaureate, compared to a quarter of all pupils, and that 10.7% had been permanently or temporarily excluded from school: Biba Kang, *Poor teenagers more likely to be excluded than get five good passes*, The Times, 22 August 2018, https://www.thetimes.co.uk/article/poor-teenagers-more-likely-to-be-excluded-than-get-five-good-passes-nw66jxgkf

[40] Of those pupils with the highest attainment at the end of primary school, 52% from low income families achieve 5 x A* and A grades at GCSE, compared with 72% of their more affluent peers: Education Endowment Foundation, *The Attainment Gap 2017*, July 2018, https://educationendowmentfoundation.org.uk/public/files/Annual_Reports/EEF_Attainment_Gap_Report_2018_-_print.pdf

[41] Between 2011 and 2017.

[42] Jo Hutchinson, David Robinson, Daniel Carr, Whitney Crenna-Jennings, Emily Hunt & Avinash Akhal, *Education in England: Annual Report 2018*, Education Policy Institute, London, July 2018, https://epi.org.uk/publications-and-research/annual-report-2018/

[43] Ibid

[44] Pupils from poor households are a third more likely to drop out of education at 16 than those from better-off families with the same GSCE results: Social Mobility Commission, *State of the Nation 2016: Social Mobility in Great Britain*, November 2016, https://assets.publishing.service.gov.uk/government/uploads/system/uploads/attachment_data/file/569410/Social_Mobility_Commission_2016_REPORT_WEB__1__.pdf

[45] Jo Hutchinson, David Robinson, Daniel Carr, Whitney Crenna-Jennings, Emily Hunt & Avinash Akhal, *Education in England: Annual Report 2018*, Education Policy Institute, London, July 2018, https://epi.org.uk/publications-and-research/annual-report-2018/

[46] Research by LKMco and Education Datalab, on behalf of the Social Mobility Commission, examining how students progress through schooling, if they go on to sixth form and university, and how their achievements translate into jobs: BBC News, *Social mobility promise 'broken' for ethnic minority children*, 28 December 2016, http://www.bbc.co.uk/news/uk-38447933

[47] 8.8% of students from more disadvantaged backgrounds drop out of university

compared to less than 5% of students from better-off families: OFFA, *Office for Fair Access Annual report and accounts 2016-17*, Controller of Her Majesty's Stationery Office, 13 July 2017, p. 10, https://assets.publishing.service.gov.uk/government/uploads/system/uploads/attachment_data/file/628293/OFFA_annual_report_and_accounts_2016-17_HC_267.pdf

[48] Social Market Foundation, *Educational inequalities in England and Wales, Commission on Inequality in Education*, SMF, January 2016, http://www.smf.co.uk/wp-content/uploads/2016/01/Publication-Commission-on-Inequality-in-Education-Initial-Findings-Slide-Pack-120116.pdf

[49] The proportion of females going to university has risen from 47% in 2012 to 55% in 2017: Sean Coughlan, *Record gender gap in university places*, BBC News, 3 October 2017, http://www.bbc.co.uk/news/education-41470331

[50] There is an hourly gender pay gap among apprentices of £1.03, a 17.6% gap. A young woman apprentice working a 35 hour week would, on average, earn £8,772.40 a year. A young man working the same hours would earn £10,674 a year. Apprentice hourly pay rates are based on a Young Women's Trust poll of 1,269 young people conducted by ComRes in 2015 and published in Young Women's Trust, *Making Apprenticeships Work For Young Women*, 2016, https://www.youngwomenstrust.org/assets/0000/2906/Making_Apprenticeships_Work_for_Young_Women.pdf

[51] Young Women's Trust research: Carole Easton, *Gendered Pay Gap*, The Times, Letters to the Editor, 8 January 2018, https://www.thetimes.co.uk/article/0c9c0722-f3dd-11e7-a789-003e705b951e

[52] The 500 comprehensive schools with the best GCSE results admit 9.4% of pupils eligible for free school meals compared with an average of 17.2% attending all schools: Alexandra Topping, *Number of pupils failing to get first choice of school expected to rise*, Guardian, 1 March 2017, https://www.theguardian.com/education/2017/mar/01/pupils-first-choice-school-national-offer-day-england-secondaries-teachers. Pupils from poorer families are half as likely as those from wealthier backgrounds to be at an outstanding secondary school. Only 15% of those from the poorest 30% of families go to primary schools judged as outstanding, compared to 27% from the wealthiest 30%. 43% of pupils attending secondary schools judged as outstanding are from the wealthiest 20% of families: Study by Teach First: Hannah Richardson *Top state schools 'dominated by richest families'*, BBC News, 1 February 2017, http://www.bbc.co.uk/news/education-39076204; and Katherine Sellgren, *Poor pupils 'less likely to be at outstanding primary'*, BBC News, 17 April 2017, http://www.bbc.co.uk/news/

education-39614276

[53] Children from low income families are less likely to attend schools rated outstanding, even if they live close to the school, as such schools are significantly under-representative of children from poorer off families in the area: Judith Burns, *Outstanding schools take too few poor pupils, study says*, BBC News, 2 August 2016, http://www.bbc.co.uk/news/education-36926766

[54] Study carried out by LKMco and Education Datalab on behalf of the Social Mobility Commission: Greg Hurst, *Secondary schools fail to push poorer pupils*, The Times, 27 February 2017, http://www.thetimes.co.uk/edition/news/secondary-schools-fail-to-push-poorer-pupils-7pwnpvrgw

[55] 7% of children attend private fee-paying schools. 25% of students go to Russell Group universities, and 40% at Oxford and Cambridge universities are from private schools: Paul Johnson, *We must beware dangers of denying our children the path to a better life*, The Times, Comment, 24 January 2017, http://www.thetimes.co.uk/edition/business/we-must-beware-dangers-of-denying-our-children-the-path-to-a-better-life-672pz870f

[56] 61% of doctors, 71% of barristers, 71% of two-star generals, 48% of senior civil servants, 51% of journalists and 345 of senior business people attended private schools: Greg Hurst, *Those old school ties still matter for judges, doctors... and actors*, 24 February 2016, page 13. Analysis by the *Chambers Student Guide* of data provided by 46 law firms on what type of school their trainees attended: Frances Gibb, *Private schools rule the roost*, The Times, 9 February 2017,http://www.thetimes.co.uk/edition/student-law/private-schools-rule-the-roost-0qpvwrd9x

[57] Greg Hurst, *Private school pupils are more likely to get extra GCSE time*, The Times, 11 February 2017, http://www.thetimes.co.uk/edition/news/private-school-pupils-are-more-likely-to-get-extra-gcse-time ncnqk9pnw. Gurpreet Narwan, Private *pupils better placed to get help for special needs*, The Times, 10 November 2017, https://www.thetimes.co.uk/article/73a82b32-c5a0-11e7-92dc-06edfbca4aab

[58] Social Mobility Commission, *State of the Nation 2016: Social Mobility in Great Britain*, November 2016, https://assets.publishing.service.gov.uk/government/uploads/system/uploads/attachment_data/file/569410/Social_Mobility_Commission_2016_REPORT_WEB__1__.pdf

[59] Study commissioned by the charity, Teach First: Greg Hurst, *Rich teenagers more likely to take on apprenticeships*, Times, 23 August 2016, https://www.thetimes.co.uk/article/rich-teenagers-more-likely-to-take-on-apprenticeships-pvgs8d8fn

[60] In the late 1990s, about 20% of households had no adults working, falling to 14.3%

in 2018, representing about three million households. In 2018 204,000 children are living in households where no-one has ever worked, compared to 32,000 in the 1990s - Office for National Statistics: Sean Coughlan, *Fewer families where no-one working*, BBC News, 29 August 2018, https://www.bbc.co.uk/news/education-45341733

[61] People brought up in workless households were 15-18% less likely to be in work than those from working families: Sam Friedman, Daniel Laurison & Lindsey Macmillan, *Social Mobility, the Class Pay Gap and Intergenerational Worklessness: New Insights from The Labour Force Survey*, Social Mobility Commission, London, 26 January 2017, http://www.lse.ac.uk/business-and-consultancy/consulting/assets/documents/social-mobility-the-class-pay-gap-and-intergenerational-worklessness.pdf

[62] Only 4% of doctors, 6% of barristers and 11% of journalists are from working-class backgrounds: Social Mobility Commission, *State of the Nation 2016: Social Mobility in Great Britain*, November 2016, https://assets.publishing.service.gov.uk/government/uploads/system/uploads/attachment_data/file/569410/Social_Mobility_Commission_2016_REPORT_WEB__1__.pdf

[63] 73% of doctors and 66% of journalists are from professional and managerial backgrounds, with only 6% and 12% respectively from working-class families: Sam Friedman, Daniel Laurison & Lindsey Macmillan, *Social Mobility, the Class Pay Gap and Intergenerational Worklessness: New Insights from The Labour Force Survey*, Social Mobility Commission, London, 26 January 2017, http://www.lse.ac.uk/business-and-consultancy/consulting/assets/documents/social-mobility-the-class-pay-gap-and-intergenerational-worklessness.pdf

[64] 11,000 internships are advertised each year, but the total number available is more like 70,000: Carys Roberts, *The Inbetweeners: The New Role of Internships in the Graduate Labour Market*, Institute for Public Policy Research, April 2017, https://www.ippr.org/files/publications/pdf/inbetweeners-the-new-role-of-internships_Apr2017.pdf?noredirect=1. Of the employers who offer internships, 48% do so on an unpaid basis: offering unpaid placements: Carl Cullinane & Rebecca Montacute, *Pay As You Go? Internship pay, quality and access in the graduate jobs market*, Sutton Trust, 23 November 2018, https://www.suttontrust.com/wp-content/uploads/2018/11/Pay-As-You-Go.pdf

[65] Those in professional jobs from working-class backgrounds are paid £6,800 (or 17%) less on average each year than those from more affluent families. Even when professionals have the same educational attainment, role and experience, those from poorer families are paid an average of £2,242 less: Sam Friedman, Daniel Laurison & Lindsey

Macmillan, *Social Mobility, the Class Pay Gap and Intergenerational Worklessness: New Insights from The Labour Force Survey*, Social Mobility Commission, London, 26 January 2017, http://www.lse.ac.uk/business-and-consultancy/consulting/assets/documents/social-mobility-the-class-pay-gap-and-intergenerational-worklessness.pdf

[66] Sean Coughlan, *Work visits result in fewer young 'Neets'*, BBC News, 2 February 2017, http://www.bbc.co.uk/news/education-38842481

[67] Ibid

[68] *The Marmot Review, Fair Society, Health Lives*, 2010, London, http://www.local.gov.uk/health/-/journal_content/56/10180/3510094/ARTICLE

[69] National Audit Office, *Tackling inequalities in life expectancy in areas with the worst health and deprivation*, 2010, http://www.nao.org.uk/wp-content/uploads/2010/07/1011186.pdf

[70] Ibid

[71] People in the lowest household income bracket (earning less than £1,200 per month) are much more likely to have experienced mental ill-health (73%) than those in the highest bracket of more than £3,701 a month (59%). An overwhelming majority of people out of work (85%) said they had experienced a problem, significantly higher than those who were in employment (66%) and retired people (53%): NatCen, *Surviving or Thriving? The State of the UK's Mental Health*, Mental Health foundation, May 2017, https://www.mentalhealth.org.uk/publications/surviving-or-thriving-state-uks-mental-health

[72] Young people from lower income families are 50% far more likely than those from higher income groups to attend accident and emergency: Lucia Kossarova, Dr Ronny Cheung, Dr Dougal Hargreaves & Eilís Keeble, *Briefing December 2017 Admissions of inequality: emergency hospital use for children and young people*, Nuffield Trust, 2017, https://www.nuffieldtrust.org.uk/files/2017-12/nt-admissions-of-inequality-web.pdf

[73] More than twice as many children from poorer families are obese in England than those from better off backgrounds, a gap which is growing wider : NHS Digital, *Obesity prevalence increases in reception age primary school children*, 19 October 2017, https://digital.nhs.uk/news-and-events/news-archive/2017-news-archive/obesity-prevalence-increases-in-reception-age-primary-school-children. In 2015/2016, 40% of children in England's most deprived areas were overweight or obese, compared to 27% in the most affluent areas: The Royal College of Paediatrics and Child Health, State of Child Health Report 2017, RCPCH, January 2017, https://www.rcpch.ac.uk/sites/default/

files/2018-05/state_of_child_health_2017report_updated_29.05.18.pdf

[74] 29% of children eligible for free school meals have good oral health compared to 40% of those who aren't eligible for free school meals: John Appleby, Robert Reed & Leonora Merry, *Root causes: quality and inequality in dental health*, Nuffield Trust & The Health Foundation, November 2017, http://www.qualitywatch.org.uk/sites/files/qualitywatch/field/field_document/QW%20dentistry%20briefing_WEB.pdf

[75] The Royal College of Paediatrics and Child Health, *State of Child Health Report 2017*, RCPCH, January 2017, https://www.rcpch.ac.uk/sites/default/files/2018-05/state_of_child_health_2017report_updated_29.05.18.pdf

[76] Pupils from Indian (and Chinese) backgrounds make the most progress at school: Natalie Perera, Peter Sellen, Jo Hutchinson, Rebecca Johnes & Lance Mao, *Education in England Annual Report 2016*, Centre Forum, April 2016, http://centreforum.org/live/wp-content/uploads/2016/04/education-in-england-2016-web.pdf

[77] Pupils from Chinese (and Indian) backgrounds make the most progress at school. Pupils from Chinese heritage on average achieve two grades higher in every GCSE subject than white British children. In Key Stage 2 reading, writing and mathematics SATs, 71% of pupils from Chinese backgrounds achieved the 'expected standard': Ibid

[78] Black children, although starting school at an average level, fall behind, and are the worst performing ethnic group at GCSE. Young black people, despite starting school with the same level of mathematics and literacy as other ethnic groups, are most likely to fail mathematics GCSE, and have the lowest outcomes in science, mathematics and technology A-levels. Boys of Black Caribbean heritage perform substantially worse than their female peers: Bart Shaw, Loic Menzies, Eleanor Bernardes, Sam Baars, Philip Nye & Rebecca Allen, *Ethnicity, Gender and Social Mobility*, Social Mobility Commission, 28 December 2016, https://assets.publishing.service.gov.uk/government/uploads/system/uploads/attachment_data/file/579988/Ethnicity_gender_and_social_mobility.pdf

[79] In Key Stage 2 reading, writing and mathematics SATs, 45% of White British pupils overall achieved the 'expected standard': Natalie Perera, Peter Sellen, Jo Hutchinson, Rebecca Johnes & Lance Mao, *Education in England Annual Report 2016*, Centre Forum, April 2016, http://centreforum.org/live/wp-content/uploads/2016/04/education-in-england-2016-web.pdf. Only 40% of White British pupils do well in GCSEs, and the education attainment gap is widest amongst pupils from white British families: Bart Shaw, Loic Menzies, Eleanor Bernardes, Sam Baars, Philip Nye & Rebecca Allen, *Ethnicity, Gender and Social Mobility*, Social Mobility Commission, 28 December 2016, https://assets.publishing.service.gov.uk/government/uploads/system/uploads/

attachment_data/file/579988/Ethnicity_gender_and_social_mobility.pdf

[80] Around 70% cent of white British children had a 'good level of development' at aged 5. While ahead at age 5, poor white British children in England make less progress in school compared to other ethnic groups. In key stage 2 SATs 32% of White British pupils from low-income families achieved the 'expected standard'. White British pupils don't do as well in their GCSEs as those who speak English as a second language: Natalie Perera, Peter Sellen, Jo Hutchinson, Rebecca Johnes & Lance Mao, *Education in England Annual Report 2016*, Centre Forum, April 2016, http://centreforum.org/live/wp-content/uploads/2016/04/education-in-england-2016-web.pdf. White boys from poorer backgrounds perform badly throughout the education system and are the worst performers at primary and secondary school: Bart Shaw, Loic Menzies, Eleanor Bernardes, Sam Baars, Philip Nye & Rebecca Allen, *Ethnicity, Gender and Social Mobility*, Social Mobility Commission, 28 December 2016, https://assets.publishing.service.gov.uk/government/uploads/system/uploads/attachment_data/file/579988/Ethnicity_gender_and_social_mobility.pdf. Social Market Foundation, *Educational inequalities in England and Wales, Commission on Inequality in Education*, SMF, January 2016, http://www.smf.co.uk/wp-content/uploads/2016/01/Publication-Commission-on-Inequality-in-Education-Initial-Findings-Slide-Pack-120116.pdf. White British children of poor families are two thirds of a grade lower in the 8 'core' GCSE subjects, and perform worse than any other group: Bart Shaw, Sam Baars & Loic Menzies (LKMco), Meena Parameshwaran & Rebecca Allen (Education Datalab), *Low income pupils' progress at secondary school*, Social Mobility Commission, 27 February 2017, https://assets.publishing.service.gov.uk/government/uploads/system/uploads/attachment_data/file/594363/Progress_at_Secondary_School_report_final.pdf

[81] Of those in the lowest income brackets, 1 in 10 white working class young people, 3 in 10 black Caribbean, 5 in 10 Bangladeshis, and 7 in 10 Chinese, go to university: Bart Shaw, Loic Menzies, Eleanor Bernardes, Sam Baars, Philip Nye & Rebecca Allen, *Ethnicity, Gender and Social Mobility*, Social Mobility Commission, 28 December 2016, https://assets.publishing.service.gov.uk/government/uploads/system/uploads/attachment_data/file/579988/Ethnicity_gender_and_social_mobility.pdf.

[82] Young black people are the least likely ethnic group to achieve a good degree and most likely to drop out of university: Ibid. At some universities black students were much less likely to get a first or upper second class degree than their white peers; date from the Higher Education Statistics Agency for 2015-16: Sian Griffiths, *Black students less likely to get a first*, The Sunday Times, 8 October 2017, https://www.

thetimes.co.uk/edition/news/black-students-less-likely-to-get-a-first-n9g77k7z6

[83] Black Caribbean pupils are permanently excluded from school three times as often as white British pupils: GOV.UK, *Ethnicity facts and figures website, Government Race Audit*, October 2017, https://www.ethnicity-facts-figures.service.gov.uk/. Black children are most likely to be excluded from school: Bart Shaw, Loic Menzies, Eleanor Bernardes, Sam Baars, Philip Nye & Rebecca Allen, *Ethnicity, Gender and Social Mobility*, Social Mobility Commission, 28 December 2016, https://assets.publishing. service.gov.uk/government/uploads/system/uploads/attachment_data/file/579988/ Ethnicity_gender_and_social_mobility.pdf

[84] GOV.UK, *Ethnicity facts and figures website, Government Race Audit*, October 2017, https://www.ethnicity-facts-figures.service.gov.uk/

[85] Black Caribbean boys are nine times more likely to be sentenced to prison than young white people: Ministry of Justice Analytical Services, *Exploratory analysis of 10-17 year olds in the youth secure estate by black and other minority ethnic groups*, Ministry of Justice, September 2017, https://assets.publishing.service.gov.uk/government/ uploads/system/uploads/attachment_data/file/641481/Exploratory-analysis-of-10-17- year-olds-in-the-youth-secure-estate-by-bame-groups.pdf

[86] Bart Shaw, Loic Menzies, Eleanor Bernardes, Sam Baars, Philip Nye & Rebecca Allen, *Ethnicity, Gender and Social Mobility*, Social Mobility Commission, 28 December 2016, https://assets.publishing.service.gov.uk/government/uploads/system/ uploads/attachment_data/file/579988/Ethnicity_gender_and_social_mobility.pdf

[87] Natalie Perera, Peter Sellen, Jo Hutchinson, Rebecca Johnes & Lance Mao, *Education in England Annual Report 2016*, Centre Forum, April 2016, http://centreforum.org/ live/wp-content/uploads/2016/04/education-in-england-2016-web.pdf

[88] Bart Shaw, Loic Menzies, Eleanor Bernardes, Sam Baars, Philip Nye & Rebecca Allen, *Ethnicity, Gender and Social Mobility*, Social Mobility Commission, 28 December 2016, https://assets.publishing.service.gov.uk/government/uploads/system/ uploads/attachment_data/file/579988/Ethnicity_gender_and_social_mobility.pdf

[89] Although the education attainment of black and Asian Muslim young people and those from Bangladeshi and Pakistani backgrounds is better than those from other ethnic groups including white British pupils, they are almost twice as likely to be unemployed as whites. Less than two-thirds of people from ethnic minorities are in employment, compared to three-quarters of white people. While those from an Indian background are nearly as likely to have a job as white people, those of Pakistani and Bangladeshi origin are the least likely to be in employment: GOV.UK, *Ethnicity facts*

and figures website, Government Race Audit October 2017, https://www.ethnicity-facts-figures.service.gov.uk/. Bangladeshi and Pakistani graduates are about 12% less likely, and Indian and Black Caribbean graduates 5% less likely, to be employed than white British graduates: Kathleen Henehan & Helena Rose, *Black and ethnic minority workers needs a bigger living standards reward for their astounding progress in getting degrees*, Resolution Foundation, 7 October 2017, https://www.resolutionfoundation. org/media/blog/black-and-ethnic-minority-workers-needs-a-bigger-living-standards-reward-for-their-astounding-progress-in-getting-degrees/

[90] People from black and minority ethnic backgrounds are less likely to get professional and managerial jobs, even if they are similarly or better qualified: GOV.UK, *Ethnicity facts and figures website, Government Race Audit* October 2017, https://www. ethnicity-facts-figures.service.gov.uk/. Although the education attainment of black and Asian Muslim young people and those from Bangladeshi and Pakistani backgrounds is better than those from other ethnic groups including white British pupils, they are 'significantly less likely to be employed in managerial or professional jobs than their white counterparts': Bart Shaw, Loic Menzies, Eleanor Bernardes, Sam Baars, Philip Nye & Rebecca Allen, *Ethnicity, Gender and Social Mobility*, Social Mobility Commission, 28 December 2016, https://assets.publishing.service.gov.uk/government/ uploads/system/uploads/attachment_data/file/579988/Ethnicity_gender_and_social_ mobility.pdf

[91] People from black and minority ethnic backgrounds on average earn less in the same type of job than their white colleagues: GOV.UK, *Ethnicity facts and figures website, Government Race Audit*, October 2017, https://www.ethnicity-facts-figures.service. gov.uk/. Young women from Pakistani and Bangladeshi backgrounds in particular, despite doing well at school and university, are paid less than women from other ethnic minorities. Research puts this down to 'workplace discrimination, particularly against Muslim women': Bart Shaw, Loic Menzies, Eleanor Bernardes, Sam Baars, Philip Nye & Rebecca Allen, *Ethnicity, Gender and Social Mobility*, Social Mobility Commission, 28 December 2016, https://assets.publishing.service.gov.uk/government/uploads/ system/uploads/attachment_data/file/579988/Ethnicity_gender_and_social_mobility. pdf. People from black and minority ethnic backgrounds working in the professions, except those of Chinese heritage, earn less than their white counterparts doing similar jobs: Dr. Sam Friedman, Dr. Daniel Laurison & Dr. Lindsey Macmillan, *Social Mobility, the Class Pay Gap and Intergenerational Worklessness: New Insights from The Labour Force Survey*, Social Mobility Commission, 26 January 2017, https://www.

scribd.com/document/337644345/Social-Mobility. Compared to the average income of a white British household, Bangladeshi families earn £8,900 less, Pakistani families £8,700 less, and black African families £5,600 less: Adam Corlett, *Diverse outcomes Living standards by ethnicity*, Resolution Foundation, August 2017, https://www.resolutionfoundation.org/app/uploads/2017/08/Diverse-outcomes.pdf

[92] Social Mobility Commission, *State of the Nation 2016: Social Mobility in Great Britain*, November 2016, https://assets.publishing.service.gov.uk/government/uploads/system/uploads/attachment_data/file/569410/Social_Mobility_Commission_2016_REPORT_WEB__1__.pdf

[93] The proportion of the national output produced by London and the south-east has increased from around 33% in 1997 to 37.7% in 2015, and is forecast to rise to 40% in 2022. By contrast the proportion of the country's output produced by all other regions is expected to decline: Larry Elliott, *TUC urges parties to deliver growth across UK*, Guardian Financial, 28 April 2017, p. 31

[94] North-east England and the West Midlands had the lowest levels of income, both 20% lower than in the south-east: Resolution Foundation report: Adam Corlett & Stephen Clarke, *Living Standards 2017, The past, present and possible future of UK incomes*, Resolution Foundation, February 2017, https://www.resolutionfoundation.org/app/uploads/2017/01/Audit-2017.pdf

[95] Since 1965, about 1.2m. more people have died before the age of 75 in the north of England than in the south, and this gap in premature deaths is growing larger: Iain E Buchan, Evangelos Kontopantelis, Matthew Sperrin, Tarani Chandola & Tim Doran, *Research report, North-South disparities in English mortality 1965–2015: longitudinal population study*, published in the Journal of Epidemiology & Community Health (DOI: 10.1136/10.1136/jech-2017-209195), August 2017, http://jech.bmj.com/content/early/2017/07/14/jech-2017-209195. Between 2014 and 2016, 3,530 more men and 1,881 more women aged between 25 and 44 died in the north than in the south, when population and age are taken into account: Evangelos Kontopantelis, Iain Buchan, Roger T. Webb, Darren M. Ashcroft, Mamas A. Mamas & Tim Doran, *Disparities in mortality among 25–44-year-olds in England: a longitudinal, population-based study*, Lancet Public Health 2018, published online 30 October 2018, https://www.thelancet.com/action/showPdf?pii=S2468-2667%2818%2930177-4

[96] Social Market Foundation, *Educational inequalities in England and Wales, Commission on Inequality in Education*, SMF, January 2016, http://www.smf.co.uk/wp-content/uploads/2016/01/Publication-Commission-on-Inequality-in-Education-

Initial-Findings-Slide-Pack-120116.pdf. 29% of white working class boys from deprived neighbourhoods in England go on to take A-levels or AS-levels, compared with 46% of white boys who come from the same economic background, but who live in more affluent areas: Pam Sammons, Katalin Toth & Kathy Sylva, *Background to success, Differences in A-level entries by ethnicity, neighbourhood and gender*, Sutton Trust, November 2015, https://www.suttontrust.com/wp-content/uploads/2015/11/Background-to-Success-Final-1.pdf. In the 2018 Key Stage 2 literacy and mathematics tests the gap between the highest and lowest performing local authorities was stark - in Richmond-upon-Thames 80% of pupils met the expected standards; 52% in Peterborough; with a national average of 65%. The gap in attainment between the best and worst local authority in 2018 was 28 percentage points, three percentage points more than in 2017: Richard Adams, *KS2 results show widening gulf between strongest and weakest primary schools*, Guardian, 4 September 2018, https://www.theguardian.com/education/2018/sep/04/ks2-results-primary-schools-performance

[97] For pupils born in 1970 there was a stronger correlation between academic attainment and social background than where you lived. In the next generation (those born in 2000) there is a much stronger link between attainment and location, than family background and income: Social Market Foundation, *Educational inequalities in England and Wales, Commission on Inequality in Education*, SMF, January 2016, http://www.smf.co.uk/wp-content/uploads/2016/01/Publication-Commission-on-Inequality-in-Education-Initial-Findings-Slide-Pack-120116.pdf

[98] A far larger proportion of children and young people are in care in the north of England than the south. There are 92 per 10,000 children under the age of 18 in care in the north-east; 49 in the east of England – Department for Education: Alison Holt, *Child protection services near crisis as demand rises*, BBC News, 6 November 2018, https://www.bbc.co.uk/news/education-46049154

[99] Department for Education: Rachel Schraer, *Is there a north-south divide in England's schools?* BBC News, 31 March 2018, https://www.bbc.co.uk/news/education-43544255

[100] Migration study by the Centre for Economic Policy Research: Richard Ford, *Brain drain created north-south divide*, The Times, 4 December 2018, https://www.thetimes.co.uk/article/brain-drain-created-north-south-divide-kvvmsrtmv

[101] Luke Raikes, Leah Millward & Sarah Longlands, *State of the North 2018, Reprioritising the Northern Powerhouse,* Institute of Public Policy Research, December 2018, https://www.ippr.org/files/2018-12/sotn-2018-web.pdf

[102] Social Mobility Commission, *Time For Change: An Assessment of Government*

Policies on Social Mobility 1997-2017, June 2017, https://assets.publishing.service.gov.uk/government/uploads/system/uploads/attachment_data/file/622214/Time_for_Change_report_-_An_assessement_of_government_policies_on_social_mobility_1997-2017.pdf

[103] OECD, *A Broken Social Elevator? How to Promote Social Mobility*, OECD Publishing, Paris, June 2018, https://read.oecd-ilibrary.org/social-issues-migration-health/broken-elevator-how-to-promote-social-mobility_9789264301085-en#page1

Chapter 8: The arguments for change

[1] Since 1988 the proportion of GCSEs achieved at the top grades has increased from around 40% to nearly 70%: Guardian Datablog, *How have GCSE pass rates changed over the exams' 25 year history?* 17 September 2012, https://www.theguardian.com/news/datablog/2012/sep/17/gcse-exams-replaced-ebacc-history-pass-rates; and Richard Adams, *GCSE results 2015: pass rate rises but A* grades dip*, Guardian, 20 August 2015, https://www.theguardian.com/education/2015/aug/20/gcses-results-2015-english-pass-rate-rises-jump-a-c-grades

[2] Overall participation in higher education was 19.3% in 1990 - National Committee of Inquiry into Higher Education (Dearing Report) Report 6, *Widening participation in higher education for students from lower socio-economic groups and students with disabilities*, table 1.1: Paul Bolton, *Education: Historical statistics Standard Note: SN/SG/4252*, House of Commons Library, 2012, https://researchbriefings.parliament.uk/ResearchBriefing/Summary/SN04252. The participation rate of 17-20 year olds was 40% in 2013/14: Department for Business, Innovation and Skills, *Statistics First Release, Participation Rates in Higher Education: Academic Years 2006/2007 – 2013/2014 (Provisional), Supplementary Table B*, p. 21, https://assets.publishing.service.gov.uk/government/uploads/system/uploads/attachment_data/file/458034/HEIPR_PUBLICATION_2013-14.pdf#page=21

[3] Kirstie Donnelly, managing director of City & Guilds, Guardian Letters, *UK education is eroded by the Ebacc, academies and tuition fees*, 14 August 2017, www.theguardian.com/politics/2017/aug/14/uk-education-is-eroded-by-the-ebacc-academies-and-tuition-fees. Dr. Tony Breslin, Chair of Industry Qualifications, Letter to the Editor, The Times, *Core creativity*, 11 August 2017, p. 28. John Kampfner, Chief Executive of the Creative Industries Federation, *Britain's got talent but we are not providing the skills*, The Times, Comment, 5 June 2017, https://www.thetimes.co.uk/past-six-days/2017-06-05/business/britains-got-talent-but-we-are-not-providing-the-skills-lgt5rqf09

[4] John Seddon, *Systems Thinking in the Public Sector, the failure of the reform regime…
and a manifesto for a better way* (Triarchy Press, Axminster, UK, 2008) p. vi

[5] For more detailed accounts of systems thinking see *The Fifth Discipline, The Art &
Practice of The Learning Organization*, Peter M. Senge, (Century Business, London,
1993); Jake Chapman, *Systems Failure, Why governments must learn to think differently*
(Demos, London, 2004); John Seddon, *Systems Thinking in the Public Sector, the failure
of the reform regime… and a manifesto for a better way* (Triarchy Press, Axminster,
UK, 2008); and Gillian Tett, *The Silo Effect, Why putting everything in its place isn't
such a bright idea* (Little, Brown Book Group, London, 2015)

[6] Jake Chapman, *Systems Failure, Why governments must learn to think differently*
(Demos, London, 2004) p. 21

[7] Ibid, p. 22

[8] Ibid, p. 20

Chapter 9: Promoting lifelong learning for all

[1] Quoted in Dr. Carol H. Sawyer, Barbara Walling & Maria Cristina Bombelli, *Learning
to Learn: Meeting the Challenge of Change, An Experience-Based Paper*, http://iff.
ac.at/oe/media/documents/Paper_24_Sawyer_Walling_Bombelli.pdf

[2] Dr. Stanley N. Graven & Dr. Joy V. Browne, *Auditory development in the foetus
and infant*, Newborn and Infant Nursing Reviews, volume 8, issue 4, December 2008,
pgs. 187-193, https://www.sciencedirect.com/science/article/pii/S1527336908001347.
Ruth Fridman, *The Maternal Womb: The First Musical School for the Baby*, Journal
of Prenatal & Perinatal Psychology & Health, volume 15, No. 1, https://www.questia.
com/library/journal/1P3-1373447681/the-maternal-womb-the-first-musical-school-
for-the. Anthony J. De Casper & William P. Fifer, *Of human bonding: Newborns
prefer their mothers' voices*, Science, volume 208, issue 4448, pgs. 1174-1176, 6 June
1980, http://bernard.pitzer.edu/~dmoore/psych199s03articles/Of_Human_Bonding.
pdf. Gina Kolata, *Studying learning in the womb*, Science, volume 225, issue 4659,
pgs. 302-303, 20 July 1984, https://cpb-us-w2.wpmucdn.com/sites.stedwards.edu/
dist/6/230/files/2013/02/CD_CatintheHatArticle-1sgsylv.pdf

[3] Paul Ryan, *Lifelong learning: Potential and constraints with special reference to
policies in the United Kingdom and Europe*, International Labour Organisation,
2003, http://www.ilo.org/wcmsp5/groups/public/---ed_emp/---ifp_skills/documents/
publication/wcms_103988.pdf

[4] Allen Tough, *The Adult's Learning Projects: a fresh approach to theory and practice*

in adult learning (Ontario Institute for Studies in Education, Toronto, 1971). Naomi Sargant, *Learning and 'Leisure', A study of adult participation in learning and its policy implications* (National Institute of Adult Continuing Education, Leicester, 1991). Sarah Beinart, and Patten Smith, *National Adult Learning Survey 1997, Research Report 49* (Prentice Hall/Harvester Wheatsheaf, London, 1998). Ivana La Valle and Steven Finch, *Pathways in Adult Learning Survey, Research Brief 137* (Department for Education and Employment, London, 1999)

[5] Adapted from Knowledge Jump website, *Informal and Formal Learning*, http://www. knowledgejump.com/learning/informal.html

[6] Katherine Sellgren, *Fall in UK adults engaged in learning, survey finds*, BBC News, 13 May 2011, http://www.bbc.co.uk/news/education-13362994

[7] Organisation for Economic Cooperation and Development, *Terms, Concepts and Models for Analysing the Value of Recognition Programmes*, RNFIL - Third Meeting of National Representatives and International Organisations, 2 - 3 October 2007, Vienna, Austria, http://www.oecd.org/edu/skills-beyond-school/41834711.pdf

[8] OECD, *Recognition of Non-formal and Informal Learning*, http://www.oecd.org/edu/skills-beyond-school/recognitionofnon-formalandinformallearning-home.htm

[9] DepartmentforEducation,April2012,www.education.gov.uk/childrenandyoungpeople/families/a00203160/role-of-parents-in-childslearning

[10] UNICEF, *The formative years: UNICEF's work on measuring early childhood*, New York, US, https://www.unicef.org/earlychildhood/files/Brochure_-_The_Formative_Years.pdf

[11] Maria Evangelou, Kathy Sylva, Maria Kyriacou, Mary Wild & Georgina Glenny, *Early Years Learning and Development Literature Review*, Department for Children, Schools and Families, 2009, http://dera.ioe.ac.uk/11382/2/DCSF-RR176.pdf. Iram Siraj-Blatchford & John Siraj-Blatchford, *Improving children's attainment through a better quality of family-based support for early learning*, Centre for Excellence and Outcomes in Children's and Young People's Services (C4EO), London, 2009, http://archive.c4eo.org.uk/themes/earlyyears/familybasedsupport/files/c4eo_family_based_support_kr_2.pdf

[12] Kathy Sylva, Edward Melhuish, Pam Sammons, Iram Siraj-Blatchford & Brenda Taggart, *The Effective Provision of Pre-School Education Project*, Department for Education and Science, London, 2004, http://eprints.ioe.ac.uk/5309/1/sylva2004EPPEfinal.pdf

[13] Dame Clare Tickell, *The Early Years: Foundations for life, health and learning, An*

Independent Report on the Early Years Foundation Stage to Her Majesty's Government, 2011, http://www.educationengland.org.uk/documents/pdfs/2011-tickell-report-eyfs.pdf

[14] Philip Hensher, *Rejecting Oxbridge isn't clever – it's a mistake*, Independent, 20 January 2012, https://www.independent.co.uk/voices/commentators/philip-hensher/philip-hensher-rejecting-oxbridge-isnt-clever-its-a-mistake-6292041.html

[15] Richard Adams, *Private schools in UK attracting record numbers of students*, Guardian, 1 May 2015, https://www.theguardian.com/education/2015/may/01/private-schools-in-uk-attracting-record-numbers-of-students

[16] Ibid

[17] Analysis by the *Chambers Student Guide* of data provided by 46 law firms on what type of school their trainees attended: Frances Gibb, *Private schools rule the roost*, The Times, 9 February 2017, http://www.thetimes.co.uk/edition/student-law/private-schools-rule-the-roost-0qpvwrd9x. Paul Johnson, *We must beware dangers of denying our children the path to a better life*, The Times Comment, 24 January 2017, http://www.thetimes.co.uk/edition/business/we-must-beware-dangers-of-denying-our-children-the-path-to-a-better-life-672pz870f

[18] Independent schools claim that the private education sector contributes £11.7b. a year and 275,000 jobs to the economy: Nicola Woolcock, *Private schools are vital to state education, says head*, The Times, 2 October 2017, https://www.thetimes.co.uk/article/3c538874-a6d9-11e7-b9a3-2cac9d6c85bd

[19] Private schools are entitled to 80% relief on business rates, valued at around £165m. per annum: Hannah Richardson, *Private school business rate relief warning from Labour*, BBC News, 25 November 2014, http://www.bbc.co.uk/news/education-30181920

[20] It is estimated that the exemption of private school fees from VAT is worth around £1.6b: Labour Party, *Funding Britain's Future*, London, May 2017, http://labour.org.uk/wp-content/uploads/2017/10/Funding-Britains-Future.pdf

[21] Lord Adonis has proposed, for example, that there should be a special tax on private schools of 25%: Nicola Woolcock, *Tax private schools to pay state teachers, says Lord Adonis*, The Times, 9 December 2017, https://www.thetimes.co.uk/article/314ef8c0-dc47-11e7-aacd-025601055216

[22] Following the 2006 Charities Act the Charities Commission issued guidance on the activities private schools would have to engage in to justify their charitable status. A successful legal challenge by the Independent Schools Council removed the Charities Commission's ability to enforce this guidance; the judicial review concluding that 'trustees of a charitable independent school should decide what was appropriate in their

particular circumstances'. The judicial review also concluded that a private school's charitable status 'depends on what it was established to do, not what it does': Catherine Fairbairn, *Charitable status and independent schools*, House of Commons Library, 19 September 2017, https://researchbriefings.parliament.uk/ResearchBriefing/Summary/SN05222. Archie Bland, *Private schools are doing laughably little to justify their charitable status*, Independent, 23 September 2013, http://www.independent.co.uk/voices/comment/private-schools-are-doing-laughably-little-to-justify-their-charitable-status-8835283.html

[23] The Conservative government in a 2016 green paper and the Conservative Party in their 2017 general election manifesto committed to requiring private schools to justify their charitable status by sponsoring academies, partnering with state schools and having bursaries for children from low-income families: Rosemary Bennett, *Private schools will keep charitable status*, The Times, 13 September 2017, https://www.thetimes.co.uk/edition/news/private-schools-will-keep-charitable-status-9zpm5nhnj

[24] For example there are claims from private school heads that the Scottish government's decision to remove the relief on business rates could in net terms end up incurring more public funding. They argue that it would take only 3% of pupils currently educated privately to opt into the state sector to wipe out the £5m. gained by ending business rate relief: Simon Johnson, *SNP decision to charge Scottish private schools business rates 'will cost taxpayer double'*, Sunday Telegraph, 17 December 2017, http://www.telegraph.co.uk/news/2017/12/17/snp-decision-charge-scottish-private-schools-business-rates/

[25] John Lyons Charity Supplementary School website, http://johnlyonscharity.org.uk/initiatives/schools/

[26] http://www.supplementaryeducation.org.uk/

[27] Home-schooling is legal in England and Wales under the 1944 Education Act, which was consolidated into the 1996 Education Act.

[28] Section 7 of the 1996 Education Act

[29] 37,000 children were educated at home in 2015, nearly two-thirds more than in 2009: Branwen Jeffreys, *Rising numbers of pupils home educated*, BBC News, 21 December 2015, http://www.bbc.co.uk/news/education-35133119. 57,800 children were home-schooled in 2018, an increase of 27% on the 45,500 in 2017 - The Association of Directors of Children's Services: Nicola Woolcock, *Schools force pupils to focus on GCSE curriculum from age of 11*, The Times, 16 November 2018, https://www.thetimes.co.uk/article/schools-force-pupils-to-focus-on-gcse-curriculum-from-age-of-

11-qz6cxl0zh

[30] Branwen Jeffreys, *Illegal schools: Ministers promise crackdown*, BBC News, 14 March 2018, http://www.bbc.co.uk/news/education-43409151.

[31] Kiran Gill, with Harry Quilter-Pinner & Danny Swift, *Making the difference, Breaking the link between school exclusion and social exclusion*, Institute for Public Policy Research, October 2017, https://www.ippr.org/files/2017-10/making-the-difference-report-october-2017.pdf. In a submission to a House of Commons committee, the Association of Directors of Children's Services (ADCS) reported that a minority of headteachers in England, due to worries about inspections, exam league table positions and losing their jobs because of academy takeovers, are persuading parents to educate their children at home so as to avoid an exclusion on their record: Hannah Richardson, *Parents being talked into homeschooling troubled children*, BBC News, 6 February 2018, http://www.bbc.co.uk/news/education-42943997

[32] Lord Agnew, *Shutting illegal schools protects children and helps bridge social divides*, The Times, Comment, 15 March 2018, https://www.thetimes.co.uk/article/b049d362-27cd-11e8-acc5-262aff1ca7a6. Branwen Jeffreys, *Illegal schools: Ministers promise crackdown*, BBC News, 14 March 2018, http://www.bbc.co.uk/news/education-43409151. Harry Yorke, *Plan for home school register dropped*, Daily Telegraph, 15 March 2018, p.2

[33] The statutory duty on local authorities to secure access to a local youth service offer is contained in Section 507B, inserted into the Education Act 1996 by section 6 of the Education and Inspections Act 2006. It requires that 'Every local authority in England must, "so far as reasonably practicable", secure for qualifying young persons in the authority's area access to sufficient educational and leisure-time activities which are for the improvement of their well-being.'

[34] Peter Walker, *Labour vows to make provision of youth services compulsory*, Guardian, 31 July 2018, https://www.theguardian.com/society/2018/jul/31/labour-vows-to-make-provision-of-youth-services-compulsory

[35] The Albemarle Report was the product of the committee established by the Minister of Education in November 1958, chaired by the Countess of Albemarle.

[36] Adam Offord, *Youth services cut by £387m in six years*, Children and Young People Now, 12 August 2016, http://www.cypnow.co.uk/cyp/news/1158579/youth-services-cut-by-gbp387m-in-six-years. UNISON, *Damage, A future at risk, Cuts in youth services*, August 2016, https://www.unison.org.uk/content/uploads/2016/08/23996.pdf

[37] National Youth Agency, *Youth services in England: Changes and trends in the provision*

of services, November 2014, http://www.nya.org.uk/wp-content/uploads/2015/01/Youth-services-in-England-changes-and-trends.pdf

[38] Association of Colleges website, https://www.aoc.co.uk/about-colleges/research-and-stats/key-further-education-statistics.

[39] The Association of Colleges says that from 2009 to 2019, college funding has fallen by about 30%: Hannah Richardson, *The students who fear for their ambitions amid college cuts*, BBC News, 17 October 2018, https://www.bbc.co.uk/news/education-45875984

[40] Branwen Jeffreys, *Further education college finances face double whammy*, BBC News, 17 September 2018, https://www.bbc.co.uk/news/education-45524935

[41] The specialist designated institutions are City Lit, Fircroft College, Hillcroft College, the Mary Ward Centre, Morley College, Northern College, Ruskin College, the Working Men's College and the Workers' Educational Association. They offer a wide range of adult education courses for over 130,000 students across the country and receive funding directly from the Skills Funding Agency.

[42] 86% of adult learning providers judged good or outstanding following Ofsted inspections: Ofsted, *The Annual Report of Her Majesty's Chief Inspector of Education, Children's Services and Skills 2014/15*, Ofsted, December 2015 p. 68, https://www.gov.uk/government/publications/ofsted-annual-report-201415-education-and-skills

[43] 1 in 2 adults with no qualifications are in work compared to more than 9 in 10 graduates. On average those with Level 2 qualifications earn around 8% more than people without Level 2 qualifications: National Learning and Work Institute, *Skills and poverty Building an anti-poverty learning and skills system*, National Learning and Work Institute (England and Wales), Leicester, September 2016, p.5, http://learningandwork.org.uk/sites/niace_en/files/files/Skills%20%20Poverty%20Sep%2016.pdf. By 2024 the number of jobs in the UK is expected to rise by about 1.8m., mainly for highly qualified managers and professionals; and only 2% of those in employment will have no formal qualifications: UK Commission for Employment and Skills, *Working Futures 2014 – 2024*, UKCES, Wath-upon-Dearne, 2014, https://www.gov.uk/government/uploads/system/uploads/attachment_data/file/514285/Working_Futures_Headline_Report_final_for_web__PG.pdf. In the years ahead, skills and qualifications will play an increasingly central role in determining individual employability, career progression and earnings potential: CBI, *Building a Better Off Britain: Improving Lives by Making Growth Work for Everyone,* Confederation of British Industry, November 2014, http://news.cbi.org.uk/news/our-package-of-measures-to-build-a-better-off-britain/

[44] Office for National Statistics, https://www.ons.gov.uk/peoplepopulationandcommunity/

populationandmigration/populationestimates/datalist

[45] Organisation for Economic Cooperation and Economic Development, *Building Skills for All: A Review of England – Policy Insight from the Survey of Adult Skills*, OECD, Paris, 2016, p.5, https://www.oecd.org/unitedkingdom/building-skills-for-all-review-of-england.pdf. More than 5m. lack both functional literacy and numeracy: National Learning and Work Institute, *Skills and poverty Building an anti-poverty learning and skills system*, National Learning and Work Institute (England and Wales), Leicester, September 2016, p.5, http://learningandwork.org.uk/sites/niace_en/files/files/Skills%20%20Poverty%20Sep%202016.pdf

[46] National Learning and Work Institute, *Skills and poverty Building an anti-poverty learning and skills system*, National Learning and Work Institute (England and Wales), Leicester, September 2016, p.5, http://learningandwork.org.uk/sites/niace_en/files/files/Skills%20%20Poverty%20Sep%202016.pdf

[47] Ibid

[48] BIS, *Impact of Poor Basic Literacy and Numeracy on Employers, Research Paper 266,* Department for Business, Innovation & Skills, London, February 2016

[49] Out of 24 countries surveyed, the UK was ranked 12th for numeracy and 17th for literacy - OECD skills survey. Out of 34 countries the UK was ranked 19th for low skills, 24th for intermediate skills, and 11th for high skills (degree level) - OECD skills survey of 34 countries: National Learning and Work Institute, *Skills and poverty Building an anti-poverty learning and skills system*, National Learning and Work Institute (England and Wales), Leicester, September 2016, p.5, http://learningandwork.org.uk/sites/niace_en/files/files/Skills%20%20Poverty%20Sep%202016.pdf

[50] The number of those aged over 24 years on Level 3 (A-level equivalent) and Level 4 courses has dropped by 86%; from 400,000 in 2012/13 to 57,100 in 2013/2014: D. Hughes, *Basic Skills Bulletin*, 169 (edited by D. Coryton), Education Publishing Company, Crediton, 2014. Ofsted, *The Annual Report of Her Majesty's Chief Inspector of Education, Children's Services and Skills 2014/15*, December 2015, https://www.gov.uk/government/uploads/system/uploads/attachment_data/file/483347/Ofsted_annual_report_education_and_skills.pdf. Between 2010 and 2017 the number of adults achieving level four awards (a Higher National Certificate or above) fell by 75% from 19,600 to 4,900: *Night schools can give those 'left behind' a leg up*, David Lammy, The Times, 13 January 2017, http://www.thetimes.co.uk/past-six-days/2017-01-13/news/night-schools-can-give-those-left-behind-a-leg-up-zv5vvwhv2.

[51] Laura McInerney, *Cappuccino with extra Italian? Pop-up classes give new buzz to*

adult learning, Guardian Education, 21 February 2017, p. 32, https://www.theguardian.com/education/2017/feb/21/pop-up-classes-adult-learning-further-education

[52] Ibid

[53] Two separate funding streams have now been merged into a single 'Adult Education Budget'. Those areas of the country that have agreed devolution deals with the government (such as Greater Manchester and Merseyside) are taking on the responsibility for commissioning adult education provision from 2018-19.

[54] BIS, *Skills Funding Agency Priorities and Funding for the 2016 - 2017 Financial Year,* Department of Business, Innovation and Skills, London 15 December 2015, https://www.gov.uk/government/uploads/system/uploads/attachment_data/file/485969/BIS-15-615-skills-funding-letter-2016-to-2017.pdf

[55] Employers and adult learners are not meaningfully involved in the planning of adult education: Dr Deirdre Hughes OBE, Karen Adriaanse & Dr Sally-Anne Barnes, *Adult Education, Too important to be left to chance, Research Report for the All Party Parliamentary Group for Adult Education (APPG) – Inquiry into Adult Education,* Warwick Institute for Employment Research, University of Warwick, July 2016, https://warwick.ac.uk/fac/soc/ier/research/adult_education/adult_education_too_important_to_be_left_to_chance.pdf

[56] The National Careers Service is the publicly funded careers service for adults and young people (aged 13 or over) in England, and has been operating since April 2012. The Service provides information, advice and guidance on learning, training, career choice, career development, job search, and the labour market. It can be accessed online, by telephone, and face to face (for people aged 19 and over).

[57] Dr Deirdre Hughes OBE, Karen Adriaanse & Dr Sally-Anne Barnes, *Adult Education, Too important to be left to chance,* Warwick Institute of Employment Research, University of Warwick, A report commissioned by the All Party Parliamentary Group for Adult Education, July 2016, https://warwick.ac.uk/fac/soc/ier/research/adult_education/adult_education_ier_report_final_2401018.pdf

[58] Most adults would like to read more, and active support needs to be provided to national and local initiatives such as those promoted by the Reading Agency to encourage people to read or read more often. The Reading Agency has called on 'book lovers across the country to give a good book to someone who doesn't read often': The Reading Agency, *Talking fiction? Research reveals our reading habits and hang*-ups, The Reading Agency website, Friday 21 April 2017, https://readingagency.org.uk/news/media/talking-fiction-research-reveals-nations-reading-habits-and-hang-ups.html

[59] These university-style loans introduced in 2013 cover the cost of learning at Level 3 or above for people aged 19 and over, with people repaying once they earn over £26,000 per year. Only £140m. of the £400m. set aside for loans for adult students has been taken and help is not available for people wanting to study pre A level courses: Laura McInerney, *Cappuccino with extra Italian? Pop-up classes give new buzz to adult learning,* Guardian Education, 21 February 2017, p. 32, https://www.theguardian.com/education/2017/feb/21/pop-up-classes-adult-learning-further-education

[60] Since the introduction of advanced learning loans in 2013 the number of people learning at Level 3 has fallen by at least a third: National Learning and Work Institute, *Skills and poverty Building an anti-poverty learning and skills system*, National Learning and Work Institute (England and Wales), Leicester, September 2016, pgs. 6 & 7, http://learningandwork.org.uk/sites/niace_en/files/files/Skills%20%20Poverty%20Sep%2016.pdf

[61] An 'education savings account' that adults could access throughout their lives, proposed by the Special Designated Institutions: Dr Deirdre Hughes OBE, Karen Adriaanse & Dr Sally-Anne Barnes, *Adult Education, Too important to be left to chance*, Warwick Institute of Employment Research, University of Warwick, A report commissioned by the All Party Parliamentary Group for Adult Education, July 2016, https://warwick.ac.uk/fac/soc/ier/research/adult_education/adult_education_ier_report_final_2401018.pdf

[62] A 'lifelong learning fund' proposed by David Lammy MP: Laura McInerney, *Cappuccino with extra Italian? Pop-up classes give new buzz to adult learning,* Guardian Education, 21 February 2017, p. 32

[63] A 'flexible loans system that would allow people to pay for training throughout their lives' advocated by Baroness Wolf: Rachel Sylvester & Alice Thomson, *Universities minister was kept in dark about pledge to freeze tuition fees*, The Times, 18 October 2017, https://www.thetimes.co.uk/article/d59fa746-b378-11e7-bd81-0feeb2b41cb4

[64] National Learning and Work Institute, *Skills and poverty Building an anti-poverty learning and skills system*, National Learning and Work Institute (England and Wales), Leicester, September 2016, http://learningandwork.org.uk/sites/niace_en/files/files/Skills%20%20Poverty%20Sep%2016.pdf

[65] The proposed programme is based on the one the Learning and Work Institute trialled with support from the Department for Business, Innovation and Skills in 13 areas, which increased engagement. The programme would differ from others as it would be 'co-designed' with adult learners, and cover all the capabilities in the one course rather than separate qualifications. This would require doubling the number on similar

courses at an extra cost of £200m. each year. Additionally there would be an expansion in the number of low-level English for Speakers of Other Languages (ESOL) classes aimed at enabling the existing 850,000 people who have ESOL needs and new migrants to learn English: Ibid, pgs. 7 & 8.

[66] The level of public funding would be tailored to individual need. There would be incentives (including through the benefits and tax systems) for people to invest in their own learning and 'top ups' for those on low incomes. Information about the employment, earnings and other outcomes of past students would be made available to help people make decisions about their future learning: Ibid, pgs. 8 & 9.

[67] This service would work with each person, and with the agreement of her/his employer, to prepare a personalised action plan: Ibid, pgs. 9 & 10.

[68] In the 2015-16 academic year - 2.28m. students studying at UK higher education institutions; undergraduate 1.75m.; postgraduate 532,970; full time 1.7m.; part time 540,285; students from the UK 1.84m.; students from outside the UK 438,015: Universities UK website, *Higher education in numbers*, http://www.universitiesuk. ac.uk/facts-and-stats/Pages/higher-education-data.aspx

[69] 49% of 17 to 30-years-old, living in England, in higher education for the first time in UK institutions and then staying in HE for at least 6 months: GOV.UK website, National Statistics, *Participation rates in higher education: 2006 to 2016*, https://www. gov.uk/government/statistics/participation-rates-in-higher-education-2006-to-2016. 27% of all 18-year-olds go to university: Richard Adams, *Almost half of all young people in England go on to higher education*, Guardian, 28 September 2017, https:// www.theguardian.com/education/2017/sep/28/almost-half-of-all-young-people-in-england-go-on-to-higher-education

[70] As at 25 August 2017, 133,280 18-year-old women from the UK had secured a university place in the UK, compared with 103,800 men of this age. The difference is the largest recorded. The gap of 36% between women and men is an increase from 35% the year before and 31% five years ago. In 2017 across the UK, 27.3% of all young men are expected to go to university this year compared with 37.1% of women: BBC News, *Record proportion of women on university courses in UK*, 28 August 2017, http://www. bbc.co.uk/news/education-41066973

[71] Disadvantaged students are defined as those from the poorest backgrounds, areas where few people attend university and certain ethnic groups; and those with disabilities and have been in care: Hannah Richardson, *Top universities to face pressure over admissions*, BBC News, 7 September 2018, https://www.bbc.co.uk/news/education-45436113

[72] Rachel Sylvester & Alice Thomson, *Universities minister was kept in dark about pledge to freeze tuition fees*, The Times, 18 October 2017, https://www.thetimes.co.uk/article/d59fa746-b378-11e7-bd81-0feeb2b41cb4

[73] Young people from the most disadvantaged areas are now 43% more likely to go to university than they were in 2009: Rachel Sylvester & Alice Thomson, *Universities minister was kept in dark about pledge to freeze tuition fees*, The Times, 18 October 2017, https://www.thetimes.co.uk/article/d59fa746-b378-11e7-bd81-0feeb2b41cb4. Since the raising of the cap on tuition fees to £9,000 the participation rate in higher education of disadvantaged students aged 19 has increased by 4.8 percentage points: Daniel Mahoney, *Wealthy Graduates: The Winners from Corbyn's Tuition Fees Policy*, Economic Bulletin, Number 97, Centre for Policy Studies, 4 August 2017, https://www.cps.org.uk/files/reports/original/170804093031-WealthyGraduatesTheWinnersfromCorbynsTuitionFeesPlan.pdf

[74] *The undergraduate funding system in England*, Universities UK Parliamentary briefing, September 2017, http://www.universitiesuk.ac.uk/policy-and-analysis/reports/Documents/2017/briefing-undergraduate-funding-england.pdf

[75] 20% from the poorest income families accepted university places in 2017. 11% from the poorest income families were in university in 2006: UCAS, *Interim assessment of UCAS acceptances for the 2017 cycle, four weeks after A level results day*, September 2017 UCAS Analysis and Research, https://www.ucas.com/file/125591/download?token=twyb2Mur

[76] Social Mobility Commission, *State of the Nation 2016: Social Mobility in Great Britain*, November 2016, https://assets.publishing.service.gov.uk/government/uploads/system/uploads/attachment_data/file/569410/Social_Mobility_Commission_2016_REPORT_WEB__1__.pdf

[77] Emran Mian & Ben Richards, *Widening participation*, Social Market Foundation, 23 March 2016, http://www.smf.co.uk/wp-content/uploads/2016/03/Social-Market-Foundation-Widening-Participation-HE-data-pack-FINALv2.pdf

[78] The proportion of disadvantaged students attending Russell Group universities increased by only 1 percentage point from 2010 to 2017. During the same period the percentage of pupils from disadvantaged neighbourhoods attending three Russell Group universities actually fell: Labour Party's analysis of Higher Education Statistics Agency data: Jessica Elgot, *Government accused of 'total failure' to widen elite university access*, Guardian, 15 August 2018, https://www.theguardian.com/education/2018/aug/15/government-accused-of-total-failure-to-widen-elite-university-

access. Seven of the Russell Group universities are admitting a smaller proportion of disadvantaged students than they were 10 years ago: Chris Havergal, *Elite universities 'going backwards' on widening access*, Times Higher Education Supplement, 18 February 2016, https://www.timeshighereducation.com/news/elite-universities-going-backwards-widening-access

[79] Nicola Woolcock, *Tough targets on poor students*, The Times, 7 September 2018, https://www.thetimes.co.uk/article/tough-targets-on-poor-students-3cw3c8vjg

[80] Kate McCann, *Two-thirds of students drop 'soft' degrees after a year*, Daily Telegraph, 21 September 2017, p. 8, https://www.telegraph.co.uk/news/2017/09/21/two-thirds-students-dropping-courses-top-uk-universities-new/

[81] Dave Phoenix, *Let's bridge the divide between academic and technical education*, Guardian, 18 July 2017, https://www.theguardian.com/higher-education-network/2017/jul/18/lets-bridge-the-divide-between-academic-and-technical-education

[82] Mature students are classified as those who start their courses when aged 21 or over.

[83] 80% of part-time higher education students are in employment: Report by the Office for Fair Access (Offa): Aftab Ali, *Head of UCU says 'rapid' drop points to a 'failure of the student finance system' to meet different needs*, Independent, 11 May 2016, http://www.independent.co.uk/student/into-university/decline-in-part-time-and-mature-student-numbers-revealed-in-promoting-access-to-higher-education-a7024816.html

[84] Ibid

[85] The number of mature students has halved since 2006: Office for Fair Access (Offa): Aftab Ali, *Head of UCU says 'rapid' drop points to a 'failure of the student finance system' to meet different needs*, Independent, 11 May 2016, http://www.independent.co.uk/student/into-university/decline-in-part-time-and-mature-student-numbers-revealed-in-promoting-access-to-higher-education-a7024816.html. Between 2010-11 and 2016-17 the number of undergraduate part-time students in England has declined by 51%: CBI and Universities UK, *The Economic Case for Flexible Learning, Main Findings and Policy Recommendations*, 26 October 2018, https://www.universitiesuk.ac.uk/policy-and-analysis/reports/Documents/2018/the-economic-case-for-flexible-learning.pdf

[86] OECD, *Education at a Glance 2018: OECD Indicators, United Kingdom country notes*, OECD Publishing, https://read.oecd-ilibrary.org/education/education-at-a-glance-2018/united-kingdom_eag-2018-70-en#page1

[87] Call for the national inquiry into access and admissions made by the University and Colleges Union (UCU): Aftab Ali, *Decline in part-time and mature student*

numbers revealed in access to higher education report 'a scandal', Independent, 11 May 2016, http://www.independent.co.uk/student/into-university/decline-in-part-time-and-mature-student-numbers-revealed-in-promoting-access-to-higher-education-a7024816.html

[88] MillionPlus, The Association of Modern Universities, *Forgotten Learners: building a system that works for mature students*, *Research Report*, Million Plus, London, March 2018, http://www.millionplus.ac.uk/documents/Forgotten_learners_building_a_system_that_works_for_mature_students.pdf

[89] Sean Coughlan, *'Wasted potential' of mature students*, BBC News, 14 March 2018, http://www.bbc.co.uk/news/education-43388911

[90] When fees were trebled in England in 2012 universities received additional funding of about £3,000 per full-time student.

[91] In 2017-18 this equated to £833.5m., just under a quarter of the total 'additional' income from fees: Jack Grove, *How can widening participation best be achieved?* Times Higher Education Supplement, 7 December 2017, https://www.timeshighereducation.com/features/how-can-widening-participation-best-be-achieved

[92] In addition to the widening access work undertaken by individual universities in 2017 the Higher Education Funding Council introduced a £60 million National Collaborative Outreach Programme, led by universities in conjunction with colleges and charities and providing outreach initiatives in areas where higher education take-up is low: Jack Grove, *How can widening participation best be achieved?* Times Higher Education Supplement, 7 December 2017, https://www.timeshighereducation.com/features/how-can-widening-participation-best-be-achieved

[93] House of Commons Committee of Public Accounts, *The higher education market*, House of Commons, 15 June 2018, https://publications.parliament.uk/pa/cm201719/cmselect/cmpubacc/693/693.pdf

[94] For example the programme run by Villiers Park Educational Trust, which operates in areas where there is not a local university, working intensively with around 800 students who have been identified by their schools at age 14: Jack Grove, *How can widening participation best be achieved?* Times Higher Education Supplement, 7 December 2017, https://www.timeshighereducation.com/features/how-can-widening-participation-best-be-achieved

[95] The Russell Group of universities, for example, argue for a restoration of maintenance grants for students from lower income backgrounds: BBC News, *University chief wants to bring back maintenance grants*, 6 August 2018, https://www.bbc.co.uk/news/

education-45079654

[96] Alex Usher & Robert Burroughs, *Targeted Tuition Fees: Is means-testing the answer?* Higher Education Policy Institute, September 2018, https://www.hepi. ac.uk/wp-content/uploads/2018/09/HEPI-Targeted-tuition-fees-Is-means-testing-the-answer-Report-112.pdf

[97] House of Commons Committee of Public Accounts, *The higher education market*, House of Commons, 15 June 2018, https://publications.parliament.uk/pa/cm201719/cmselect/cmpubacc/693/693.pdf

[98] David Willets, *A University Education* (OUP, Oxford, 2017)

[99] Comprising academics, students and employer representatives.

[100] Universities and colleges participating in TEF receive one of three awards available - *Gold* for delivering consistently outstanding teaching, learning and outcomes for its students. It is of the highest quality found in the UK; Silver for delivering high quality teaching, learning and outcomes for its students. It consistently exceeds rigorous national quality requirements for UK higher education; and Bronze for delivering teaching, learning and outcomes for its students that meet rigorous national quality requirements for UK higher education: *About the TEF*, Higher Education Funding Council for England, http://www.hefce.ac.uk/lt/tef/whatistef/teffaq/

[101] The Office for Students started operating in April 2018, with responsibility, amongst other things, for 'teaching standards': Department for Business Innovation & Skills, *Case for Creation of The Office For Students, A new public body in place of the Higher Education Funding Council for England (HEFCE) and the Office for Fair Access (OFFA)*, June 2016, https://www.gov.uk/government/uploads/system/uploads/attachment_data/file/527757/bis-16-292-ofs-case-for-creation.pdf

[102] Survey of more than 15,000 full-time UK undergraduates: Alex Buckley, Ioannis Soilemetzidis & Nick Hillman, *The 2015 Student Academic Experience Survey*, Higher Education Policy Institute & Higher Education Academy, p. 30, https://www.hepi. ac.uk/wp-content/uploads/2015/06/AS-PRINTED-HEA_HEPI_report_print4.pdf

[103] In 2017 32% of students surveyed considered their university course value for money, compared to 50% in 2012: Comptroller and Auditor General Department, *The higher education market*, National Audit Office, 8 December 2017, https://www.nao.org.uk/wp-content/uploads/2017/12/The-higher-education-market.pdf.   Office for Students, *National Student Survey – NSS*, June 2018, https://www.officeforstudents.org.uk/advice-and-guidance/student-information-and-data/national-student-survey-nss/.

[104] David Laws, *Crisis of confidence in tuition fees system*, Letters to the Editor, The

Times, 19 October 2017, https://www.thetimes.co.uk/article/8e4c94de-b432-11e7-a7ed-96e3d3dae681. UNIVERSITAS website, U21 Ranking of National Higher Education Systems 2017, 2017 ranking map, http://www.universitas21.com/ranking/map

[105] Ryan Shorthouse, *If student loan reform led to a tax cut, the Tories could be onto something*, The Times, 12 September 2017, https://www.thetimes.co.uk/edition/news/if-student-loan-reform-resulted-in-a-tax-cut-the-tories-could-be-onto-something-dv69vszhm

[106] Sonia Sodha, *How to turn Britain's universities into comprehensives*, Guardian, 17 August 2017, https://www.theguardian.com/commentisfree/2017/aug/17/britain-universities-comprehensives-academic-selection. There has also been a 1.5b. increase in capital investment since 2012: The Times, *Duff Degrees*, Leading Article, 11 December 2017, https://www.thetimes.co.uk/article/ed03e9c8-dde0-11e7-a1a7-d23b605d14fb

[107] Higher Education Statistics Agency, *Finances of Higher Education Providers 2016/17, Table A: Balance sheet*, HESA, 26 April 2018,https://www.hesa.ac.uk/data-and-analysis/publications/finances-2016-17

[108] Sean Coughlan, *Theresa May's university review will not scrap fees*, News website, 19 February 2018, http://www.bbc.co.uk/news/education-43106736

[109] Camilla Turner, *Universities 'mis-selling' scandal as some graduates are left with lower earning capacity than school leavers*, Daily Telegraph, 8 December 2017, http://www.telegraph.co.uk/education/2017/12/08/universities-mis-selling-scandal-graduates-left-lower-earning/

[110] Which? & Higher Education Policy Institute, *The Student Academic Experience Survey*, May 2013, https://www.hepi.ac.uk/wp-content/uploads/2014/02/1.Higher_Educational_Report.pdf. Alex Buckley, Ioannis Soilemetzidis & Nick Hillman, *The 2015 Student Academic Experience Survey*, Higher Education Policy Institute & Higher Education Academy, https://www.hepi.ac.uk/wp-content/uploads/2015/06/AS-PRINTED-HEA_HEPI_report_print4.pdf

[111] David Laws, *Crisis of confidence in tuition fees system*, Letters to the Editor, The Times, 19 October 2017, https://www.thetimes.co.uk/article/8e4c94de-b432-11e7-a7ed-96e3d3dae681. Buckingham University introduced two-year degrees 40 years ago, with students taking shorter holidays and studying for four terms a year instead of three: Rosemary Bennett, *Three-year degrees encourage 'high-drink, low-work' culture, says Sir Anthony Seldon*, The Times, 15 August 2017, https://www.thetimes.co.uk/edition/news/three-year-degrees-encourage-high-drink-low-work-culture-says-sir-anthony-seldon-t2k68hdqm

[112] The new university in Hereford opening in autumn 2018 specialising in engineering and undertaking masters programmes in three rather than four years: Greg Hurst, *New university to abandon lectures and charge £12,000*, The Times, 5 September 2016, http://www.thetimes.co.uk/past-six-days/2016-09-05/news/new-university-to-abandon-lectures-and-charge-12-000-383ltgt95

[113] Rosemary Bennett, *Three-year degrees encourage 'high-drink, low-work' culture, says Sir Anthony Seldon*, The Times, 15 August 2017, https://www.thetimes.co.uk/edition/news/three-year-degrees-encourage-high-drink-low-work-culture-says-sir-anthony-seldon-t2k68hdqm

[114] Buckingham University received 1,474 applications for two year degree courses for the 2017-18 academic year compared with 1,340 in 2016-17, and accepted 284, a 31% year-on-year increase. Birmingham City University had 250 applications for two year degree courses starting this autumn compared with 106 in 2016-17. The universities of Staffordshire, Greenwich and Northampton also increases in students taking two-year degrees: Rosemary Bennett, *More students cut costs by choosing two-year degrees*, The Times, 14 August 2018, 12:01am, https://www.thetimes.co.uk/article/more-students-cut-costs-by-choosing-two-year-degrees-vvwsxw2vv

[115] Harry Yorke, *Students to save £25,000 under radical plans for new two-year degrees*, Sunday Telegraph, 10 December 2017, http://www.telegraph.co.uk/news/2017/12/10/students-save-25000-radical-plans-new-two-year-degrees/

[116] Richard Tice & Tariq Al-Humaidhi, *Timebomb, How the University Cartel is Failing Britain's Students*, UK 2020 Limited, September 2017, http://www.uk2020.org.uk/wp content/uploads/2017/09/JRTI5635_UK_higher_education_timebomb_report_170830_WEB.pdf

[117] The Times, *No Mean Fee*, Leading Article, 13 September 2017, https://www.thetimes.co.uk/edition/comment/no-mean-fee-w67lfrb35

[118] Roughly one-third of the cost of higher education is funded directly by the government (via the Higher Education Funding Council) and two-thirds by students paying tuition fees, funded mainly through the loans system. Maximum tuition fees are currently £9,250 each year, but used as the de facto amount by virtually every institution. On leaving university graduates start repaying their loans when they are earning a salary in excess of £25,000 (increased from £21,000 in April 2018), paying 9% of their income above this amount. Interest is set at the Retail Price Index (RPI) rising on a stepped basis up to a maximum of RPI plus three percent when earnings exceed £41,000. Loans outstanding after thirty years are written off by the government:

The undergraduate funding system in England, Universities UK Parliamentary briefing, September 2017, http://www.universitiesuk.ac.uk/policy-and-analysis/reports/ Documents/2017/briefing-undergraduate-funding-england.pdf; and Rachel Sylvester, *Richer graduates have the most to gain from freezing or ending university tuition fees*, The Times, 18 October 2017, https://www.thetimes.co.uk/article/bbcd4bde-b378-11e7-bd81-0feeb2b41cb4. It is projected that 83% of graduates will fail to repay their debt in full and 45% of loans will be written off: Chris Belfield, Jack Britton & Laura van der Erve, *Higher Education finance reform: Raising the repayment threshold to £25,000 and freezing the fee cap at £9,250*, Institute of Fiscal Studies, 3 October 2017, https://www.ifs.org.uk/publications/9964

[119] Held by 6m. UK students and graduates: Rosemary Bennett, *Student loans chief Steve Lamey sacked amid complaints*, The Times, 9 November 2017, https://www.thetimes.co.uk/article/7eacf86a-c4c3-11e7-92dc-06edfbca4aab

[120] House of Lords Economic Affairs Committee, *Treating Students Fairly: The Economics of Post-School Education*, House of Lords, 11 June 2018, https://publications.parliament.uk/pa/ld201719/ldselect/ldeconaf/139/139.pdf and; Richard Tice & Tariq Al-Humaidhi, *Timebomb, How the University Cartel is Failing Britain's Students*, UK 2020 Limited, September 2017, http://www.uk2020.org.uk/wp content/uploads/2017/09/JRTI5635_UK_higher_education_timebomb_report_170830_WEB.pdf

[121] Anthony Reuben, *Could student loans ruling mean the system is redesigned?* BBC News, 16 December 2018, https://www.bbc.co.uk/news/education-45889703

[122] About 300,000 new places will be needed at universities over the next 12 years. The 18-year-old population has been declining steadily for a number of years, but from 2020 it will increase again, rising by nearly 23% by 2030, pushing up demand for university places by 50,000. A further 350,000 places will be needed to keep pace with the existing growing participation rate, but other factors may reduce that by 50,000. Currently, more women than men go to university, but if males were to increase their rates of participation, 500,000 extra places would be needed in total by 2030: Bahram Bekhradnia & Diana Beech, *Demand for Higher Education to 2030*, HEPI Report 105, Higher Education Policy Institute, March 2018, https://www.hepi.ac.uk/wp-content/uploads/2018/03/HEPI-Demand-for-Higher-Education-to-2030-Report-105-FINAL.pdf

[123] Paul Johnson, *The murky world of student loans, the national debt and a fiscal illusion*, The Times, Comment, 19 February 2018, https://www.thetimes.co.uk/article/a3817068-14d1-11e8-96d8-811fd4bb2b55. The debt is sold off and the way this has been done has been criticised for unnecessarily losing hundreds of millions of

pounds to the national exchequer: Sir Amyas Morse KCB, Comptroller and Auditor General, *Investigation into oversight of the Student Loans Company's governance, and management of its former chief executive*, National Audit Office, 8 May 2018, https://www.nao.org.uk/wp-content/uploads/2018/05/Investigation-into-oversight-of-the-Student-Loans-Companys-governance.pdf

[124] Philip Aldrick, Student loan sell-off 'had £600m cost for taxpayer', The Times, 20 July 2018, https://www.thetimes.co.uk/article/student-loan-sell-off-had-600m-cost-for-taxpayer-qkkx300pf#top.

[125] Sean Coughlan, *Student loan ruling adds £12bn to government borrowing*, BBC News, 17 December 2018, https://www.bbc.co.uk/news/education-46591500

[126] In October 2017 prime minister, Theresa May, announced that there would be a 'major review' of English university funding: John Morgan, *PM May announces 'major review' of English university funding*, Times Higher Education Supplement, 4 October 2017, https://www.timeshighereducation.com/news/pm-may-announces-major-review-english-university-funding. The review is being carried out by British author and equities broker, Philip Augar.

[127] *Richer graduates have the most to gain from freezing or ending university tuition fees*, Rachel Sylvester, The Times, 18 October 2017, https://www.thetimes.co.uk/article/bbcd4bde-b378-11e7-bd81-0feeb2b41cb4

[128] There is speculation that the Augar review is considering cutting tuition fees to £6,500: Sean Coughlan, *Are students overpaying for tuition fees?* BBC News, 14 November 2018, https://www.bbc.co.uk/news/education-46180849

[129] Rachel Sylvester, *Richer graduates have the most to gain from freezing or ending university tuition fees*, , The Times, 18 October 2017, https://www.thetimes.co.uk/article/bbcd4bde-b378-11e7-bd81-0feeb2b41cb4

[130] Andy Green & Geoff Mason, *The Case for an All-Age Graduate Tax in England, LLAKES Research Paper 61*, Centre for Research on Learning and Life Chances (LLAKES), UCL Institute of Education, London, September 2017, https://www.llakes.ac.uk/sites/default/files/61.%20Green%20and%20Mason_0.pdf. The Times, *Analysis: which works best? Graduate tax or student loans?* 20 October 2017, https://www.thetimes.co.uk/edition/news/universities-analysis-which-works-best-graduate-tax-or-student-loans-0ft2zdb8k

[131] Difficulties in managing a graduate tax would include defining who is a graduate, what rate of tax should be used given that over time there have been different student funding arrangements, and claiming from graduates working abroad: The Times, *Analysis: which works best? Graduate tax or student loans?* 20 October 2017, https://

www.thetimes.co.uk/edition/news/universities-analysis-which-works-best-graduate-tax-or-student-loans-0ft2zdb8k

[132] Times Higher Education Supplement, *Should universities be a force for social good?* 30 November 2017, https://www.timeshighereducation.com/hub/p/should-universities-be-force-social-good

[133] Around 60 universities sponsor academies.

[134] Edge Hill University, Lancashire: Anna Fazackerley, *2VCs: Should universities be forced to sponsor schools?* Guardian, 12 July 2017, https://www.theguardian.com/higher-education-network/2017/jul/04/2vcs-should-universities-be-forced-to-sponsor-schools. London South Bank University: Times Higher Education Supplement, *Should universities be a force for social good?* 30 November 2017, https://www.timeshighereducation.com/hub/p/should-universities-be-force-social-good

[135] OECD, *Education at a Glance 2013: OECD Indicator A1: To What Extent have People Studied?* From Graph A1.1 – Population that has attained tertiary education (2011) (www.oecd.org), http://www.russellsage.org/sites/default/files/Fig10_Comparative_hires_0.png

[136] Allison Dickinson, *Online learning: not just for jobs*, Guardian Education, 10 January 2017, p. 36

[137] OU established in 1969; most degrees completed over 6 years, total tuition fees around £17,000: Open University website, http://www.open.ac.uk/courses/fees-and-funding

[138] Open University website, http://www.open.ac.uk/courses/fees-and-funding

[139] Sean Coughlan, *University offers fully fledged science degree online for £5,650*, BBC News, 6 March 2018, http://www.bbc.co.uk/news/education-43288793. The OU has developed its own Mooc platform, *FutureLearn*: Harriet Swain, *'This change will be the end of the Open University as we know it'*, Guardian, 20 October 2015, https://www.theguardian.com/education/2015/oct/20/open-university-strike-ou-regional-centres-moocs

[140] The coalition government cut £90m. off the OU's grant: Laura McInerney, *Gove's education reforms make second chances a thing of the past*, Guardian, 14 October 2013, https://www.theguardian.com/education/2013/oct/14/gove-education-reforms-failing-children. The funding cuts caused fees to more than treble (full-time from £1,540 to £5,000 per year, and part-time from £770 to £2,500): Sarah Harris, *Now Open University triples tuition fees to £5,000 a year*, MailOnline, 24 September 2011, http://www.dailymail.co.uk/news/article-2041243/Now-Open-University-triples-tuition-

fees-5-000-year.html

[141] Harriet Swain, *'This change will be the end of the Open University as we know it'*, Guardian, 20 October 2015, https://www.theguardian.com/education/2015/oct/20/open-university-strike-ou-regional-centres-moocs. Chris Havergal, *Open University posts £7m loss as student numbers slump*, Times Higher Education Supplement, 3 March 2016, https://www.timeshighereducation.com/news/open-university-posts-ps7m-loss-student-numbers-slump. In March 2018 the OU announced plans to cut 41 undergraduate and postgraduate degree courses, leaving only 71 degrees available: Diane Taylor, *Open University plans major cuts to number of staff and courses*, Guardian, 21 March 2018, https://www.theguardian.com/education/2018/mar/21/open-university-plans-major-cuts-to-number-of-staff-and-courses

[142] We first came across the term 'learning organisation' in Peter Senge's book *The Fifth Discipline*, initially published in 1990, in which he presents a new and fundamentally different way of leading and managing organisations: Peter M. Senge *The Fifth Discipline, The Art and Practice of the Learning Organisation* (Century Business, London, 1993) p. 4.

[143] Ibid, p. 7

[144] Chris Pratt, *Re-inventing Leadership, Building sustainable success in organisations* (Wilton65, Berkshire, UK, 2016) p. 165

[145] Ibid, pgs. 167 and 168

[146] Jan U. Hagen, *Confronting Mistakes, Lessons from the Aviation Industry when Dealing with Error* (Palgrave Macmillan UK, London, 2013)

[147] Chris Pratt, *Re-inventing Leadership, Building sustainable success in organisations* (Wilton 65, Berkshire, UK, 2016) p. 169

[148] GOV.UK website, *Training and study at work: your rights*, https://www.gov.uk/training-study-work-your-rights

[149] GCSE grades A to C (4 to 9 under the new grading system)

[150] Section 63A of the Employment Rights Act 1996

[151] The Education and Skills Act 2008

[152] Unionlearn with the TUC website, Union Learning Fund, https://www.unionlearn.org.uk/union-learning-fund

[153] Ibid

[154] The geographical areas for the lifelong learning partnerships would be determined by Parliament following consultation. Our starting point would be a lifelong learning partnership for each of the 152 local authorities that have responsibility for the provision

of all local government services i.e. metropolitan districts, London boroughs, unitary authorities, Isles of Scilly and county councils.

[155] Including information and advice services, libraries, prison services and Jobcentre Plus.

[156] Including early years education, schools, colleges, adult education, universities.

[157] Examples of initiatives aimed at engaging men in learning are the Sheds programmes in Australia (Barry Golding website, Men's Sheds, https://barrygoanna. com/mens-sheds/), Ireland (Lucia Carragher *Men's Sheds in Ireland Learning through community contexts*, The Netwell Centre School of Health & Science Dundalk Institute of Technology, February 2013, http://menssheds.ie/wp-content/uploads/2013/10/ Men%E2%80%99s-Sheds-in-Ireland-National-Survey.pdf) and the UK (UK Men's Sheds Association website, https://menssheds.org.uk/)

[158] An example of the use of non-conventional venues learning is Costa coffee shops: Laura McInerney, *Cappuccino with extra Italian? Pop-up classes give new buzz to adult learning,* Guardian Education, 21 February 2017, p. 32

[159] For example the Reading Agency campaign calling on 'book lovers across the country to give a good book to someone who doesn't read often': Survey of 2,000 UK adults by The Reading Agency: BBC News, *Too busy to read? You're not the only one,* http://www.bbc.co.uk/news/entertainment-arts-39653776

[160] *Lifelong learning: Potential and constraints with special reference to policies in the United Kingdom and Europe*, Paul Ryan, International Labour Organisation, 2003 http://www.ilo.org/wcmsp5/groups/public/---ed_emp/---ifp_skills/documents/ publication/wcms_103988.pdf

Chapter 10: Building strong families

[1] Mel Ainscow, *Towards Self-Improving School Systems, Lessons from a city challenge* (Routledge, Abingdon, UK, 2015) p. 89

[2] Department for Communities, Learning and Local Government, *The Fiscal Case for Working with Troubled Families*, 2013, www.gov.uk/government/uploads/system/ uploads/attachment_data/file/79377/20130208_The_Fiscal_Case_for_Working_with_ Troubled_Families.pdf

[3] There were 1.9m. adult victims of domestic violence in the year ending March 2017, 1.2m. of them women. Almost 100 women in England and Wales were killed in 2017 by a partner or former partner. Reported cases of partner abuse rose by 23% between 2015 and 2016: The Office of National Statistics: Alice Thomson, *Domestic violence*

needs a #MeToo moment, The Times, 21 February 2018, https://www.thetimes.co.uk/article/5996c438-1677-11e8-a427-78e8af199a96

[4] Alexandra Topping, *Councils struggling to cope with surge in child protection referrals*, Guardian, 17 February 2018, https://www.theguardian.com/society/2018/feb/17/councils-struggling-cope-surge-child-protection-referrals-domestic-violence

[5] Including voluntary sector and community organisations, youth offending service, child and adolescent mental health, school attendance officers, youth service, schools, careers, drug & alcohol services, various health services, Job Centre Plus, debt advice services, adult social care, adult mental health services, adult learning and skills, housing services, police and community safety, CAFCASS, special educational needs, fire and rescue service, children's centres and children's social care.

[6] *Home-Start* is a leading family support service with 16,000 volunteers, supporting 30,000 families and 60,000 children. There are 269 local, independent Home-Starts. Central to Home-Start's work is the volunteers, all of whom are parents, who spend around two hours a week in a family's home 'supporting them in the ways they need'. Home-Start also support families in groups, organises day trips and parties, and facilitates family members accessing local services.

[7] National Institute of Adult Continuing Education *Family Learning Works, The Inquiry into Family Learning in England and Wales*, NIACE, 2013, https://www.learningandwork.org.uk/wp-content/uploads/2017/01/The-Inquiry-into-Family-Learning-in-England-and-Wales-Summary.pdf

[8] Research by the Social Mobility Commission: *Half of teenagers 'never been in a theatre'*, Sean Coughlan, BBC News, 5 April 2017, http://www.bbc.co.uk/news/education-39479035

[9] Children of parents who have low levels of education are eight times more likely to have poor literacy skills than those whose parents have higher levels of education: Organisation for Economic Co-operation and Development, *Survey of Adult Skills, First Results, England and Northern Ireland*, 2013

[10] 5m. adults in England with difficulties in everyday English; 8m. with difficulties with basic mathematics: Department for Business, Innovation and Skills, *Skills for Life Survey*, 2011, www.gov.uk/government/publications/2011-skills-for-life-survey

[11] Ofsted, *An evaluation of the benefits of family learning for participants, their families and the wider community*, 2009, www.ofsted.gov.uk/resources/family-learning

[12] Parental involvement with school such as helping with homework and attending school events, is more than four times as important as socio-economic class in

influencing children's academic performance: Dr. Alex Nunn, Dr. Steve Johnson, Dr. Sunya Monro, Dr. Tim Bickerstaffe & Sarah Kelsey, *Factors influencing social mobility, Research Report No. 450*, Department for Work and Pensions, London, https://www.researchgate.net/publication/237102825_Factors_influencing_social_mobility

[13] National Institute of Adult Continuing Education, *Family Learning Works, The Inquiry into Family Learning in England and Wales*, NIACE, 2013, https://www.nationalnumeracy.org.uk/sites/default/files/family_learning_works_2013.pdf, p. 18

[14] By 2011 over 10,000 fewer parents and carers were involved in family learning than there were in 2009, a drop of 6.7%; a decline which has continued since: National Institute of Adult Continuing Education, *Family Learning Works, The Inquiry into Family Learning in England and Wales*, NIACE, 2013, https://www.nationalnumeracy.org.uk/sites/default/files/family_learning_works_2013.pdf, p. 25. Department for Business, Innovation and Skills, *Data Service statistical first release*, June 2013

[15] Supporting Parents on Kids' Education in Schools

[16] Professor Kathy Sylva, Stephen Scott, Vasiliki Totsika, Katharina Ereky-Stevens & Carolyn Crook, *Training parents to help their children to read: A randomised control trial*, British Journal of Educational Psychology, September 2008, volume 78, number 3, https://onlinelibrary.wiley.com/doi/epdf/10.1348/000709907X255718, pgs. 433-455

[17] National Institute of Adult Continuing Education, *Family Learning Works, The Inquiry into Family Learning in England and Wales*, NIACE, 2013, https://www.nationalnumeracy.org.uk/sites/default/files/family_learning_works_2013.pdf, p. 21

[18] Organisation for Economic Cooperation and Development, *What can parents do to help their children succeed in school? Pisa in Focus 2011/10*, OECD, November 2011

[19] Ibid

[20] 64% of parents never share books with their babies. More than half of families do not own a single baby book: Study of parents of babies at 7 months and under, carried out by ICM Research and The Fatherhood Institute on behalf of Booktrust, in June 2012: Katy Morton, *Bookstart campaign encourages parents to enjoy books with babies*, Nursery World website, 13 June 2012, https://www.nurseryworld.co.uk/nursery-world/news/1106117/bookstart-campaign-encourages-parents-enjoy-books-babies

[21] Bookstart is administered by Booktrust, an independent charity dedicated to encouraging people of all ages and cultures to engage with books. It is sponsored by over 25 children's publishers, with funding provided by the Department for Education. In 2011 the government reduced its funding to Bookstart by half to £13.5 million over two years: BBC News, *Bookstart funding confirmed two months after U-turn row*, 26

February 2011, http://www.bbc.co.uk/news/uk-12586839

[22] Thomas G. O'Connor & Stephen B.C. Scott, *Parenting and outcomes for children*, Joseph Rowntree Foundation, 2007, https://www.jrf.org.uk/sites/default/files/jrf/migrated/files/parenting-outcomes.pdf

[23] For example in arguing for programmes to encourage parents to play a more active role in their children's education, former Conservative education secretary Justine Greening recognises that 'the government fears being accused of taking a nanny state approach to education if it asks parents to do more to support children's learning at home': Caroline Wheeler, *Poor, white pupils need more help at home*, The Sunday Times, 6 May 2018, https://www.thetimes.co.uk/article/poor-white-pupils-need-more-help-at-home-w8p7l7ltj

[24] Dr. Barbie Clarke & Fatima Younas, *Helping Parents to Parent*, Social Mobility Commission, 20 February 2017, https://assets.publishing.service.gov.uk/government/uploads/system/uploads/attachment_data/file/592452/Helping_Parents_to_Parent_report.pdf

[25] Ibid

[26] Geoff Lindsay, Steve Strand, Mairi Ann Cullen, Stephen Cullen, Sue Band, Hilton Davis, Gavan Conlon, Jane Barlow & Ray Evans, *Research Report DFE-RR121(a), Parenting Early Intervention Programme Evaluation*, Department for Education, May 2011, https://assets.publishing.service.gov.uk/government/uploads/system/uploads/attachment_data/file/182715/DFE-RR121A.pdf

[27] Families and Schools Together (FAST), Positive Parenting Program (Triple P), Strengthening Families Programme 10-14 (SFP 10-14), Strengthening Families, Strengthening Communities (SFSC) and The Incredible Years. In one study all seventy parents interviewed said that the parenting classes they had attended 'had helped them' and that they 'had noticed an improvement in their children's behaviour': Cristina Odone, *Can parenting be taught*, Guardian Family, 20 May 2017, p. 5, https://www.theguardian.com/lifeandstyle/2017/may/20/can-parenting-be-taught

[28] Geoff Lindsay, Steve Strand, Mairi Ann Cullen, Stephen Cullen, Sue Band, Hilton Davis, Gavan Conlon, Jane Barlow & Ray Evans, *Research Report DFE-RR121(a), Parenting Early Intervention Programme Evaluation*, Department for Education, May 2011, https://assets.publishing.service.gov.uk/government/uploads/system/uploads/attachment_data/file/182715/DFE-RR121A.pdf

[29] Richard Layard & Judy Dunn, *A Good Childhood: Searching for Values in a Competitive Age* (Penguin, London, 2009)

[30] UNICEF, *The formative years: UNICEF's work on measuring early childhood*, New York, US, https://www.unicef.org/earlychildhood/files/Brochure_-_The_Formative_Years.pdf

[31] Maria Evangelou, Kathy Sylva, Maria Kyriacou, Mary Wild & Georgina Glenny, *Early Years Learning and Development Literature Review*, Department for Children, Schools and Families, 2009, http://dera.ioe.ac.uk/11382/2/DCSF-RR176.pdf. Iram Siraj-Blatchford & John Siraj-Blatchford *Improving children's attainment through a better quality of family-based support for early learning*, Centre for Excellence and Outcomes in Children's and Young People's Services (C4EO), London, 2009, http://archive.c4eo.org.uk/themes/earlyyears/familybasedsupport/files/c4eo_family_based_support_kr_2.pdf

[32] 734,000 in school reception classes; 352,600 in school nurseries; 539,000 in before and after school clubs; 267,600 childminding; and 1.2 million places in private nurseries, crèches, parent and toddler groups, and playgroups. These places are managed by around 90,000 different private, voluntary, school and individual early years and childcare providers, and run by approximately 452,100 staff including childminders: GOV.UK, Official Statistics, Children and early years providers survey: 2016, https://www.gov.uk/government/statistics/childcare-and-early-years-providers-survey-2016. All childcare providers excluding parent and toddler groups, nannies and short-term crèches, have to be registered by Ofsted, who inspect providers based on the early years foundation stage (EYFS). Children are assessed (through a professional observing them) between ages two and three and at the end of the school year they reach age five: GOV.UK WEBSITE, https://www.gov.uk/early-years-foundation-stage

[33] Parents in the UK spend nearly 34% of their income on childcare, nearly three-times the OECD average, making it the most expensive childcare of all OECD countries: Organisation for Economic Co-operation and Development, *Society at a Glance 2016*. Daniel Martin, *UK childcare is the most expensive in the world: Families now spend a third of their income on nurseries and childminders*, The Daily Mail, 11 October 2016, http://www.dailymail.co.uk/news/article-3831626/UK-childcare-expensive-world-Families-spend-income-nurseries-childminders.html. BBC News Reality Check team, *Childcare: Do UK parents pay the most in the world?* BBC News, 13 February 2018, http://www.bbc.co.uk/news/uk-42966047

[34] All Party Parliamentary Group on Children's Centres, *Family Hubs: The Future of Children's Centres Strengthening family relationships to improve Life Chances for everyone*, July 2016, https://democracy.leeds.gov.uk/documents/s150825/app%208%20

appg%20on%20childrens%20centres%20-%20family%20hubs%20report%20final.pdf

[35] Ibid, p. 23

[36] Manjit Gheera, Christine Gillie, Steven Kennedy, Robert Long & Antony Seely, *Government support for childcare under the Labour Government 1997-2010*, House of Commons Library, 29 January 2014, http://researchbriefings.parliament.uk/ResearchBriefing/Summary/SN06382#fullreport

[37] About 40% of parents.

[38] In September 2017.

[39] £250 million (2.7%) of the additional £9b. of government funding for this extra 15 hours free education and childcare will go to go families most in need. The highest earning half of the population will receive 75% of this funding: Lucy Powell MP, *A lost generation, why social mobility in the early years is set to go backwards*, Social Market Foundation, London, August 2017, https://www.dropbox.com/s/k8ap3uo1wg3qaz7/A%20Lost%20Generation.pdf

[40] Greg Hurst, *Pledge of 30 hours 'free' childcare will cost parents dear*, The Times, 1 September 2017, https://www.thetimes.co.uk/edition/news/pledge-of-30-hours-free-childcare-will-cost-parents-dear-6616n25pj. Catherine Gaunt, *Lower staff: child ratios to bring down costs, says DfE*, Nursery World, 30 November 2015, https://www.nurseryworld.co.uk/nursery-world/news/1154964/lower-staff-child-ratios-to-bring-down-costs-says-dfe. Many nurseries have increased fees for provision for younger children and charging for such things as meals and nappies to make up the shortfall of government funding: Hannah Richardson, *Parents shelling out for 'free' nursery scheme*, BBC News, 18 January 2018, http://www.bbc.co.uk/news/education-42639258

[41] The average charge for a child in Britain aged under 2 to attend nursery part-time, for 25 hours a week, is £122 in 2018 - up 7% on the previous year. For a child aged two to attend for 25 hours, the cost is £119 a week, up 6%. The study by the Family and Childcare Trust suggests that the price rises could be down to the new policy that offers parents 30 hours of free childcare for children aged three and four: Olivia Rudgard, *Free childcare pushing annual nursery costs beyond £6,300, report suggests*, Daily Telegraph, 28 February 2018, https://www.telegraph.co.uk/news/2018/02/28/free-childcare-pushing-annual-nursery-costs-beyond-6300-report/

[42] The research suggests five key policy levers for facilitating quality early years provision – frameworks for 'quality goals and regulations' and the curriculum; staff effectiveness; engaging families; and data, research and monitoring. A quality framework sets out standards on such areas as staff-child ratios, indoor/outdoor space,

staff qualifications, and the frequency and quality of relationships between staff and children and their parents: Organisation for Economic Cooperation and Development, *Starting Strong III - A Quality Toolbox for Early Childhood Education and Care*, January 2012, http://www.oecd.org/edu/school/49325825.pdf

[43] The staff-child ratios in nurseries for those under the age of two is 1 to 3, and for childminders 1 to 2 for under ones and 1 to 3 for under twos.

[44] For example, Dr. John Bowlby, *Attachment and loss Volume 2: Separation - Anxiety and Anger* (Pimlico, London, 1998)

[45] Approved childcare is a childminder, playscheme, nursery or school registered with Ofsted. Currently parents can get financial help from the government for 'approved' childcare for children under the age of 11. This includes Tax-Free Childcare, where the government pays £2 for every £8 parents pay for childcare. No financial help is provided for parents who choose to look after their young children at home: GOV.UK, *Help paying for childcare* website, https://www.gov.uk/help-with-childcare-costs/tax-credits

[46] Frank Field MP *Mothers and Work*, The Times, Letters to the Editor, 16 January 2018, https://www.thetimes.co.uk/edition/comment/challenge-to-the-parole-board-over-rapist-nl2t6j7g6

[47] In Finland paid parental leave (after a child's birth) is four months for mothers and nine weeks for fathers.

[48] Study by the OECD: Charles Bremner, *Finland is first country where fathers do most of the childcare*, The Times, 9 December 2017, https://www.thetimes.co.uk/article/e102d384-dc4e-11e7-aacd-025601055216.

[49] Fiona Bruce MP & Lord Farmer, *Manifesto for the Family*, The Times, Letters to the Editor, 6 September 2017, https://www.thetimes.co.uk/edition/comment/organ-donation-and-the-role-of-next-of-kin-glpgr37jr

[50] Conservative MPs & Peers, *A Manifesto to Strengthen Families, Policies for a Conservative Government to strengthen families*, August 2017, http://www.strengtheningfamiliesmanifesto.com/assets/Family_Manifesto.pdf

[51] Councils responsible for the provision of all local government services in their area.

Chapter 11: Supporting school improvement

[1] Professor Robin Alexander, Director of the Cambridge Primary Review, in 2008 – quoted in Michael Bassey, *Political impact: from the least state-controlled to the most in 24 years*, Free schools from government control.com website, http://www.free-school-from-government-control.com/political.html

[2] OECD, *How are schools held accountable?*, in, *Education at a Glance: OECD Indicators*, OECD Publishing, http://www.oecd.org/edu/skills-beyond-school/48631582.pdf

[3] Ibid

[4] NSPCC, *Under pressure, ChildLine Review, What's affected children in April 2013 – March 2014*, NSPCC, 2014

[5] María Teresa Flórez & Pamela Sammons, *Assessment for learning: effects and impact* (CfBT Education Trust and Oxford University Department of Education, 2013) https://www.educationdevelopmenttrust.com/~/media/EDT/Reports/Research/2013/r-assessment-for-learning-2013.pdf

[6] Paul Black & Dylan Wiliam, *Inside the Black Box Raising Standards Through Classroom Assessment*, (King's College London School of Education, 6 November 2001), https://weaeducation.typepad.co.uk/files/blackbox-1.pdf

[7] Only four out of 35 OECD countries have national tests in primary schools: OECD, *How are schools held accountable?* Education at a Glance: OECD Indicators, OECD Publishing, http://www.oecd.org/edu/skills-beyond-school/48631582.pdf

[8] Ibid

[9] Lord Baker of Dorking, Letter to Editor, The Times, *Value of Studying for GCSEs*, 11 September 2017, https://www.thetimes.co.uk/edition/comment/vice-chancellors-and-high-university-salaries-m62kq5rt3

[10] Ibid

[11] Tim Brighouse & David Woods, *How to improve your school* (Routledge, London, 1999) pgs. 121 & 122

[12] NAHT, *Instead - evaluating for the future*, Leadership Focus, The Magazine for NAHT and NAHT Edge Members, Issue 73, May 2016

[13] Professor William Richardson & Dr Sue Sing, *The impact of practical and 'vocational' learning on academically-able young people aged 11–16*, Edge Foundation, 2011, http://citeseerx.ist.psu.edu/viewdoc/download?doi=10.1.1.736.9734&rep=rep1&type=pdf

[14] Richard Garner, *Curriculum 'stuck in Victorian era'*, Independent, 31 October 2011, https://www.independent.co.uk/news/education/education-news/curriculum-stuck-in-

victorian-era-6255031.html

[15] Professor William Richardson & Dr Sue Sing, *The impact of practical and 'vocational' learning on academically-able young people aged 11–16*, Edge Foundation, 2011, http://citeseerx.ist.psu.edu/viewdoc/download?doi=10.1.1.736.9734&rep=rep1&type=pdf

[16] The National Archives, Records of the National Curriculum Council, http://discovery.nationalarchives.gov.uk/details/r/C136

[17] Nicola Woolcock, *Music lessons make children feel clever*, The Times, 27 May 2017, https://www.thetimes.co.uk/edition/news/music-lessons-make-children-feel-clever-jtgr6vdkd

[18] Department for Education, *Personal, social, health and economic education guidance*, https://www.gov.uk/government/publications/personal-social-health-and-economic-education-pshe/personal-social-health-and-economic-pshe-education#personal-social-health-and-economic-education

[19] Ibid

[20] Ofsted, *Bold beginnings: The Reception curriculum in a sample of good and outstanding primary schools*, November 2017, https://assets.publishing.service.gov.uk/government/uploads/system/uploads/attachment_data/file/663560/28933_Ofsted_-_Early_Years_Curriculum_Report_-_Accessible.pdf

[21] Ibid

[22] Nicola Woolcock, *Primary pupils 'turned off reading by complex tests'*, The Times, 1 May 2017, https://www.thetimes.co.uk/edition/news/tough-tests-stunt-primary-pupils-progress-say-mps-0gh7nxsvz

[23] Universities UK, *Solving Future Skills Challenges*, August 2018, https://www.universitiesuk.ac.uk/policy-and-analysis/reports/Documents/2018/solving-future-skills-challenges.pdf

[24] The World Economic Forum website, *The Fourth Industrial Revolution: what it means, how to respond*, https://www.weforum.org/agenda/2016/01/the-fourth-industrial-revolution-what-it-means-and-how-to-respond/

[25] World Economic Forum, *The 10 skills you need to thrive in the Fourth Industrial Revolution*, World Economic Forum website, https://www.weforum.org/agenda/2016/01/the-10-skills-you-need-to-thrive-in-the-fourth-industrial-revolution/

[26] World Economic Forum, *The Future of Jobs Employment, Skills and Workforce Strategy for the Fourth Industrial Revolution*, Global Challenge Insight Report, January 2016, World Economic Forum, http://www3.weforum.org/docs/WEF_Future_of_Jobs.pdf

[27] Report by Winchester University commissioned by the Royal Academy of

Engineering, which studied the effects of three pilot schemes to unite the worlds of education and engineering, which ran in England and Scotland from 2014 to 2016 across 33 schools and a further education college, and involved 3,000 pupils and 84 teachers: Professor Bill Lucas, Dr. Janet Hanson, Dr. Lynne Bianchi & Dr Jonathan Chippindall, *Learning to be an Engineer Implications for schools, A report for the Royal Academy of Engineering*, March 2017, https://www.raeng.org.uk/publications/reports/learning-to-be-an-engineer

[28] Daniel Rigney, *The Matthew Effect: How advantage begets further advantage* (Columbia University Press, New York, 2010)

[29] Oxford University Press, *Why Closing the Word Gap Matters: Oxford Language Report*, April 2018, http://fdslive.oup.com/www.oup.com/oxed/Oxford-Language-Report.PDF?region=uk

[30] The Scottish Survey of Literacy and Numeracy (SSLN), published in May 2017 showed that secondary pupils were almost twice as likely to read things regularly on electronic devices as books. Four in 10 older pupils believe that 'reading is boring'. 12% read magazines very often while 14% regularly read non-fiction books: Daniel Sanderson, *Pupils should ditch devices and read for pleasure, schools told*, 11 May 2017, The Times, https://www.thetimes.co.uk/edition/scotland/pupils-should-ditch-devices-and-read-for-pleasure-schools-told-20pr2j236.

[31] In PISA mathematics tests of 15 and 16 year olds in 70 countries UK pupils were ranked 27th: Organisation for Economic Co-operation and Development, *PISA 2015 Results , Excellence and equity in education, volume I*, OECD Publishing, Paris, 2016, p. 5, https://www.oecd-ilibrary.org/docserver/9789264266490-en.f?expires=1530130847&id=id&accname=guest&checksum=55157E04D2F19378A38A5FFE66636D64

[32] The government has offered to provide training, textbooks and advice about 'Chinese-style maths teaching' to nearly half of England's primary schools, at a cost of £42m: Greg Hurst, *Pupils will be taught maths the Chinese way*, The Times, 12 July 2016, p. 1.

[33] Mastery maths focuses on 'whole-class teaching and on pure rather than applied maths', and requires pupils to focus on a limited number of concepts each school year rather than going rapidly through a large range of mathematical disciplines (as is the practice generally in the UK): Rosemary Bennett & Greg Hurst, *Pupils will be taught maths the Chinese way*, Times, 12 July 2016, page 1. *Chinese-style textbooks fail to make the grade*, The Times, 15 August 2017, https://www.thetimes.co.uk/edition/news/chinese-style-textbooks-fail-to-make-the-grade-fpfdvhdsd. Basic arithmetic in the early years, for example, is covered more slowly than it is in the UK. Children

have to have a strong grasp of multiplication and division before they move on to learn about fractions in year 4 or 5: Harry Low, *Should all countries use the Shanghai maths method?* BBC World Service, 20 January 2017, http://www.bbc.co.uk/news/magazine-38568538

[34] *Report of Professor Sir Adrian Smith's Review of Post-16 Mathe*matics, Department for Education, July 2017, https://www.gov.uk/government/uploads/system/uploads/attachment_data/file/630488/AS_review_report.pdf

[35] Sally Weale, *Labour: we'll end compulsory GCSE maths and English resits*, Guardian, 20 November 2018, https://www.theguardian.com/education/2018/nov/20/labour-vow-end-compulsory-maths-english-retakes

[36] Department for Education, *Mathematics GCSE subject content and assessment objectives*, 2013, https://assets.publishing.service.gov.uk/government/uploads/system/uploads/attachment_data/file/254441/GCSE_mathematics_subject_content_and_assessment_objectives.pdf

[37] Camilla Turner, *Scrap maths GCSE because it is too difficult for less able students, says architect of the modern exam system*, Daily Telegraph, 15 May 2018, https://www.telegraph.co.uk/education/2018/05/15/scrap-maths-gcse-difficult-less-able-students-says-architect/

[38] John Kampfner, *Britain's got talent but we are not providing the skills*, The Times, Comment, 5 June 2017, p. 38, https://www.thetimes.co.uk/past-six-days/2017-06-05/business/britains-got-talent-but-we-are-not-providing-the-skills-lgt5rqf09

[39] Mike Pattenden, *Lack of IT staff leaving companies exposed to hacker attacks*, Guardian, 25 December 2017, https://www.theguardian.com/technology/2017/dec/25/lack-of-it-staff-leaving-companies-exposed-to-hacker-attacks

[40] In 2017 54% of secondary schools do not offer computer science GCSE; 11% of GCSE students in England took computer science, and only 20% of these are girls. Since 2014 30,000 fewer girls have obtained a computing qualification by the age of 16: The Royal Society, *After the reboot: computing education in UK schools,* November 2017, https://royalsociety.org/~/media/policy/projects/computing-education/computing-education-report.pdf; and Peter E.J. Kemp, Miles G. Berry & Billy Wong, The Roehampton Annual Computing Education Report: Data from 2017, University of Roehampton, London, June 2018, https://www.bcs.org/upload/pdf/computing-education-report.pdf. 7,000 fewer students took GCSE computer science and ICT in 2017 than did in 2016: Lord Baker of Dorking, Letter to the Editor, The Times, 13 November 2017, https://www.thetimes.co.uk/article/d7601de6-c7c7-11e7-b529-95e3fc05f40f

[41] In 2016 the total number of girls taking either ICT or computer science GCSE fell by 12% compared to 2015: Mark Bridge, *Girls put off by new computer science GCSE*, The Times, 20 December 2016, http://www.thetimes.co.uk/edition/news/girls-put-off-by-new-computer-science-gcse-pnvsqtbj6

[42] The Royal Society, *After the reboot: computing education in UK schools*, https://royalsociety.org/~/media/policy/projects/computing-education/computing-education-report.pdf

[43] Nicola Woolcock, *Schools are told to make science go with a bang*, The Times, 10 August 2017, https://www.thetimes.co.uk/edition/news/schools-are-told-to-make-science-go-with-a-bang-6v33b70wz

[44] Judith Burns, *School budget squeeze 'is reducing pupils' subject choice'*, BBC News, http://www.bbc.co.uk/news/education-39527183.

[45] In 2016 53.5% of pupils were entered for at least one creative arts subject in 2016, down from 55.9% in 2015 and a high of 57.1% in 2014. It is the lowest proportion in the past 10 years: Rebecca Johnes, *Entries to arts subjects at Key Stage 4*, Education Policy Institute, September 2017, https://epi.org.uk/publications-and-research/entries-arts-subjects-key-stage-4/.

[46] In England, 53.5% of pupils in 2016 had five GCSEs at A*-C grade including English and mathematics without retakes at the end of compulsory schooling at age 16: *Education and Training Statistics for the United Kingdom 2017*, SFR64/2017, 9 November 2017, Department for Education and National Statistics, https://www.gov.uk/government/statistics/education-and-training-statistics-for-the-uk-2017

[47] Philip Collins, *Let's keep A levels but scrap outdated GCSEs*, The Times, 18 August 2017, https://www.thetimes.co.uk/edition/comment/let-s-keep-a-levels-but-scrap-outdated-gcses-c7gw207vq

[48] *Education and Training Statistics for the United Kingdom 2017*, SFR64/2017, 9 November 2017, Department for Education and National Statistics, https://www.gov.uk/government/statistics/education-and-training-statistics-for-the-uk-2017

[49] Mike Baker, *Why Tomlinson was turned down*, BBC News, 26 February 2005, http://news.bbc.co.uk/1/hi/education/4299151.stm

[50] Department for Education and Skills, *14-19 Curriculum and Qualifications Reform Final Report of the Working Group on 14-19 Reform*, DfES Publications, October 2004, http://www.educationengland.org.uk/documents/pdfs/2004-tomlinson-report.pdf

[51] Grades 1-3 under new GCSE grading system

[52] Grades 4-9 under new GCSE grading system

[53] The Guardian, *Key points: the Tomlinson report*, 18 October 2004, https://www.theguardian.com/education/2004/oct/18/1419education.furthereducation1

[54] Mike Baker, *Why Tomlinson was turned down*, BBC News, 26 February 2005, http://news.bbc.co.uk/1/hi/education/4299151.stm

[55] Ibid

[56] Philip Collins, *Let's keep A levels but scrap outdated GCSEs*, The Times, 18 August 2017, https://www.thetimes.co.uk/edition/comment/let-s-keep-a-levels-but-scrap-outdated-gcses-c7gw207vq

[57] Mike Baker, *Why Tomlinson was turned down*, BBC News, 26 February 2005, http://news.bbc.co.uk/1/hi/education/4299151.stm

[58] Ibid

[59] Department for Education and Skills, *14-19 Curriculum and Qualifications Reform Final Report of the Working Group on 14-19 Reform*, DfES Publications, October 2004, p. 4, http://www.educationengland.org.uk/documents/pdfs/2004-tomlinson-report.pdf

[60] Research by the Education and Employers charity shows that young people who have four or more contacts with employers (including visits from employers, job shadowing or placements in the workplace) while at school are 86% less likely to be not in education, employment and training (NEET) when they leave school. School students, on average, had two such employer links. Professional families and the schools they attend are much more effective at using social connections to get access to work experience: Social Mobility Commission: Sean Coughlan, *Work visits result in fewer young 'Neets'*, BBC News, 2 February 2017, http://www.bbc.co.uk/news/education-38842481

[61] Oliver Wright, *Careers advice fails pupils, CBI warns*, The Times, 29 December 2017, https://www.thetimes.co.uk/article/c5cd02d6-ec18-11e7-ad3e-1cc26d7d8b0c

[62] More than half of secondary and around a fifth of primary schools are now academies: The Observer, *The Observer view on the Tories starving schools of funding*, Editorial, 27 January 2018, https://www.theguardian.com/commentisfree/2018/jan/27/observer-view-how-tories-starving-schools-funding

[63] Ibid

[64] As at January 2018 more than 35,000 children were being taught in schools that were rated inadequate almost a year previously and had not been converted into academies: Sir Amyas Morse, KCB Comptroller and Auditor General, *Converting maintained schools to academies*, National Audit Office, 20 February 2018,https://www.nao.org.uk/wp-content/uploads/2018/02/Converting-maintained-schools-to-academies.

pdf. 'In order for the MAT model to succeed there needs to be a greater number of sponsors in the system. Certain areas of the country are struggling to attract new sponsors and small rural schools, largely in the primary sector, are at risk of becoming isolated. There is also growing concern for 'untouchable' schools which trusts refuse to take on': House of Commons Education Committee, *Multi-academy trusts,* House of Commons, 28 February 2017, https://publications.parliament.uk/pa/cm201617/cmselect/cmeduc/204/204.pdf.

[65] NAHT, *Instead - evaluating for the future*, Leadership Focus, The Magazine for NAHT and NAHT Edge Members, Issue 73, May 2016

[66] Marc Kidson & Emma Norris, *Implementing the London Challenge*, Joseph Rowntree Trust, Institute for Government, 2014, https://www.instituteforgovernment.org.uk/sites/default/files/publications/Implementing%20the%20London%20Challenge%20-%20final_0.pdf

[67] Merryn Hutchings, Charley Greenwood, Sumi Hollingworth, Ayo Mansaray & Anthea Rose, with Sarah Minty & Katie Glass, *Evaluation of the City Challenge programme*, Institute for Policy Studies in Education, London Metropolitan University for the Department of Education, June 2012, https://assets.publishing.service.gov.uk/government/uploads/system/uploads/attachment_data/file/184093/DFE-RR215.pdf

[68] Mel Ainscow, *Towards Self-Improving School Systems, Lessons from a city challenge* (Routledge, Abingdon, UK, 2015) p. 79

[69] Fiona Miller, *'Time for a new era': Headteachers start fightback against policy diktat*, Guardian Education, 26 April 2016, p. 34

[70] National Association of Headteachers, *Leadership Focus, The magazine for NAHT and NAHT edge members*, Issue 81, April 2018, Headlines Partnership Publishing, Milton Keynes, UK, pgs. 24-26

[71] Department for Education, *Schools causing concern: Guidance for local authorities and Regional Schools Commissioners on how to work with schools to support improvements to educational performance, and on using their intervention powers*, Department for Education, February 2018, https://www.gov.uk/government/uploads/system/uploads/attachment_data/file/680559/Schools_causing_concern_guidance_-_February_2018.pdf

[72] Local authority statutory responsibilities for education include school places planning, admissions, special educational needs, safeguarding, education otherwise, attendance, transport, finance and governing bodies

[73] E. Hooge, T. Burns, T. & H. Wilkoszewski., *Looking Beyond the Numbers:*

Stakeholders and Multiple School Accountability, OECD Education Working Papers, No. 85, (OECD Publishing, 2012). David Hargreaves, *A self-improving school system: towards maturity* (NCSL, Nottingham, 2012)

[74] M. Mourshed, C. Chijioke & M. Barber, *How the world's most improved school systems keep getting better*, (McKinsey & Company, 2010), https://www.mckinsey.com/industries/social-sector/our-insights/how-the-worlds-most-improved-school-systems-keep-getting-better

[75] Melanie Ehren, Jane Perryman & Ken Spours, *Accountability and school inspections* (Institute of Education, University of London, June 2014) https://ris.utwente.nl/ws/portalfiles/portal/5119299

[76] Christine Gilbert, *Towards a self-improving system: the role of school accountability* (NCSL, Nottingham, 2012), http://dera.ioe.ac.uk/14919/1/towards-a-self-improving-system-school-accountability-thinkpiece%5B1%5D.pdf

[77] Melanie Ehren, Jane Perryman & Ken Spours, *Accountability and school inspections* (Institute of Education, University of London, June 2014) https://ris.utwente.nl/ws/portalfiles/portal/5119299

[78] Ibid

[79] An analysis by the Local Government Association of Department for Education data shows that 12 councils will face a shortfall in places from 2018/19; 23 in 2019/20, 41 in 2020/21, 57 in 2021/22; and 66 in 2022/23: Louis Emanuel, *Councils want to force free schools to expand*, The Times, 1 September 2017, https://www.thetimes.co.uk/edition/news/councils-want-to-force-free-schools-to-expand-8rv2jgtmf

[80] Shan Scott, Chief Adjudicator, *Office of the Schools Adjudicator Annual Report September 2015 to August 2016*, Office of the Schools Adjudicator, November 2016, pgs. 5, 8 & 26 - 28, https://assets.publishing.service.gov.uk/government/uploads/system/uploads/attachment_data/file/585915/OSA_Annual_Report_2016.pdf, Shan Scott, Chief Adjudicator, *Office of the Schools Adjudicator Annual Report, September 2016 to August 2017*, Office of the Schools Adjudicator, February 2018, pgs. 4 & 25-33, https://assets.publishing.service.gov.uk/government/uploads/system/uploads/attachment_data/file/680003/2017_OSA_Annual_Report_-_Final_23_January_2018.pdf. Hannah Richardson, *The children in care left without a school place*, BBC News, 23 October 2017, http://www.bbc.co.uk/news/education-41664460

[81] Sir Amyas Morse KCB, Comptroller and Auditor General, *Converting maintained schools to academies*, National Audit Office, 20 February 2018, https://www.nao.org.uk/wp-content/uploads/2018/02/Converting-maintained-schools-to-academies.pdf

[82] Sir Amyas Morse KCB Comptroller and Auditor General, *Capital funding for schools*, National Audit Office, 20 February 2017, https://www.nao.org.uk/wp-content/uploads/2017/02/Capital-funding-for-schools.pdf

[83] Jon Andrews, *School performance in academy chains and local authorities – 2017*, Education Policy Institute, June 2018, p. 9, https://epi.org.uk/publications-and-research/performance-academy-local-authorities-2017/

[84] House of Commons Committee of Public Accounts, *Retaining and developing the teaching workforce,* House of Commons, 24 January 2018, https://publications.parliament.uk/pa/cm201719/cmselect/cmpubacc/460/460.pdf

[85] These initiatives are estimated to have cost £555m.

[86] House of Commons Committee of Public Accounts, *Retaining and developing the teaching workforce,* House of Commons, 24 January 2018, https://publications.parliament.uk/pa/cm201719/cmselect/cmpubacc/460/460.pdf

[87] Nicola Woolcock, *Schools plug gaps with unqualified teachers*, The Times, 6 January 2018, https://www.thetimes.co.uk/edition/news/schools-plug-gaps-with-unqualified-teachers-dnlqmvn3h

[88] For example, although there have been tax-free bursaries of £30,000 to attract graduates to train as mathematics teachers, the numbers on these courses has fallen by over a quarter. The government plan to invest a further £1.3 billion in such bursaries by 2020: The Times, Leading Article, *More Teachers, Please*, 9 January 2018, https://www.thetimes.co.uk/article/9c9bd37c-f4b7-11e7-a789-003e705b951e

[89] 108,800 bursaries were awarded between 2009-10 and 2015-16; 101,000 qualified, but 11% didn't end up teaching in state schools; a 'wasted' cost of at least £44m. The cost could be much higher as the calculation was made using the minimum bursary of £4,000: Nicola Woolcock, *Millions wasted on teacher training bursaries for graduates who never teach*, The Times, 26 October 2018, https://www.thetimes.co.uk/article/millions-wasted-on-teacher-training-bursaries-for-graduates-who-never-teach-08r8l632s

[90] House of Commons Committee of Public Accounts, *Retaining and developing the teaching workforce,* House of Commons, 24 January 2018, https://publications.parliament.uk/pa/cm201719/cmselect/cmpubacc/460/460.pdf

[91] Rosemary Bennett, *MPs condemn 'sluggish' response to teacher exodus*, The Times, 31 January 2018, https://www.thetimes.co.uk/article/eb80ac16-0609-11e8-8e80-008642e5faa1

[92] Sean Coughlan, *Heads worried tuition fee pledge for teachers to be dropped*, BBC

News, 22 June 2017, http://www.bbc.co.uk/news/education-40371953

[93] Henry Zeffman & Nicola Woolcock, *Tory conference: Party freezes student fees in £11bn drive to win youth vote*, The Times, 2 October 2017, https://www.thetimes.co.uk/article/983962d6-a6e7-11e7-b9a3-2cac9d6c85bd

[94] Rosemary Bennett, *MPs condemn 'sluggish' response to teacher exodus*, The Times, 31 January 2018, https://www.thetimes.co.uk/article/eb80ac16-0609-11e8-8e80-008642e5faa1

[95] David Foster, *Teacher recruitment and retention in England*, House of Commons Library, 4 June 2018, http://researchbriefings.parliament.uk/ResearchBriefing/Summary/CBP-7222#fullreport

[96] Camilla Turner, *Teachers promised fewer hours and no new tests in charm offensive to reduce their workload*, Daily Telegraph, 10 March 2018, https://www.telegraph.co.uk/news/2018/03/10/teachers-promised-fewer-hours-no-new-tests-charm-offensive-reduce/

[97] Speech by Her Majesty's Chief Inspector of Schools and Children Services, Amanda Spielman, to the Association of School and College Leaders Annual Conference 2018, 10 March 2018, Birmingham: Sean Coughlan, *Damian Hinds to cut workload to tackle teacher shortage*, BBC News, 10 March 2018, http://www.bbc.co.uk/news/education-43345857

[98] Charles Clarke, *Grasping the nettle: Labour's challenge on public sector reform*, May 2012

[99] These school-based teaching training programmes include *School Direct* and *Postgraduate Teaching Apprenticeship* (schools recruit and train teachers on the job, in partnership with other schools or a university); *School-centred initial teacher training* (delivered by groups of 'teaching'' schools); *Future Teaching Scholars* (for 'exceptional' mathematics or physics A-level students); *Teach First* (charity that trains teachers to work in schools in low-income communities); *Premier Pathways* (paid two-year programme); *Now Teach* (specifically for those who are employed and want a career change into teaching); *Researchers in Schools* (for researchers who have completed or nearing completion of a PhD); *Early years initial teacher training* (for those who want to specialise in teaching 0-5 year olds).

[100] In 2017 31% of teacher trainees on the Teach First programme were switching careers, compared with 22% in 2011: Nicola Woolcock, *New middle-aged teachers targeted to boost schools*, The Times, 29 December 2017, https://www.thetimes.co.uk/article/c5cd02d6-ec18-11e7-ad3e-1cc26d7d8b0c

[101] For example, Teach First, the largest of the graduate recruiters, has 1,750 graduates on teacher training at a cost of £76m: Hannah Fearn, *Teach First: why does it divide opinion?* Guardian, 14 January 2014, https://www.theguardian.com/education/2014/jan/14/why-is-teach-first-scheme-so-controversial

Chapter 12: Skilling up the nation

[1] On average 50% of young people in the most developed countries follow vocational routes, and in Germany 75%; in the UK this is 30%: Peter Wilby, *The government seems posed to get it all wrong again on technical skills*, Guardian Education, 31 May 2016, p. 35

[2] Oliver Wright & Greg Hurst, *Technical colleges flop as they fail to recruit pupils*, Times, 18 October 2016, p. 20, https://www.thetimes.co.uk/article/technical-colleges-flop-as-they-fail-to-recruit-pupils-5mn3rhl7p

[3] Seven UTCs have closed due to low student numbers: Sally Weale, *£9m Greater Manchester college closes after three years due to lack of pupils*, Guardian, 7 February 2017, https://www.theguardian.com/education/2017/feb/07/greater-manchester-university-technical-college-closes-three-years

[4] 55% of UTCs are running at less than half capacity: Survey by Schools Week of 26 UTCs, April 2017: Rosemary Bennett, *Technical colleges are half empty*, The Times, 1 May 2017, https://www.thetimes.co.uk/edition/news/tech-colleges-mvdhhzzhf

[5] Of the UTCs that have been inspected by Ofsted, one was outstanding, six good, and six inadequate: Robert Lea, *Baker laments 'snobbery' against technical colleges*, The Times, 30 January 2017, http://www.thetimes.co.uk/past-six-days/2017-01-30/business/baker-laments-poor-support-for-vital-technical-education-8rh6889qg

[6] In the national ratings that measure pupils' progress between the ages of 11 and 16, three UTCs were at the national average, seven below, and 16 well below: Robert Lea, *Baker laments 'snobbery' against technical colleges*, The Times, 30 January 2017, http://www.thetimes.co.uk/past-six-days/2017-01-30/business/baker-laments-poor-support-for-vital-technical-education-8rh6889qg

[7] Out of 1,292 students leaving UTCs in 2016, 44% went on to university (national average 38%); 29% into apprenticeships (national average 8.4%); and only 5 applied for jobseeker's allowance, compared 1 in 9 nationally: Robert Lea, *Baker laments 'snobbery' against technical colleges*, The Times, 30 January 2017, http://www.thetimes.co.uk/past-six-days/2017-01-30/business/baker-laments-poor-support-for-vital-technical-education-8rh6889qg

[8] National Centre on Education and the Economy, Centre on International Education Benchmarking website, *Finland: Career and Technical Education*, http://ncee. org/what-we-do/center-on-international-education-benchmarking/top-performing-countries/finland-overview/finland-school-to-work-transition/

[9] Robert Lea, *Baker laments 'snobbery' against technical colleges*, The Times, 30 January 2017, http://www.thetimes.co.uk/past-six-days/2017-01-30/business/baker-laments-poor-support-for-vital-technical-education-8rh6889qg

[10] Department of Education and Skills, *14-19 Curriculum and Qualifications Reform Final Report of the Working Group on 14-19 Reform*, DfES Publications, October 2004, http://www.educationengland.org.uk/documents/pdfs/2004-tomlinson-report.pdf

[11] David Willets, *A University Education* (OUP, Oxford, 2017)

[12] David Charter, *The journeyman years still happen for 35 traditional German trades*, 25 January 2017, http://www.thetimes.co.uk/past-six-days/2017-01-25/elite-apprenticeships/the-journeyman-years-still-happen-for-35-traditional-german-trades-tjp3s3gbw

[13] Sarah Snelson & Kat Deyes, *BIS Research Paper Number 296, Understanding the Further Education Market in England*, Department of Business, Innovation and Skills, London, July 2016, https://assets.publishing.service.gov.uk/government/uploads/system/uploads/attachment_data/file/544310/bis-16-360-fe-market-england.pdf

[14] Accredited by 160 awarding organisations. 40% of students are studying for a level 2 qualification: Sarah Snelson & Kat Deyes (Frontier Economics), *BIS Research Paper Number 296, Understanding the Further Education Market in England*, Department of Business, Innovation and Skills, London, July 2016, https://assets.publishing.service. gov.uk/government/uploads/system/uploads/attachment_data/file/544310/bis-16-360-fe-market-england.pdf

[15] Ibid

[16] Ibid

[17] 70% of learners in further education travel less than 10km. from their home to the site of their provider, with 50% travelling less than 6km: Ibid

[18] House of Commons Committee of Public Accounts, *Overseeing financial sustainability in the further education sector*, The Stationery Office Limited, 16 December 2015, https://publications.parliament.uk/pa/cm201516/cmselect/cmpubacc/414/414.pdf

[19] Ibid

[20] In 2012 the university undergraduate was funded at £8,400 per annum and the full time further education college student aged 19 to 24 at £2,150: House of Lords Select

Committee on Social Mobility Report of Session 2015–16, *Overlooked and left behind: improving the transition from school to work for the majority of young people*, The Stationery Office Limited, 8 April 2016, p. 59, https://publications.parliament.uk/pa/ld201516/ldselect/ldsocmob/120/120.pdf

[21] Helena Kennedy QC, *Learning Works, Widening Participation in Further Education*, Further Education Funding Council, 1997, p. 1, https://core.ac.uk/download/pdf/9063796.pdf

[22] Voice website, http://blog.voicetheunion.org.uk/?p=12558

[23] Institute for Fiscal Studies website, *Higher Education Funding, Reforms to student finances will have complex and far-reaching effects*, http://election2015.ifs.org.uk/higher-education

[24] Sally Weale, *More cuts to further education will push colleges 'over the precipice'*, Guardian, 24 November 2015, https://www.theguardian.com/education/2015/nov/24/further-education-cuts-colleges-spending-review

[25] House of Commons Committee of Public Accounts, *Overseeing financial sustainability in the further education sector,* The Stationery Office Limited, 16 December 2015, https://publications.parliament.uk/pa/cm201516/cmselect/cmpubacc/414/414.pdf

[26] University and College Union, *What will 24% cuts mean to further education in England?* June 2015, http://www.fefunding.org.uk/files/2015/03/FE_cuts_briefing_June15.pdf

[27] Polly Toynbee, *Britain's skills failure shows the hollowness of May's immigration pledge*, Guardian, 4 December 2018, https://www.theguardian.com/commentisfree/2018/dec/04/britain-skills-failure-theresa-may-immigration-brexit

[28] House of Commons Committee of Public Accounts, *Overseeing financial sustainability in the further education sector,* The Stationery Office Limited, 16 December 2015, https://publications.parliament.uk/pa/cm201516/cmselect/cmpubacc/414/414.pdf

[29] Ibid

[30] David Foster, *Further Education: Post- 16 Area Reviews*, House of Commons Library Briefing Paper Number 7357, 28 March 2017

[31] Voice website, http://blog.voicetheunion.org.uk/?p=12558

[32] David Foster, *Further Education: Post- 16 Area Reviews*, House of Commons Library Briefing Paper Number 7357, 28 March 2017

[33] The Further Education Funding Council for England (FEFC) was a non-departmental public body of the (then) Department for Education and Skills which allocated funding to colleges, and set national policy for and exercised quality control of the sector,

between 1992 and 2001.

[34] In evidence to the economic affairs committee of the House of Lords in January 2018, Lord Baker presented findings of a government study showing that the number one thing that employers look for when recruiting is work experience (cited by 66%), followed by vocational qualifications (52%) and then academic qualifications (48%): Alexandra Frean, *Apprenticeships can bridge skills gap and offer a second chance*, The Times, Comment, 17 January 2018, https://www.thetimes.co.uk/edition/business/apprenticeships-can-bridge-the-skills-gap-across-the-generations-fgqpqjw8h

[35] Alice Thomson, *Snobbery is killing the apprenticeship dream*, The Times, 24 January 2018, https://www.thetimes.co.uk/article/a9e88cd6-0075-11e8-a2b0-4e5c7848ab02

[36] Alexandra Frean, *How to break into the big four accountancy firms*, The Times, 24 January 2018, https://www.thetimes.co.uk/edition/elite-apprenticeships/how-to-break-into-the-big-four-accountancy-firms-0z5qr7l5b

[37] Rosemary Bennett, *Elite apprenticeships: The smart way to get hands-on experience and stay debt-free*, The Times, 24 January 2018, https://www.thetimes.co.uk/edition/elite-apprenticeships/elite-apprenticeships-the-smart-way-to-get-hands-on-experience-and-stay-debt-free-6bfvwvn5j

[38] Survey of 1,001 15 to 18 year-olds undertaken in August 2017 - ECA/JTL/Joint Industry Board poll: Excellence in Electrotechnical & Engineering Services website, *YouGov Poll: Just 8% of students advised to seek apprenticeships*, ECA, 24 August 2017, https://www.eca.co.uk/news-and-events/news/2017/aug/yougov-poll-just-8-of-students-advised-to-seek?dm_i=36D7,K0M8,3KLMN8,239T3,1

[39] Sir Peter Lampl *Need to Encourage Apprenticeships*, The Times, Letters to the Editor, 24 January 2018, https://www.thetimes.co.uk/edition/comment/plastic-packaging-and-ways-of-reducing-it-l3r7vsrnn

[40] Almost three quarters of companies are recruiting apprentices, up from two thirds in 2014; compared with one third that are recruiting graduates, down from two thirds four years ago - Research by the manufacturing body, EEF: Miles Costello & James Hurley, *You're hired! Apprentices answer new industry call*, The Times, 17 December 2018, https://www.thetimes.co.uk/article/you-re-hired-apprentices-answer-new-industry-call-m2qzb0gpv

[41] Alice Thomson, *Snobbery is killing the apprenticeship dream*, The Times, 24 January 2018, https://www.thetimes.co.uk/article/a9e88cd6-0075-11e8-a2b0-4e5c7848ab02

[42] Alice Thomson, *Why university is not the only option*, The Times, 24 January 2018, https://www.thetimes.co.uk/edition/elite-apprenticeships/why-university-is-not-the-

only-option-dmb0f53bz

[43] Research by the housebuilder, Redrow, found that low wages were the biggest deterrent to young people starting apprenticeships, with 42% saying that higher first-year wages would persuade them to take up an apprenticeship: Emily Gosden, *Fears over apprenticeship targets as numbers fall*, The Times, 5 March 2018, https://www.thetimes.co.uk/article/7dcb8e46-1fec-11e8-a25c-0a92182647c9

[44] An apprentice aged under 19 years of age in their first year of an apprenticeship is legally entitled to at least the apprenticeship National Minimum Wage of £3.70 per hour. Apprentices aged 19 or over who have completed the first year of their apprenticeship are legally entitled to at least the National Living and Minimum Wage rates relevant to their age group, which are 19 to 20 years, £5.90; 21 to 24 years, £7.38; and 25 years & over, £7.83: HM Government website, Industrial Strategy, The National Living Wage and National Minimum Wage - GOV.UK, https://checkyourpay.campaign.gov.uk/#are_you_an_apprentice_

[45] Survey by ComRes for the Young Women's Trust of present and recent apprentices found that two in five apprentices spent more on the role than they earned. In some cases, it found that apprentices on the minimum wage were 'being exploited by being given the same work and responsibilities as non-trainee workers': Young Women's Trust, *Young Women & Apprenticeships: Still Not Working?* Young Women's Trust, London, November 2017, https://www.youngwomenstrust.org/assets/0000/8200/Young_Women_and_apprenticeships.pdf

[46] A survey of MPs by ComRes for the Young Women's Trust found that only one in five MPs thought that the apprentice minimum wage was enough to live on: Young Women's Trust, *Young Women & Apprenticeships: Still Not Working?* Young Women's Trust, London, November 2017, https://www.youngwomenstrust.org/assets/0000/8200/Young_Women_and_apprenticeships.pdf

[47] Health, business, engineering, retail and construction were the most popular sectors for new apprentices in England last year. Most starts were in two of those sectors, which accounted for 277,330 between them: health, public services and care; business, administration and law: Lora Jones, *Apprenticeships: Eight things you need to know*, BBC News, 21 February 2018, http://www.bbc.co.uk/news/business-42977824

[48] Although the overall number of apprentices starting new programmes has seen a drop, more apprentices are starting advanced or higher level programmes in England. In 2016-17, 53% of apprenticeship starts were at intermediate level, 40% at advanced level and the remaining 7% at higher level. The proportion of higher and advanced

level apprenticeships has climbed steadily from 37% in 2011-12 to 47% in the last academic year: Lora Jones, *Apprenticeships: Eight things you need to know*, BBC News, 21 February 2018, http://www.bbc.co.uk/news/business-42977824

[49] Six in 10 apprenticeships for those aged under 25 are at level 2 and only a quarter of these trainees move to a level 3 apprenticeship. Sir Peter Lampl, *Need to Encourage Apprenticeships*, The Times, Letters to the Editor, 24 January 2018, https://www.thetimes.co.uk/edition/comment/plastic-packaging-and-ways-of-reducing-it-l3r7vsrnn

[50] The Times, *Training Failing*, Leading Article, 23 January 2018, https://www.thetimes.co.uk/article/ac1dc2e8-ffb5-11e7-a2b0-4e5c7848ab02

[51] Tom Richmond, *The great training robbery, Assessing the first year of the apprenticeship levy*, Reform Research Trust, April 2018, https://reform.uk/research/great-training-robbery-assessing-first-year-apprenticeship-levy

[52] Oliver Wright & Rosemary Bennett, *Scandal of inadequate apprenticeships*, The Times, 23 January 2018, https://www.thetimes.co.uk/article/afd9f4b0-ffbf-11e7-a2b0-4e5c7848ab02

[53] Oliver Wright & Rosemary Bennett, *Scandal of inadequate apprenticeships*, The Times, 23 January 2018, https://www.thetimes.co.uk/article/afd9f4b0-ffbf-11e7-a2b0-4e5c7848ab02

[54] In 2017 Ofsted inspected 189 apprenticeship training providers responsible for 187,000 apprentices; 6% were judged as outstanding, 43% good, 40% required improvement, and 11% inadequate. This compares to 9% of schools judged to require improvement and 2% as inadequate in 2017: Oliver Wright & Rosemary Bennett, *Scandal of inadequate apprenticeships*, The Times, 23 January 2018, https://www.thetimes.co.uk/article/afd9f4b0-ffbf-11e7-a2b0-4e5c7848ab02. Between September 2017 and February 2018, Ofsted inspected 55 training providers finding 33 of them to be good or outstanding, 16 requiring improvement, and six inadequate; 40%, therefore, being inadequate or requiring improvement. 33,000 apprentices were with providers judged to be good or outstanding; 80% of the overall places inspected during this period were good or outstanding: Speech by Ofsted's chief inspector, Amanda Spielman, the quality of apprenticeships, changes in the sector and Ofsted's role to the Annual Apprenticeships Conference, Birmingham, 22 March 2018, published 23 March 2018, GOV.UK website, https://www.gov.uk/government/speeches/amanda-spielman-speech-to-annual-apprenticeships-conference

[55] Ofsted - The proportion of apprentices being taught by inadequate training providers increased to 20% in 2017; 37,000 apprentices: Oliver Wright & Rosemary Bennett,

Scandal of inadequate apprenticeships, The Times, 23 January 2018, https://www.thetimes.co.uk/article/afd9f4b0-ffbf-11e7-a2b0-4e5c7848ab02

[56] Speech by Ofsted's chief inspector, Amanda Spielman, the quality of apprenticeships, changes in the sector and Ofsted's role to the Annual Apprenticeships Conference, Birmingham, 22 March 2018, published 23 March 2018, GOV.UK website, https://www.gov.uk/government/speeches/amanda-spielman-speech-to-annual-apprenticeships-conference

[57] Jude Burke, *Revealed: Six more apprenticeship providers banned from taking new recruits*, FE Week, 15 October 2018, https://feweek.co.uk/2018/10/15/revealed-six-more-apprenticeship-providers-banned-from-taking-new-recruits/

[58] Government research into apprenticeships found 10% of apprentices did not even know they were on the scheme: The Times, *Training Failing*, Leading Article, 23 January 2018, https://www.thetimes.co.uk/article/ac1dc2e8-ffb5-11e7-a2b0-4e5c7848ab02

[59] Oliver Wright & Rosemary Bennett, *Scandal of inadequate apprenticeships*, The Times, 23 January 2018, https://www.thetimes.co.uk/article/afd9f4b0-ffbf-11e7-a2b0-4e5c7848ab02

[60] The Times, *Training Failing*, Leading Article, 23 January 2018, https://www.thetimes.co.uk/article/ac1dc2e8-ffb5-11e7-a2b0-4e5c7848ab02

[61] 56% of apprentices continue being employed at the end of their training - Department for Education/CIPS: Alexandra Frean & Thomas Mackie, *Support for apprentice levy goes up in flames*, The Times, 11 January 2018, https://www.thetimes.co.uk/article/88889090-f648-11e7-9cfd-f28094b4d5ce

[62] Under the levy system organisations can select any provider who is registered to undertake their off-the-job training. There are now more than 2,000 registered providers, compared to around 900 before the introduction of the levy: Oliver Wright & Rosemary Bennett, *Scandal of inadequate apprenticeships*, The Times, 23 January 2018, https://www.thetimes.co.uk/article/afd9f4b0-ffbf-11e7-a2b0-4e5c7848ab02

[63] Angela Rayner, *Young people who don't go to university are being let down too*, Shadow Education Secretary, The Times, 29 August 2017, https://www.thetimes.co.uk/edition/news/young-people-who-do-not-go-to-university-are-being-let-down-too-whjjxnzff

[64] Meg Hillier MP, Chair of the House of Commons Public Accounts Committee, *The scandal of inadequate apprenticeships*, The Times, Letters to the Editor, 26 January 2018, https://www.thetimes.co.uk/article/the-scandal-of-inadequate-apprenticeships-brzkxbmdz

[65] Ofsted had concerns about Learndirect's poor training standards and financial management in spring 2015, but didn't make the decision to inspect it until November 2016. Following an inspection in March 2017 Learndirect was rated 'inadequate'. Learndirect then applied for and were granted a super injunction to prevent Ofsted from publishing its report and even it to the government. The report was supressed for four months until the injunction was lifted. Even when the report was published, Learndirect continued to receive government funding including £95m. in the 2017-18 financial year. Leardirect's contract was not terminated and they will continue to train apprentices and other trainees and receive large amounts of public money until their contract ends in the summer of 2018. Despite all of this, Learndirect has in effect re-constituted itself as a new legal entity – Learndirect Apprenticeships Ltd, and is managing training contracts: Branwen Jeffreys, *Learndirect 'should face investigation', says senior MP*, BBC News, 11 September 2017, http://www.bbc.co.uk/news/education-41231483; House of Commons Committee of Public Accounts, *The monitoring, inspection and funding of Learndirect Ltd,* House of Commons, 26 February 2018, https://publications. parliament.uk/pa/cm201719/cmselect/cmpubacc/646/646.pdf; Dominic Ponsford, *FE Week successfully challenges training giant Learndirect's legal gag on revealing damning Ofsted report*, The Press Gazette, 14 August 2017; and Meg Hillier MP, Chair of the House of Commons public accounts committee, *The scandal of inadequate apprenticeships*, The Times, Letters to the Editor, 26 January 2018, https://www. thetimes.co.uk/article/the-scandal-of-inadequate-apprenticeships-brzkxbmdz

[66] BBC News, *Learners let down by Learndirect, say MPs*, 2 March 2018, http://www. bbc.co.uk/news/education-43241486

[67] Branwen Jeffreys, *Learndirect 'should face investigation', says senior MP*, BBC News, 11 September 2017, http://www.bbc.co.uk/news/education-41231483

[68] Alexandra Frean, *Levy to blame for slump in apprentices, employers say*, 23 February 2018, The Times, https://www.thetimes.co.uk/article/a0901294-181c-11e8-a427-78e8af199a96

[69] Jonty Bloom & Karen Hoggan, *Apprenticeship numbers fall by 59% after levy imposed*, BBC News, 23 November 2017, http://www.bbc.co.uk/news/business-42092171

[70] Lora Jones, *Apprenticeships: Eight things you need to know*, BBC News 21 February 2018, http://www.bbc.co.uk/news/business-42977824

[71] Ibid

[72] 97% of small accountancy companies said taking on apprentices had been good value for money; 90% that apprentices helped boost productivity at 90%; and half said

they preferred to recruit apprentices rather than university graduates: Association of Accounting Technicians website, *Majority of smaller businesses realise the value of apprenticeships*, 5 March 2018, https://www.aat.org.uk/aat-news/majority-of-smaller-businesses-realise-the-value-of-apprenticeships

[73] The levy is unpopular with more than half of those employers who have to pay it: The Times, *Training Failing*, Leading Article, 23 January 2018, https://www.thetimes.co.uk/article/ac1dc2e8-ffb5-11e7-a2b0-4e5c7848ab02. The Chartered Management Institute: Emily Gosden, *Fears over apprenticeship targets as numbers fall*, The Times, 5 March 2018, https://www.thetimes.co.uk/article/7dcb8e46-1fec-11e8-a25c-0a92182647c9

[74] Alexandra Frean, *Levy to blame for slump in apprentices, employers say*, 23 February 2018, The Times, https://www.thetimes.co.uk/article/a0901294-181c-11e8-a427-78e8af199a96

[75] 42% of companies offer apprenticeships: Department for Education: CIPS: Alexandra Frean & Thomas Mackie, *Support for apprentice levy goes up in flames*, The Times, 11 January 2018, https://www.thetimes.co.uk/article/88889090-f648-11e7-9cfd-f28094b4d5ce

[76] While the government estimated the new levy would affect 2% of employers, a survey by the Chartered Institute for Personnel and Development suggested about a third currently pay the apprenticeship levy: Lora Jones, *Apprenticeships: Eight things you need to know*, BBC News, 21 February 2018, http://www.bbc.co.uk/news/business-42977824

[77] Steve Rotheram, *I trained as a bricklayer but we need more than warm words about apprenticeships*, The Times, 6 March 2018, https://www.thetimes.co.uk/article/e087546e-208e-11e8-8ccc-a83211a65142

[78] A survey by the Chartered Institute for Personnel and Development indicated that 22% of employers don›t know whether they have to pay the levy or not: Lora Jones, *Apprenticeships: Eight things you need to know*, BBC News, 21 February 2018, http://www.bbc.co.uk/news/business-42977824; and Department for Education/CIPS: Alexandra Frean & Thomas Mackie, *Support for apprentice levy goes up in flames*, The Times, 11 January 2018, https://www.thetimes.co.uk/article/88889090-f648-11e7-9cfd-f28094b4d5ce

[79] Institute of Directors: Lora Jones, *Apprenticeships: Eight things you need to know*, BBC News, 21 February 2018, http://www.bbc.co.uk/news/business-42977824

[80] 40% of companies surveyed said the apprenticeship levy 'won't make any difference to the amount of training we offer': Department for Education: CIPS: Alexandra Frean

& Thomas Mackie, *Support for apprentice levy goes up in flames*, The Times, 11 January 2018, https://www.thetimes.co.uk/article/88889090-f648-11e7-9cfd-f28094b4d5ce

[81] 19% of companies surveyed said they were writing off the levy as a tax and not using it for training: Department for Education - CIPS: Alexandra Frean & Thomas Mackie, *Support for apprentice levy goes up in flames*, The Times, 11 January 2018, https://www. thetimes.co.uk/article/88889090-f648-11e7-9cfd-f28094b4d5ce. 1 in 10 of the Institute of Directors' members written the levy off as a tax: Lora Jones, *Apprenticeships: Eight things you need to know*, BBC News, 21 February 2018, http://www.bbc.co.uk/news/business-42977824

[82] 33% of companies surveyed said they were developing a new apprenticeship programme: Department for Education - CIPS: Alexandra Frean & Thomas Mackie, *Support for apprentice levy goes up in flames*, The Times, 11 January 2018, https:// www.thetimes.co.uk/article/88889090-f648-11e7-9cfd-f28094b4d5ce

[83] Alice Thomson, *Why university is not the only option*, The Times, 24 January 2018, https://www.thetimes.co.uk/edition/elite-apprenticeships/why-university-is-not-the-only-option-dmb0f53bz

[84] Jonty Bloom & Karen Hoggan, *Apprenticeship numbers fall by 59% after levy imposed*, BBC News,
23 November 2017, http://www.bbc.co.uk/news/business-42092171

[85] Alistair Osborne, *'Radical' scheme is a total shambles*, The Times, Business Commentary, 11 January 2018, https://www.thetimes.co.uk/article/c36af7fc-f648-11e7-a789-003e705b951e. Steve Rotheram, *I trained as a bricklayer but we need more than warm words about apprenticeships*, The Times, 6 March 2018, https://www.thetimes.co.uk/article/e087546e-208e-11e8-8ccc-a83211a65142

[86] Alexandra Frean & Thomas Mackie, *Support for apprentice levy goes up in flames*, The Times, 11 January 2018, https://www.thetimes.co.uk/article/88889090-f648-11e7-9cfd-f28094b4d5ce

[87] 75% of manufacturers have complained in an EEF survey that they are unable to spend the money now tied up in their apprenticeship levy fund. More than one-third see no benefit at all from the scheme: Iain Dey, *Apprentice levy is nothing more than a tax*, The Sunday Times, 25 February 2018, 12:01am, https://www.thetimes.co.uk/edition/business/iain-dey-apprentice-levy-is-nothing-more-than-a-tax-v5c9rx3fw

[88] Alice Thomson, *Snobbery is killing the apprenticeship dream*, The Times, 24 January 2018, https://www.thetimes.co.uk/article/a9e88cd6-0075-11e8-a2b0-4e5c7848ab02

[89] Alexandra Frean & Thomas Mackie, *Support for apprentice levy goes up in flames*,

The Times, 11 January 2018, https://www.thetimes.co.uk/article/88889090-f648-11e7-9cfd-f28094b4d5ce. Alistair Osborne, *'Radical' scheme is a total shambles*, The Times, Business Commentary, 11 January 2018, https://www.thetimes.co.uk/article/c36af7fc-f648-11e7-a789-003e705b951e

[90] For example out of 67 students on a part-time business course for executives at Cranfield University's School of Management, 61 have had their places funded by money from the apprenticeship levy: Kaya Burgess, *Trainees' levy used to fund top executives*, The Times, 9 October 2017, https://www.thetimes.co.uk/article/65214d14-ac5f-11e7-8f75-2b6f1159f66f. In response to demand from employers universities are running around 40 MBA courses being funded from the apprenticeship levy at a total cost of £26m.: Nicola Woolcock, *Universities cash in with courses for 'apprentices'*, The Times, 5 May 2018, https://www.thetimes.co.uk/article/universities-cash-in-with-courses-for-apprentices-ncb9q5h06

[91] Jude Burke, *DfE urgently seeking answers to why level two apprenticeships fell by 38%*, FE Week, 6 December 2018, https://feweek.co.uk/2018/12/06/dfe-seeks-to-improve-understanding-of-huge-level-2-apprenticeships-drop/

[92] Martin Birchall, *Employer levy concern must be addressed*, The Times, 24 January 2018, https://www.thetimes.co.uk/edition/elite-apprenticeships/employer-levy-concern-must-be-addressed-9ckqcwhfm

[93] Alistair Osborne, *'Radical' scheme is a total shambles*, The Times, Business Commentary, 11 January 2018, https://www.thetimes.co.uk/article/c36af7fc-f648-11e7-a789-003e705b951e

[94] Robert Lea, *Budget 2018: Unpopular apprenticeship levy 'still too rigid' despite reforms*, The Times, 30 October 2018, https://www.thetimes.co.uk/article/budget-2018-unpopular-apprenticeship-levy-still-too-rigid-despite-reforms-2ljbjp2sg

[95] Alexandra Frean & Thomas Mackie, *Support for apprentice levy goes up in flames*, The Times, 11 January 2018, https://www.thetimes.co.uk/article/88889090-f648-11e7-9cfd-f28094b4d5ce

[96] Oliver Wright, *Apprentice levy is not enough to train an engineer, say bosses*, The Times, 30 April 2018, https://www.thetimes.co.uk/article/apprentice-levy-is-not-enough-to-train-an-engineer-say-bosses-3c20xz6zg

[97] Between August and October 2017 there were 11,600 higher level apprenticeship starts, an increase of 26.8% compared to 2016, with 2,200 taken up by school leavers aged under 19: Rosemary Bennett, *Doubts grow over apprenticeship levy as numbers drop*, The Times, 26 January 2018, https://www.thetimes.co.uk/article/42b22a2a-0220-

11e8-a2b0-4e5c7848ab02

[98] Alexandra Frean, *Levy to blame for slump in apprentices, employers say*, 23 February 2018, The Times, https://www.thetimes.co.uk/article/a0901294-181c-11e8-a427-78e8af199a96

[99] Sean Coughlan, *Theresa May's university review will not scrap fees*, BBC News, 19 February 2018, http://www.bbc.co.uk/news/education-43106736

[100] Rosemary Bennett, *Parents told not to look down on apprenticeships*, The Times, 24 January 2018, https://www.thetimes.co.uk/article/f24d4678-008a-11e8-9de1-e6776d524215

[101] Rosemary Bennett, *Elite apprenticeships: The smart way to get hands-on experience and stay debt-free*, The Times, 24 January 2018, https://www.thetimes.co.uk/edition/elite-apprenticeships/elite-apprenticeships-the-smart-way-to-get-hands-on-experience-and-stay-debt-free-6bfvwvn5j. The average pay of a higher level apprentice one year after completing the apprenticeship is £27,200; 65% more than the average pay of £16,500 for those with a degree one year after graduating. After two years the difference narrows to 26% - £27,800 compared to £22,000: Longitudinal Educational Outcomes dataset: Alexandra Frean, *Apprenticeships can bridge skills gap and offer a second chance*, The Times, Comment, 17 January 2018, https://www.thetimes.co.uk/edition/business/apprenticeships-can-bridge-the-skills-gap-across-the-generations-fgqpqjw8h

[102] Rosemary Bennett, *Parents told not to look down on apprenticeships*, The Times, 24 January 2018, https://www.thetimes.co.uk/article/f24d4678-008a-11e8-9de1-e6776d524215

[103] Alice Thomson, *Snobbery is killing the apprenticeship dream*, The Times, 24 January 2018, https://www.thetimes.co.uk/article/a9e88cd6-0075-11e8-a2b0-4e5c7848ab02

[104] Higher and Degree [apprenticeship] Vacancy Listing March 2018, https://assets.publishing.service.gov.uk/government/uploads/system/uploads/attachment_data/file/696600/Apps-Campaign-Listing-290318.pdf. Rosemary Bennett, *Parents told not to look down on apprenticeships*, The Times, 24 January 2018, https://www.thetimes.co.uk/article/f24d4678-008a-11e8-9de1-e6776d524215

[105] In 2016-17, health, business, engineering, retail and construction were the most popular sectors for new apprentices in England last year. Most starts were in two of those sectors, which accounted for 277,330 between them: health, public services and care; business, administration and law: Lora Jones, *Apprenticeships: Eight things you need to know*, BBC News website, 21 February 2018, http://www.bbc.co.uk/news/

business-42977824

[106] Speech by Ofsted's chief inspector, Amanda Spielman, *The quality of apprenticeships, changes in the sector and Ofsted's role*, to the Annual Apprenticeships Conference, Birmingham, 22 March 2018, published 23 March 2018, GOV.UK website, https://www.gov.uk/government/speeches/amanda-spielman-speech-to-annual-apprenticeships-conference

[107] A good example of this is the Key6 Group that Ofsted inspected as a newcomer to the apprenticeship market and found that it was 'not fit for purpose' with the large majority of trainees unaware that they were apprentices: Ofsted, *Report of monitoring visit to Key6 Group Limited, 15–16 February 2018*, https://reports.ofsted.gov.uk/inspection-reports/find-inspection-report/provider/ELS/1273215

[108] Meg Hillier, MP, Chair, Public Accounts Committee, based on the evidence that the committee considered as part of their review of LearnDirect, says that 'more and more companies are setting themselves up as training providers and Ofsted says that it will struggle to keep tabs on these': *The scandal of inadequate apprenticeships*, The Times, Letters to the Editor, 26 January 2018, https://www.thetimes.co.uk/article/the-scandal-of-inadequate-apprenticeships-brzkxbmdz

[109] Speech by Ofsted's chief inspector, Amanda Spielman, *The quality of apprenticeships, changes in the sector and Ofsted's role*, to the Annual Apprenticeships Conference, Birmingham, 22 March 2018, published 23 March 2018, GOV.UK website, https://www.gov.uk/government/speeches/amanda-spielman-speech-to-annual-apprenticeships-conference

[110] House of Commons Committee of Public Accounts, *The monitoring, inspection and funding of Learndirect Ltd,* House of Commons, 26 February 2018, https://publications.parliament.uk/pa/cm201719/cmselect/cmpubacc/646/646.pdf

[111] Institute of Apprenticeships website, Search the Apprenticeship Standards, https://www.instituteforapprenticeships.org/apprenticeship-standards/. Alexandra Frean & Thomas Mackie, *Support for apprentice levy goes up in flames*, The Times, 11 January 2018, https://www.thetimes.co.uk/article/88889090-f648-11e7-9cfd-f28094b4d5ce

[112] House of Commons Committee of Public Accounts, *The monitoring, inspection and funding of Learndirect Ltd,* House of Commons, 26 February 2018, https://publications.parliament.uk/pa/cm201719/cmselect/cmpubacc/646/646.pdf

[113] More than half of employers are calling for the apprenticeship to be replaced. Only 20% of the employers that pay the levy support the system and 19% do not plan to use it to develop apprenticeships: Research by the Chartered Institute of Personnel and

Development, only 20 per cent of the employers that pay the levy support the system. Nineteen per cent do not plan to use it to develop apprenticeships: Alexandra Frean & Thomas Mackie, *Support for apprentice levy goes up in flames*, The Times, 11 January 2018, https://www.thetimes.co.uk/article/88889090-f648-11e7-9cfd-f28094b4d5ce

[114] 53% of employers want the levy to be replaced with a broader training tariff : Research by the Chartered Institute of Personnel and Development involving a survey of more than a 1,000 employers: Alistair Osborne, *'Radical' scheme is a total shambles*, The Times, Business Commentary, 11 January 2018, https://www.thetimes.co.uk/article/c36af7fc-f648-11e7-a789-003e705b951e

[115] Alexandra Frean & Thomas Mackie, *Support for apprentice levy goes up in flames*, The Times, 11 January 2018, https://www.thetimes.co.uk/article/88889090-f648-11e7-9cfd-f28094b4d5ce

[116] There are calls, for example from the Association of Employment and Learning Providers, for the full costs of off-the-job training for all 16-24 year old apprentices to be met from public funding: Jonty Bloom & Karen Hoggan, *Apprenticeship numbers fall by 59% after levy imposed*, BBC News website, 23 November 2017, http://www.bbc.co.uk/news/business-42092171

[117] Alexandra Frean & James Hurley, *The 'huge reform' yet to prove that it is up to the job*, The Times, 5 March 2018, https://www.thetimes.co.uk/article/8131f00a-1fd5-11e8-8ccc-a83211a65142. Nicola Woolcock, *Campaign to build the engineers of tomorrow*, The Times, 24 January 2018, https://www.thetimes.co.uk/edition/elite-apprenticeships/campaign-to-build-the-engineers-of-tomorrow-m57hgr678

[118] Alexandra Frean & Thomas Mackie, *Support for apprentice levy goes up in flames*, The Times, 11 January 2018, https://www.thetimes.co.uk/article/88889090-f648-11e7-9cfd-f28094b4d5ce

[119] As part of the Chancellor's 2018 Spring statement it was announced that the 'education secretary will release up to £80 million to help small businesses take on apprentices': Martin Strydom, *Spring statement: the main points at a glance – Skills*, The Times, 13 March 2018, https://www.thetimes.co.uk/article/ccc730c4-26bb-11e8-acc5-262aff1ca7a6

[120] Angela Rayner, *Young people who don't go to university are being let down too*, The Times, 29 August 2017, https://www.thetimes.co.uk/edition/news/young-people-who-do-not-go-to-university-are-being-let-down-too-whjjxnzff

[121] Alexandra Frean & Thomas Mackie, *Support for apprentice levy goes up in flames*, The Times, 11 January 2018, https://www.thetimes.co.uk/article/88889090-f648-11e7-

9cfd-f28094b4d5ce

[122] GOV.UK, Education and Skills Funding Agency website, About Us, https://www.gov.uk/government/organisations/education-and-skills-funding-agency/about

[123] Institute of Apprenticeships website, https://www.instituteforapprenticeships.org/about/what-we-do/

[124] Local enterprise partnerships are partnerships between local authorities and businesses. They decide what the priorities should be for investment in roads, buildings and facilities in the area: GOV.UK, *2010 to 2015 government policy: Local Enterprise Partnerships (LEPs) and enterprise zones*, 8 May 2015, https://www.gov.uk/government/publications/2010-to-2015-government-policy-local-enterprise-partnerships-leps-and-enterprise-zones/2010-to-2015-government-policy-local-enterprise-partnerships-leps-and-enterprise-zones

[125] Transferring these functions sub-regionally would have the support of Mayors such as Steve Rotherham (Merseyside) and Andy Burnham (Greater Manchester): Steve Rotherham, *I trained as a bricklayer but we need more than warm words about apprenticeships*, The Times, 6 March 2018, https://www.thetimes.co.uk/article/e087546e-208e-11e8-8ccc-a83211a65142

[126] QS Top Universities website, World University Rankings 2019, https://www.topuniversities.com/university-rankings/world-university-rankings/2019

[127] 84% of students are 'content with their degree courses' - The National Student Survey undertaken by the Higher Education Funding Council for England of the 2017 final-year students: Office for Students website, National Student Survey – NSS, https://www.officeforstudents.org.uk/advice-and-guidance/student-information-and-data/national-student-survey-nss/get-the-nss-data/

[128] On average graduates earn £9,500 a year more or £170,000 to £250,000 over their lifetimes than non-graduates. Those with master's degree earn £317,000 on average more over a life-time, and those with a doctorates, £409,000 more. Analysis by the Russell Group and London Economics: Rosemary Bennett, *Top university degree adds £177,000 to graduates' lifetime pay*, The Times, 2 November 2017, https://www.thetimes.co.uk/article/2ba475e4-bf46-11e7-8bb9-94e1372175c0. The average impact of graduating from higher education on earnings at age 29 is estimated to be 28% for women and 8% for men: Chris Belfield, Jack Britton, Franz Buscha, Lorraine Dearden, Matt Dickson, Laura van der Erve, Luke Sibieta, Anna Vignoles, Ian Walker & Yu Zhu, *The impact of undergraduate degrees on early-career earnings Research report*, Institute for Fiscal Studies, November 2018, https://assets.publishing.service.gov.uk/

government/uploads/system/uploads/attachment_data/file/759278/The_impact_of_
undergraduate_degrees_on_early-career_earnings.pdf

[129] *This country needs all the graduates it can get*, Alice Thomson, The Times, 18 October
2017, https://www.thetimes.co.uk/article/7cee015e-b37a-11e7-a7ed-96e3d3dae681

[130] House of Commons Education Committee, *Value for money in higher education,*
House of Commons, 5 November 2018, https://publications.parliament.uk/pa/
cm201719/cmselect/cmeduc/343/343.pdf

[131] Edwina Dunn, *UK skills shortage: Misconception about STEM subjects are failing
young people,* CITY A.M. website, 5 February 2016, http://www.cityam.com/233916/
uk-skills-shortage-misconception-about-stem-subjects-are-failing-young-people

[132] Employers are increasingly concerned that graduates lack work experience and have
'poorly developed soft skills': Rosemary Bennett, *Elite apprenticeships: The smart
way to get hands-on experience and stay debt-free*, The Times, 24 January 2018, https://
www.thetimes.co.uk/edition/elite-apprenticeships/elite-apprenticeships-the-smart-
way-to-get-hands-on-experience-and-stay-debt-free-6bfvwvn5j

[133] Since 2015 universities have been allowed to admit as many students as they want:
Jonathan Paige, *University entry is a 'free for all'*, The Times, 12 August 2017, https://
www.thetimes.co.uk/edition/news/university-entry-a-free-for-all-as-unconditional-
offers-more-than-double-in-five-years-mmfcb97rk

[134] House of Commons Committee of Public Accounts, *The higher education market,*
House of Commons, 15 June 2018, https://publications.parliament.uk/pa/cm201719/
cmselect/cmpubacc/693/693.pdf

[135] Each year only 2% of students transfer to another university: House of
Commons Committee of Public Accounts, *The higher education market,* House of
Commons, 15 June 2018, https://publications.parliament.uk/pa/cm201719/cmselect/
cmpubacc/693/693.pdf

[136] Examples of universities that have expanded are Surrey and Swansea (which have
doubled their student numbers), Coventry, Reading and Aston (more than 50%),
and 'dozens' of others (more than 30%). 17 universities have suffered a decline in
student numbers of more than 10% since 2012, including five of more than 20%.
Examples include London Metropolitan (34%), Southampton Solent and Cumbria
(24%), Bedfordshire and Huddersfield (18%) and East London and Kingston (26%).
So called 'elite' universities are taking students who in previous years would have
gone to 'middle-tier' institutions, which are taking students from 'lower-tier' ones.
Many of the universities that have lost students have growing multi-million pound
deficits: Rosemary Bennett & Ryan Watts, *Universities on the brink in struggle to*

attract students, The Times, 2 November 2018, https://www.thetimes.co.uk/article/universities-on-the-brink-in-struggle-for-students-tp2lv6jbk

[137] Analysis by The Times of data from Higher Education Statistics Agency returns, 2016-17: Rosemary Bennett, Nicola Woolcock & Ryan Watts, University debt: credit crunch looms as debt spirals, 3 January 2019, The Times, https://www.thetimes.co.uk/article/university-debt-credit-crunch-looms-as-debt-spirals-2vm65hpq5

[138] Report of the Office for National Statistics in 2013, and research commissioned by the Chartered Institute of Personnel and Development 2015: Katie Allen,*UK graduates are wasting degrees in lower-skilled jobs*, Guardian, 25 May 2017, https://www.theguardian.com/business/2015/aug/19/uk-failed-create-enough-high-skilled-jobs-graduates-student-debt-report; and Jason Groves, *Revealed: Half of all university graduates are languishing in low-skilled jobs which do not need a degree*, Daily Mail, 20 August 2015, http://www.dailymail.co.uk/news/article-3203675/Half-university-graduates-languishing-low-skilled-jobs-not-need-degree.html. Emma Simpson, *Will doing a degree land you a career?* Business correspondent, BBC News, 16 November 2017, http://www.bbc.co.uk/news/business-42003418

[139] Half of employers surveyed by the Association of Graduate Recruiters believed that newly qualified graduates do not have the skills to start employment as they lack people skills and a fundamental understanding of the world of work: BBC News, *Graduates aren't skilled enough, say employers*, 15 March 2017, http://www.bbc.co.uk/newsbeat/article/39268144/graduates-arent-skilled-enough-say-employers. House of Commons Business, Innovation & Skills Committee, and Education Committee, *Education, skills and productivity: commissioned research*, The Stationery Office Limited, 5 November 2015, pgs. 23–27, https://publications.parliament.uk/pa/cm201516/cmselect/cmbis/565/565.pdf

[140] There is a STEM unemployment rate of 8% compared to the national unemployment rate of 4.3%: Study by the Chartered Institute of Personnel and Development: Alexandra Frean, *KPMG snubs universities by offering own digital degrees*, The Times, 6 January 2018, https://www.thetimes.co.uk/edition/business/kpmg-snubs-universities-by-offering-own-digital-degrees-k9jcdrd78

[141] Ibid

[142] Chartered Institute of Personnel and Development, *Policy report, Over-qualification and skills mismatch in the graduate labour market*, CIPD, London, August 2015, https://www.cipd.co.uk/Images/over-qualification-and-skills-mismatch-graduate-labour-market_tcm18-10231.pdf

[143] Chris Belfield, Jack Britton, Franz Buscha, Lorraine Dearden, Matt Dickson, Laura van der Erve, Luke Sibieta, Anna Vignoles, Ian Walker & Yu Zhu, *The impact of undergraduate degrees on early-career earnings Research report*, Institute for Fiscal Studies, November 2018, https://assets.publishing.service.gov.uk/government/uploads/system/uploads/attachment_data/file/759278/The_impact_of_undergraduate_degrees_on_early-career_earnings.pdf

[144] Neil O'Brien, Will Tanner & Guy Miscampbell, A question of degree, UK Onward, 7 January 2019, https://www.ukonward.com/wp-content/uploads/2019/01/J6493-ONW-A-Question-Of-Degree-190104.pdf

[145] John Caudwell, *Our obsession with sending people to university is holding us back*, Daily Telegraph, p.28, 15 August 2018, https://www.telegraph.co.uk/business/2018/08/15/obsession-sending-people-university-holding-us-back/

[146] Speech by Robert Halfon MP to the Centre for Social Justice on 5 February 2018: Hannah Richardson, *Many graduates earn 'paltry returns' for their degree*, BBC News, 5 February 2018, http://www.bbc.co.uk/news/education-42923529

[147] Chartered Institute of Personnel and Development, Policy report, *Over-qualification and skills mismatch in the graduate labour market*, CIPD, August 2015, https://www.cipd.co.uk/Images/over-qualification-and-skills-mismatch-graduate-labour-market_tcm18-10231.pdf

[148] Higher Education Statistics Agency (HESA), Finances, https://www.hesa.ac.uk/data-and-analysis/providers/finances

[149] In 2016 27,160 people started on higher level apprenticeships, which can lead to degree equivalent qualifications. Of those starting higher level apprenticeships there were 1,800 school leavers; most were aged 25 or over: Greg Hurst, *More high-level apprenticeships are on their way*, Times, http://www.thetimes.co.uk/past-six-days/2017-01-25/elite-apprenticeships/more-high-level-apprenticeships-are-on-their-way-pg0q0j6j5

[150] Employers have for many years sponsored individuals on degree courses. Degree apprenticeships, recruited directly by companies and splitting their time between the workplace and study are at an early stage with fewer than 5,000 students. Degree apprentices usually spend 80% of their time in the workplace and 20% studying. By September 2017 4,850 had started degree apprenticeships in such areas as chartered management, manufacturing engineering, nuclear science and aerospace engineering: Nicola Woolcock, *Apprentices profit from paid degree courses*, The Times, 9 October 2017, https://www.thetimes.co.uk/article/92be8ba6-ac5f-11e7-8f75-2b6f1159f66f

[151] For example companies like Dyson run their own degree courses: Richard Adams,

James Dyson says tuition fees hit students with debt at 'worst time', Guardian, 13 September 2017, https://www.theguardian.com/education/2017/sep/13/james-dyson-tuition-fees-students-loan-debt. Employers such as Accenture, BT, Ford, Goldman Sachs, Glaxosmithkline, IBM, John Lewis, KPMG, Lloyds Bank and Virgin Media have their own apprentice degree programmes in digital technology: Alexandra Frean, *KPMG snubs universities by offering own digital degrees*, The Times, 6 January 2018, https://www.thetimes.co.uk/edition/business/kpmg-snubs-universities-by-offering-own-digital-degrees-k9jcdrd78

[152] Research by ICM found that businesses reported that those with a higher apprenticeship are 25% more employable than those who took an alternative route into a career: James Hurley, *How to avoid debt and start your career in engineering*, Times, 25 January 2017, http://www.thetimes.co.uk/past-six-days/2017-01-25/elite-apprenticeships/how-to-avoid-debt-and-start-your-career-in-engineering-82jvv0s2n. To tackle specific skills shortages, starting in September 2018, the accountancy firm, PWC, has entered into an arrangement with Leeds and Birmingham universities to place 40 apprentices on computer science degrees 'tailored to the company's specifications so that students graduate with the technical and problem-solving skills that employers complain graduates often lack'. The apprentices will work at PWC during vacations and during the third year of their four year course: Nicola Woolcock, *Apprentices profit from paid degree courses*, The Times, 9 October 2017, https://www.thetimes.co.uk/article/92be8ba6-ac5f-11e7-8f75-2b6f1159f66f.

[153] Pupils' engagement with mathematics and science declines during secondary school – 74% amongst girls and 56% amongst boys: Edwina Dunn, *UK skills shortage: Misconception about STEM subjects are failing young people*, CITY A.M. website, 5 February 2016, http://www.cityam.com/233916/uk-skills-shortage-misconception-about-stem-subjects-are-failing-young-people. 20% of those on A-level physics programmes are girls, which has been the case for the last 20 years: Sarah Haythornthwaite, *'We are wasting the huge potential girls have in STEM careers'*, Times Education Supplement, 30 May 2017, https://www.tes.com/news/school-news/breaking-views/we-are-wasting-huge-potential-girls-have-stem-careers

[154] Edwina Dunn, *UK skills shortage: Misconception about STEM subjects are failing young people*, CITY A.M. website, 5 February 2016, http://www.cityam.com/233916/uk-skills-shortage-misconception-about-stem-subjects-are-failing-young-people

155 The numeracy skills of England's 16 to 19 year olds are ranked 22nd out of 23 developed countries: Edwina Dunn, *UK skills shortage: Misconception about STEM*

subjects are failing young people, CITY A.M. website, 5 February 2016, http://www.cityam.com/233916/uk-skills-shortage-misconception-about-stem-subjects-are-failing-young-people

[156] Ibid

[157] Girls outperform boys in A-Level STEM subjects, with a higher percentage achieving A or A* grades in 2016. There are significantly fewer girls than boys choosing STEM subjects beyond GCSE: Social Market Foundation, *Jobs of the future Research*, EDF Energy, August 2017, https://www.edfenergy.com/sites/default/files/jobs-of-the-future.pdf

[158] In 2011 1.6% of girls did A-level physics compared with 6.1% of boys. In 2016, 1.9% of girls chose A-level physics compared with 6.5% of boys; no girls at all studied physics in 44% of schools in England; and 8% of girls and 12.3% of boys took mathematics A-level. The gender balance at physics A-level in England's schools has changed little in decades, with only 20% being female: Institute of Physics, *Why not physics? A snapshot of girls' uptake at A-level*, IoP, May 2018, http://www.iop.org/publications/iop/2018/file_71495.pdf.

[159] Rosemary Bennett, *Girls give up on sciences after A level*, The Times, 15 January 2018, https://www.thetimes.co.uk/article/09a5ec66-f97a-11e7-9a34-94e1b34681c3

[160] 12% of engineering and technology graduates are female: Government News Release, *Government and industry join forces to help get more women and girls in STEM*, 9 August 2013, https://www.gov.uk/government/news/government-and-industry-join-forces-to-help-get-more-women-and-girls-in-stem. In 2016/17 only 8% of STEM apprenticeships were women, who constitute over 50% of all apprenticeships: National Audit Office 2018: Lorraine Candy, *Family: how to help teens choose their GCSE and A-level subjects*, The Sunday Times, 4 March 2018, https://www.thetimes.co.uk/article/07afb632-1c7d-11e8-8523-de565c87c927

[161] Josie Gurney-Read, *STEM skills should be 'integrated across the curriculum'*, Daily Telegraph, 18 March 2014, http://www.telegraph.co.uk/education/educationnews/10706162/STEM-skills-should-be-integrated-across-the-curriculum.html

[162] Ibid

[163] Sarah Haythornthwaite, *'We are wasting the huge potential girls have in STEM careers'*, Times Education Supplement, 30 May 2017, https://www.tes.com/news/school-news/breaking-views/we-are-wasting-huge-potential-girls-have-stem-careers

[164] In 2017, 41% of A-level entries were in STEM subjects, compared to 40% in 2016: Dan Matthews, *How to inspire the next STEM generation*, Daily Telegraph, 21

February 2018, http://www.telegraph.co.uk/business/boeing-uk/inspiring-the-next-stem-generation/

[165] The number of girls taking Stem subjects at A-levels has increased by over 17% since 2010: Jane Wakefield, *Government urged to act over computer science GCSEs*, BBC News, 10 November 2017, http://www.bbc.co.uk/news/technology-41928847

[166] Nicola Woolcock, *University hopes women with arts A levels will flock to engineering*, The Times, 20 April 2018, https://www.thetimes.co.uk/article/university-new-model-in-technology-and-engineering-nmite-hopes-women-with-arts-a-levels-will-flock-to-engineering-bg5dzrznx

[167] *Wakeham Review of STEM Degree Provision and Graduate Employability*, April 2016, https://assets.publishing.service.gov.uk/government/uploads/system/uploads/attachment_data/file/518582/ind-16-6-wakeham-review-stem-graduate-employability.pdf

[168] While three in four UK businesses report a shortage of digital skills, STEM graduates are more likely to be unemployed six months after graduation than those from other disciplines. Compared with a national unemployment rate of 4.3%, STEM graduate unemployment rates are 8% for computer science graduates and 6% for those with degrees in physical science, engineering and technology and mathematical science. Research suggests that many STEM graduates lacked the 'soft' employability skills, such as critical thinking, problem-solving and working in teams that employers are looking for: Chartered Institute of Personnel and Development, *Policy report: The graduate employment gap: expectations versus reality*, CIPD, November 2017, https://www.cipd.co.uk/Images/the-graduate-employment-gap_2017-expectations-versus-reality_tcm18-29592.pdf

[169] Steve Lucas, *Digitally Skilled Workers Needed For UK's Future, Reveals O2*, Development Economics, 3 September 2013, https://developmenteconomics.co.uk/digitally-skilled-workers-needed-for-uks-future-reveals-o2/

[170] Matt Warman, *Digital economy needs 750,000 workers*, Daily Telegraph, 3 September 2013, https://www.telegraph.co.uk/technology/news/10281733/Digital-economy-needs-750000-workers.html

[171] Digital Economy Act 2017

[172] Department for Education, *Improving adult basic digital skills: Government consultation*, 18 October 2018, https://consult.education.gov.uk/post-16-basic-skills-team/improving-adult-basic-digital-skills/supporting_documents/Improving%20adult%20basic%20digital%20skillsconsultation.pdf

[173] £30m. for digital skills; £34m. for training builders: Andrew Ellson, *Budget 2017: Retraining scheme to boost productivity*, The Times, 23 November 2017, https://www.thetimes.co.uk/article/aa60c15e-cfd0-11e7-b1ec-8503a5941b97

[174] Harry de Quetteville, *Teaching tech*, Daily Telegraph, 19 March 2018, https://www.telegraph.co.uk/technology/teaching-tech/

[175] House of Lords Select Committee on Digital Skills, *Make or Break: The UK's Digital Future*, The Stationery Office Limited, 17 February 2015, https://publications.parliament.uk/pa/ld201415/ldselect/lddigital/111/111.pdf

[176] Ibid

[177] Steve Hughes, *Brain Gain, How to Attract, Retain and Reconnect Digital Talent*, Vodafone, London, 21 March 2018, https://mediacentre.vodafone.co.uk/pressrelease/brain-gain/. Nick Jeffery, *There are plenty of ways we can stop the brain-drain of digital* talent, The Times, Comment, 21 March 2018, https://www.thetimes.co.uk/article/fb4c0768-2c5a-11e8-b7e0-bf91416644a6

[178] Report on government commissioned review of industrial digitalisation, led by the UK chief executive of Siemens, Jürgen Maier, which brings together in a series of recommendations the views and input from over 200 firms and organisations, including Rolls-Royce, Accenture and Cambridge and Newcastle universities. The review is suggesting that an agreement between government and industry could put Britain at the forefront of new technologies such as robotics, artificial intelligence, 3D printing, augmented and virtual reality, giving a much needed productivity boost and a net gain of 175,000 highly skilled, better paid jobs: Angela Monaghan, *Fourth industrial revolution could unlock £445bn for UK, report reveals*, Guardian, 30 October 2017, https://www.theguardian.com/business/2017/oct/30/fourth-industrial-revolution-could-unlock-445bn-for-uk-report-reveals

[179] *Shadbolt Review of Computer Sciences Degree Accreditation and Graduate Employability*, 16 May 2016, https://assets.publishing.service.gov.uk/government/uploads/system/uploads/attachment_data/file/518575/ind-16-5-shadbolt-review-computer-science-graduate-employability.pdf

[180] To be called Made Smarter UK Commission

[181] Jürgen Maier review: Angela Monaghan, *Fourth industrial revolution could unlock £445bn for UK, report reveals*, Guardian, 30 October 2017, https://www.theguardian.com/business/2017/oct/30/fourth-industrial-revolution-could-unlock-445bn-for-uk-report-reveals

[182] Funded and managed by the Education and Skills Funding Agency, the NCS's remit

is to provide information, advice and guidance on learning, training, career choice, career development, job search, and the labour market, and can be accessed online, by telephone, and face to face (but only for those aged 19 and over).

[183] The National Careers Council was established in May 2012 by the Skills Minister to advise Government on careers provision for young people and adults in England.

[184] National Careers Council, *An Aspirational Nation: Creating a culture change in careers provision*, June 2013, https://assets.publishing.service.gov.uk/government/uploads/system/uploads/attachment_data/file/354644/bis-13-919-national-careers-council-report-an-aspirational-nation-creating-a-culture-change-in-careers-provison.pdf; and National Careers Council, *Taking action: Achieving a culture change in careers provision*, September 2014, https://feweek.co.uk/wp-content/uploads/2014/09/EET_National_Careers_Council_Report.pdf

[185] National Careers Council, *Taking action: Achieving a culture change in careers provision*, September 2014, pgs. 2, 3 & 4, https://feweek.co.uk/wp-content/uploads/2014/09/EET_National_Careers_Council_Report.pdf

[186] The evaluation of the contribution of the National Careers Service found that the employment outcomes of its customers were actually worse in the first months post-support. In the sixth month after receiving service support, customers spent 3.5% less time in employment than peers who did not access the service. The gap later narrows, but even in the 24th month after intervention, those who receive support spent an average of 2% less time in employment: Marguerita Lane, Gavan Conlon, Viktoriya Peycheva, Iris Mantovani & Shantayne Chan, *An economic evaluation of the National Careers Service Research report*, Department for Education, March 2017, https://assets.publishing.service.gov.uk/government/uploads/system/uploads/attachment_data/file/603929/National_Careers_Service_economic_evaluation.pdf

[187] Controlling for other factors, schools which held formal external quality awards for their careers provision had on average 2% more pupils achieving 5 A-C GCSEs, including English and mathematics; a 0.5 percentage point less persistent absence rate; and 1.5% more gaining 3 A levels – Tristram Hooley, Jesse Matheson & A.G. Watts, *Advancing ambitions: The role of career guidance in supporting social mobility*, The Sutton Trust & University of Derby, October 2014, https://www.suttontrust.com/wp-content/uploads/2014/10/Advancing-Ambitions-16.10-1.pdf

[188] The Education Act 2011

[189] House of Commons Education Committee, *Careers guidance for young people: The impact of the new duty on schools*, The Stationery Office Limited, 23 January 2013,

https://publications.parliament.uk/pa/cm201213/cmselect/cmeduc/632/632.pdf

[190] Peter Walker, *Careers advice reforms led to worrying deterioration in standards, say MPs*, Guardian, 23 January 2013, https://www.theguardian.com/education/2013/jan/23/careers-advice-reforms-mps

[191] Tristram Hooley, Jesse Matheson & A.G. Watts, *Advancing ambitions: The role of career guidance in supporting social mobility*, The Sutton Trust & University of Derby, October 2014, https://www.suttontrust.com/wp-content/uploads/2014/10/Advancing-Ambitions-16.10-1.pdf

[192] Many pupils feel that current careers provision within the school environment is irrelevant and often doesn't keep pace with demand. 84% of 14-19 year olds would like more advice from their school or college regarding future options: Study, conducted by the Association of Accounting Technicians: Josie Gurney-Read, *Poor careers advice failing to address STEM skills 'crisis'*, Daily Telegraph, 28 October 2014, https://www.telegraph.co.uk/education/educationnews/11192026/Poor-careers-advice-failing-to-address-STEM-skills-crisis.html

[193] Barnardos, *Helping the inbetweeners: Ensuring careers advice improves the options for all young people*, Barnardos, August 2013, p.19, http://www.barnardos.org.uk/helping_the_in_betweeners.pdf

[194] Between 2009-10 and 2012-13, council spending on careers has fallen by £228m., with many Connexions services closed: Tristram Hooley, *Inspire children with good careers advice and they do better at school*, The Conversation UK website, 17 October 2014, http://theconversation.com/inspire-children-with-good-careers-advice-and-they-do-better-at-school-33104

[195] *How careers advice has become 'a ghost service': Pupils are being forced to phone premium rate phone lines for guidance rather than have face-to-face meetings*, The Daily Mail, 28 August 2013, http://www.dailymail.co.uk/news/article-2403498/Careers-advice-National-Careers-Service-forces-pupils-pay-premium-phone-line-rates-says-Barnardos.html

[196] Sarah Snelson & Kat Deyes, *BIS Research Paper Number 296, Understanding the Further Education Market in England*, Department of Business, Innovation and Skills, London, July 2016, https://assets.publishing.service.gov.uk/government/uploads/system/uploads/attachment_data/file/544310/bis-16-360-fe-market-england.pdf

[197] House of Commons Committee of Public Accounts, *The higher education market*, House of Commons, 15 June 2018, https://publications.parliament.uk/pa/cm201719/cmselect/cmpubacc/693/693.pdf

[198] Censuswide, on behalf of the AAT, conducted an online survey of 17-18 year olds leaving school or college after completing their A-levels in the summer of 2018: Association of Accounting Technicians website, *School leavers say careers advice remains 'insufficient' despite Government commitments*, AAT, 9 January 2018, https://www.aat.org.uk/about-aat/press-releases/school-leavers-say-careers-advice-remains-%E2%80%98insufficient%E2%80%99-despite-government

[199] Only 43% say they use a careers adviser for information and guidance: Ibid

[200] Only 50% had heard of the information provided by the National Careers Service: Ibid

[201] Nicola Woolcock, *Careers advisers condemned for wasting money*, The Times, 3 December 2018, https://www.thetimes.co.uk/article/careers-advisers-condemned-for-wasting-money-rj5fbsg7l

[202] 72% of young people had knowledge of university entrance, but only 36% of apprenticeships: Association of Accounting Technicians website, *School leavers say careers advice remains 'insufficient' despite Government commitments*, AAT, 9 January 2018, https://www.aat.org.uk/about-aat/press-releases/school-leavers-say-careers-advice-remains-%E2%80%98insufficient%E2%80%99-despite-government

[203] Jude Burke, *Anne Milton finally unveils much-delayed careers strategy*, FE Week, 4 December 2017, https://feweek.co.uk/2017/12/04/milton-finally-launching-much-delayed-careers-strategy/

[204] Paul Offord, *Careers and Enterprise Company slammed for multimillion-pound research spending*, FEWEEK, 16 May 2018, https://feweek.co.uk/2018/05/16/careers-and-enterprise-company-grilled-on-multi-million-pound-research-spending/

[205] Dr Deirdre Hughes OBE, Karen Adriaanse and Dr Sally-Anne Barnes, *Adult Education, Too important to be left to chance*, Warwick Institute of Employment Research, University of Warwick, A report commissioned by the All Party Parliamentary Group for Adult Education, July 2016, https://warwick.ac.uk/fac/soc/ier/research/adult_education/dh_adult_education_full_report.pdf

[206] Nearly four out of five 14 to 16-year-olds would consider a career in a science, technology, engineering and maths (STEM) related industry, but more than half of those surveyed admitted that they knew very little about the type of jobs on offer. 52% of mathematics and science teachers surveyed said that they do not know what STEM-related businesses are looking for in new employees. 62% of UK businesses feel that Britain are facing a skills gap in the industry with the current number of recruits failing to meet future demand. 67% of STEM employers said there had been little improvement in the situation over the past 5 years; 34% said they felt the situation had

in fact worsened: Study carried out by Nestlé UK & Ireland: Josie Gurney-Read, *Poor careers advice failing to address STEM skills 'crisis'*, Daily Telegraph, 28 October 2014, https://www.telegraph.co.uk/education/educationnews/11192026/Poor-careers-advice-failing-to-address-STEM-skills-crisis.html

[207] House of Lords Select Committee on Digital Skills, *Make or Break: The UK's Digital Future*, The Stationery Office Limited, 17 February 2015, https://publications.parliament.uk/pa/ld201415/ldselect/lddigital/111/111.pdf

[208] Oliver Wright, *Careers advice fails pupils, CBI warns*, The Times, 29 December 2017, https://www.thetimes.co.uk/article/c5cd02d6-ec18-11e7-ad3e-1cc26d7d8b0c

[209] Tristram Hooley, Jesse Matheson & A.G. Watts, *Advancing ambitions: The role of career guidance in supporting social mobility*, University of Derby and The Sutton Trust, October 2014, https://www.suttontrust.com/wp-content/uploads/2014/10/Advancing-Ambitions-16.10-1.pdf

[210] Dr Deirdre Hughes OBE, Karen Adriaanse and Dr Sally-Anne Barnes, *Adult Education, Too important to be left to chance*, Warwick Institute of Employment Research, University of Warwick, A report commissioned by the All Party Parliamentary Group for Adult Education, July 2016, https://warwick.ac.uk/fac/soc/ier/research/adult_education/dh_adult_education_full_report.pdf

[211] Research shows that output per hour in industries where at least one quarter of the workforce is paid less than two thirds of the median wage, was up to 30% lower in the UK than other European countries. Poor skills and management were cited as the main causes. More productive countries provided more on-the-job training and had better management practices: John Forth & Ana Rincon Aznar, *Productivity in the UK's low-wage industries*, Joseph Rowntree Foundation & The National Institute of Economic and Social Research, York, February 2018,https://www.niesr.ac.uk/sites/default/files/publications/ForthAznar%20productivity.pdf

[212] On-the-job training has been declining, or stagnating, since before the financial crisis of 2008: Ana Rincón Aznar, John Forth, Geoff Mason, Mary O'Mahony & Michele Bernini, *UK skills and productivity in an international context,* Department for Business, Innovation and Skills, National Institute of Economic and Social Research, December 2015, https://assets.publishing.service.gov.uk/government/uploads/system/uploads/attachment_data/file/486500/BIS-15-704-UK-skills-and-productivity-in-an-international_context.pdf, p. 7. UK Commission for Employment and Skills, *Employer Skills Survey 2013: UK Results, Evidence Report 81*, UKCES, January 2014, https://www.gov.uk/government/publications/ukces-employer-skills-survey-2013

Manufacturers are cutting training and skills budgets more now than at any point since the 2008 financial crisis - CBI's industrial trends survey: Tim Wallace, *Manufacturers slash training budgets at fastest pace since financial crisis*, Daily Telegraph, 25 July 2018, https://www.telegraph.co.uk/business/2018/07/24/manufacturers-slash-training-budgets-fastest-pace-since-financial/

[213] Over the past 10 to 12 years, the proportion of workers who have undertaken learning activities in the previous 13 weeks has declined from nearly a third to just over a quarter. Between 2005 and 2015, spending on retraining and raising skills was lower in the UK than in any other EU country. While spending on skills training in the UK averages less than 0.1% of gross domestic product, other EU countries typically spend 0.5% to 1% or more: Research for the National Institute of Economic and Social Research in collaboration with the Centre for Vocational Education Research: David Smith, *We must act now to prevent the skills gap becoming unbridgeable*, The Times, Comment, 24 January 2018, https://www.thetimes.co.uk/article/b4a7b8b6-004a-11e8-9de1-e6776d524215

[214] The duration of training activities has fallen (and is now typically less than a week). Workers studying and training for a qualification has dropped from 16% to less than 12%: Ibid

[215] 71% of employers don't train first-time managers: Chartered Management Institute, *Leadership for Change, CMI's Management Manifesto*, CMI, June 2017, https://www.managers.org.uk/~/media/Files/PDF/CMI-Management-Manifesto.pdf. Poor management and leadership are estimated to cost UK businesses £84b.: Chartered Management Institute, *Leadership for Change, CMI's Management Manifesto*, CMI, June 2017, https://www.managers.org.uk/~/media/Files/PDF/CMI-Management-Manifesto.pdf

[216] Martin Strydom, *Spring statement: the main points at a glance – Skills*, The Times, 13 March 2018, https://www.thetimes.co.uk/article/ccc730c4-26bb-11e8-acc5-262aff1ca7a6

[217] Speech by Damian Hinds, secretary of state for education, at the Education World Forum in London, 2124 January 2018: Sean Coughlan, *Hinds says schools face digital challenge*, BBC News, 22 January 2018, http://www.bbc.co.uk/news/education-42781375

[218] Gordon Rayner, *Grammar school expansion will create up to 16,000 new places, Education Secretary reveals*, Daily Telegraph, 11 May 2018, https://www.telegraph.co.uk/politics/2018/05/10/grammar-school-expansion-will-create-16000-new-places-educationsecretary/

[219] Lord Sandy Leitch, Leitch Review of Skills, *Prosperity for all in the global economy - world class skills*, Executive Summary and Foreword, Her Majesty's Stationery Office, December 2006, pgs. 3-5, https://www.gov.uk/government/uploads/system/uploads/attachment_data/file/354161/Prosperity_for_all_in_the_global_economy_-_summary.pdf

Chapter 13: Tackling underachievement

[1] Central Advisory Council for Education (England), *Half Our Future, A Report of the Central Advisory Council for Education (England)* (Ministry of Education, Her Majesty's Stationery Office, London, 1963), http://www.educationengland.org.uk/documents/newsom/newsom1963.html

[2] Benjamin Disraeli was a novelist and Conservative politician, serving twice as prime minister in 1868, and between 1874 and 1880.

[3] Benjamin Disraeli, Prime Minister of the United Kingdom, Speech in the House of Commons on 15 June 1874: Hansard, 15 June 1874, Commons Sitting, Education, Science, and Art— Minister of Education, Motion for a Select Committee, HC Deb 15 June 1874 volume 219 cc1589-623, http://hansard.millbanksystems.com/commons/1874/jun/15/motion-for-a-select-committee

[4] Central Advisory Council for Education (England), *Half Our Future, A Report of the Central Advisory Council for Education (England)* (Ministry of Education, Her Majesty's Stationery Office, London, 1963) pgs. xiii, xiv & xvi-xviii, http://www.educationengland.org.uk/documents/newsom/newsom1963.html

[5] Ibid, pgs. xvi-xviii

[6] *Education and Training Statistics for the United Kingdom 2017*, SFR64/2017, 9 November 2017, Department for Education and National Statistics, © Crown copyright 2017, https://www.gov.uk/government/statistics/education-and-training-statistics-for-the-uk-2017

[7] *Ibid*

[8] Department for Education and National Statistics, *Education and Training Statistics for the United Kingdom 2017*, SFR64/2017, 9 November 2017, https://www.gov.uk/government/statistics/education-and-training-statistics-for-the-uk-2017

[9] For example, only 102 out of 3,526 secondary schools had a Progress 8 score that was better for free school meal pupils than non-free school meal pupils: *Revealed: The schools where the poorest pupils make most progress*, Jess Staufenberg, Schools Week, 3 February 2018, https://schoolsweek.co.uk/revealed-the-schools-where-the-poorest-

pupils-make-most-progress/. Education Endowment Foundation, *The Attainment Gap 2017*, EEF, 2017, https://educationendowmentfoundation.org.uk/public/files/Annual_ Reports/EEF_Attainment_Gap_Report_2018_-_print.pdf

[10] OECD (2016), *PISA 2015 Results (Volume I): Excellence and Equity in Education,* PISA, OECD Publishing, Paris. http://dx.doi.org/10.1787/9789264266490-en

[11] English 16 to 19 year-olds are the worst of 23 developed nations in literacy and 22nd of 23 in numeracy: Małgorzata Kuczera, Simon Field Hendrickje & Catriona Windisch, *OECD Skills Studies, Building Skills for All: A Review of England Policy Insights from the Survey of Adult Skills*, OECD, 2016, http://www.oecd.org/unitedkingdom/building-skills-for-all-review-of-england.pdf

[12] Dave Phoenix, *Let's bridge the divide between academic and technical education*, Guardian, 18 July 2017, https://www.theguardian.com/higher-education-network/2017/jul/18/lets-bridge-the-divide-between-academic-and-technical-education

[13] Helena Kennedy QC, *Learning Works: Widening Participation in Further Education* (The Further Education Funding Council, Coventry, 1997) p. 21, http://dera.ioe. ac.uk/15073/2/Learning%20works%20-%20widening%20participation%20in%20 further%20education%20(Kennedy%20report).pdf

[14] The National Literacy Trust estimates that 5.1 million adults in England are functionally illiterate, meaning that they have a reading age of 11 or below and can understand only the most straightforward, short texts on familiar topics: Anita Singh, *Millions of British adults are functionally illiterate but problem is ignored, Dame Gail Rebuck warns*, Daily Telegraph, 5 January 2019, https://www.telegraph.co.uk/news/2019/01/05/ millions-british-adults-functionally-illiterate-problem-ignored/

[15] Sir Michael Wilshaw, *Unseen children: access and achievement 20 years on*, Ofsted, 2013, p. 4, https://www.gov.uk/government/uploads/system/uploads/attachment_data/ file/379157/Unseen_20children_20-_20access_20and_20achievement_2020_20years _20on.pdf

[16] Bart Shaw, Sam Baars, Loic Menzies, Meena Parameshwaran & Rebecca Allen, *Low income pupils' progress at secondary school*, Social Mobility Commission, London, 27 February 2017, https://assets.publishing.service.gov.uk/government/uploads/system/ uploads/attachment_data/file/594363/Progress_at_Secondary_School_report_final.pdf

[17] Richard Adams, *Ofsted chief: families of white working-class children 'lack drive' of migrants*, Guardian, 22 June 2018, https://www.theguardian.com/education/2018/jun/21/ families-white-working-class-children-economic-burden-lack-drive-of-migrants

[18] Ibid

[19] Nadeem Badshah, *White British five-year-olds bottom of class in reading*, The Times, 19 November 2018, https://www.thetimes.co.uk/article/white-british-five-year-olds-bottom-of-class-in-reading-05dxn83kw

[20] 94% of pupils said they felt good about school in year 3, 91% in year 7 and 84% in year 9. 93% had positive attitudes to teachers in year 3, 90% in year 7 and 84% in year 9. 90% had positive attitudes to school attendance in year 3, 89% in year 7 and 82% in year 9. 32% of year 9 pupils said they were bored at school, compared with 19% in year 3: Survey of 31,873 primary and secondary pupils in England and Wales in the year to April 2016 - GL Assessment, *Pupil Attitudes to Self and School Report 2016*, GL Assessment, September 2016, https://www.gl-assessment.co.uk/sites/gl/files/images/PASS-report-UK.pdf

[21] Ofsted, *Key Stage 3: the wasted years?* September 2015, Ofsted, https://www.gov.uk/government/uploads/system/uploads/attachment_data/file/459830/Key_Stage_3_the_wasted_years.pdf

[22] Richard Pring, Geoff Hayward, Ann Hodgson, Ken Spours, Jill Johnson, Ewart Keep, Gareth Rees, Alis Oancea, Stephanie Wilde, Susannah Wright, & Joanne Hazell, *The Nuffield Review of 14–19 Education and Training: Final report Education for All: the Future of Education and Training for 14–19 year-olds* (Routledge, 2009), http://www.nuffieldfoundation.org/sites/default/files/files/Nuffield%20Report28-04-09%20final%20to%20print.pdf

[23] Laura McLarty & Rhetta Moran, *Equality and Human Rights Commission Research Report Series 26: Engaging all young people in meaningful learning after 16: A qualitative study* (2009), Equality and Human Rights Commission, Manchester, UK, 2009, https://www.equalityhumanrights.com/sites/default/files/research_report_26_engaging_all_young_people_in_meaningful_learning_after_16_a_qualitative_study.pdf

[24] Ofsted, *Key Stage 3: the wasted years?* September 2015, Ofsted, https://www.gov.uk/government/uploads/system/uploads/attachment_data/file/459830/Key_Stage_3_the_wasted_years.pdf

[25] Department for Education, *Schools, pupils and their characteristics: January 2018*, Statistical Publication, 28 June 2018, https://assets.publishing.service.gov.uk/government/uploads/system/uploads/attachment_data/file/719226/Schools_Pupils_and_their_Characteristics_2018_Main_Text.pdf

[26] Tom Whipple, *A naughty pupil can cost classmates £75,000 in pay*, The Times, 19 September 2016, http://www.thetimes.co.uk/edition/news/a-naughty-pupil-can-cost-

classmates-75-000-in-pay-bxvbzq0g3

[27] Kiran Gill, with Harry Quilter-Pinner & Danny Swift, *Making the Difference, Breaking the Link between School Exclusion and Social Exclusion*, Institute for Public Policy Research, October 2017,https://www.ippr.org/files/2017-10/making-the-difference-report-october-2017.pdf

[28] Ibid

[29] 3,900 pupils were permanently excluded from schools in England in 2012-13, and 6,685 in 2015-16; a 40% increase: Ibid. Between 2012 and 2015 permanent exclusions rose by 25%, from 4,630 to 5,800; and fixed-term exclusions by 13%, from 267,520 to 302,980. In some areas the increase has been 300%. The number of days pupils were excluded fixed-term also increased from an average of 4.18 days to 4.38: Laurence Cawley & Daniel Wainwright, *Barnsley and Middlesbrough see pupil exclusion rises of 300%*, BBC News, 4 October 2016, http://www.bbc.co.uk/news/uk-england-37340042. 7,720 pupils were permanently excluded in 2016/17 compared to 6,685 in 2015/16; 15% increase. There were 381,865 fixed-period exclusions in 2016/17, a 13% increase on 2015/16: GOV.UK website, National Statistics, *Permanent and fixed-period exclusions in England: 2016 to 2017*, Department for Education, published 19 July 2018, https://www.gov.uk/government/statistics/permanent-and-fixed-period-exclusions-in-england-2016-to-2017. ,

[30] 83% of permanent exclusions are from secondary schools: Ibid

[31] Kiran Gill, with Harry Quilter-Pinner & Danny Swift, *Making the Difference, Breaking the Link between School Exclusion and Social Exclusion*, Institute for Public Policy Research, October 2017,https://www.ippr.org/files/2017-10/making-the-difference-report-october-2017.pdf

[32] Statutorily alternative provision is defined as that for 'pupils who are unable to receive suitable education (usually due to exclusion or illness) by schools'. It is a broad term covering a wide variety of types of educational settings included pupil referral units, alternative provision academies and free schools, hospital schools, including those run by charities and other independent organisations. In the context of this book alternative provision relates to education for those excluded from mainstream schools: House of Commons Education Committee, *Forgotten children: alternative provision and the scandal of ever increasing exclusions,* House of Commons, 18 July 2018, https://publications.parliament.uk/pa/cm201719/cmselect/cmeduc/342/342.pdf

[33] 6,685 pupils were permanently excluded from schools in England in 2015-16; 48,000 pupils were being educated in the alternative provision sector, which caters for pupils

excluded from school: Kiran Gill, with Harry Quilter-Pinner & Danny Swift, *Making the Difference, Breaking the Link between School Exclusion and Social Exclusion*, Institute for Public Policy Research, October 2017,https://www.ippr.org/files/2017-10/making-the-difference-report-october-2017.pdf

[34] Ibid. In a submission to a House of Commons committee, the Association of Directors of Children's Services (ADCS) reported that a minority of headteachers in England, due to worries about inspections, exam league table positions, losing their jobs and academy takeovers, are persuading parents to educate their children at home so as to avoid an exclusion on their record: Hannah Richardson, *Parents being talked into homeschooling troubled children*, BBC News, 6 February 2018, http://www.bbc.co.uk/news/education-42943997

[35] Kiran Gill, with Harry Quilter-Pinner & Danny Swift, *Making the Difference, Breaking the Link between School Exclusion and Social Exclusion*, Institute for Public Policy Research, October 2017, https://www.ippr.org/files/2017-10/making-the-difference-report-october-2017.pdf. Warwick Mansell, *The academy trusts whose GCSE students keep disappearing*, Guardian, 6 November 2018, https://www.theguardian.com/education/2018/nov/06/academy-trusts-gcse-students-disappearing-prior-to-exams. Half of the 19,000 GCSE-aged pupils that dropped off school rolls between 2016 and 2017 did not reappear on another school roll, and may have been 'off-rolled' by schools in Years 10 and 11: Amanda Spielman, *The Annual Report of Her Majesty's Chief Inspector of Education, Children's Services and Skills 2017/18*, Ofsted, 4 December 2018, https://assets.publishing.service.gov.uk/government/uploads/system/uploads/attachment_data/file/760991/29523_Ofsted_Annual_Report_2017-18_WEB.pdf

[36] Kiran Gill, with Harry Quilter-Pinner & Danny Swift, *Making the Difference, Breaking the Link between School Exclusion and Social Exclusion*, Institute for Public Policy Research, October 2017, https://www.ippr.org/files/2017-10/making-the-difference-report-october-2017.pdf

[37] Bart Shaw, Sam Baars, Loic Menzies, Meena Parameshwaran & Rebecca Allen, *Low income pupils' progress at secondary school*, Social Mobility Commission, 27 February 2017, https://assets.publishing.service.gov.uk/government/uploads/system/uploads/attachment_data/file/594363/Progress_at_Secondary_School_report_final.pdf

[38] GOV.UK website, National Statistics, *Permanent and fixed-period exclusions in England: 2016 to 2017*, Department for Education, published 19 July 2018, https://www.gov.uk/government/statistics/permanent-and-fixed-period-exclusions-in-england-2016-to-2017

[39] Boys of black Caribbean origin are more than three times as likely as other boys to be permanently excluded: Caroline Wheeler & Sian Griffiths, *Education secretary Damian Hinds warns that schools must curb expulsions*, The Sunday Times, 11 March 2018, https://www.thetimes.co.uk/article/317a2c2a-24a9-11e8-a283-1b5f066ae234

[40] Kiran Gill, with Harry Quilter-Pinner & Danny Swift, Making the Difference, *Breaking the Link between School Exclusion and Social Exclusion*, Institute for Public Policy Research, October 2017, https://www.ippr.org/files/2017-10/making-the-difference-report-october-2017.pdf

[41] Ibid. Children with special educational needs are about four times as likely to be permanently excluded. Those with autism are twice as likely to be permanently excluded as other children: Caroline Wheeler and Sian Griffiths, *Education secretary Damian Hinds warns that schools must curb expulsions*, The Sunday Times, 11 March 2018, https://www.thetimes.co.uk/article/317a2c2a-24a9-11e8-a283-1b5f066ae234.

[42] In 2015-16 14 children under the age of five, including 4 aged three and 6 aged four, were sent to pupil referral units because of their disruptive behaviour in nursery or school: Department for Education, *Schools, pupils and their characteristics: January 2017, SFR 28/2017*, 29 June 2017, https://assets.publishing.service.gov.uk/government/uploads/system/uploads/attachment_data/file/650547/SFR28_2017_Main_Text.pdf

[43] Kiran Gill, with Harry Quilter-Pinner & Danny Swift, *Making the Difference, Breaking the Link between School Exclusion and Social Exclusion*, Institute for Public Policy Research, October 2017, https://www.ippr.org/files/2017-10/making-the-difference-report-october-2017.pdf

[44] House of Commons Education Committee, *Forgotten children: alternative provision and the scandal of ever increasing exclusions,* House of Commons, 18 July 2018, https://publications.parliament.uk/pa/cm201719/cmselect/cmeduc/342/342.pdf

[45] Ibid

[46] Caroline Wheeler & Sian Griffiths, *Education secretary Damian Hinds warns that schools must curb expulsions*, The Sunday Times, 11 March 2018, https://www.thetimes.co.uk/article/317a2c2a-24a9-11e8-a283-1b5f066ae234

[47] Ibid

[48] Vic Goddard, Headteacher of Passmores Academy, Essex: *'We batter them with kindness': schools that reject super-strict values*, Josh Halliday, Guardian, 27 February 2018, https://www.theguardian.com/education/2018/feb/27/schools-discipline-unconditional-positive-regard

[49] Sutton Trust, Ipsos Mori Young People Omnibus Survey 2018, Private Tuition

Polling 2018, https://www.suttontrust.com/wp-content/uploads/2018/07/Private-Tuition-Polling-2018.pdf

[50] One in three pupils received private tuition for specific GCSE exams; nearly half for school work in general; and more than one in four for entrance exam to private or grammar schools: Ibid

[51] Far more have received private tuition in London (one in five) than the rest of the country: Ibid

[52] More than one in five pupils from more advantaged households received private tuition, compared to less than 1 in 5 from less well-off households: Ibid

[53] 56% of Asian pupils, 42% of Black pupils, and 25% of white pupils had private tuition: Ibid

[54] 31% from two parent families had private tuition, compared to 24% from single parent households: Ibid

[55] Ibid

[56] John Jerrim, *Extra Time Private tuition and out-of-school study, new international evidence*, Sutton Trust, London, September 2017, https://www.suttontrust.com/wp-content/uploads/2017/09/Extra-time-report_FINAL.pdf

[57] Part 3 of the Children and Families Act 2014

[58] Department for Education Press release, Reforms for children with SEN and disabilities come into effect, 1 September 2014, https://www.gov.uk/government/news/reforms-for-children-with-sen-and-disabilities-come-into-effect

[59] Amanda Spielman, *The Annual Report of Her Majesty's Chief Inspector of Education, Children's Services and Skills 2017/18,* Ofsted, 4 December 2018, https://assets.publishing.service.gov.uk/government/uploads/system/uploads/attachment_data/file/760991/29523_Ofsted_Annual_Report_2017-18_WEB.pdf

[60] Department for Education & Department of Health, *Special educational needs and disability code of practice: 0 to 25 years, Statutory guidance for organisations which work with and support children and young people who have special educational needs or disabilities*, January 2015, https://assets.publishing.service.gov.uk/government/uploads/system/uploads/attachment_data/file/398815/SEND_Code_of_Practice_January_2015.pdf

[61] Department for Education Press release, Reforms for children with SEN and disabilities come into effect, 1 September 2014, https://www.gov.uk/government/news/reforms-for-children-with-sen-and-disabilities-come-into-effect

[62] Amanda Spielman, *The Annual Report of Her Majesty's Chief Inspector of Education, Children's Services and Skills 2017/18,* Ofsted, 4 December 2018, https://assets.

publishing.service.gov.uk/government/uploads/system/uploads/attachment_data/
file/760991/29523_Ofsted_Annual_Report_2017-18_WEB.pdf

[63] Department for Education & Department of Health, *Special educational needs and disability code of practice: 0 to 25 years, Statutory guidance for organisations which work with and support children and young people who have special educational needs or disabilities*, January 2015, https://assets.publishing.service.gov.uk/government/uploads/system/uploads/attachment_data/file/398815/SEND_Code_of_Practice_January_2015.pdf

[64] Ibid

[65] The Children and Families Act 2014 replaced special educational needs statements and Learning Difficulty Assessments with EHCPs.

[66] Amanda Spielman, *The Annual Report of Her Majesty's Chief Inspector of Education, Children's Services and Skills 2017/18,* Ofsted, 4 December 2018, https://assets.publishing.service.gov.uk/government/uploads/system/uploads/attachment_data/file/760991/29523_Ofsted_Annual_Report_2017-18_WEB.pdf

[67] Ibid

[68] Sian Griffiths, *£350m boost for pupils with special needs*, The Sunday Times, 16 December 2018, https://www.thetimes.co.uk/article/350m-boost-for-pupils-with-special-needs-ksp7ln5p2

14 Conclusion: a manifesto for learning

[1] 69.4% of GCSE entries in 2012 awarded A*-C grades compared to 41.9% in 1988: Joint Council for Qualifications – quoted in Data Blog, Guardian, https://www.theguardian.com/news/datablog/2012/sep/17/gcse-exams-replaced-ebacc-history-pass-rates#data. Grades awarded for GCE A-level entries: A*-A 11.4% 1989, 26.3% 2017; A*-B 26.6% 1989, 55.1% 2017; A*-C 43.0% 1989, 79.4% 2017: Joint Council for Qualifications website, Exam results, A levels, https://www.jcq.org.uk/examination-results/a-levels; and Student Performance Analysis, National percentage figures for A level grades, http://www.bstubbs.co.uk/a-lev.htm

[2] The number of students in university education increased from around 600,000 in 1996 to 2.28m. in 2016: Tejvan Pettinger, *Number of students at university in UK*, Economics website, 14 September 2011, http://www.economicshelp.org/blog/3190/education/number-of-students-at-university-in-uk/. Universities UK, *Higher education in numbers*,http://www.universitiesuk.ac.uk/facts-and-stats/Pages/higher-education-data.aspx

[3] Tony Robbins, Life Coach

[4] Billy Camden, *DfE to consult on level 4 and 5 T-levels for introduction from 2022, FE*

Week, 6 December 2018, https://feweek.co.uk/2018/12/06/dfe-to-develop-new-suite-of-higher-technical-qualifications/

[5] Damian Hinds, *More bedtime stories and no phones at the dinner table*, The Times, 14 November 2018, https://www.thetimes.co.uk/article/more-bedtime-stories-and-no-phones-at-the-dinner-table-9zs0mt375. Pippa Crerar, *Children starting school 'cannot communicate in full sentences'*, Guardian, 31 July 2018, https://www.theguardian.com/education/2018/jul/31/damian-hinds-social-mobility-children-school-screen-time

[6] GOV.UK, Statement from the new Prime Minister Theresa May, Published 13 July 2016, https://www.gov.uk/government/speeches/statement-from-the-new-prime-minister-theresa-may

[7] Sian Griffiths, *Schools inspector threatens D-minus for 'exam factories'*, The Sunday Times, 12 August 2018, https://www.thetimes.co.uk/article/schools-inspector-threatens-d-minus-for-exam-factories-rvp3jrnbd

[8] At the end of May 2018 the most senior civil servant at the Department for Education, the permanent secretary, Jonathan Slater, took the most unusual step of lodging a formal objection to plans by the government to introduce the first T levels in two years-time because they were being rushed and that the courses risked being of poor quality. Mr. Slater asked for a delay in implementation and a 'ministerial direction' from the Education Secretary, saying that it will be 'very challenging' to ensure they are taught to a high standard: Nicola Woolcock, *T levels have employers scratching their heads*, The Times, 30 May 2018, https://www.thetimes.co.uk/article/t-levels-have-employers-scratching-their-heads-69ljgvcg2. Even the minister responsible, Anne Milton, has said that 'as a mother of four, she would advise her own children to wait until the system (of T-levels) had bedded in': Oral evidence by Anne Milton, skills minister, to the House of Commons Education Committee, 17 July 2018 – quoted in Rosemary Bennett, *Skills minister shows lack of confidence in T level*, The Times, 18 July 2018, https://www.thetimes.co.uk/article/skills-minister-anne-milton-shows-lack-of-confidence-in-t-level-bn9xrt3dl. The CBI has expressed concern that T-levels 'are not ready and are being rushed through': Sian Griffiths, *Parents told T-levels may not help get a job*, The Sunday Times, 27 May 2018, https://www.thetimes.co.uk/article/parents-told-t-levels-may-not-help-get-a-job-ctwhfm8fs

[9] Richard Adams & Heather Stewart, *Damian Hinds pledges to help teachers overwhelmed by excessive workload*, Guardian, 21 July 2018, https://www.theguardian.com/education,2018/jul/20/hinds-pledges-to-help-schools-reduce-teacher-stress-to-retain-staff